Vienna

Vienna

Art and Architecture

Edited by Rolf Toman
Photography by Gerald Zugmann and Achim Bednorz

h.f.ullmann

FRONT COVER:
Joseph Maria Olbrich
Secession Building, 1918
Detail of the front façade, dome with gold-plated laurel leaf.
Photo: Gerald Zugmann

BACK COVER:
Andreas Streit
Palais Equitable on the Stock-im-Eisen-Platz
Staircase, 1890-91.
Photo: Gerald Zugmann

FRONTISPIECE:
Theophil Hansen
Parliament, 1774-83, Entrance hall
Photo: Gerald Zugmann, Vienna

© 2008 Tandem Verlag
h.f.ullmann is an imprint of Tandem Verlag GmbH

Concept and Design: Rolf Toman, Espéraza
Editing: Barbara Borngässer, Paris; Birgit Beyer, Cologne
Photography: Gerald Zugmann, Vienna; Achim Bednorz, Cologne
Picture Research: Monika Bergmann, Fenja Wittneven, Cologne
Cover Design: Peter Feierabend, Cologne

Original title: *Wien, Kunst und Architektur*
ISBN 978-3-8331-4892-7

© 2008 for the English edition:
Tandem Verlag GmbH
h.f.ullmann is an imprint of Tandem Verlag GmbH

Translation from German: Paul Fletcher, Isabell Hull, Petra Kopp, Jan Neumann, Dai Roberts,
Christine Shuttleworth, Peter Spurgeon, Jackie Smith, Edgar Schmitz, in association with
Chanterelle Translations, London
Editor of the English-language edition: Josephine Bacon, Chanterelle Translations, London
Typesetting: Chanterelle Translations, London
Project Coordination: Bettina Kaufmann und Kristin Zeier

Printed in China
ISBN 978-3-8331-4893-4

10 9 8 7 6 5 4 3 2 1
X IX VIII VII VI V IV III II I

www.ullmann-publishing.com

Contents

Gustav Peichl
Overview of Viennese Architecture

Vienna is different — or is it? In no other European city do national and cultural contradictions clash like they do in the capital of the former Austro-Hungarian Empire. Nowhere else was or is the importance of the *genius loci* as pronounced as it is in Vienna.

Intellectual brilliance in both arts and sciences has always had a place in the city. The self-image of the Viennese is characterized by the cheerfully pessimistic philosophy of "live and let live," which has provided fertile soil for their great artistic and architectural achievements. This is evident from the many famous artists, scientists, and architects who have lived and worked in the city.

Vienna is the city of Sigmund Freud. It should not be assumed that it is merely coincidence that Freud developed his theory and practice of psychoanalysis in Vienna. The debate continues to rage as to whether it had to have been developed in Vienna, where Sigmund Freud was working, or whether it could not have evolved equally well elsewhere. It is certain, however, that a remarkable correlation exists between psychoanalysis, the sociopolitical climate, and architecture in Vienna. As Freud himself has said: "Art is the expression of a higher talent. It affords insights into the realm that few may enter and stirs you with indefinable power. One can never completely explain its effect but one feels it." Otto Wagner, the founder of classical modernism in architecture, had a different perspective: "Everything modern must conform to the new materials and the demands of today if it is to suit Modern Man. It must reflect our own better, democratic, self-confident and astute self."

Architects do a great deal to influence and shape their environment. Good architecture has always relied on its utility value as well as its outward appearance. The quality of a building is determined by the "mood" and poetic beauty it expresses as part of its function. According to Vitruvius (25 A.D.) "Architecture only deserves praise when it combines usefulness and comfort, longevity and beauty."

The effective presence of design elements constitutes a peculiarity of Viennese architecture. Ornaments dominate the design in a playful, but sometimes formalistic and exaggerated manner.

Different trends and contrasting personalities emerge from a survey of Vienna and its architectural heritage. There is the bold philosophical thought and understated architecture of Ludwig Wittgenstein (in the "Haus Kundmanngasse") or the formalistic imagination of Otto Wagner (the Post Office Savings Bank and the Steinhof church). The most convincing architectural solutions and the most intriguing contradictions of modern Vienna are based on the classical motifs of Otto Wagner and the clear and concise designs of the buildings of Adolf Loos.

RIGHT:
Karl König
Haus der Industrie,
4, Schwarzenbergplatz, 1906–09
Detail of large meeting hall.

OPPOSITE:
Gabriele Montani, Johann Lukas von Hildebrandt
St. Peter's church, 1702–33

The new Haas-Haus by
Hans Hollein (1985) and St.
Stephen's Cathedral
(commenced in 1230)

With the end of the baroque period, ca. 1780, the Viennese *haute bourgeoisie* assumed, to a degree, the role of the nobility, a development which in architecture was reflected in the buildings of the so-called Biedermeier period and the classical period. Josef Kornhäusl was one of Vienna's leading architects during the Biedermeier period. His work can be seen as leading the way toward the modernist architecture of Adolf Loos. Clear and unadorned structures were characteristic of Kornhäusl and helped to shape the building culture of his time.

The mid-nineteenth century marked Vienna's rise as a metropolis. When the city's defenses and bastions were razed to the ground in 1850, the resulting expansion and inclusion of the suburbs constituted the greatest venture in Viennese building and urban development seen until this time. The double ring road known as the Ringstrasse, with its prestigious buildings, constituted the first large-scale example of Viennese urban development.

Architecture has always been a major factor in Austria, lending important impulses to artistic and cultural development, and this is particularly true of Vienna, where the cityscape is dominated by the exuberance of the Baroque (1600–1760), the Napoleonic era (prior to 1848), the ring roads of 1848–1890 with their rapid industrial development, the expansion prior to 1918 and, most importantly, the social housing projects of the inter-war period between 1918 and 1938.

This last was a ground-breaking and pioneering development in social housing in Europe. The conservative English weekly *The*

Spectator called the program "a miracle." "Karl-Marx-Hof," one of the most famous complexes of the type, built in the 1930s, became a symbol of the struggle for progress and democracy. The large-scale projects and urban modernization schemes, on the other hand, were unable to achieve the socio-political and architectural standards of the earlier decades.

For Vienna, once one of the most important and also most autonomous cities in the world, the turn of the nineteenth century constituted a culmination point in urban development, although it took years before the intellectual and cultural achievements of this period, such as Viennese art deco style known as Jugendstil, were properly recognized and appreciated. Vienna's greatest artists of the period were themselves overshadowed by their contemporaries. The work of Otto Wagner and Adolf Loos, who are recognized today as being among the founders of modern architecture, dates from as long ago as the beginning of the twentieth century, yet neither Wagner nor Hoffmann were awarded the recognition they deserved at the time, and certainly not in their home city.

The splendid artefacts, especially the creative achievements of the Secession and the Wiener Werkstätten, were only accepted by a small section of the society, because of their exclusive style and intrinsic value. It was the liberal upper classes alone who proved to be receptive and cosmopolitan in outlook. The cheerful formal rigor and decorative arrangement of detail in the almost sensuous buildings of Josef Hoffmann contrast with the urban and social concerns of the great *Wiener*

Otto Wagner
Balustrade of a building at
40 Wienzeile

View of the Ringstrasse at night
from the Imperial Hotel

Otto Wagner
Post Office Savings
Bank, 1903

Josef Hoffmann
Skywa-Primavesi Villa, 1913

Wohnhöfe, the residential apartments centered around a courtyard, which were typical of the first decades of the twentieth century.

More than members of any other profession, the architect is caught up in the dichotomy between rationality and emotion. His work has first and foremost to fulfill a function, but as an artist the architect is also responsible for the sensual appeal of his work. The erotic "desire for creation in beauty" as Plato put it, determines the actions of the architect, who even now is able to draw on the latest technological developments.

Vienna is still a city which inspires creativity in music, theater, and the fine arts. In the area of "the visual arts," the Viennese are tremendously proud of the small, scaled-down features of recent buildings, such as stores or bars. However, the attitude to large-scale projects, such as office and apartment block megaliths, is one of shame.

Thanks to the city's architectural colleges and the variety of architectural theories they expound, a climate has evolved that is characterized by a general aspiration to quality. Vienna is picky, even stubborn; the worldwide architectural fashion for postmodernism bitten by the decoration bug has almost completely bypassed the city. The "smart-and-sloping" fashion promoted by the deconstructivists was also frowned upon.

It is typical of Vienna that every building has evolved from a mixture of traditional forms and context-specific requirements. The result of this "Vienna Mix" is determined by two components: on the one hand, by the new appreciation of traditional forms and on the other hand, new ideas and the specific requirements of the building.

Vienna is different! And special!

Adolf Loos
Steiner House, 1910

Karl Ehn
Karl-Marx-Hof, 1926

ILLUSTRATIONS ON PP. 10-11:
View of the Michaeler wing of the Hofburg and the steeple of St. Michael's Church (left).

Ehrenfried Kluckert

Viennese Art and Architecture from Classical Antiquity to the Renaissance

Traces of Classical Antiquity and the Early Middle Ages

Vienna's origins are hidden beneath streets and alleys, churches and townhouses and are almost inaccessible today. Still, it is worthwhile searching for clues of the city's ancient past, for instance in the center of the old part of town, to the west of Marc-Aurel-Strasse, where the marketplace of what was once the Roman fort of Vindobona is located. Remnants of ancient walls found during excavation work bear witness to the city's Roman past. These remains can still be viewed today. Access to the site is via the house at no. 3.

In around 15 BC, the Romans conquered the kingdom of Noricum and established their headquarters on the banks of the Danube. It was thanks to Marcus Aurelius that the boundary along the Danube was made secure and that Vindobona could prosper. This emperor has often been called "the philosopher in the purple." Although he was a successful military strategist, he had nothing in common with the type of soldier-emperor who dominated Roman foreign policy from the third century AD onward. Marcus Aurelius, who was influenced by Stoic philosophy, contemplated a world governed by reason and was the author of many philosophical treatises. In 180 AD, he died in Vindobona. The cause of death is said to have been the Plague. In the street bearing his name, high up on the corner of Salzgasse, a statue commemorates this remarkable Roman emperor.

Remnants of the Roman fort have also recently been discovered at Michaelerplatz, opposite the entrance to the Hofburg, the royal residence. These seem to be parts of a bastion or other building outside the actual fort. The Viennese architect Hans Hollein surrounded these foundations with walls and a railing, which leave the Roman ruins visible, beside the remnants of a medieval fountain and a nineteenth-century building. Many exhibits from the Roman period are displayed at the Kunsthistorisches Museum and the Historisches Museum. In addition to some well-preserved bronze artefacts, the gravestone of Flavius Draccus in the Historisches Museum is of particular interest. It is one of those very rare Roman memorials that still show traces of the original brightly colored painting. The style is typical of the transition from Celtic to Roman art, which occurred during the first century AD (ill. p. 13, upper left).

The Hoher Markt is something of a connecting link between Antiquity and the Middle Ages. It is possible that this was the center of town in the early Middle Ages, after the Romans had been driven out by the Markomanni at the end of the second century. Although the Romans succeeded in recapturing the ruined Vindobona and even introduced viticulture under Emperor Probus, they were forced to surrender to the Germanic tribes who tried to storm the fort in the fourth century and later settled in the area of the former Roman camp. The block of houses that is enclosed to the west by Tiefer Graben, to the south by the Naglergasse and Graben streets, to the east by the Kramergasse and Rothgasse and to the north by the elevation between the churches of Maria am Gestade and St. Ruprecht's, is a fairly accurate demarcation of the modest medieval settlement

During the fifth and sixth centuries, the town had witnessed the upheaval of the *Völkerwandering* (Migration of Peoples), then between 791 and 797 Charlemagne's wars against the Avars. After his victory, Vienna and the eastern territories were incorporated into his empire as the Carolingian East March. To define this East March more clearly and to specify the point at which the Middle Ages began in Vienna, one has to delve into Bavarian history. Bavarian counts controlled parts of what today is Upper and Lower Austria as early as the sixth century. The first Irish and Scottish missionaries reached the area around Vienna during the seventh century. Then the Avars and Slavs advanced and drove out the Bavarians. Nevertheless, the first monasteries were founded in the eighth century, at Mondsee in 748 and at Kremsmünster in 777.

Urban development, building, and sculpture in the High Middle Ages

Missionaries presumably also built St. Ruprecht's, Vienna's first church, in the eighth century. Its foundations, which are constructed of Roman materials, rise above a former bastion that was part of the northern defenses of the fort. The nave and the lower part of the steeple date from the eleventh century. The church's existence is documented for the first time in 1161. At the same time, Romanesque alterations were made to the nave. The flat timbered ceiling, which has been restored several times, and the late Gothic vaulted choir have been preserved. The transept of the right-hand chapel has a beautiful ribbed vault. There is a sharp contrast between the Gothic architecture and the round-arched arcades in the squat Romanesque west tower (ill. p. 13, upper right). The arches are subdivided by small columns with heavily cushioned capitals.

Until the eighteenth century, a Romanesque crucifix, dating from between 1170 and 1180 hung in the church. It is among the oldest surviving Viennese artifacts (ill. p. 13, lower right). The long figure of Christ is worked in great detail, as can be seen in the arrangement of the cloth, the rib-cage, and the meticulously shaped pointed beard. The crucifix was acquired by the Abbey of Melk and can be viewed today at Melkerhof Chapel in Vienna. Nowadays, the church of St. Ruprecht appears to be overshadowed by

Tombstone of a Roman knight
from Gaul, T. Flavius Draccus
1st century AD, limestone, height:
90 in (225 cm)
Historisches Museum, Vienna

Hoher Markt
Etching, 16th century
Historisches Museum, Vienna

the tall, imposing houses of the Baroque and the nineteenth century. At the time, however, the church must have appeared to travelers arriving from the north, that is, from the Danube, as a signal of an auspicious Christian settlement. Viennese trade and travel at that time was directed mainly northward.

A walk from St. Ruprecht's to the Hoher Markt and then on along the Tuchlauben toward St. Peter's covers what in medieval times constituted Vienna, which incidentally was called "Wenia." Looking at the pompous Baroque splendor of St. Peter's, designed by Johann Lukas von Hildebrandt, it is easy to forget that this was previously the site of another church of tremendous importance for the town's history. Archeologists have been able to determine its groundplan, which was located about seven steps below the level built upon in 1676. On the basis of its rectangular form, they have deduced that it was a late Roman hall church, dating from the fourth century. It is likely that an irregular village developed around this early church, and this constituted the initial core of what later became Vienna. A first reconstruction of this early church could have occurred in 792 on Charlemagne's orders, after his victory over the Avars who had driven out the Bavarian settlers.

The settlement expanded from St. Peter's northward in the direction of St. Ruprecht's. Historians suspect that here, under the maze of narrow lanes, there stood a bastion within the Roman walls which still exist today. Both settlements would have merged during the ninth century. The annals of Salzburg mention a first battle between Bavarians and Hungarians *ad Uueniam* in 881, in which the Hungarians were beaten, albeit not conclusively.

St. Ruprecht's Church
West steeple, ca. 1130/70

Crucifix, ca. 1170/80
Melkerhof Chapel

Stained-glass window with saints' cross showing Heinrich II Jasomirgott, around 1300, Brunnenhaus

Exposed Romanesque capital from the Schottenkirche
Museum im Schottenstift

Romanesque column, ca. 1177
Museum im Schottenstift

Romanesque Madonna, 1250
Repainted in the 19th century
Museum im Schottenstift

Between 907, the year of the Battle of Bratislava, and 991, when they were driven out, the Hungarians controlled Vienna. Whether they settled within the area of the city itself is unclear, but it has been ascertained that they founded settlements in the surrounding area.

After Otto I beat the Hungarians at Lechfeld in 955, most of the East March, with the exception of Vienna and the eastern territories, were reintegrated into the Holy Roman Empire. A short time later, in 976, the counts of Babenberg were granted the East March as a fee, and in 996 they are mentioned as margraves of "Ostarrichi." Vienna and the surrounding area were only liberated in 981, when the Bavarian Duke Heinrich der Zänker ("the squabbler") advanced with his army and recaptured the city. The eastern border of the empire had thus once again been pushed back eastward of the Vienna Woods.

In the course of the eleventh century, more and more people moved to Vienna and the area available for settlement had to be extended. The burghers therefore erected a solid wall within the boundaries of the Roman fort, which ran roughly along the present Parisergasse, in other words, still to the east of the later Babenberg castle at Am Hof. Outside of the Roman fort, another new settlement developed, actually more of a village standing in a meadow, in the area of what are now Bäckerstrasse and Sonnenfelsgasse. These streets still bear the outlines of the long, oval marketplace, around which the buildings were grouped.

At that time, however, Vienna was not yet the royal capital. The Babenberg noblemen resided at Klosterneuburg and kept their distance from the town, which was controlled by two families, the Formbachers and the Sieghards, until in 1130 the Babenberg Margrave Leopold III seized power in the city. A reliable date is provided by a document dated 1137, in which Leopold IV is mentioned in the context of the *civitas* Vienna. A few years later, in 1156, the Austrian margravate became a duchy, with Vienna as the residence of the Babenberg dynasty. The first Duke of Austria was Heinrich II Jasomirgott (ill., upper left), who a year before, while still at Regensburg, had summoned Irish Benedictine monks from Iona in Scotland. The Schottenkirche (Church of the Scots) at the Freyung was named for them. The church was built in the Romanesque style. The east wing was completed as early as 1177, the year in which Jasomirgott died. His family buried him in the crypt of his church. The consecration of the building, however, did not take place until 1200, many years after his death.

Only a few parts of the Schottenkirche, such as the triapsial termination of the choir, still remain of the original Romanesque building. In the southern choir chapel, the so-called "Romanesque Chapel," a number of features of the original building remain, for example the pillar with its octagonal shaft and a volute capital (ill. center right) which was originally part of the monastery cloister. Uncovered fragments of arch with delicately structured cushioned capitals and high imposts also point to a late twelfth-century date (ill. opposite, above). A sculpture of the Madonna, which was brightly painted in the nineteenth century, is clearly identifiable as late Romanesque (ill. opposite, below). The church was altered and partly rebuilt in the fourteenth and fifteenth centuries. This included work on the transept, whose tower collapsed in 1635. From 1638 through 1648 the building was rebuilt in the Baroque style. A painted medallion, which is part of a late fifteenth-century family tree of the Babenbergs, provides some indication of what the building may have looked like at that time. (ill. right).

Jasomirgott also built a royal castle, which was located at Am Hof, today the largest open space in the city center, which stands next to the Freyung, a former Babenberg residence which no longer exists. Today, Märkleinsches Haus, built according to plans by Johann Lukas von Hildebrandt, is located at the site. It is easy to imagine the various events at court which took place in these grand and spacious grounds. Sources report splendid festivities and jousting tournaments. The poet Walther von der Vogelweide, who probably first visited Vienna in 1196 and who is said to have returned to the city again and again, came here to compete in a singing contest against the *minnesinger* (troubadour) Reinmar von Hagenau.

With the foundation of the Schottenkloster (Scottish Monastery) and the extension of the parish of St. Stephen's, founded in 1147, the layout of medieval Vienna gradually emerged. By the end of the twelfth century, the area to the south of Graben, with its five side-streets between Kärntnerstrasse and Kohlmarkt, had also been incorporated. In order to afford sufficient protection to the new settlement along the line between the present Michaelerplatz and Albertinaplatz, not just a wall but presumably a gate and perhaps even a bastion would have been considered. Leopold V is said to have surrounded the settlement with a wall between 1180 and 1198, for which the finance came from the ransom for the release of the English king, Richard the Lionheart, who was captured in 1192 at Erdberg and held prisoner at Aggstein castle. In ca. 1200, Leopold VI also built a new castle, probably on the site of the present Hofburg, near the Stallburg.

By this time, the *civitas* Vienna had become one of the leading centers of trade in Europe. It was thanks to Leopold that in 1221, Vienna received its city charter and became a place of permanent settlement (ill. right). This meant that henceforward, foreign merchants who warehoused their goods in Vienna had to sell them to Viennese merchants within a period of two months. This lead to further economic growth and laid the foundations of modern Vienna as a thriving center of trade.

ILLUSTRATION ABOVE:
Hans Part and other artists
Babenberg family tree, medallion containing the oldest depiction of the Schottenkirche at the Freyung, 1489-92
Klosterneuburg, College Museum

ILLUSTRATION BELOW:
Duke Leopold the Glorious grants Vienna its city charter on October 18, 1221
Austrian National Library

Above: St. Michael's Church, around 1200
14th-century Steeple
Right: Interior with alterations from the Baroque with partial 19th-century restoration of original Gothic features

St. Michael's Church

Around 1200, the former court parish church of St. Michael's was rebuilt as a basilica with two transepts. An earlier building has been dated to ca. 1100. An obvious medieval feature among the many Baroque alterations to the church is the slender Gothic steeple. The remains of frescos on the triumphal arches leading to the choir date from around 1350 and depict scenes from the Last Judgment, showing Christ and the apostles. On the northern wall of the square-ended choir, remnants of other paintings from that era can be seen. The oldest paintings in the church, however, can be found on the southern wall of the steeple chapel. St. Cosmas, St. Damian, and St. Thomas were probably painted around 1300, or slightly earlier, by Viennese masters. On the west wall, a fresco of the same period depicts the Archangel Michael weighing souls in the balance at the Last Judgment. Mary and the Devil are looking on, watching attentively as the scales rise and fall.

St. Michael's Church
Interior west wall with fresco of the archangel Michael at the Last Judgement, ca. 1300

Maria am Gestade

Another church, Maria am Gestade at Salvator-gasse, is important because of its particular location within the city. The steep steps of the Am Gestade and Marienstiege lanes lead up to the small forecourt of the church, with its narrow façade and portal topped by a filigreed baldaquin. The position of the church thus resembles that of St. Ruprecht's, which is probably also why the addition *am Gestade* (on the bank) was made to the dedication. The bank referred to is that of the Danube, on which the church was located.

Maria am Gestade was originally founded as a church for the bargees, who, approaching the city by water, would recognize their destination from a great distance by the slender steeple and towering west façade of the church. The same is true, of course, for traders approaching the city with their carts from the direction of the Vienna Woods. Maria am Gestade was located on high ground just within the city walls, making its elegant outline a city landmark.

The church is first mentioned in a document dating from 1158. There was an earlier church on the site dating from ca. 1030, and archeologists have even discovered the remains of Roman walls within its foundations. The choir of the present church dates from between 1330 to 1369 (ill. p. 19), the nave from 1394 to 1414. The filigree steeple, which is of the same period, is topped by a delicate open lantern and decorated with pinnacles, crockets, and gargoyles. The stained-glass windows of the choir, which are well worth seeing, originated around the middle of the fourteenth century. At some point in the fourteenth century, an unknown artist carved two more Gothic figures from sandstone. These were to become important for the development of medieval sculpture in

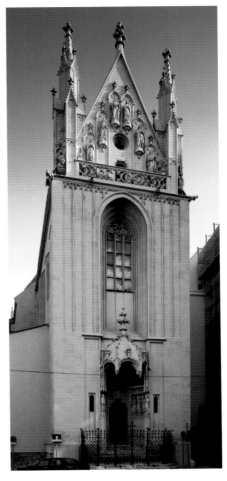

Maria am Gestade, mid-12th to early 15th century
West façade and steeple
Cupola by Michael Knab
1394-1427

Panel paintings from a winged altar
Annunciation (far left)
Coronation (left)

Maria am Gestade
High Gothic stone sculptures in the nave: Mary (left) and the Archangel Gabriel (right) at the center of an Annunciation scene

Lower Austria (ill. p. 18). The statues of Mary and the Archangel Gabriel are the focus of a scene depicting the Annunciation. The graceful figures appear weightless and animated. The many folds in the robes make them appear as if they are floating rather than standing. The locks of their hair are arranged in geometrical patterns. Some historians suspect that these sculptures come from a Bavarian workshop, as Maria am Gestade was the headquarters of a church official from Passau. This, however, appears unlikely as the Viennese sculptures are so much more elegant and graceful than their Bavarian counterparts.

Two late Gothic panel paintings were probably painted around 1460 in a Viennese workshop (ill. p. 17, below). There may be a link to the so-called Scots Master, whose altars originated around that time (see ill. pp. 34–35). A shared esthetic is apparent in the style and composition, as well as in the subject-matter. These paintings indicate stronger Dutch influence, even more than in those of the Scots Master, so that it is tempting to view them as having been produced by the studios of Rogier van der Weyden or Dirk Bouts. The paintings, on a gold ground, depict the Annunciation and the Crowning of The Virgin.

ILLUSTRATION OPPOSITE:
Maria am Gestade, mid-12th to early 15th century
View of the choir, 1330-69

The Minorite Church

The Minorites, who were Franciscans, reached Vienna in the early thirteenth century. They founded a monastery here as well as the church of Maria Schnee. The monastery, however, soon had to make way for the dynastic, court, and state archive.

The main portal of the church is one of Vienna's most precious Gothic treasures. It dates from the fourteenth century and is flanked by a small belfry. The tripartite tympanum of the portal depicts the Crucifixion, and is the work of the Franciscan monk, Jakobus of Paris. During excavations for the construction of the Viennese subway system, the foundations of a Gothic chapel were discovered to the east of the transept. From these, it was possible to reconstruct the ground plan, using stones from the original chapel. These remains can now be visited and, with a little imagination, visualize the size of the original compound.

ILLUSTRATION OPPOSITE:
Minorite Church, pre-1339 to 1380, east view

The Minorite Church
Main portal with tympanum by Jacobus of Paris

The church burnt down several times in quick succession and in 1230, except for the west wing, was completely rebuilt on the same groundplan. In 1258, while the clergy was actually preparing for the consecration, yet another fire devastated the church. St. Stephan's was finally consecrated without further mishap in 1263. Friedrich II, the last of the Babenberg dukes, nicknamed "the Squabbler", who initiated the rebuilding, did not, however, live to see it completed. He fell at the battle against the Hungarians on the Leitha in 1246.

The so-called Giant Gate at the west side of church and the choir gallery recall Friedrich's rule. Here, on the northern wall of the former Babenberg Gallery, remains of frescoes dating from ca. 1290 can still be seen. They depict Christ in the Mandorla. Below him, are the towers and pinnacles of the architecture of Heavenly Jerusalem and a group of figures whose significance is unclear. Historians suspect that the scene depicts the investiture of Albrecht I by King Rudolf I of Habsburg. If this is the case, then the scene depicts an important moment in Austrian history, because Albrecht's ascent to the throne marks the first instance of a Viennese becoming a king of Germany.

Today, only parts of the foundations and the ground floor of the west steeples at the entrance to the west portal of the thirteenth century building remain. Incidentally, these are also called Heathen Towers, after the heathen shrine which is said to have stood on this site.

The Romanesque west section is easy to reconstruct today. In place of the pointed central gothic window there was a rose window. The

ILLUSTRATION OPPOSITE:
St. Stephan's Cathedral,
from 1230

Sculptures from the 12th century integrated into the 13th-century Giant Gate.

St. Stephan's Cathedral, west façade, 1230/40-1263

St. Stephan's Cathedral

By the first half of the thirteenth century, Vienna had expanded to the size of the present city center. St. Stephan's, the symbol of the city, towered above it, even then. The church, lovingly called *Steffl* (Little Stephen) by the Viennese, is the heart of the city and the most important Medieval ecclesiastical building in Austria. It is an impressive example of the interweave of Romanesque and Gothic, and in the case of the cathedral it is very difficult to disentangle the two. This may be a result of the relative speed with which the original church was extended and altered.

St. Stephan's was founded in the 1130s as a parish church of the Passau diocese. The first consecration of the east wing of the church took place in 1147. The nave was completed in 1160. The church was laid out as a basilica with two transepts, two mighty west steeples and a square choir which terminated in an transept. The large transepts also had apses.

two steeples were connected by a blind arcade, which was roofed over by a low triangular gable, the top of which would have reached up to the present Gothic central window.

In the few years which it took to complete the Late Romanesque cathedral, the groundwork for the ascendancy of the Habsburg dynasty was laid. After the death of the last of Babenberg duke, King Ottokar II of Bohemia laid claim to the throne of both countries. Only after Rudolf I of Habsburg had been elected king could the Babenberg lands be wrested from Ottokar.

A stained-glass choir window dating from 1390 (today in the collection of the Historisches Museum) shows Rudolf sitting under a canopy holding a scepter and the shield of the imperial eagle (ill. right). This is the first in a series of such portraits of Habsburg kings. This monumental row of royal portraits is most likely the work of a Viennese court artist, who was probably influenced by developments in Viennese sculpture.

A comparison illustrates this very well. The sculptures on the Giant Gate date from the thirteenth century. The tympanum shows Christ in Majesty; over the door and in the arch grotesques crouch below dignified apostles (ill. upper left). Even the stonemason and the canon are present in this portal. Composition, facial characteristics, and other details point to this being the work of a studio in Bamberg. The sculptures on one of the gates at Bamberg Cathedral (between 1229 and 1231) show many similarities to the apostle figures of the Giant Gate. Incidentally, the portal's name derives from the finding of a bone of a mammoth during construction. The workers of the time thought they had found the bone of a giant who had died during Noah's Flood.

St. Stephan's was largely reconstructed in Gothic style in the fourteenth century. In 1304, work was begun on the large choir (ill. p. 25). The new building was dedicated thirty-six years later. Albrecht I, the son of Rudolf I of Habsburg, who was elected German king in 1298, is listed as the patron. Work was completed under his son, Albrecht II. The section of the building called the Albertine Choir is named for him. Rudolf IV, son of Albrecht II, commissioned the building of the Gothic nave and the widening of the aisles in 1359. This king, who is also called "the Founder," contributed substantially to the political and economic growth of Vienna. He regulated and maximized tax revenue, promoted trades and crafts, and founded and furthered the *Universitas Literarum* along the lines of the university in Prague. The university received its charter on March 12, 1365; the charter is written in German and Latin.

King Rudolf I
Painting on glass, ca. 1390
St. Stephan's Cathedral,
former choir
Historisches Museum, Vienna

ILLUSTRATION LEFT:
St. Stephan's Cathedral,
Giant Gate
Apostles and grotesques in the
arch (above)

St. Stephan's Cathedral,
Singer Gate
Detail depicting scenes from the life
of St. Paul
1359-65 (below)

ILLUSTRATION OPPOSITE:
St. Stephan's Cathedral, view of
the Albertine Choir, 1304-40

Rudolf is shown holding a model of the cathedral building in his hand on the two aisle portals, the northern Bishop's Gate and the southern Singer Gate, which are located directly behind the west façade of St. Stephen's (ill. left). These models, the first representations of St. Stephan's, show different views of the cathedral, and the Albertine choir is greatly simplified. A portrait of Rudolf, who was the son-in-law of the Emperor Charles IV, who lived in Prague, has survived; it is by an unknown Viennese master (ill. p. 29). Together with a portrait of King John of France, which originated at around the same time, it is one of the earliest individual portraits.

The height and width of the church interior are unusual in scale (ill. right). The distance between the west portal and the choir is about 400 feet (100 m). The pillars of the nave are massive and appear monumental. The windows, on the other hand, are tall and slender. They are framed by pilasters with foliage consoles and roofed over by delicate three-faceted fillets. The vault of the nave is not much higher than those of the aisles; the older choir, on the other hand, is a hall choir with a simple ribbed vault. To reconcile the two contrasting building styles, the architect constructed a slender blind arcade to suggest a dynamic rise.

The eastern central window of the choir depicts a crucifixion scene in bright blues and purples. This is probably the most valuable Gothic exhibit in the cathedral and dates from ca. 1340.

The sculptures of the middle choir, the figures of St. Lawrence, St. Stephen, St. Christopher, St. Catherine, and John the Baptist, are similar in style. They probably once belonged to a much larger group depicting all the saints. The so-called *Dienstbotenmadonna* (Servants' Madonna) on the right of the transept (ill. p. 27 upper left) is considered to be one of the most charming Madonnas of its time. Created in 1320 to 1325, it reflects the elegance of court art, while at the same time shows great sensitivity in the portrayal of the affection the mother is showing to the child. It is likely that the statue was once a devotional figure belonging to the Lady Altar in the women's choir.

The altar tomb of Rudolf IV, the cathedral's patron, who died in 1365, can be found in the main choir in the crypt which Rudolf had built especially to house tombs of the members of the House of Habsburg. He and his wife, Katharina of Bohemia, the daughter of Emperor Charles IV, are shown on the tomb. Both figures appear to float rather than lie. The tomb is considered a prime example of the Gothic Viennese stonemasons' art (ill. left).

ILLUSTRATION ABOVE:
St. Stephan's Cathedral, Singer Gate, 1359-65. Rudolf IV with a model of the cathedral

ILLUSTRATION BELOW:
St. Stephan's Cathedral. Altar tomb of Rudolf IV and his wife, ca. 1360

St. Stephan's Cathedral
Man of Sorrow, around 1420-30

The sculptures of the Bishop's Gate closely resemble those of the choir in style, and have been linked to a Prague workshop. The tympanum depicts the Death of Mary and her coronation in heaven. The lower figures are individual portraits of Rudolf's IV brother, Albrecht III, and his wife Elisabeth of Bohemia.

Other items from St. Stephen's can be found today in the Cathedral and Diocesan Museum. The strangely three-dimensional group of figures of the Deposition (ill. upper right) probably comes from a passion cycle created ca. 1330 to 1340. The figures of Mary and John the Baptist (ill. right) belonged to a crucifixion scene dating from the early 15th century.

After the death of Rudolf IV in 1365, his brother Albrecht III became the patron of the continuing reconstruction of the cathedral. Between 1380 and 1390, the southern choir steeple was raised up to the second story and adorned with a large number of sculptures.

In 1400 the first draft was submitted for the monumental single steeple which can still be seen today. Its construction, which marked the transition from the Middle Ages to the Renaissance, was completed around 1433.

Gothic painting

The panel paintings of Klosterneuburg mark the spectacular beginnings of Gothic painting in Vienna. They were painted by artists from Viennese workshops, so that the existence of a reputable Viennese school can be assumed. In 1322, a fire at the abbey church at Klosterneuburg substantially damaged and partly destroyed the unique enamel panels which Nikolaus of Verdun had created for an ambo in 1181. For this reason, it was decided to reassemble the panels so as to create a winged altar instead, and to attach new panel paintings at the back of this altar. Provost Stephan von Sierndorf in 1324 commissioned four such paintings. One of them shows two scenes, *The Three Maries at the Grave* and *Noli me tangere* (ill. p. 29, upper right). The Viennese master seems to have been familiar with Giotto's frescoes in the Arena Chapel in Padua, since the Italian master's use of perspective and principles of composition seem to have guided the painter. The reverse perspective of the grave and the Giottoesque hill landscape are particularly notable. The other panel paintings also show influences of Giotto, so that one is justified in assuming that these paintings are evidence of a first critical appraisal of Giotto's work north of the Alps.

The surprisingly early portrait paintings have already been mentioned in the context of the portrait of Duke Rudolph IV (ill. p. 29, lower left). In a further panel painting depicting the Crucifixion, the painter incorporated a portrait of the patron, Provost Stephan von Sierndorf. The Italian influences, which once again are identifiable in this painting, can be explained in terms of the political ambitions of the House of Habsburg, which were then directed southward.

While the restoration work at Klosterneuberg in Carinthia was proceeding, parts of Friuli and Trieste fell to Austria. The fourteenth-century conquests of what is now Italy certainly influenced Viennese art, and this influence spread as far north as Prague, where around the middle of the century the Master of Hohenfurth began to draw on the elegant figures and decorative compositional elements of Viennese works of art.

At the beginning of the century, a number of important workshops producing illuminated manuscripts had established themselves, whose high standard of quality is comparable to that of the Wenzel workshop in Prague which also flourished at that time. The first court miniature was the *Rationale Durandi*, commissioned by Duke Albrecht III around 1385. Its first pages are in the so-called "soft style" characteristic of Bohemia, whereas later pages already show a definite French influence.

The Vienna court illuminators maintained very close links with Klosterneuburg, as is apparent from the Klosterneuburg Bible, which dates

Angel with Thurible,
Stained-glass window,
ca. 1340
St. Stephan's Cathedral and
Diocesan Museum

Master Nikolaus
Holy Trinity
Page from codex CCI 67 fol. 3v,
1421 - 1424
Museum of the College at
Klosterneuburg

Viennese Master (?)
Portrait of Duke Rudolf IV the
Founder, 1360 - 1365
Painting on wood, 18 x 12 in
(45 x 30 cm).
St. Stephan's Cathedral and
Diocesan Museum

from the first decades of the fourteenth century. In the many surviving bills for work done we get a real sense of the personalities of the artists behind the works of art. One of these artists was Master Nikolaus, who was active in Vienna up to ca. 1430 and who was also involved in the creation of the *Rationale Durandi*. The shapes

and colors of his illumination of the Holy Trinity, completed between 1421 and 1424 (ill. upper left), still show signs of Bohemian influences which, however, were slowly loosing ground in response to developments in southern Dutch painting. Some aspects of the design of the ornamentation are also reminiscent of Franco-Flemish manuscript illustrations.

It is also worth taking a brief look at medieval crafts, although few examples have survived to the present day. There is evidence of the existence of goldsmithing workshops from as early as 1170, which points both to the city's prosperity and to the self-assurance of its rulers. When Leopold VI described the city to Pope Innocent III as the largest in Germany apart from Cologne, he was referring not just to the city's topography but more importantly to its economic power.

One of the oldest objects produced in a Viennese goldsmith's workshop is a Romanesque chalice, which may have been made as early as the thirteenth century. It is fashioned from gold-plated copper, and the stem is decorated with leaves and half-circles.

It has also been proven that the altar by Nikolaus of Verdun at Klosterneuburg was repaired and restructured in a leading Viennese goldsmith's workshop in 1331 after being damaged in the fire. A silver processional cross, the work of a Viennese silversmith dating from the mid fourteenth century and now in the possession of Schnütgen Museum in Cologne, also bears witness to the high standard of Viennese craftsmanship at the time.

Rear view of the Klosterneuburg Altar:
The three Maries at the Grave and Noli me tangere 1330 - 31 Painting on wood, 40 x 47 in (102 x 120 cm), Museum of the College at Klosterneuburg

Viennese workshop
Processional cross, 14th century
Schnütgen Museum, Cologne

St. Stephan's Cathedral
North tower, 1467

Hans Puchsbaum
Draft of the northern steeple in
elevation, around 1400
Historisches Museum der
Stadt Wien.

Moving into the Renaissance

After Duke Albrecht V came to power in 1411, the city again experienced a cultural revival, although it was accompanied by general unrest. Emergency taxes and military spending were burdens on the citizens and stifled economic initiative. Merchants from southern Germany dominated the capital market. Dissatisfaction and dissent grew and found an outlet in civic unrest, which was soon directed against the Jews, who lived in a ghetto near the old castle at Am Hof. The persecution of the Jews culminated in an appalling massacre of 1420 in which more than 200 men and women were burned at the stake outside the city walls, and the ghetto was dispersed.

The social and economic turmoil of those years was accompanied by intrigue among the political leadership. Emperor Friedrich III, guardian of his son Albrecht who was still a minor, strove to assume the regency of Vienna. The result was continuous factional fighting, in the course of which Archduke Albrecht VI laid claim to the city. Civil war broke out in 1461,

and the castle came repeatedly under siege. Eventually, in 1463, Albrecht VI emerged as the winner of the conflict, although he died the same year.

Throughout this eventful period, St. Stephan's Cathedral acquired more or less the form it has today. To return to the history of its construction and its appearance in the Late Middle Ages, while the interior is characterized mainly by tall Gothic structures, the outside, apart from the sculptures of the portal, is dominated by late Gothic stylistic elements. The stonework of the cathedral, the walls of the nave, the buttresses, and the choir give the impression of an imposing "architectural mountain range", with the mighty southern spire appearing almost to stand as a separate bell tower.

The most significant new building and reconstruction works were begun In the first half of the fifteenth century. Before 1440, workers had been busy with the brickwork on the outer walls of the nave. At the same time, the new transept was built. Finally, plans were presented for a new design of the west façade. The west gallery was to be restructured and the façade as a whole made bigger and broken through, to allow a large middle window to be built. We cannot be certain whether an extension with two steeples on the east side was still being envisioned at that time.

In 1467, work commenced on the north tower (ill. left). The foundation stone had been laid seventeen years previously, a definite indication of the indecision which prevailed as to the final structure and height of the tower. A draft of the northern steeple in elevation, from the Viennese stonemasons' lodge, illustrates the dimensions originally envisioned. It was actually planned to make this tower even slightly higher than its southern counterpart.

At around the same time Vienna became a diocese, which was perhaps what prompted the sudden start of work on the tower. Work was stopped in 1511, however, and a Renaissance story added to the flat-topped tower. Exactly two hundred years later, in 1711, a twenty-ton bell was added, the so-called *Pummerin* (Boomer).

The transition to Renaissance style is visible in the interior mainly in the rich ornamentation of the pillars. The biblical figures and saints probably date from between 1435 and 1490. The names of the sculptors are unknown, but it seems that there were several, each with his own individual style and techniques. The great Lady-altar, built in 1447, with its sculptures in the shrine and its splendidly painted outer wings, bears witness to the transition from the Gothic to the early modern period (ill. p. 31, right). It comes from a Viennese workshop and was a donated to the church by King Friedrich

III. For this reason, it is also often called Friedrich's altar. Friedrich III, who became emperor in 1452, had his motto *A E I O U* (*Austria erit in orbe ultima*) inscribed in the altar, thereby documenting for the first time the House of Habsburg's pretensions to universal power. The graceful poses of the sculptures and their loosely flowing robes are typical of the early fifteenth century. The saints and biblical figures in the altar wings are painted in a similar fashion.

For the creation of his tomb (ill. p. 33, above), Friedrich III in 1467 summoned the famous Niclaes Gerhaert of Leyden, who was then working in Strasbourg. The aged sculptor, however, only managed to complete the creation of a model before he died in Vienna in 1473. His son completed the work, which the Emperor did not live to see as he died in 1493. The monumental tomb, which can only be compared to that of Maximillian, his son, at Innsbruck, was completed in 1513 and was placed in the southern choir chapel. This is where the emperor found his final resting-place.

Viennese Master (?)
Lady-altar, 1447
St. Stephan's Cathedral,
north choir

ILLUSTRATION LEFT:
Late Gothic pillar ornamentation
Nave, St. Stephan's Cathedral

In 1511, the city appointed Anton Pilgram as
master builder for the cathedral. Pilgram, who
was both a sculptor and an architect, was born
in Brno (Brünn) in 1465, and for many years
worked in southwest Germany, where,
amongst other things, he constructed the chan-
cel of St. Kilian's at Heilbronn. He only arrived in
Vienna toward the end of his life, but shortly
before his death he created his most significant
work, the organ bracket and pulpit of St.
Stephan's Cathedral.

The organ bracket, next to the northern
transept pillar, shows the artist himself, holding
a par of compasses and a set-square. The organ
itself was dismantled in 1720. The pulpit, which
was created between 1514 and 1515, shows in
the balustrade the four Fathers of the church,
saints Gregory, Ambrose, Jerome, and Augustine, who, as the "pillars of the Church," represent correct doctrine. Lizards and toads on the
parapet of the stairs symbolize, as in the Middle
Ages, the evil of the world, which is conquered
by the Church Fathers. Posing as "the man at
the window," Anton Pilgram has immortalized
himself in this self-portrait, which shows the
artist's independence and is a reference to the
dawning of the modern age.

The intensely realistic representation of the
human form and the unusual variety of shapes
and movement differ from the Gothic style of
representation, which tended to idealize and to
ignore individual facial characteristics. Pilgram's
art was based on an intensive critical appraisal
of the late medieval workshops of the Upper
Rhine valley, and especially the work of Niclaes
Gerhaert, whose broad-shouldered figures and
coarse faces live on in Pilgram's own work.

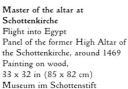
Master of the altar at
Schottenkirche
Flight into Egypt
Panel of the former High Altar of
the Schottenkirche, around 1469
Painting on wood,
33 x 32 in (85 x 82 cm)
Museum im Schottenstift

Depictions of the city

A number of depictions of the city present a picture of the late medieval St. Stephan's Cathedral and the surrounding buildings. One of these is the background to an altar painting by the Scottish master (so-called after an altar he built for the Schottenkirche) depicting the flight into Egypt (ill. above), showing medieval Vienna. The artist probably placed himself on one of the hills in the southwest of the city to study the details and sketch the city outline. The southern steeple and the west façade are clearly recognizable, as well as the choir and the church roof. Even the gable of the nave, completed at this time, can be made out. To the right of the rock the rounded steeple of Maria am Gestade soars unmistakably. The steeple rising above the horizon to the left of St. Stephan's is probably that of St. Michael's. The neighboring Hofburg can be made out as a massive fortress with two towers. Further to the left, marking the southwest section of the city, one can see the choir steeple of the Minorite church. The panel paintings of the Scottish altar constitute one of the outstanding works of late Gothic painting in Vienna. This monumental altar has wings which when open depict the life of Mary in 16 panels and when

closed show the passion of Christ in eight panels. The passion scenes are placed in an urban context and follow motifs by Rogier van der Weyden or Dirk Bout. As in the medieval passion plays, the characters are placed in front of buildings or in the entrances of houses. The scenes depicting Christ's entry into Jerusalem, the carrying of the cross, the Crucifixion and the mourning of Christ (ills. p. 35) have backgrounds which recall the Danube valley and the softly rolling hills of the Vienna Woods.

Another altar painting by the same artist, identified by some art historians as Wolfgang Kremser, and belonging to the same altar, depicts the meeting between Mary and Elisabeth (ill. above). The setting for meeting is Kärntnerstrasse. The viewer looks down that street toward St. Stephan's and recognizes the façade with the two Heiden Towers. The church to the left is St. Peter's before it was rebuilt, of course, during the Baroque period.

A further depiction of Vienna on a medallion dates from 1489 and is part of the Babensberg family tree from Klosterneuburg already mentioned above. It depicts the death of Friedrich the Quarrelsome in the battle against the Hungarians in 1246. Here too Vienna is the background for the picture.

Master of the altar at
Schottenkirche
Visitation of Mary
Panel of the former High Altar of
the Schottenkirche, ca. 1469
Painting on wood, 34 x 33 in
(85 x 82 cm)
Museum im Schottenstift

ILLUSTRATION OPPOSITE:
Master of the Altar at
Schottenkirche
The Mourning of Christ
Panel of the former High Altar of
the Schottenkirche, ca. 1469
Painting on wood, 34 x 33 in
(85 x 82 cm)
Collection of the Österreiche
Galerie

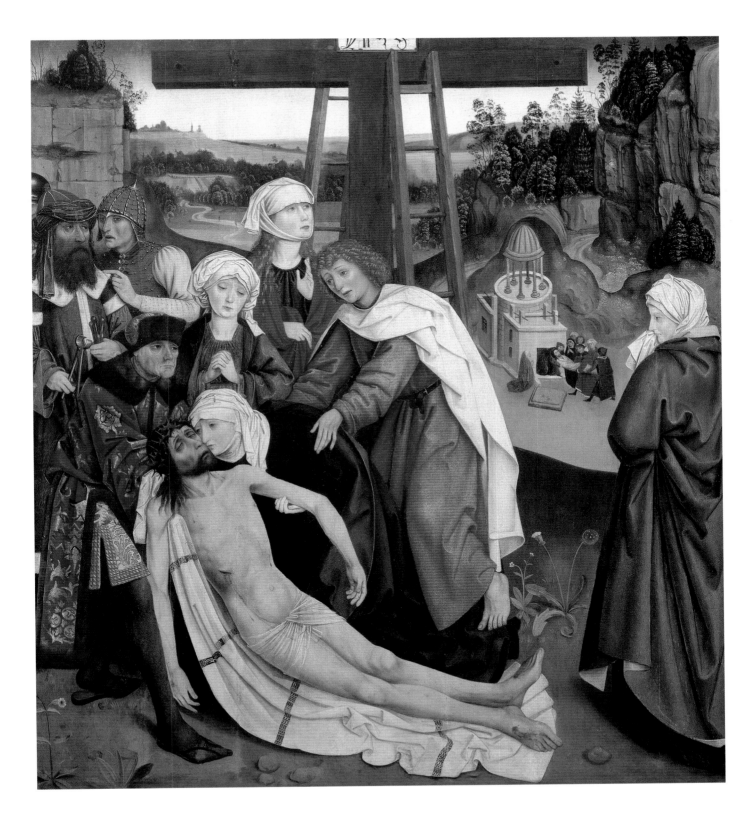

Scenes from the alter in the Schottenaltar   35

The Renaissance

Vienna in the Late Middle Ages was a wealthy and elegant city. The most significant building projects had mainly been completed. Even some of the city homes of the burghers resembled splendid palaces. This is pointed out in a letter written by Enea Silvio Picolomini, later Pope Pius II, dating from 1438, in which he states: "The houses of the burghers are tall and roomy, decorative, well and solidly built, with pleasant halls and enormous rooms, which they call parlors, and which are heated because the winters are very cold. There are glass windows everywhere. Doors and railings are generally made of iron. Birds sing in the parlors, and they contain many wonderful objects. Wide stables are open to horses and all kinds of draft animals. The houses have tall gables. They are tastefully and splendidly ornamented, and generally painted both inside and out. They are built of stone, but sadly the roofs are mostly of shingles, not tiles. When you visit a burgher, you would think you were visiting a nobleman."

According to this description some of these homes of the burghers were not just comfortable, but quite luxurious. The increase in bourgeois wealth is one of the characteristic features of the early Renaissance, and becomes obvious, above all, in the interior decoration and furnishings of the houses.

This was positively repellent to those who considered themselves the guardians of high morals and to religious zealots. One sermon by the Viennese university lecturer, Georg Tudel von Giengen, from around 1460 deals with the immoral and decadent tastes of the well-to-do. Tudel criticizes the design of townhouse bedrooms, and especially of the beds themselves. In spite of—or perhaps because of—this critique, the document is of singular importance as an indication of the changing tastes characteristic of the Renaissance in Vienna. To quote from the sermon, "Sixth, it is sinful to have the canopy above it painted with shameless pictures, whence comes great sin and woe. One finds numerous impudent persons who have made such shameless paintings for themselves that these can not be spoken of. And other innocent people, seeing these, might be led into temptation. If man wants to adorn his canopy or bed with paintings, these should be of the bitter passion of Christ, and of the Cross and of the Last Judgement, causing him to atone and lament for his sins."

Even while enjoying these delights, Vienna also faced a difficult and bloody challenge. On September 22, 1529, the Turks, under their Sultan Suleiman I, stood before the gates of the city. Three years earlier, they had beaten the Hungarians in the battle of Mohács and had conquered Budapest. Now the Viennese were

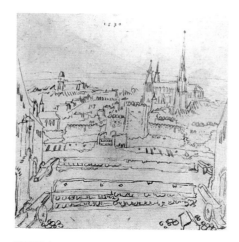

Wolf Huber
The Turkish siege of Vienna, 1530
Ink drawing, Albertina Collection.

awaiting the onslaught of the mighty Turkish army. The city had been weakened by a dreadful fire, which had broken out four years earlier and had destroyed more than one third of all the buildings. Rebuilding was costly and slow. Moreover, the medieval bastions had to be re-enforced and even rebuilt in many places. As news of the approaching Ottoman army reached the city, many burghers fled in haste. Among them were the members of the City Council, who thus avoided being drafted into the defense of the city. As the suburbs had to be destroyed to give the artillery a clear view of the attacking Turkish army, their inhabitants made for the inner city. Disputes over ownership and protection arose while, at the same time, the military high command under Count Nicklas Salm, appointed by Ferdinand, had difficulties in mustering a trained army capable of defending Vienna.

Fortunately, Count Palatine Phillip arrived at the fortress literally at the last minute with an army of 17,000 men, mainly Germans and Spaniards. Now, at least, there was a chance, albeit slim, of successfully defending the city.

The Turkish attack was directed against the Kärntner Gate, and succeeded in making dangerously large breaches in the city wall. Thanks to the heroic defense lead by Count Salm, however, the attackers were eventually beaten back on October 15. The prudent Count was also fortunate in the weather, which did much to prevent the Turkish attack. The first winter storms, which included deluge-like rainfall, forced Suleiman to call off the siege of the city, and the Turkish army withdrew. There was no immediate danger from the Turks for the time being, but people were convinced that the Ottoman advance could be repeated.

A drawing by Wolf Huber, who together with Albrecht Altdorfer is seen as one of the founders

of the so-called "Danube School," shows a view of the city as seen from the south (ill. left). The towers of St. Ann's can be made out in front of St. Stephan's Cathedral. This chapel was probably built around 1320, and after 1531 it was extended into a convent of the Order of St. Clare The small church does not exist any more; it was demolished in 1887. The tower of the Kärntner Gate, hotly contested during the Turkish siege, can also be seen clearly in Huber's drawing. It stands between the battlements of the city walls. The large holes in the wall were the result of grenade bombardment, at which the Turks were experts. The drawing is a unique document and shows the heavy losses suffered by the city in warding off the attack.

Another principal figure of the "Danube School" was Lucas Cranach the Elder, who had also resided in Vienna, although he had done so two decades earlier and only for a short time. There is evidence of his presence in the city between 1502 and 1504. What could have enticed the young painter from Kronach in Upper Franconia to come to Vienna? Famous master painters in whose workshops the young painter might have trained did not exist in Vienna at that time, but could be found in many other European cities. The young Albrecht Dürer, for example, went to Colmar, to study the work of the great Martin Schongauer, and later to Venice to learn about new developments in Renaissance art. Perhaps Cranach sought contact with the imperial court of Maximillian I which was a major source of stimulation for the arts and sciences. Vienna was then the largest German city, and capital of the German and Roman empire.

An important early work by Lucas Cranach, which also illustrates this atmosphere of humanist learning, is his portrait of Dr. Johan Cuspinian, rector of the university from 1501, whose final resting-place can be found to the left of the entrance to St. Stephan's. In the painting, the scholar is portrayed as a poet inspired by the dramatic world of nature. His hand rests on a book, which symbolizes his superior knowledge (ill. p. 37, left). We know that Cuspinian specifically instructed the painter to use an astrological constellation for the painting's background. The star shining through the trees is Saturn, the planet of melancholy, reflection, and genius. The merciless owl with the oriole in its claws also makes reference to a Saturnian disposition. The bathing figures in the background, on the other hand, are indicative of the influence of the moon, linked to the water element. All these are symbols of the planetary influences which the scholar believed himself to be under.

The living landscape reappears in the portrait of Cuspinian's wife, Anna Putsch, with its use of the symbols and allegories of the sitter's horoscope. The burning castle in the background and

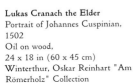

Lukas Cranach the Elder
Portrait of Johannes Cuspinian,
1502
Oil on wood,
24 x 18 in (60 x 45 cm)
Winterthur, Oskar Reinhart "Am
Römerholz" Collection

the falcon attacking a swan in flight symbolize the influence of the planet Mars on her disposition and the young woman's choleric temperament. Anna Putsch, who had only married the young scholar one year previously and who is depicted in the dress of a Viennese aristocrat, was the daughter of the treasurer to Maximillian I, whom Cuspinian served as a diplomat. In the painting, she holds a carnation in her hand and appears somewhat introverted and self-conscious. Her husband, on the other hand, glancing upward curiously and rather stubbornly, appears both self-confident and approachable.

It is possible that the artist intended the double portrait to symbolize the dichotomy between the medieval and the modern world. This dichotomy would be apparent not just in the poses and expressions of the sitters, but also in the contrast between the humanist and astrological elements of the pictures on the one hand and the symbolic backgrounds on the other. These show particularly Gothic landscapes, with castles towering above steep mountain cliffs. The characteristics

of landscape painting to be seen here, such as exaggerated rock formations, lush green trees, and snow-covered mountain ranges seen in the distance, were adopted by Albrecht Altdorfer and became characteristic of the Danube School.

It is difficult to pinpoint exactly when the Renaissance can be said to have begun in Vienna. Certainly the brief influence of Lucas Cranach the Elder had introduced a modern note. His iconographic and stylistic momentum helped to foster the new direction art was to take in the Renaissance. Cranach's artistic ideas were advanced considerably by the university under the patronage of the Habsburg king, Maximillian I, who became emperor in 1508. The influence of Burgundy, the northern cradle of the Renaissance, was determined by Maximillian's marriage to Maria, daughter of Charles the Bold, Duke of Burgundy. Italian cultural influences were also felt after Maximillian's second marriage, to Maria Bianca Sforza, niece of Lodovico, the Milanese ruler. Maximillian's aim was to extend his political influence and expand his power base.

Lukas Cranach the Elder
Portrait of Anna Putsch, 1502
Oil on wood, 24 x 18 in
(60 x 45 cm).
Winterthur, Oskar Reinhart "Am
Römerholz" Collection

Salvator Chapel
Porch, around 1525

The marriage of Philip the Fair, Maximillian's son, to Johanna, daughter of the Catholic king of Castile and Queen of Aragon, meant that Spain and its territories, including the kingdom of Naples and its overseas colonies, were now also part of the House of Habsburg, along with territories in Burgundy and Italy. Previously, under the Peace of Bratislava in 1491, Maximillian had secured for the Habsburgs the succession to the thrones of Bohemia and Hungary. Philipp, Archduke of Austria and briefly King of Castile, died in 1506. His son, Charles I of Castile and Aragon, became Emperor Charles V in 1519. Until he abdicated in 1556, Charles V ruled an empire on which, as he himself put it, "the sun never set." Charles V, born in Ghent in 1500, could be said to be neither Viennese nor Austrian, in fact, if anything, he was Dutch or Burgundian. When, on the death of his father Philip in 1516, he came into the Habsburg inheritance, he ruled over his vast empire from El Escorial, his palace near Madrid.

The political development, which was to fundamentally change the course of European history, began in Vienna. In 1522, Emperor Charles V bequeathed his Habsburg inheritance to his brother, Ferdinand of Austria, who later married Anna, the sister of the last king of Bohemia and Hungary, Ludwig II. When Ludwig fell in battle at Mohács, Ferdinand succeeded to the throne of Bohemia and in 1529, after the Turkish withdrawal from Vienna and Hungary, also gained control of Hungary. The enormous empire had become divided into two parts. Ferdinand I, German king from 1533 and Holy Roman Emperor after his brother's abdication, ruled over the hereditary Habsburg lands, which included possessions in the southwest of what is now Germany and parts of Burgundy. The other half of the empire, which included Spain and its colonies, Naples, Milan, the Duchy of Burgundy, and the Netherlands, fell to Philip II, son of Charles V, after Charles himself died in 1568.

The Renaissance in Vienna appears as a period of transition between the Late Middle Ages and the Baroque. The burgeoning humanism, the artistic awakening brought about by the "Danube School," and the European expansion of the Habsburg empire and its consequent division can be said to have been innovative factors both politically and artistically. The forms of expression they found, however, were limited artistically.

A number of reasons prevented the kind of cultural rebirth which took place in other countries. Firstly, there was the Turkish threat, which was finally overcome and ended in the expulsion of the Turkish forces. This required the rebuilding of the rebuilding of the suburbs and of the fortifications of the city itself.

Vienna was also inextricably linked to the major developments in European history which occurred in the first half of the sixteenth century. The more significant of these included Martin Luther's posting of the Theses at Wittenberg (1517), which effectively started the Reformation; the Peasants' Revolt (1524-25); the formation of the Catholic League (1538), and finally the Council of Trent, which triggered the Counter-Reformation. Europe, torn apart by religious and social upheaval, stood on the brink of the Thirty Years War.

Hofthaler (after J Francolin)
The Imperial Castle, 1560
Albertina Collection

Historia Frederici et Maximilliani
Siege of the Hofburg by the
Viennese in 1462
Dynastic, Court, and State
Archive

Hofburg
Swiss Gate, 1552

After the division of the Empire, King Ferdinand I had to make new plans for Vienna as his city of residence. He may have had plans to this effect as early as 1525, but a fire devastated large parts of the city. Rebuilding the city as quickly as possible took precedence over the expansion of the castle. Unlike the city of Klagenfurth, for instance, where a similar fire had resulted in a comprehensive program of urban redevelopment, in Vienna the opportunity was not grasped because of the huge expense involved in the reconstruction of the city's fortifications which had been destroyed as a result of the battles with the Turks. As a consequence, Vienna does not possess the typical grid layout of other royal cities of residence in mainland Europe.

The years of disruption between the great fire and the Turkish threat did, however, produce one gem of the Renaissance — the Salvator Chapel (ill. p. 38, above). Its portal, with its delicate acanthus arabesques and the slender pillars with Corinthian capitals, is a rare example of Italianate Renaissance style in Vienna, and the tympanum with its paneled arch resembles those of the Florentine Quattrocento.

The Hofburg

In 1533, Ferdinand I, then still only King of Bohemia, decided to relocate the most important royal offices from Prague to Vienna. The time had finally come to rebuild and extend the royal castle, the Hofburg. As already mentioned, the Bohemian King Ottokar had begun construction on the center section of the present Hofburg in the area of the Schweizerhof, in 1275.

Whether or not Ferdinand intended to incorporate the older castle of Leopold VI is unclear. Having ousted Ottokar in 1278, Rudolf I completed the building. This oldest part of the castle was a four-winged complex with powerful angled towers and a chapel which was extended in the fifteenth century and whose transept protrudes from the façade. An engraving from 1517 from the *Historia Friderici et Maximilliani* depicts the siege of the castle and the royal family by angry Viennese in 1462 (ill. upper left) and is probably the work of a Viennese master of the Danube School. The hurried style hardly allows

Samual von Hoogstraten
Inner Ward and Amalienburg,
1652
Museum of the History of Art

Hofburg
View of the arcades of the Stallburg
1558 onward

for any detailed observation of the state of the building, but the dimensions of the medieval Hofburg and one of the towers can be recognized quite clearly.

Ferdinand I extended this part of the Hofburg and transformed it into a magnificent Renaissance castle. The Swiss Gate (ill. p. 39, right) and the wing between the Schweizerhof and the inner ward were built in 1552 under the royal master builder Pietro Ferrabosco. The three-quarter columns of the Swiss Gate are inlaid with strong metal rings. The entrance is covered by a depressed mirrored vault, which is decorated with gargoyles, coats of arms, and ornaments. Incidentally, these parts of the Hofburg were only given their present names in the middle of the eighteenth century, after the Swiss troops serving Franz I, husband of the Empress Maria Theresia.

The Stallburg with its splendid court arcades (ill. right) was built in 1562, when Ferdinand's son, the archduke and later emperor, Maximillian II, returned from Spain to become King of Germany. It housed the royal stables and later the royal picture galleries. The Tournament Book of 1561 contains a vivid depiction of the interior of the apartments in the

sixteenth century. The illustration by Hanns von Francolin is entitled "Luncheon of His Roman Imperial Majesty on June 13, 1560 at the Viennese Castle" and depicts opulent Renaissance décor and mounted, intarsiated ornaments. The massive paneled ceiling and the large tapestries on the walls of the room are also clearly recognizable.

In 1575, Pietro Ferrabosco presented the Emperor Rudolf II with plans for a new castle, later called the Amalienburg (ill. above) after Amalie, wife of Emperor Joseph I. It is situated opposite the Swiss Court and was completed in 1588. The two buildings are not connected; presumably they each bordered the old city wall which ran along their south-facing walls. The older part of the Hofburg, the Swiss Court, and the Amalienburg were situated around the inner ward, where Emperor Maximillian II, founder of the Spanish Riding School in 1572, held horse races. The old and the new castle were eventually linked by the first Emperor of the Baroque period in Vienna, Leopold I. The so-called Leopoldine Section, an imposing castle complex, was built between 1660 and 1666 and was modeled on the royal residence in Munich.

Map of the Hofburg

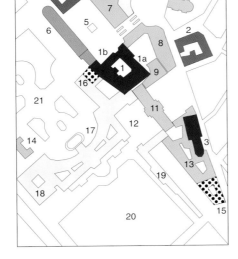

1 Swiss Court
1a Treasury
1b Swiss Gate
2 Stallburg
3 Augustine Chapel
4 Amalienburg
5 Inner Ward
6 Leopoldine Section
7 Chancellery
8 Spanish Riding
    School
9 Ballroom
10 St. Michael's Church
11 Royal Library
12 Library Courtyard
13 Augustine Monastery
14 Outer Gate
15 Albertina
16 Ceremonial Hall
17 Neue Burg
18 Ethnology Museum
19 Orangery
20 Royal Garden
21 Heldenplatz

 Middle Ages

16th century

 17th century

 18th century

 1800 - 1850

1850 - 1900

Maximillian II, who took an interest in the arts and sciences, also had a summer residence built outside the city walls, the plans for which were drawn up by Pietro Ferrabosco. The New Building, as it was called, was meant to astound and impress European diplomats. Construction commenced in 1569. Maximillian II, who died in 1576, did not live to see the finished work, which was only completed eleven years later under his successor, Rudolf II. By that time, though, Rudolf had already left Vienna, which was being torn apart by religious upheaval, and had moved the court to Prague.

The magnificent castle and its gardens no longer exist, and the few remaining walls cannot do justice to the grandeur of what used to be the largest palace complex in a city north of the Alps. Maximillian II, following the examples of the Italian princes of the Renaissance, had tried to combine the pleasures of court life with the seriousness of scientific pursuit. The luxurious apartments housed valuable collections and small libraries, while the gardens with their fountains and sculptures were filled with exotic flora and fauna.

Aerial photograph showing parts of the Hofburg (Neue Burg, Heldenplatz, Outer Gate) as well as the Museum of Fine Arts and the Museum of Natural History (in the foreground)
All buildings date from the 19th century.

Apart from the Renaissance sections of the Hofburg, only one city house of that time survives, the so-called "Palais Porcia" on the Herrengasse. It is said to have been built at the end of the sixteenth century, although not for the owner whose name it bears and who acquired it much later. The coat of arms in the center of the two-story row of arcades in the courtyard names Georg Andreas, Baron of Hofkirchen, as the first owner. He was, however, unable to complete the building himself due to lack of funds. His brother-in-law, Losensteiner, provided the necessary capital and in return acquired the privilege of placing his family coat of arms next to that of the baron. The delicate arcades in the courtyard and the ornaments adorned with musical instruments and weaponry which decorate the arcade spandrels are reminiscent of the late Italian Renaissance (ill. left). The same is true of the triangular gable and the ornaments of the main facade, which already lean heavily toward the Baroque (ill. p. 53).

The only Viennese church with a Renaissance façade is located on the picturesque Franziskanerplatz (ill. p. 43). The Franciscan church is dedicated to St. Jerome and was built between 1603 and 1611. The steep volute gable adorned with slender pyramids, the almost Gothic, ogival windows, and the porch are all reminiscent of late Gothic churches with renaissance décor, such as can be found in southern Germany.

Vienna never fully embraced the Renaissance style. Individual examples of Renaissance architecture, sculpture, and painting are scattered throughout different parts of the city. There are several reasons for this. For one thing, the split in the House of Habsburg and the subsequent relocation of the court from Vienna to Spain and Bohemia certainly played a mayor part. Also, the reformist and scientifically inclined Maximillian II introduced the Reformation to Vienna, and the Counter-Reformation did not take hold until later. During the siege of the city by the Turks, many churches that had been built beside the city walls were destroyed, and the religious orders in the city were in disarray. Protestant preachers hardly encountered any Catholic opposition, and the majority of Viennese converted to the new form of Christianity. Undercurrents of religious conflict persisted, however. In 1551, King Ferdinand made a decisive move to strengthen the Counter-Reformation by inviting the Jesuits to Vienna. When they took up residence in the former Carmelite monastery at Am Hof, this provided a significant stimulus for the Catholic faith to reassert itself in Vienna.

ILLUSTRATION OPPOSITE:
Bonaventura Daum
Franciscan Church, 1603

ILLUSTRATIONS LEFT:
ABOVE:
Palais Porcia, around 1600
Renaissance arcades in
the courtyard

BELOW:
Courtyard of Haus 1 at 7,
Bäckerstrasse
before 1587

Ehrenfried Kluckert

Art and Architecture in the Seventeenth and Eighteenth Centuries. Baroque and Rococo

Historical development

The development of the architectural style known as court Baroque is generally associated with the period of the Thirty Years' War, yet while this generalization may hold true for many European countries, it is inapplicable in Vienna. Prague, rather than Vienna, had been the Habsburg capital since 1582, when it was chosen as the seat of government by Rudolf II, in order to escape the religious disputes in Vienna.

This move profoundly affected the fate of the Habsburg dynasty. Emperor Ferdinand II fought on the side of Catholic League, founded in 1609. Despite the bitter resistance of the Protestant cities, Rudolf's brother Matthias secured his succession in Bohemia and Hungary in 1612, supported by Cardinal Klesl and by his successor, Ferdinand. In secret negotiations it was agreed that Ferdinand would inherit the Spanish throne should Philip III die without a male heir, while Bohemia and Hungary would fall to Spain should Ferdinand fail to produce a male heir to the Imperial throne. This dubious political move was designed to strengthen the Catholic League and feed the European ambitions of the Habsburg dynasty. The victory of the Counter-Reformation seemed assured.

These arrangements constituted a violation of the freedom of religion that Rudolf II had guaranteed to the Bohemian cities in the so-called Letter of Majesty. Protests ensued, and the 1618 Defenestration of Prague launched the insurrection of the Bohemian Estates. The Thirty Years' War had begun. Matthias died one year later. His successor, Emperor Ferdinand II, who had once again chosen Vienna as his place of residence, had to deal with the Protestants, in the form of the army of the Bohemian Estates. He received a delegation at the Hofburg but was not prepared to make any concessions in matters of religion. Faced with this situation, Count Thurn, the commander of the Estates army, appeared before the walls of Vienna; he had captured the suburbs and hoped to storm the city with the support of the Viennese Protestants. The Viennese, however, denied him the necessary assistance. The walls held fast and the Bohemians were finally forced to retreat.

Emperor Ferdinand II now allied himself with the head of the Catholic League, Duke Maximilian of Bavaria. In 1620 he was victorious over the Protestant King Frederick of Bohemia, the so-called "Winter King," at the Battle of the White Mountain, which put an end to Protestant domination of Bohemia and Moravia. Ferdinand then definitively gave up his residence in Prague and moved the court to Vienna. His powers were completely restored when on March 6, 1629 he issued the Edict of Restitution, reclaiming all the ecclesiastical possessions which had been confiscated by the Protestants.

The Counter-Reformation violently imposed by the Habsburgs' absolutist policies encountered

hardly any resistance in Vienna that year, since the city also seemed to have been spared the turmoil of war. Suddenly, in the last years of the war, just before the Treaty of Westphalia in 1648, a Swedish army, under the command of the victorious Lennart Torstenson, reached the gates of city, establishing itself on the northern bank of the Danube. The fortifications proved insurmountable, however, and when the expected Protestant reinforcements did not materialize the Swedes retreated. This army, reinforced by Transylvanian troops, subsequently headed for the "alternative capital" of Prague, which was besieged for long weeks and months — until the last day of the war. The long-awaited peace, negotiated on October 24, 1648, saved the inhabitants of Prague from the almost certain destruction of their city.

Ferdinand did not live to see the end of the war, for he had died in 1637. Perhaps age had mellowed him slightly, or perhaps he had learned something from the political unrest, because two years before he died, with the Peace of Prague, he renounced the Edict of Restitution.

Even though the city of Vienna did not suffer directly from the war, the towns and villages of the surrounding area had been plundered and destroyed, a state of affairs which hampered the development of trade for many years. The financial resources of the Viennese merchants were still too modest to support a thoroughgoing economic recovery and the city only developed very slowly in the early Baroque period.

First came the tentative construction or renovation of ecclesiastical buildings, a manifestation of both the triumph of the Counter-Reformation and the revival of the city as the imperial residence under Ferdinand. It is Leopold I, not Ferdinand, who deserves to be called the first Baroque emperor, for neither Ferdinand II, nor Ferdinand III who succeeded him in 1637, were able to muster the financial resources to carry out the first great Baroque project, the extension of the Hofburg. This was left to Leopold I.

Yet the Leopoldine period was marked not so much by extensive construction work as by feasts and celebrations. Leopold was a great patron of the arts; dance, music, drama, and opera were among his favorite forms of entertainment. Only once the Turkish danger was definitively over could an extensive building program be undertaken. It was under the emperor Charles VI that Baroque Vienna finally emerged — mainly the work of Johann Bernhard Fischer von Erlach and Johann Lukas von Hildebrandt.

Two years after the defeat of the Turks by Prince Eugene at Zenta in 1697, the Peace of Karlowitz awarded Austria-Hungary the province of Transylvania and the greater part of Slovenia and Croatia. With victory over the Turks and the establishment of Habsburg supremacy in Europe came an economic revival which helped provide

Emperor Leopold I (1640–1705). Crowned in 1658, Leopold is regarded as the first Baroque emperor.

17th-century History

the financial resources to rebuild the outskirts of the city that had been razed to the ground by the advancing Turks. Particular attention was paid to the rebuilding and extension of the Josefstadt, with the handsome square in front of the Piaristen church. At the same time, a smaller settlement developed on the land of the Bürgerspital hospital. Around 1700, Prince Liechtenstein acquired the land on approximately the site of today's Ninth District, around the picturesque Strudlhofstiege steps, and had part of it divided into building-plots. The neighboring Althangrund was also used for buildings. Paradoxically, the rebuilding of Vienna took place outside the city walls, with the suburbs clearly separated from the city center by the Glacis, a "green belt" around the city, which the emperor surrounded with new fortifications, the Linienwall, still recalled today by the line of the Gürtelstrasse.

By the time of his death, the emperor Charles VI had become unpopular with his subjects, as a result of the wars he waged far away from Vienna which had led to shortages and price rises. The state coffers had been drained by military entanglement in the War of the Spanish Succession (1701–17) and the constant battles against the Turks, at Belgrade for example, where Prince Eugene was once again able to celebrate a brilliant victory in 1717. Vienna's merchant class could not afford to act as financial backers indefinitely. By 1705, the imperial ministers had established credit institutions such as the Stadt-Banco.

While this may have gained the confidence of the population, it was not enough to satisfy the state's enormous appetite for credit. Economic upturns alternated with recessions, from which the artisans suffered most, leading to revolts that were bloodily suppressed by the army. These social evils led to the setting up of economic commissions which recommended the introduction of reforms to enable the commoners of the city to enjoy economic prosperity by bringing their incomes more into line with those of the upper classes and the nobility.

When Charles VI died at La Favorita in 1740, the economic situation had generally been stabilized and the social conditions of the population had improved, while the building of Baroque Vienna was almost complete. There now began the "female rule," which the Viennese so despised initially, of the daughter of the deceased emperor. Maria Theresia, Queen of Bohemia and Hungary as well as Archduchess of Austria, was the wife of Franz Stephan of Lorraine, the future Emperor Franz I.

In the first year of the Empresses' reign, the Elector Charles Albert of Bavaria waged war against her, since he refused to recognize her legitimate claim to the Habsburg territories. The War of the Austrian Succession began with the invasion of Habsburg Silesia by the Prussian King

Frederick II, the Great. An alliance between Prussia and France gave the Bavarian Elector a free hand to storm Prague and have himself elected Holy Roman Emperor under the name of Charles VII. At the same time as she had to cope with events in the European theatre of war, Maria Theresia had to face her first crucial test in the defense of Vienna by confronting the advancing armies of the Elector of Bavaria. The city could hardly have withstood a serious military assault, but Charles Albert fortunately spared it, by marching from St. Pölten to Moravia.

A year later, by the time the Empress gave birth to a son, the future Joseph II, the mood in Vienna had changed. Maria Theresia was now not only merely tolerated or respected but held in great affection. Furthermore, she was seen as a woman who was economical with the citizens' money. No major building projects were undertaken during her reign, with the exception of the Schönbrunn Palace, her favorite residence. Maria Theresia also favored the arts, though not in the pompous, overblown style of her predecessor Leopold I, preferring the more intimate pleasures of domestic entertainments. She played music with her children, and even enjoyed handicrafts.Not even formal occasions were nearly as lavish as they had been two generations earlier. The scientific interests of her husband, Franz Stephan, the future emperor, found expression in the growth of the imperial collection of scientific instruments.

Maria Theresia reformed and modernized her empire by uniting her extensive territories under a single civil service; her capital Vienna also benefited from this reorganization. A census performed in 1757 counted 175,000 inhabitants of the city. Maria Theresia ordered the Vienna city council to register land holdings in the city and to undertake a first numbering of houses. She was also responsible for instituting a regular postal service, the so-called *klapperpost* (rattle post), named for the rattle that announced the arrival of the postman.

Under the Empress, Austria moved into a new age of liberalism and enlightenment. Torture and serfdom were abolished, and religious intolerance was no longer the rule.

In Vienna, reforms were introduced which were designed to bring growth and prosperity, to the city. The Prater and the Augarten were made into public parks for the enjoyment of the citizens. On an economic level, the administration now differentiated between commercial ventures serving the city's domestic needs and the production of goods for export abroad.

The greatest achievement of the Theresian reforms, however, was the reorganization of educational and scientific institutions. By displacing the Jesuit order which had hitherto controlled teaching and research in the university, the gates of institutions of higher learning were thrown

Johann Gottfried Auerbach
Emperor Charles VI in the regalia of the Order of the Golden Fleece
Kunsthistorisches Museum

Franz Xavier Pelenko, Maria Theresia, Franz I, Stephan and Archduke Joseph
Heeresgeschichtliches Museum

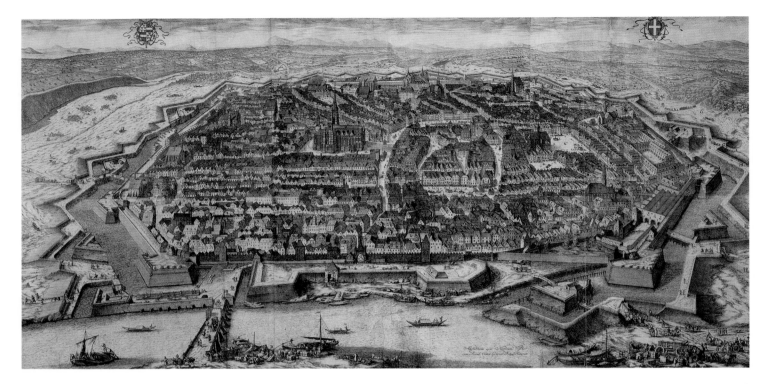

open to scholars and scientists of international repute. One example of the repercussions was the setting up by the Dutch physician Gerard van Swieten, who was appointed to Vienna in 1745, of the first medical clinic. Van Swieten also founded the *Ältere Wiener Medizinische Schule* (Higher Viennese School of Medicine). Maria Theresia also founded the *Ritterakademie* (Knights' Academy) and the *Orientalische Akademie* (Oriental Academy) which were designed to provide suitable training for young noblemen destined for the diplomatic service.

For forty years, Maria Theresia held the fate of the Habsburg dynasty in her hands. She showed herself to be a wise ruler who succeeded, despite the trappings of royalty, in retaining a warm and natural personality.

The Baroque Cityscape

Vienna's cityscape shows numerous points of contact between the Gothic and the Baroque. Jacob Hoefnagel's copperplate engraving of 1609, which offers a bird's eye view of the city, shows that many of the narrow lanes of medieval Vienna had survived (Illustration above). Only the fortifications had been renovated. The city wall, originally constructed in ca. 1300 can be seen here to have survived only on the Danube side, while the remainder had been replaced by a curtain wall and bastions constructed after the Italian model.

The population of Vienna had grown considerably since the defeat of the Turks, partly due to the influx of court officials and servants. The courtiers were only rarely prepared to live out in the suburbs, so the Viennese coped by adding more stories to their town-houses. Buildings of three or four floors were sometimes increased to up to seven stories high. Vienna grew vertically — a bizarre, even a unique, phenomenon for the sixteenth and seventeenth centuries, as far as urban development was concerned. Contemporary travelers reported in amazement on the tall buildings of the city on the Danube whose façades could not even be seen in their entirety because of the narrowness of the streets.

This shortage of accommodation appears to have been particularly acute in certain years, as can be inferred from the imperial court's offer of financial incentives to citizens willing to embark upon construction ventures. This measure promoted the building of the vertical extensions already discussed, as well as encouraging the construction of new housing to replace older dwellings which no longer satisfied the public health regulations.

It was the responsibility of the city's chief quartermaster to ensure that all citizens fulfilled what was called their *Hofquartierspflicht* (court accommodation duty), which required them to accommodate court servants at an extremely advantageous rent as far as the tenants were concerned.

It is understandable that many families tried to avoid this imposition, but they could only gain exemption if they extended their existing houses or built new ones, or contributed financially to the construction of accommodation in the city wall bastions to house the city guard.

The early seventeenth century cityscape had numerous Gothic features. For instance, on the Stephansplatz which abuts the north aisle of the cathedral, there is the facade of the late thirteenth century presbytery. In 1723, this became the archbishop's palace and today it houses the diocesan museum.

Strangely, a Gothic choir breaks through the facade, a relic of the medieval presbytery which projects from the outer wall like a foreign body from the past (Illustration opposite, bottom left). When the palace was rebuilt after burning down in 1627 the external decoration of the choir was also altered in the style of the early Baroque, the apse being adorned with delicately ornamented oval oculi and windows provided with triangular and segmental pediments, without however, any attempt being made to integrate it into the regularity of the Baroque facade.

The palace was rebuilt between 1632 and 1641 under the bishops Anton Wolfrath and Friedrich Philipp, Count Breuner, to plans by the Italian Giovanni Coccapani. The early Baroque pattern of the building still survives in the clear separation between the different stories and in the almost

17th-century Architecture

Pietro de Pomis
Graz, Mausoleum of Ferdinand II
Begun in 1614.

PREVIOUS PAGE:
**Jacob Hoefnagel, Johann
Nicolaus Visscher**
A birds-eye view of Vienna
looking north, 1609.

unadorned design of the windows. The corners in ashlar, the bracketed cornice, and the curve of the arches on the square side with their prominent keystones are reminiscent of Renaissance styles —an exception in Viennese Baroque architecture. The façade was renovated in the early eighteenth century under Bishop Sigmund, Count Kollnitsch, who was later elevated to the rank of prince-bishop. The dominant first floor was given a rich stucco decoration. The alternating forms of the wing-like open pediments ornamented in rocaille are decorated with shell-shapes and provided with corner volutes. Beneath the window-sills of the second floor, there are curving bands of decoration with scrolled ends.

Cardinal Melchior Klesl had already introduced many new Catholic religious orders to the city in the sixteenth century, hoping not only to stem the advance of the Reformation but to drive it out completely from Vienna and eventually from throughout the Habsburg empire. He found support from Ferdinand I, who in 1554 placed the university under state control and handed over the education system to the Jesuits. In 1622, Ferdinand II, another resolute enemy of Protestantism, merged the University and the Jesuit school.

Carmelites and Hospitaliers also came to Vienna during the sixteenth century, settling in the Leopoldstadt. Later on, the Paulines also made themselves at home on the Wieden and the Servites settled on the Rossau. The Jesuits and the Dominicans both contributed churches to the city.

The Counter-Reformation can thus be seen to be, without any doubt, the first as well as the strongest driving force in the development of early Baroque culture. Many medieval religious buildings, such as the Schottenkirche and the Michaelerkirche, were given a baroque

renovation. The design of the Stadtpalais is also strongly influenced by this new architecture.

It must be admitted, however, that Viennese Baroque architecture of the early seventeenth century was by no means avant-garde and innovative for its day; quite the contrary. The architecture of the Counter-Reformation was already firmly entrenched in Salzburg, where it had gained its first foothold in the Habsburg territories north of the Alps. Salzburg cathedral, built by Santino Solari between 1614 and 1628, is a good example of the new architectural style (Illustration right). The architects derived the design of the facade and the structure of the interior from Roman church building.

Graz also has a monument of significance in the development of Baroque church-building, namely, the mausoleum of Ferdinand II, also begun in 1614 (illustration left). Ferdinand, archduke of the Steinmark before his coronation as emperor and, as has been said, already a forceful supporter of the Counter-Reformation, commissioned a design from Pietro de Pomis. De Pomis was probably the first architect north of the Alps to opt for an oval plan. The mausoleum, a funerary chapel attached to the Katharinenkirche, is a two-story building covered with an oval cupola in the Italian style. The eastern facade is also derived from the Italian Baroque tradition. Structural elements, such as the three-quarter columns, pilasters, window frames, and sills project three-dimensionally, and the alternation of triangular and segmental pediments is rigidly maintained. The final, broad-arched segmental pediment is located above the triangular pediment of the attic, a design borrowed from the façade of the Jesuits' mother-church in Rome, the Gesù.

Santino Solari
Salzburg Cathedral, 1614–28

Giovanni Coccapani
Archbishop's Palace, 1632 – 41
Façade with late-Gothic choir
(left) and inner courtyard (above)

The first Baroque churches in Vienna also share these architectural features. As an example, the façade of the Jesuits' university church, which was the work of several unknown master-builders, was renovated and altered by Carlo Antonio Carlone in 1631, and further transformed by Andrea Pozzo at beginning of the eighteenth century (Illustration right). In parts, the design takes its inspiration from Salzburg Cathedral, even down to the detailing. Like its Salzburg counterpart, the two-story façade, with its triangular pediment supported by volutes, strongly protruding sills, and alternating segmented and triangular pediments over the windows, gives a "broad shouldered" impression. The twin towers are a little awkward, being poorly proportioned in relation to the height of the façade; this is also the case in Salzburg. It has to be said, however, that the towers were only completed during the 1680s. The Jesuitenkirche in Vienna is thus the first twin-towered Baroque building in Austria.

The interior of the university church, the so-called "templum academicum," is a simple rectangular space with side-chapels, which is also comparable to the Salzburg model. Reference to Salzburg gives pause for thought, since the design is not derived from Il Gesù, the Jesuits' "original church" in Rome, as had been the case in other examples. The Austrian connection appears to have been stronger — possibly an indication of the search for an independent architectural style.

In redesigning the venerable Schottenkirche, the Italian architects Marco Spazio and Carlo Antonio Carlone — the latter was also in charge of the construction work — certainly studied the façade of the Jesuitenkirche in detail, but they adapted it to the required proportions. They were responsible for a first phase of work from 1638 to 1641. Further changes were made under Silvestro Carlone from 1643 onward. He it was who gave it the Baroque appearance which today makes it one of the most delightful of Viennese ecclesiastical buildings (Illustration top left).

The close correspondence with the Jesuitenkirche church is astonishing. Identical features include the regular articulation with pilasters, the double arrangement of windows in both stories, the emphasis on the central axis by means of a portal, a dominant upper-story window, and the projecting cornice between the two stories. With the broken segmental pediment of the main portal and the niche set within it the architects were quoting, as a reference to the Jesuits as it were, a motif from the University church.

While the façade of the Jesuitenkirche remains almost rigid in aspect, the Italians sought to create movement and harmony of proportion by creating the central section of the Schottenkirche façade. The way in which the wings are recessed made it possible to top them with truncated

Carlo Antonio Carlone
Andrea Pozzo
Jesuitenkirche (The University
Church), begun in 1626,
1703–1707

Carlo Antonio Carlone
Schottenkirche, 1638–41 and
1643–48,
View from the south-west

Bernardo Bellotto (Canaletto)
View of the Freyung, from the
south-east, around 1759,
Oil on canvas,
46 x 60 in (116 x 152 cm),
Kunsthistorisches Museum

towers, which rise only slightly higher than triangular pediment of the central section. The principal bell tower rises slenderly behind the apse;
with its subdivided, bulbous dome, it contrasts
with the linear consistency of the side-towers

The architects had to take the church's location
into consideration. While only the west façade of
the Jesuitenkirche is visible to the observer, in the
case of the Schottenkirche both the south and the
west façades needed an architecturally effective
design. Bellotto's painting of 1759 (Illustration p.
48) shows the position of the church in relation to
the "Freyung" Platz, just as it can be seen today.
The left corner tower relates to the west frontage
and thus acts as a kind of urban architectural hinge.
At this point, the square extends onto the bastion
and thus to the city limits. The tower takes on a
kind of topographic role – in a biblical sense, too, as
the symbol of the gates to the heavenly Jerusalem.
The prominent transept and the bell-tower placed
in front of the choir function as sacred emblems of
majesty and dominate the Freyung.

At the beginning of the seventeenth century
ecclesiastical architecture began to manifest
slightly more diversity which points toward an
increasing independence of architectural
language, but Rome undoubtedly remains the
dominant model.

The plan of the Dominikanerkirche, which was
also built in this period (illustration. bottom and
right) is, after St. Stephan's cathedral, the second
largest church in Vienna, shows an interesting
variation on that of the Roman church of Il Gesù
(Illustration bottom right). The architect responsible for the plans is unknown, though some
sources suggest that the design is the work of the
Italian Giovanni Giacomo Tencala, who did much

of his work in Vienna. The church was built
between 1631 and 1634, Jakob Spatz and Antonio Canevale directing the construction. The
upper story of the two-story façade is framed by
powerful volutes and crowned by a triangular pediment. The steps to the portal and its broken segmental pediment above, as well as the large central window of the upper story with its parapet
linked to a cornice, can be seen as free variations
on motifs of Il Gesù.

This church in Rome was not only a model for
later Jesuit churches, it provided a model for the
whole church architecture of the Counter-Reformation. Giacomo della Porta's façade, with its
emphasis on the central axis, became the prototype north of the Alps as well. One of the
most striking and, in those days, most architecturally innovative motifs was Il Gesù's triangular
pediment set into a monumental segmental
pediment—a dominant architectural feature
which also crowned the façade of Ferdinand II's
mausoleum in Graz. The architect of the

**Giacomo Barozzi da Vignola and
Giacomo della Porta**
Il Gesù, Rome, 1568–84

Dominikanerkirche did not make use of this motif, instead placing a triangular pediment over the door in lively contrast to the segmental pediment over the dominant window.

The spatial plan of Il Gesù was only adopted in part for the Dominikanerkirche in Vienna. The nave, with its flanking chapels, is traversed by a compressed "transept," the whole surmounted by a cupola, though without a drum, unlike the Roman church on which it is based. It is entirely possible that the model here was the Carmelite church, whose construction had been begun only a few years before. This church in Leopoldstadt is dedicated to Saint Joseph, and is thought to be the earliest Baroque church in Vienna (Illustration. top). Its three-story, vertically stressed façade can hardly be ascribed to an Italian model, though it bears some resemblance at most to Carlo Maderno's Santa Susanna in Rome, though only in the strict articulation by pilasters and the framing of the upper stories by volutes.

Otherwise, Maderno's building has two floors and is more spatial and dynamic in the design of its façade. Compared with the Jesuitenkirche church, the Karmeliterkirche church is more pleasing and more harmonious in its proportions. This

is certainly a consequence of the traditional architectural principle of tapering the mass of the building toward the top, and, in addition, the obligatory concentration of members around the central axis, recognizable in the placing of double pilasters on either side of the main portal.

The distinctively rapid transition from Gothic to Baroque in Vienna, with the Renaissance representing only a brief intermezzo, is impressively demonstrated by a comparison of the Franziskanerkirche, completed in 1611, and the Karmeliterkirche, begun about 15 years later. The church on the Franziskanerplatz, which is still distinguishably late medieval (illustration. p. 43) stands right next to an ecclesiastical building erected only a few years later in an accomplished Baroque style. This physical proximity is as disconcerting as the temporal, as if a village church had been built in the traditional style with a modern vicarage built alongside at the same time.

The beginnings of Baroque architecture in Vienna were cautious and began at a relatively late stage. The Baroque style drew its inspiration from Italy, via Salzburg and Graz, but it very quickly — if not always happily — developed its own architectural language.

The Splendor of the Baroque

The period of Baroque splendor, known as "Vienna gloriosa," began around 1658, when Leopold I received the imperial crown. A few years later, he commissioned the Italian Filiperto Lucchese to provide an extension to the Hofburg. At that time, the Hofburg consisted of a number of disparate buildings. There was the Stallburg, set apart from the Schweizerhof, and facing it the Amalienburg, to which it was joined on the southern flank only by a wall and a set of buildings, as can be seen in an engraving of 1560.

Plans for the new complex were submitted to the emperor for approval in 1660. They provided for an elongated building which would link the Amalienburg castle to the nucleus, the Schweizerhof (illustration. p. 51, top). The wing by Domenico and Carl Martino Carlone was built by 1666, but two years later it was damaged by fire so that a new building had to be planned. This was designed by Giovanni Pietro Tencala, together with Lodovico Burnacini, and completed in 1681 under Domenico Carlone.

The unusual elongated construction, soon to be known as the Leopoldine Wing, was articulated by regularly spaced giant pilasters but was

17th-century Architecture

PREVIOUS PAGE:
Karmeliterkirche (Josephskirche), ca. 1623, façade and interior looking east

Domenico and Carl Martino Carlone, Giovanni Pietro Tencala
View of the Leopoline Wing, 1660–81

Filiperto Lucchese, Carl Antonio Carlone
"Am Hof" or "Zu den Neun Engelschören" church, 1662

very sparsely decorated. The roof cornice with its massive brackets is noteworthy, however. The flat capitals of the pilasters terminate beneath the mezzanine in a narrow cornice, to be echoed in the walls below, articulated by scaly pilasters tapering toward the bottom. The capitals are surmounted by voluminous brackets which support the top cornice.

The *Am Hof* or *Zu den Neun Engelschören* (The Nine Angel Choirs) church (Illustration bottom right), the Jesuits' *Casa Professa*, was renovated in association with the Leopoldine Wing. The building had originally been a Carmelite church, built ca. 1400. The emperor Ferdinand II had made finance available for construction in 1627, but in 1662, two years after work began on the Leopoldine Wing, Filiperto Lucchese was commissioned to redesign the façade, and it was Carlone who supervised the building.

Lucchese drew his inspiration from Roman and Venetian ecclesiastical buildings, taking from them the giant pilasters, powerful volutes, and broken segmental pediments. A few motifs came from the original Gesù of the Jesuits, such as the prominent volutes of the upper story. The three-dimensionality of the façade was enhanced by the relief of the ornamentation and the strongly projecting cornices and pilasters.

The Leopoldine Wing seems to have set the tone for other palaces in Vienna. As the first Baroque imperial palace of the capital, it not only provided the model but also the topographical point of reference for the later construction projects of the nobility.

For the Viennese aristocracy, in architectural competition with the imperial house, it seemed particularly attractive to acquire land as close as possible to the Hofburg palace, and this is why the first Baroque extension to the Hofburg has to be understood as a significant architectural signal, initiating the gradual transformation of the Viennese cityscape.

The change was not essentially the result of the church-building of the first decades of the seventeenth century, and the early Baroque churches stood out curiously amid the late medieval Gothic town-houses that were to shape the streets and squares of Vienna for many years to come.

It was also a matter of location. Churches were generally built in squares, less commonly on the streets, and their contribution to enlivening the architectural scene was thus limited. The building of mansions and palaces in the city, on the other hand, caused a fundamental change in the appearance of the streets, for five or six town-houses had to be pulled down in order to make room for a palatial residence of appropriate scale.

Here again, it was Salzburg that attracted the attention of the Emperor and the Viennese nobility. The southern city's highly ambitious archbishop,

Wolf Dietrich von Raitenau, wanted to turn the city into the "Rome of the North." The rebuilding of Salzburg under the reign of von Raitenau, from 1596 through 1619, inspired by the palazzos of Rome, provided the beginnings of a model for the transformation of a medieval city into a Baroque capital. The bishop's, later archbishop's, palace on the Stephansplatz and of course the Leopoldine Wing of the Hofburg can be seen as Vienna's initial response to the spate of building activity in Salzburg.

In the decades that followed, it was the distinguished palaces of the nobility that were responsible for the decisive transformation of the Viennese cityscape. At the edge of the city, on the Minoritenplatz, not far from the Hofburg, and as it were as a continuation of the Leopoldine Wing, Konrad Balthasar, Count Starhemberg, bought a town-house in 1661 which he then demolished and caused to be rebuilt in the Baroque style by 1687 (illustration top). At a time when the neighboring Hofburg still stood isolated, this three-story building with mezzanine above, and powerful bracketed cornice must have looked like a grand urban castle.

With its giant pilasters, which in the manner of Palladio rise from the high plinth and extend beyond the principal stories, and with its rusticated ground floor, it radiates the dignity and confidence of its owner.

The principal façade borders the Minoritenplatz square; the long side is formed of 13 bays articulated by pilasters. These are almost playfully broken up by the broken segmental pediments of the windows and the forms arranged like caryatids under the cornice. In the succeeding period this contrast, which may be sought in vain in the architecture of Roman Baroque palaces, became a characteristic feature of Viennese town palaces. Dignity and charm in captivating unity – this is how one might characterize the architectural rhetoric of this palace, which alongside the Leopoldine Wing of the Hofburg is one of the most outstanding early Baroque buildings in Vienna.

Almost at the same time as the Hofburg was extended, the *Deutschordenshaus* was built in the city center, near the cathedral. This was constructed for the Order of Teutonic Knights, which had been resident in Vienna since the

Folbert Van Alten Allen
Birds-eye view of the city of Vienna from the west, ca. 1680
Historisches Museum der Stadt Wien

Deutschordenshaus with church
Engraving by J. A. Corvinus after S. Kleiner
Department of Historical Monuments, Austrian Government

thirteenth century and is the first building incorporating a church dating from this period. In 1667, Carlo Canevale produced plans for a Baroque building which provided for the integration of the medieval chapel. The building was widened from 1679 to 1682, but work had to be halted as a result of the Turkish threat. Only in 1720, under the direction of Anton Erhard Martinelli, could the complex be extended and completed (illustration bottom). The portals date from the seventeenth century. Half a century later the pilaster articulation was "modernized" and the windows provided with alternating segmented and triangular pediments.

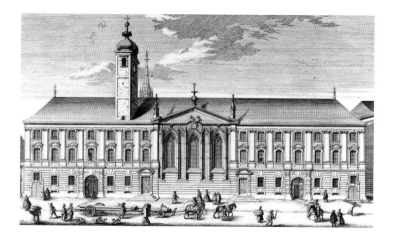

The Turkish Siege of 1683

During the seventeenth century, the suburbs of Vienna — the Josefstadt, the Liechtental, the Schottenfeld, and the Rossau — gradually expanded, and the capital was surrounded by a garland of townhouses, picturesque squares with proud churches, hospitals, and garden palaces — which stood, however, at a considerable distance from the bastion, separated from it by a wide expanse of meadows and rivers.

Folbert van Alten Allen's copperplate print of ca. 1680, which is engraved on six plates and assembled in two rows, gives a birds-eye view of Vienna just before the Turkish siege of 1683 (illustration top). It is important evidence for any discussion of the city's development, in that it documents the situation before the suburbs were torn down for security reasons on the approach of the Ottoman army. And this was not all, for tall buildings in the inner city that stood close to the fortifications — the theatre in the Hofburg complex, for example — were also burned down.

The view is from the west. The Währinger Strasse runs from the left and from the bottom right the Alser Strasse runs leftward, that is toward the western part of the bastion, to the Schottentor gate. Behind it towers the unmistakable Schottenkirche. In the right-hand part of the city, the Leopoldine Wing can clearly be seen to the left of the Minoritenkirche, and the Michaelerkirche stands above the Hofburg on the right. The imposing fortifications are complete — this being probably the main reason for the production

PREVIOUS PAGE:
Unknown artist
Kara Mustafa Pasha, ca. 1696
Oil on canvas,
30 x 20 in (75 x 49 cm)
Historisches Museum der Stadt
Wien

Charles Allard
Ernst Rüdiger, Count Starhem-
berg, ca. 1690
Copperplate engraving,
28 x 17 in (52 x 42 cm)
Historisches Museum der Stadt
Wien

and deliberate dissemination of this panoramic view — and appear to be an invincible defensive complex. Unfortunately, this would have been a mistaken assumption.

In the last days of March 1683, a mighty army left Adrianople (Edirne) under the command of Kara Mustafa (illustration. p. 54, center right) and headed for the Habsburg capital. An alliance of European powers had to be assembled in great haste against the renewed Turkish threat. The forces of the Polish King Jan Sobieski and the imperial army under the command of Duke Karl of Lorraine were at the ready. However, so great was the superiority of the Turks that the western armies were forced to retreat and Vienna once again found itself under siege.

In 1680, the Emperor appointed Ernst Rüdige, Count Starhemberg as military commander of the city, making him responsible for its defense. The Count had served as a colonel in the imperial army since 1668 but he only 16,000 men at his disposal, as Vienna's population had been drastically reduced by a terrible outbreak of the Black Death (bubonic plague) which ravaged the city in 1679.

The Pasha's army reached Vienna on July 14, 1683, and an enormous camp of more than 25,000 tents surrounded the city. Attacks were concentrated on the area between the Burgtor and the Schottentor gates. The Turks, pastmasters in the undermining of fortifications, destroyed the forward bastions and inflicted heavy damage

on the walls. In the city, an outbreak of dysentery thinned out the ranks of the defenders, while the relieving armies of the Polish king and Charles of Lorraine only advanced slowly. The despondent defenders would hardly be able to withstand an assault. They expected the city walls to be stormed, and at the end of August Count Starhemberg made the first preparations for the expected combat within the city itself.

The Turks seemed to be confident of taking Vienna. A sketch-plan from the secret archives of the Grand Vizier Aynaci Süleyman Pasha shows Vienna already conquered, the Cathedral depicted as topped with the Islamic crescent moon. Vienna is surrounded by the Ottoman tented cities. The upper part depicts the hills of the Vienna Woods, and beneath them the Grand Vizier's quarters, indicated by the sacred banner emblazoned with the green double-edged sword.

Turkish confidence grew when the invaders conquered the ravelins, the embankments in front of the fortified walls, which they called the "magic mound." Now it could only be a matter of hours, days at the most, before they could definitively storm the city. So sure was he of his victory that the Grand Vizier delayed starting the final attack. Almost at the same time, on the night of September 9, the commanders of the relieving armies which had marched from the Kahlenberg signaled their arrival, and soon the heights of the Vienna Woods were occupied by 65,000 soldiers, all allied to the Viennese. The

Franz Geffels
The decisive battle, 1683
Oil on canvas,
74 x 109 in (184 x 272 cm)
Historisches Museum der Stadt
Wien

Turks were completely unaware of the scale of the task which faced them, and only made preparations which would adequately deal to meet the approaching army under the command of the Polish King Jan Sobieski. This was their undoing. Franz Geffel's fantastic panorama of the battle (illustration p. 55) shows the Christian troops rushing down from the heights of the Vienna Woods onto the many thousands of Turkish tents below. The besieged city can be seen in the distance as well as the sap-trenches that ran up to the extensive fortifications.

The weak Ottoman defense was quickly overcome, and Karl of Lorraine and his powerful forces pushed on toward Nussdorf and destroyed a large part of the Turkish army which was completely taken by surprise. He was able to turn the broad enemy line, and on the evening of September 12, the great Ottoman army was put to flight.

That same night, the Grand Vizier Kara Mustafa had Ibrahim Pasha, "the man responsible for Nussdorf," executed. Yet the Grand Vizier shared the same fate a few weeks later when the Sultan, convinced of his commander-in-chief's neglectful conduct of the war, had Kara Mustafa strangled in Belgrade.

Vienna had been saved once again. Furthermore, the victory over the Turks was so decisive that Austria could be confident of not having to face the same danger from the Ottomans for a long time to come. The Habsburgs re-conquered Hungary, and the Balkan countries also awaited the advance of the victorious army to liberate them from the Turkish yoke. Austria thus became a great power with land holdings all over central and eastern Europe.

The Lobkowitz and Liechtenstein Palaces

After this mercifully brief interruption by war in 1683, building in Vienna was resumed with increased vigor. As has already been said, the Viennese nobility wanted to build their own palaces as close as possible to the Hofburg. Of course, the number of building plots near the Hofburg was severely limited, and in the late seventeenth and early eighteenth centuries, the princes either had to settle within the narrow confines of the city or make use of the outer districts on the other side of the Hofburg, where there was even plenty of room for generously proportioned gardens.

The next town palace to be built near the court was that of Count Dietrichstein, which now bears the name of its subsequent owner, Prince von Lobkowitz (illustration above). At the end of 1684, the Count commissioned three designs. After much thought, he opted for the plan submitted by the architect Giovanni Pietro Tencala. It is by no means clear that the Count was particularly enthusiastic about securing the services of Tencala, the imperial architect and court engineer, who did much work in Vienna on spectacular palaces. In any case, the Count's hesitation throws a significant light on his own position as patron. It was the Count who decided on the size and shape of the project, and it was the architect's job to take care of the technical side and to make suggestions for decoration. The Baroque client, whether emperor, king, or duke, saw himself not only as a statesman or military commander but also, in some respects, as a creative artist.

The architect's task in the case of the Lobkowitz Palace was not simple, as the building was to fill a space which at the end of the seventeenth century was seen as a linchpin of the cityscape. The palace was to be located between the Augustinian monastery and the Kapuzinerkirche. Johann Bernhard Fischer von Erlach's Imperial Library had yet to be built, so the southern aspect of the city still looked very patchy and disparate. At the point where the Dorotheengasse and the Spiegelgasse reached the city limits, the fortifications turned at an angle, forming a bulwark known as the Augustinerbastion. Even though they were some distance away, the Lobkowitz and Starhemberg Palaces appeared to flank the Hofburg buildings.

The palace projects like the bows of a ship at the intersection between the Augustinerstrasse and the Spiegelgasse, giving particular significance to the powerful bracketed top cornice and the ashlar blocks of the corner. According to old plans and sketches, Tencala's articulation of the façade was very restrained, but the rhythmic alternation of segmented and triangular pediments over the windows of the first floor, and individual balustrades and the small consoles beneath the window sills make for a lively effect. Between the brackets of the top cornice hang delicate, curving wreaths of fruit, supplemented in the central bay over the main entrance by a

pair of cupids holding small cartouches. The pilasters are subdivided horizontally to create rectangular fields. All in all, despite the variety of ornamentation and the associated dynamism of the façade, Tencala knew how to maintain a certain air of restrained aristocratic elegance.

A short time later, the palace would undergo minor changes when Johann Bernhard Fischer von Erlach provided the slightly projecting central section with an attic, topped by a balustrade with sculpted figures.

Fischer von Erlach was also responsible for the redesign of the portal, an architectural jewel. The pilasters and the rounded columns that stand in front of them are skewed outward. Between them, projecting from the depth of the portal, a round molded archway curves forward, hiding the projecting balustrade and flanked on either side by two decorative urns. The imposing barrel-vaulted entrance leads to the Hercules fountain. The staircase, flanked by Tuscan columns, encloses the banqueting hall. The vaulted ceiling is surprising with its cartouches and rectangular areas linked by opulent painted architectural features in an amazingly successful trompe l'oeil.

It was in this banqueting hall that in 1804, Ludwig van Beethoven conducted the première of his Eroica Symphony. The work had originally been intended for Napoleon, but was dedicated to the composer's generous patron Prince Franz Joseph von Lobkowitz when Beethoven became disillusioned by his erstwhile hero.

In another prominent position, but this time in the Herrenquartier on the opposite side of the Hofburg grounds, the Khevenhüller family planned a monumental building opposite the already completed Starhemberg Palace shortly

after the completion of the Lobkowitz Palace. However, circumstances soon forced them to sell the land. Count Dominik Andreas Kaunitz was the lucky new owner, and in 1691 he commissioned a first set of plans from the Italian Domenico Martinelli. Work started that year or the next. The plan was for a four-story building in the Roman style, built around a square inner courtyard, but Count Kaunitz was not able to enjoy his vast building plans for long. According to the land ownership records, ownership of the building-site — for the palace had not yet risen above the ground floor — changed on April 23, 1694. The new owner, Prince Johann Adam von Liechtenstein, looked for a new architect and found him in Gabriel de Gabrieli, who completed the palace in 1705 (illustration above and pp. 58-59).

The central section of the main façade, in today's Bankgasse, the former Vorderer Schenkenstrasse, is decorated with giant pilasters. Deep curving brackets link the the low mezzanine to the tall projecting cornice.

The portal of the Liechtenstein Palace is wider and even more strongly emphasized than that on the main façade of the Lobkowitz Palace. It is arranged over the width of the central section and with two double columns skewed toward the central axis it projects far into the street. The ends of the broken cornice reach out like a pair of arms. The splendid portal is completed by a bowed balustrade flanked by

and the brackets of the cornice are absent in the side sections, which are treated plainly. Beneath the top cornice, double and single brackets alternate. Articulating pilasters are entirely absent; only the windows on the main floor are provided with representative triangular pediments. This contrast and many other details are of Roman inspiration, but when looked at in conjunction with other town palaces, the gradual emergence of something like a Viennese style can be seen, of which the earliest characteristic features are the concentration of ornamentation toward the center, the richly varied design of the deep top cornices, and the rather muted but intricate decoration of the façade.

The most intriguing feature of the interior is the sculpture on Gabriel de Gabrieli's captivating staircase (Illustration left and p. 59) The staircase rises from the vestibule, via a half-landing, to the piano nobile, which receives its light from the large windows of the façade.

The series of mythological allusions is not so obviously tailor-made for the political purposes of the prince as it is at Prince Eugene's Stadtpalais. In this context, it seems to be more a matter of creating a cheerful and pleasant atmosphere. Playful putti romp about on the landings, which are linked together by elegant sweeps of rocaille. The balustrade of the staircase and of the upper floors is articulated by pillars. The putti continue to desport themselves on the triangular pediments and cornices of the walls, whose surfaces are articulated by pilasters, columns, and edicules. There are also statues of Greek gods here, including Apollo and Hermes.

Gabriel de Gabrieli
Liechtenstein Palace, 1691–1705
Staircase

sculptures on plinths. The architectural sculpture was created by Giovanni Giuliani, who taught Georg Raphael Donner. Giuliani was born in Venice in 1663 and came to Vienna in the early 1690s, where he provided sculptures for the magnificent palaces of the nobility. He taught his pupil, Georg Raphael Donner, to sculpt the rather contorted figures which seem to be struggling to escape from their location. Giuliani tried to free the bodies from the surrounding architecture by placing them on elevated plinths, thus giving them as much freedom of movement as possible. By comparison, the monumental caryatids of the portal, sculpted in the manner of Johann Bernhard Fischer von Erlach on the Minoritenplatz, are highly integrated into the architecture (illustration right), making a serious and dignified impression, in contrast to the lively architecture of the main portal.

The main portal and the central section provide a dynamic focal point. The intensity of ornamentation, the alternation of segmental and triangular pediments over the windows, and the three-dimensionality of the pilasters, capitals,

Gabriel de Gabrieli
Liechtenstein Palace, 1691–1705
Side-entrance on the
Minoritenplatz

Garden Palaces

In addition to their town palaces, the Viennese nobility and the Habsburg rulers also had so-called "garden palaces" outside the walls. By the beginning of the seventeenth century, Emperor Matthias had a summer residence built outside the gates, which he called it "La Favorita," since he preferred it to all his other residences. Emperor Leopold I had the façade of La Favorita redesigned between 1672 and 1683, but when in 1683 the Turks stood before Vienna, Ernst Rüdiger, Count Starhemberg, was forced to have it razed it to the ground for security reasons. A few years after the victory over the Turks, the Emperor decided to rebuild the palace. The architects are believed to be Lodovico Burnacini and Giovanni Tencala.

The articulation of the long façade is very flat and the ornamentation not very varied, giving it a rather monotonous effect. Only the central section is provided with giant pilasters. Viennese and foreign visitors could work up little enthusiasm for this summer palace. The author of an early eighteenth-century travel book writes: "When one hears of an imperial summer residence one imagines one will be able to admire a palace constructed with the greatest artistry; however one is forced to abandon this opinion when one sees nothing but a fairly long building which is neither wide nor tall, which may have a few quite well-furnished rooms but which is arranged in such a manner that one could hardly imagine it to be the summer residence of a great emperor."

Under Leopold, La Favorita nonetheless flourished as a center of cultural activity. Sumptuous operas were performed here, and Baroque celebrations made use of the garden, the outdoor theater, the grotto, and the tournament ground, all of which glittered with hitherto unparalleled splendor. It is said that a masked ball held at La Favorita during the visit of the Tsar of Russia

"The Imperial Favorita" engraving by G. D. Heumann after S. Kleiner, 1725 Department of Historical Monuments, Austrian Government

OPPOSITE PAGE:
Domenico Martinelli
Liechtenstein Garden Palace, 1691–1704 (now the Museum of Modern Art)
Façade (top) and Marble Hall (bottom)

Giovanni Battista Carlone, Giovanni Pietro Tencala, Lodovico Burnacini
La Favorita, Theresanische Akademie, 1615, 1687–93
TOP: The library, 1746;
BOTTOM: Trompe l'oeil perspective garden gate in wrought iron

The vaulted ceiling was designed in ca. 1706 by the Italian stucco artist Santino Bussi (illustration p. 59). The contrast between the almost completely three-dimensional figures and the flat decoration of the moldings makes this one of his masterpieces. Bussi quickly became famous, and in addition to receiving numerous prestigious commissions the title of "court artist" was bestowed upon him in 1714.

in 1698 was more magnificent than anything that had ever been seen before .

The heyday of La Favorita lasted only half a century. By around 1740, the garden and palace were in a neglected state. Maria Theresia donated the building and grounds to the Jesuits for their "Seminarium Nobilium." The Jesuits then made alterations to the palace and these have been preserved to this day.

Toward the end of the eighteenth century, Emperor Franz II had the Jesuit school closed down. It was reopened in 1797 as the *Collegium Theresianum,* an educational institution for young noblemen. Of the Baroque gardens, only parts of the grotto have survived. The garden gate with its trompe l'oeil perspective effect is a master-piece of the metalworker's art (illustration, p. 60, bottom left).

Soon after building work had begun on the Favorita, the artistically inclined Prince Johann Adam von Liechtenstein, whose town palace has already been discussed, commissioned plans for a garden palace. An initial sketch-plan was created by Johann Bernhard Fischer von Erlach, on the basis of which the Italian Domenico Martinelli, then working for Count Kaunitz, was supposed to work out new proposals. The building work was delayed, however, but after meeting the famous Roman architect Carlo Fontana the Prince asked him to draw up new plans. He remained unconvinced by these new proposals, however, and reverted to Martinelli's original project.

The building was completed in 1704 (illustration right). The slightly elevated central section of five bays is flanked on each side by wings of four plainer bays. The ground floor is dominated by the rusticated pilasters and the five archways of the central section. The rendering of the two upper floors is broken up with window moldings in high relief and associated triangular and segmental pediments. A painting by Bernardo Bellotto, dating from the middle of the eighteenth century, today in the princely collection in Vaduz, Lichtenstein, gives a very vivid picture of a sumptuous garden party and shows the palace and parts of the Viennese skyline (illustration, p. 62 top). The central axis runs from the back gate and leads via a fountain to the terrace of the belvedere, designed by Johann Bernhard Fischer von Erlach, but demolished in 1873 to make way for a new building in the Historic style. The parterres extend from the central avenue and are ornamented and planted in different ways, including knot and spiral patterns. The plantings are of box, yew, and cypress. The Count had the garden adorned with numerous sculptures. Gods and heroes of Antiquity, such as Hercules or Venus and allegorical group representations such as that of Apollo and Daphne, alternate with richly decorated vases, perched on high pedestals.

Johann Jakob Pock
St. Stephan's Cathedral,
high altar
1640–47

Seventeenth-century Baroque Sculpture

Baroque sculpture in Vienna only really began to
develop after the Turkish siege, reaching its
apogee in the eighteenth century with the work
of Georg Raphael Donner and Franz Xavier
Messerschmidt. There are, however, also seventeenth-century works remarkable for their diversity and refinement.

Baroque sculpture really began in Vienna in
1618 with the endowment by the Emperor's consort, Anna, of the Imperial chapel in the Kapuzinerkirche, about which more will be said later.

The statues on the high altar at St Stephan's
Cathedral (illustration left) were another starting
point for Viennese Baroque sculpture. These are
the work of the sculptor Johann Jakob Pock, who
was summoned to Vienna from Constance just to
create the elegantly drawn figures for the black
marble altar; he completed the work between
1640 and 1647. It seems significant that a sculptor who was not local should have been given
this major commission. Apparently, there was no
local competition for the work.

For the Mariensäule (Mary Monument) on the
Am Hof square the emperor Leopold I had a
model made by his stucco artist, Balthasar
Herold. The Virgin Mary appears atop a high
Corinthian column as if at the Apocalypse, surmounting the vanquished basilisks. Far below
her, four angels stand on a tall stone plinth, the
pedestal of the column, wielding swords and

shields to ward off the dragons at their feet (illustration bottom right). The scene illustration rates
the theme of *ecclesia militans*, the church mili-
tant, and probably refers to the dedication of the
church opposite which is called *Zu den Neun
Engelschören* (The Nine Angel Choirs). The
bronze casting was performed by Herold in 1667,
after dismantling a wooden column.

In 1679, Vienna was visited by the Black
Death, which claimed thousands of victims. During the epidemic, Emperor Leopold had praised
the construction of a shrine to avert the deadly
danger. By the time the Plague was over, the first
call on financial resources was the need to deal
with its consequences and then shortly thereafter extensive fortifications had to be built to
deal with the Turkish threat.

Consequently, it was not until 1687 that Emper-
or Leopold I laid the foundation stone for the present Pestsäule (Plague Monument) (illustration
p. 63). The design was based on plans by Matthias
Rauchmiller, who came from Radolfzell on Lake
Constance. Two years later, Johann Bernhard
Fischer von Erlach made alterations to the plinth;
the large reliefs on it are by Fischer von Erlach and
Ignaz Bendl. The cloudswept obelisk is by Paul
Strudel, who also worked on the sculptures,
together with others. including Matthias Rauchmiller, Tobias Kracker, Johann Frühwirt, and
Matthias Gunst. The comprehensive iconographic
allusions unites the Trinity on the top of the

Balthasar Herold
Mariensäule, 1667

Matthias Rauchmiller, Lodovico
Burnacini, Johann Bernhard Fischer von Erlach, Paul Strudel
and others
Pestsäule, 1693

column, with the Emperor Leopold at prayer, the
coats of arms of the House of Austria and of the
kingdoms of Hungary and Bohemia, and allegorical figures and reliefs on biblical themes which
refer to the epidemic and its defeat. The creation
of Eve in Paradise and the end of the Flood are
placed as pendants to representations of victorious Faith and the vanquished Plague. The vanquished Plague is represented by a toothless old
crone with shriveled, pendulous breasts and wrin-
kled skin who is falling headlong backward below
a figure carrying a cross and symbolizing Faith
whose gaze is turned heavenward.

Above this allegory, the Emperor kneels in
prayer, flanked by the Lamb of God and a globe of
the earth, God's empire on which the sun never
sets. The kneeling Emperor and the figure of Faith
are linked by a bronze scroll on which is inscribed

a hymn of praise. Two other scrolls containing
prayers of supplication and thanksgiving are placed
at equally significant locations on the monument,
giving unequivocal expression to the humility
before God of the Habsburg throne. It was the
Emperor himself who, as is recorded here, "conceived and composed" the three prayers.

The Pestsäule is without a doubt one of the
early masterpieces of Viennese baroque sculpture. The exemplary collaboration between the
sculptors and the architect Johann Bernhard Fischer von Erlach, and between them and Lodovico
Burnacini, who had overall direction of the project,
led to a homogenous and accomplished work of
art. With this column, Leopold I raised a monument to rule by Divine right, whose iconography
forged a powerful link between the House of Austria and "Austrian piety."

Detail of the Pestsäule:
Leopold I with allegorical figures
of Faith and the vanquished
plague

"World Theater" and Court Pastorale

Throughout Europe, Baroque Vienna was renowned as the city of ceremony and celebrations. It was here, in the city by the Danube, not in Paris, where court entertainment came to exhibit a pomp and grandeur never seen before. From triumphal entry to gentle pastoral play, court culture enjoyed an era of what Richard Alewyn has so aptly described as "tropically rampant sensuality."

As well as all the pomp and ceremony, the ostentatious processions, the magnificent banquets accompanied by firework displays, splendid opera and theater performances, ephemeral architecture also played a major part.

A document dating from 1560 records that the then emperor built a stage-set town on the banks of the Danube outside Vienna. The buildings, the defensive walls, and the towers were all made from timber. The festival, in which 900 actors took part, was called the *Stadtbelagerung* (Town Siege); the soldiers were expected to fight on both land and water. This was not meant to be some choreographed epic, rather a depiction of possible future events. One contemporary historian described the scene thus: "The defenders reviled the attackers not just verbally but also, to further provoke them, they threw bodies into the Danube. What was even more cruel and scandalous was that they shot the bodies into the air from mortars ... So as not to keep the reader in too much suspense, it should be added that these lifelike human forms were nothing more than leggings and suits of armor stuffed with straw."

Although theater and ceremonial were firmly rooted in reality, moments of illusion were necessary; however, so as not to stray too far over the border from reality, these had to be kept to a bare minimum.

It would be wrong to imagine ephemeral architecture — temporary structures — as some sort of simple backdrop architecture. Often famous architects were involved, and not merely to offer advice, they were also asked to plan and implement the project. Such commissions were not always financed by dukes and emperors, but often by wealthy merchants or even by the Vienna City Council. In 1690, municipal representatives and businessmen commissioned Johann Bernhard Fischer von Erlach to build two monumental triumphal arches. A third one was to be designed by Peter Strudel. The occasion and the theme were the return of the imperial couple and the heir to the throne after the coronation of their son Joseph as King of Rome on June 4, 1690.

Fischer's drawing represents an unexpectedly novel architectural idea for this type of construction (see illustration right). The side sections of the triumphal arch are designed as small exedra, in which arched pedestals support tall columns that extend way beyond the terminating balustrade. Similarly ornate, but more rooted in the traditional style, stands the second arch, just visible beyond the first one. Here it is shown with two stories, resembling a rather diaphanous church façade. Of course, Fischer used the ancient triumphal arch as his model, but he transformed it in such an imaginative way that he created a completely new style. The Roman decorative and narrative reliefs have a three-dimensional look, as if projecting from the wall; the figures on the balustrade and on the coping on the pillars are fully sculpted and stand in energetic poses.

When planning the triumphal arch, Fischer initially wanted to demonstrate his Italian experience. It is clear that he understood how to apply ancient models to good effect in a contemporary style and in the appropriate esthetic context from the integration of High Baroque decorative art. This sort of work served as the best possible introduction to the elevated circles of the Vienna court architects. There was also another factor. The architect saw the planning stage and the construction of ephemeral architecture as an opportunity to try out new ideas, which he could then use in later works. The spiral columns actually re-appear in a similar structural context on the Karlskirche.

Nine years later, the citizens of Vienna remembered the tremendous success of Fischer's triumphal arches and invited the architect to construct two triumphal gates for the marriage of the heir to the throne, Joseph I, to Amalia Wilhelmina

Johann Bernhard Fischer von Erlach
Design for the Gates of Honor to mark the arrival of Joseph I in Vienna, 1690
Graphische Sammlung Albertina

von Braunschweig-Lüneberg on February 24, 1699. Fischer constructed a sort of *tempietto* or small temple and designed a superb iconographic representation with Joseph as a sunlit, triumphant victor and his bride, Amalia Wilhelmina, as Juno.

The entry of the heir to the throne and his new wife followed the format of a Roman triumphal procession, but surrounded with all the ceremonial of the Vienna court. The empire is portrayed here as a universal and divinely ordained political authority. The ruler, standing under the baldequin, is portrayed as a Caesar of the Holy Roman Empire.

This short-lived fashion for illusory architecture was intended to convey the celestial grandeur of the emperor. All the usual court ceremonial was now no longer enough to project the dignity of the Imperial family. The court ritual was played out in World Theatre, i.e. the world as a stage; it was not just theatre, but also a ceremonial procession.

Another example of this style is the monumental work by the court painter, Martin von Meytens, now kept in the Ceremonial Hall in Schönbrunn Palace. It shows the entry into Vienna of Princess Isabella of Parma, bride of the future Emperor Joseph II (see illustration above).

The wedding was planned for the fall of 1760. The first imperial cavalier, Prince Joseph Wenzel von und zu Liechtenstein, was appointed to perform the wedding in Parma as a representative of the Austrian empire and to bring the bride back to Vienna. The parade was held in front of the Hofburg along the present Augustinerstrasse. Snaking along in what seems like a never-ending procession, the ranks of mounted formations moved forward. In amongst them march the musicians and the soldiers. They pass two ephemeral triumphal gates, one on the left in the foreground, the other on the far edge of the picture top right. In the center below, it is possible to identify the silver-blue carriage of the bride. She is accompanied by the Swiss Guard, who can be recognized by their black and yellow imperial uniform. Ahead rolls the golden carriage of the Liechtenstein principality with the bride's special ambassador.

The painting aroused great interest at the time, as it was accomplished with enormous attention to detail, although this was not exclusively attributable to von Meytens. Many masters and aides contributed their skills in the court studio. Every single one of the ninety-four coaches, drawn by

Martin von Meytens
Arrival of Princess Isabella of
Parma in Vienna, 1760
Oil on canvas
Schloss Schönbrunn, on loan from
the Kunsthistorisches Museum
(**Museum of the History of Art**)

six horses, in the majestic parade is represented accurately. At the time, admirers of the painting could compare the details and their realistic portrayal with newspaper reports of the event.

Such attention to detail and the sheer size of the painting ought not be taken, however, as an esthetic commonplace in Baroque painting. It was rather a political gesture, a symbolic acknowledgement of the ceremony through which the Habsburg and Bourbon dynasties were united. The picture was part of a cycle depicting the various stages of this major event. Other paintings showed the wedding ceremony itself in the Augustinerkirche, the wedding banquet, the imperial supper, and a theater performance in the Hofburg (see illustration left).

The theatre performance was the most important event in the court ceremonial of the Viennese World Theatre. Court festivities to mark major events such as weddings or coronations reached their climax in triumphal processions and a visit to the theater, since the theatrical world was an important component of a court education. But there was a clear demarcation line between entertainment and social functions, clearly laid down in the house rules at Schönbrunn. On the one hand, children were expected to perform in ballets or pastoral plays as a surprise for their parents, while on the other hand they had to attend all the festivities that accompanied theater performances to be presented to the court.

The grand performances took place either in the theater building itself or on one of the city's squares. For the court dignitaries, the splendor of Vienna unfolded in the Hofburg. This was where the Emperor felt at one with the muses and the

ILLUSTRATION OPPOSITE:
Nikolaus von Pacassi
Schönbrunn Palace Theatre
1741-49
View of the auditorium

Martin van Meytens
Theatre performance to mark the wedding of Joseph II with Isabella of Parma in Vienna, 1760
Oil on canvas
Schönbrunn Palace, on loan from the Kunsthistorisches Museum (Museum of the History of Art)

ADJACENT:
Ulrich Kraus (after Johann Waltmann)
Equine ballet in the inner Burgplatz
Engraving, beginning of the eighteenth century.
Österreichische Nationalbibliothek (Austrian National Library)

FAR RIGHT:
Nicolaus van Hoy (after a drawing by Carlo Pasetti)
Argonaut ship from the equine ballet
Engraving, beginning of the eighteenth century
Österreichische Nationalbiblio-

gods of Mount Olympus. People were happy to speak of the Imperial Roman court and to describe Vienna as the capital of the Western world. It was to demonstrate this universal claim, that World Theatre was performed The inner palace courtyard was converted into an imaginary world landscape with hills and towers. Images of clouds descended to the floor and triumphal gateways marked the various parts of the world. Then a gate would open and a ship with artificially billowing sails would make its entry (see illustration p. 66 below). Out of the ship jumped riders, accompanied by pages in silver armor. Rising from a swirl of cloud there came an allegorical figure, Fama, dressed in white and holding a trumpet in her hand to proclaim the glory of the Imperial family. The play began. Riders, squires, and pages edged forward in military formation. And then the horses of the Spanish Riding School danced on, worked through a series of intricate steps, combined in a series of daring leaps with more horses emerging through the gates, and performed their spectacular ballet.

The Emperor himself often played a part in such performances. It is said that Leopold personally practiced the most complicated maneuvers. He was proud to be known as the "Emperor of the West" and his equine ballet as "The Concert of Europe." The choreographic genius who orchestrated the horses from the imperial stud in Lipizza was senior stable master, Count Gundacker von Dietrichstein. Theatrical engineer, Alessandro Carducci, was summoned to the Vienna court from Florence and rewarded with 200,000 guilders for his trouble. He was also awarded the title of Freiherr (baron). Carlo Pasetti, responsible for the design of the square, arrived from Ferrara. Court poet, Francisco Sbarra, crafted verses and composer, Anton Berteli, took care of the musical accompaniment. The Vienna ballet, which lasted about four hours, was one of the most exciting events in a city already spoiled for festivals and ceremonial.

The heroic pastorale, the gentle descent into sentimental rural idylls which were all the rage in the mid-eighteenth century, heralded the arrival of the playful Rococo era. A transitional period was not easy to identify in Vienna. Perhaps the cultural events at the court of Maria Theresia, now directed more at the bourgeoisie, were responsible for the change. At any event, for whatever reason, pompous state events were cast aside in favor of a more pastoral court culture. But it would not be true to describe this a turning-point. The changes reflected more a novel variation on the Baroque festival, as the court continued to allow the stage to be used for World Theatre, the play which reflected the capital's universality.

Empress Maria Theresia increasingly chose to distance herself from overblow cultural pursuits, preferring instead the quieter world of the pastoral play. The Imperial festival gradually rid itself of its pathos to become a tranquil Rococo pastorale. The Schönbrunn palace theater, built by Nikolaus von Pacassi between 1741 and 1749 (see illustration page 68 above), was used for summer performances. In the words of the Empress, "there must be spectacles, we cannot live in such a grand residence without them" and so family events were held there. The actors included princes, princesses, and selected noblemen. Plays were performed by Christoph Willibald Gluck and Metastasio, a pseudonym chosen by the Roman abbot, Pietro Antonio Domenico Bonaventura Trapassi, who was the most important exponent of the Arcadian romantic lyric at court.

Pastoral plays completed the picture of cultural life at court. Vienna and the Hofburg were the backdrop for triumphal parades in honor of the Imperial House of Habsburg. Court ceremonial centered on the Viennese *Welttheater* (World Theater) but was then reduced to an almost bourgeois level to emerge as the *pastorale*. In retrospect, it is clear that the grand parades held outside the gates of Vienna for the bride, Isabella of Parma, and the accompanying marriage festivities of 1760 represented both the climax and the turning point of the Baroque festival. It is even possible to talk of these events as a farewell party for the Baroque. From then on, small-scale theatre in the form of the pastoral play and the sentimental romantic idyll were to dominate.

Johann Bernhard Fischer von Erlach

The first phase of Viennese Baroque ended with the victorious expulsion of the Turks in 1683. When did the true flowering of Baroque culture begin, the triumph of the Baroque *Gesamtkunstwerk*, the total work of art? Perhaps the court became so preoccupied with magnificent celebrations and glittering parties that it neglected the imperial capital. In any case, Leopold was not a ruler with a passion for building, though this omission had pragmatic reasons. Clearly, the reconstruction of the destroyed suburbs was a matter of greater urgency. So the Hofburg, the Habsburg's main palace, remained unaltered after 1681, the year the Leopold Wing was completed.

There was, of course, no desire to present a picture to the public of a ruling family intent merely on enjoying itself, in fact quite the opposite. A handbill circulated around Vienna with an allegorical picture showing the house of Habsburg as a late Gothic palace. It rests on two columns, the Mariensäule (Maria Column) and the Pestsäule (Plague Column), symbols of reverence and thanksgiving for God's help in overcoming the Plague and the Turkish threat. The Pestsäule in the Graben, completed in 1693, serves as a memorial to *Pietas Austriaca* (Austrian Roman Catholic piety). Providing the funds for new churches and church renovation work also served as a form of propaganda.

But how was the Habsburg capital to be portrayed to the outside world, to the rest of Europe? The Hofburg, consisting only of architectural fragments, had to stand alongside

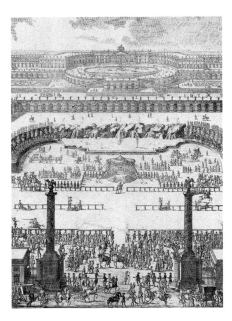

Medal with bust of Johann Bernhard Fischer von Erlach (1656-1723) by Benedikt Richter 1719

Johann Bernhard Fischer von Erlach
First sketch of the imperial palace for Schönbrunn (extract), 1688 "Entwurff einer Historischen Architectur" (Plan of Civil and Historical Architecture), Vol. IV, Plate 2

splendid new buildings in other capitals. Andreas Schlüter had built the Berlin Stadtschloss in 1698, Georg Wenzeslaus von Knobelsdorff the Potsdam Stadtschloss in 1664 and this was converted and extended in 1680. Matthäus Daniel Pöppelmann had constructed the Zwinger Palace in Dresden between 1697 and 1716.

Johann Bernhard Fischer von Erlach's plans for Schönbrunn had to be seen in this context of impressive foreign buildings. Hellmut Lorenz aptly described it as a "hypertrophic visiting card" (see illustration above). Four broad, architecturally distinct terraces extend up the gently rising hill, which is crowned by a huge concave building with side-wings, corner pavilions, and galleries. The design was clearly meant to be taken seriously but it was also a presentational device designed to impress Fischer von Erlach's illustrious patrons.

The work of Johann Bernhard Fischer marked the real flowering of Viennese Baroque. He was born in Graz in 1656, the son of a sculptor, and received the von Erlach title in 1696. At the age of fifteen, Fischer went to Rome and trained as a sculptor in the studio of the German artist, Johann Ferdinand Schor.

Schor's team worked closely with that of the Roman Baroque architect and sculptor, Gianlorenzo Bernini. At the Academia di San Luca, the leading art school in Rome, Fischer studied Bernini's works and writings. Many of Bernini's sketches were later included in Fischer's *Entwurff einer Historischen Architectur* (Plan of Civil and Historical Architecture), which was first published in 1721. Bernini's first project for the Louvre in Paris, a concave central section into which a projecting oval is incorporated, lives on in several of Fischer's garden pavilion designs. This applies particularly to the sketches for the so-called *Lust-Garten-Gebäude* (pleasure garden building), which date from around 1680 (see illustration above right). The style undergoes its first change in another drawing. Here ancient vases frame a garden palace or summer residence (see illustration right, second from top). The façade follows a sophisticated design, as a convex central section rises ornately above the concave lower floor, topped by a balustrade surmounted with figures. This unusual combination of inward and outward projecting façades preoccupied Fischer during his stay in Rome. When planning garden palaces and country houses later on, in each case he referred back to earlier sketches and made some small, but startling alterations. Furthermore, Fischer's architectural leitmotif became increasingly important in Baroque styles north of the Alps. As well as the dynamic interplay between concave and convex sections, Fischer must have grappled long and hard with Bernini's designs for the tower-flanked façade of St Peter's in Rome. The front elevation of St Peter's appears later in an altered form in Fischer's plan for Vienna's Karlskirche.

In 1683, before Fischer returned home, he visited Naples in the company of the Marchese del Carpio, from whom the young sculptor and prospective architect received his first commission, although it was only for staging festivals and producing bronze medallions. The Marchese enjoyed good relations with the Habsburg court, as he had been ambassador in Rome to the Spanish Habsburg Charles II from 1676 through 1682. A year later, he was appointed Spanish viceroy in Naples. It was in Naples that Fischer met Francesco Antonio Picchiatti, an antiquarian and architect. The latter, a follower of Cosimo Fanzagos, showed Fischer the importance of using quotations from the classics for decorating church and palace façade s. This proved to be a useful experience for Fischer in his later work.

In 1686, Fischer returned home, initially to his home town of Graz. A short time later, he was contacted by the Viennese court, courtesy of a recommendation from Naples. Fischer's name must have been treated with unusual respect, as Count Michael Althan asked in 1688 "whether the person who stayed with Cavagliere Bernini for sixteen years was called Fischer."

This prosperous nobleman was an important figure among Vienna's patrons of the arts. Such wealthy benefactors greatly appreciated local architects who had benefited from training in Italy.

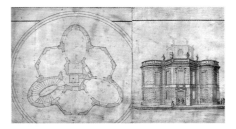

Johann Bernhard Fischer von Erlach
Codex Montenuevo
Design for a country house

Johann Bernhard Fischer von Erlach
Entwurff einer Historischen Architectur (Plan of Civil and Historical Architecture)
Two Vases and a Country House, Vol. V, Plate 10

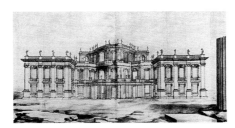

Johann Bernhard Fischer von Erlach
Design for a large country house
(Liechtenstein Palace in the Rossau)

Johann Bernhard Fischer von Erlach
Entwurff einer Historischen Architectur Belvedere Liechtenstein, Vol. V, Plate 12

Fischer was first employed as an architect and sculptor on the Pestsäule (Plague Column). He went on to design garden pavilions, altars, and fountains. It was during his first year in Vienna that he produced his imaginative design for the Imperial summer palace at Schönbrunn. However, his design did not receive the response for which he had hoped. It must have been a great disappointment to him when Johann Adam, Prince Liechtenstein, rejected his plans for a garden palace in the Rossau. The plans Fischer produced in 1688 were regarded by the prince as unsuitable (see illustration left, second from bottom). Instead Prince Johann Adam turned to Martinelli, who suggested a more traditional design for the building, a mixture of country villa and town mansion. Fischer's plans, on the other hand, resembled a Venetian palace transformed into the Bernini style. A central oval, whose lower floor was intended as a rocky grotto, extended from the recessed middle section. It was more a *maison de plaisance* than an aristocrat's mansion.

There was some consolation for the architect, however. A short time later, he was able to implement his ideas for a garden pavilion, even though the structure did not follow his original plans exactly. In 1689, a belvedere to Fischer's plans was built in the garden area opposite the palace. However this was demolished in the nineteenth century and all that remains is a drawing in Fischer's "Plan of Civil and Historical Architecture" (see illustration bottom left) and a painting by Bernardo Bellotto (see illustration page 62 top). Domenico Martinelli, a tutor at the Academy in Rome, entered the service of Prince Liechtenstein in 1690 and represented serious competition for Fischer. Praised as an architect of incomparable quality, the Italian, unlike his Austrian counterpart, was simply overburdened with commissions. This proved a particularly bitter pill for Fischer to swallow; his training in Rome should have been proof enough of the quality of his work and among the nobility he was much valued as the "local Roman."

As has already been mentioned, Emperor Leopold I had no enthusiasm for new buildings. In Fischer's opinion, the Schönbrunn Palace was completed in a half-hearted way and to "standard dimensions." Fischer's earlier inspired ideas were disregarded.

It must have come as a great relief when the Archbishop of Salzburg, Count Thun, appointed Fischer as court architect in 1694. At last he would be able to put his own imaginative plans for church buildings into practice. However, he retained his home in Vienna and only visited Salzburg for consultations with the archbishop and to supervise the work as it was being carried out.

Prince Eugene (1663-1736)
Österreichische Nationalbibliothek (Austrian National Library)

Prince Eugene's Winter Palace

In 1695, Fischer unexpectedly won a prestigious and lucrative contract, namely the construction of Prince Eugene's Winter Palace in Vienna's Himmelpfortgasse. It should first be mentioned, however, that during the last years of the seventeenth century, the style for town house façades had gradually changed. Long, monotonous frontages such as the Leopold Wing at the Hofburg, a pattern that can still be seen in the Starhemberg Palace, were now broken up by ressauts or projections. Italian architects such as Enrico Zucalli and Domenico Martinelli were summoned to Vienna, where they enjoyed the luxury of being well supplied with work and were able to adopt new approaches.

At last, Fischer had the opportunity to put his Roman experience into practice, and he did it with style. He designed a seven-bay structure which, due to the narrow lane in which it was located, had to have a flat façade. This was given a distinctive and unmistakable character by its portals. Huge double consoles supported each balcony and a lavishly decorated balustrade. In place of columns or pillars, he designed bas-reliefs showing battle scenes from classical mythology *(Aeneas and Anchises, Hercules and Anteus)*. These related to the glorious deeds of Prince Eugene (see illustration below). The tall windows of the piano nobile above the portals were also decorated, setting themselves apart from the rest of the window architecture by their reversed segmental pediments with inset cartouches. Colossal pilasters with flat composite capitals which extended from the lower floor up to the mezzanine and then abutted the cornice, broke up the façade to give it interest.

Fischer's masterpiece, however, was the staircase which, because of the complicated site, had to be completely redesigned without any preconceived ideas (see illustration page 71). The existing situation was labyrinthine. Several buildings had to be merged into one palace. The ceilings and floors had to be dismantled and then rebuilt. The staircase is, in fact, a combination of several rooms, all originating from different buildings. It was really a "house within a house."

A distinctive model, that hints at Hildebrandt's solution in the Upper Belvedere, arose out of the staircase at the Winter Palace. In both cases, the ascent and descent of the stairs are impressively staged. The complex, iconographic presentation refers to the virtues of the head of the household. With the sculpted figures of Hercules, Atlantis and other mythological characters paraded before the eyes, it is easy to imagine the heroes of Olympus. Completing the pictorial scene are wall and ceiling paintings (see illustration page 112) pointing to an imaginary goal, the apotheosis of the Prince (see illustration p.100, left). The sculptures were produced by Giovanni Giuliani, a Venetian who came to Vienna in the 1690s and worked in various palaces, usually on staircases. A glance at the ground plan reveals a confusing array of rooms left over from the original building. Fischer tried to keep to a logical sequence of rooms as far as he could. He managed to do this successfully by positioning and proportioning the banqueting room right behind the central landing to which the staircases lead. By incorporating the old building into the new, he adapted the room to the height of the piano nobile, itself determined by the façade, thereby creating a structural elegance; however, he had to alter a complex system of old rooms in order to make the new banqueting hall which

ILLUSTRATION OPPOSITE:
Prince Eugene's Winter Palace
1695, Staircase

Johann Bernhard Fischer von Erlach
Prince Eugene's Winter Palace
1695, Façade

Prince Eugene's Winter Palace
Portal reliefs with battle scenes
from ancient mythology

unfortunately longer exists, as it was later converted into a number of smaller rooms. On the other hand, it is still possible today to view the reception rooms, in particular the Blue Drawing-room (see illustration page 72/73), the prince's Parade Room, and the Red Drawing-room, the audience chamber. Prince Eugene had his own ideas as regards the interior design. The wainscoting was to be gilded and decorated with grotesques, and the doors and walls were to be covered with fine fabrics. Mirrors and oil paintings, wall-sconces, and crystal chandeliers were to be just an integral part of the splendor as was the elegant furniture. As Johann Basilius Küchelbeckler remarked in his *Allerneuester Nachricht vom Römisch-Kayserlichen Hofe* (The Latest News from the Imperial Roman Court), "nothing was spared on this palace if it could exalt his magnificence."

Suddenly, Prince Eugene changed his plans drastically. He saw Fischer's work as having been completed. It must have been both incomprehensible and depressing for the architect to have the planning and direction of the palace taken away from him so abruptly. His great local rival, Johann Lukas von Hildebrandt, was now entrusted with all the Prince's further contracts. Were there material or aesthetic reasons that caused this change of mind or was it simply princely whim? Even now, nobody knows the answer. Perhaps the appointment of Hildebrandt dates back to the 1695-96 Italian campaigns, when Prince Eugene met the young architect who was then building fortresses. Hildebrandt stuck rigidly to Fischer's scheme and did not touch the core structure. However, the Prince wanted additional wings to accommodate his library. In 1708, the eastern gallery was completed; after the acquisition of the neighboring property to the west, Hildebrandt finished the other wing in 1724.

Toward the end of the century, when Fischer had stopped working for the Prince, he became involved in serious plans for the Schönbrunn Palace (see illustration page 68 above). The land in question had belonged to the Emperor since 1686, although initially Leopold I only had plans to build a hunting lodge and spacious gardens.

In 1695, the imperial court commissioned the Frenchman, Jean Trehet, to design the gardens. A tutor working for the Emperor, Obersthofmeister Prince Salm, who was involved in the education of the heir to the throne, Joseph I, was impressed by Fischer's plans for the Palace and almost certainly by the whole imaginative project. Prince Salm persuaded the court to let him take personal charge of the architect. The work then progressed rapidly. Perhaps Fischer's idealistic plans had also impressed the Emperor, since even though the monarch had no intention of implementing such a grand scheme, he did not appear to have been against the idea of converting the planned hunting lodge into a palace. In any case,

LEFT:
Prince Eugene's Winter Palace 1695,
Blue Drawing-room

ILLUSTRATION ABOVE:
Prince Eugene's Winter Palace 1695,
Gold Cabinet and gilded door leading to one
of the state rooms

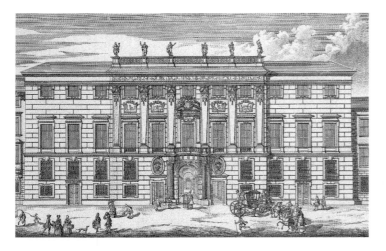

The Batthyány-Schönborn Palace

"The façade of the building which His Excellency Herr Adam Batthyan, Privy Councillor and Bannus of Croatia, built on the Schottenplatz 1700 AD." This is the inscription accompanying an engraving by J.A. Delsenbach based on Johann Bernhard Fischer von Erlach's sketch of what the Batthyány-Schönborn Palace would be like when it was completed. Work had started a year earlier near the Schottenplatz (see illustration left and right). Adam, Count Batthyány, who acquired the land in 1698, commissioned Fischer to build his new Winter Palace.

Judging by the imaginative design for the façade , it would appear that Fischer was given a free hand. In all the literature, this palace is often described as Fischer's most distinctive creation. In fact, the oculi with the candelabra next to the central portico are rather idiosyncratic and the two doors flanking the portico look odd when the façade is seen as a whole. As in Prince Eugene's Palace in the Himmelpfortgasse, Fischer positioned a window framed with pilasters and crowned with a segmental pediment in the piano nobile area above the main entrance. Allegorical figures, displaying the count's coat-of-arms, rest on the curving pediment cornice. The downward tapering pilasters, with decorative work tumbling over the capitals, help to emphasize the central projection and its five bays.

In 1740, the count's widow sold the estate to the Bishop of Würzburg, Frederick Charles, Count von Schönborn, who had the internal rooms re-designed and refurbished, so that he could accommodate his collection of paintings and library of 18,000 priceless volumes. The staircase with its ornate figures and the Red Drawing-room are the main showpiece rooms in the palace. The red, classical-style ornaments on the wall-coverings, the delicate Rococo heating-stove, and the heavy crystal chandeliers in the Red Drawing-room are among the most memorable features of all the grand drawing rooms in Vienna.

Shortly before his death in 1705, Emperor Leopold remembered Fischer's imaginative design for the Plague Column in the Graben, and commissioned the artist to plan a monument for his son, Joseph. The Emperor had promised to build this in 1702, if Joseph returned safely from the Palatinate wars against the French king. He did, indeed, return home safely and Fischer planned a monument for the Hoher Markt to consist of three columns, a high platform, and a baldaquin crown, formed from segmental pediments. In the center, beneath the baldaquin, in accordance with the imperial promise, Fischer placed a "Colossus in honor of St Joseph," a monumental fountain with a series of figures, namely the high priest

Johann Bernhard Fischer von Erlach
Batthyány-Schönborn Palace
Portal and façade detail, 1698

ILLUSTRATION OPPOSITE:
Batthyány-Schönborn Palace
View from the Red Drawing-room
into the staircase adorned with
statuary

Batthyány-Schönborn Palace
J.A. Delsenbach after a drawing
by Johann Bernhard Fischer von
Erlach, 1700
Historisches Museum der Stadt
Wien

Johann Bernhard Fischer von
Erlach
Batthyány-Schönborn Palace
Red Drawing-room, 1740

it was Leopold's idea to "add two courtyards to the *corps de logis* (central part of the building). It would then be suitable for housing the whole Imperial court." The Emperor was something of a pragmatist, however.

The marriage of Joseph lay ahead and the heir would be entitled to his own court. A hunting lodge would hardly have been appropriate. Another of the engravings in Fischer's "Historic Architecture" book shows Leopold's favored solution. The central section is extended by two side-wings, creating a spacious courtyard. The *corps de logis* was completed and habitable by 1700, when the court held a lavish reception for the heir to the throne and his wife to mark the opening of the palace. Work on the side-wings was delayed, however, due to the sudden death of Joseph I in 1711. The palace was no longer important and work was stopped. Its extension and conversion was only resumed in 1743, under Maria Theresia.

marrying Mary and Joseph — a religious allusion to the House of Habsburg and the *pietas Austriaca*. As time was of the essence, Fischer had the monument erected within a year as a marble-painted wooden construction. This temporary measure remained in place, but when it started to decay, as Joseph's interest in it waned. After his death in 1711 it faced demolition, but repairs were made and, in 1724, one year after Fischer's death, Emperor Charles VI ordered a second temporary monument to replace it. Finally, on April 14, 1732, the Imperial family replaced the wooden structure with a marble monument. Fischer's son, Joseph Emmanuel, was responsible for the final version and it can now be seen on the Hoher Markt (see illustration left).

Johann Bernhard Fischer von Erlach and Johann Lukas von Hildebrandt

One of Fischer's bitterest rivals was Johann Lukas von Hildebrandt. As mentioned earlier, Hildebrandt took over from Fischer while the latter was in charge of Prince Eugene's Winter

Palace and superseded him in various other important building projects.

Hildebrandt was generally more popular than his older colleague, so it must have been a considerable source of satisfaction for Fischer to see that in one instance at least, the younger man was willing to respect his own architectural approach. In 1697, Hildebrandt became responsible for the design and completion of the Mansfeld-Fondi Summer Palace. Taking into account the tastes of the Viennese nobility, he followed the Roman architectural style that Fischer had initially adopted. It was for this reason that he planned an oval central section, accessed from the garden by a dog-leg staircase, and flanked by two wings. Hildebrandt, however, was unable to complete the building.

In 1716, when Prince Schwarzenberg acquired the property, it was still a shell. Four years later, Fischer was given the job of completing the building, now known as Palais Schwarzenberg. What a memorable event! He altered the external appearance quite

Baroque Architecture and Johann Bernhard Fischer von Erlach

considerably by replacing the ornamented
edicules with rounded arches and by emphasizing sectional features such as the cornices
and pilasters. The decorative work typical
of Hildebrandt, which would have brought
the oval central projection into the façade,
was not carried out. Instead, Fischer turned
the central oval into an unusual and dominant feature.

The different architectural styles of these
two men who played such an important part in
the Baroque movement north of the Alps is
easy to identify in the Palais Daun-Kinsky,
which Hildebrandt built between 1713 and
1716 (see illustration page 87, right).

This palace, which stands opposite the
Schottenkirche, creates an attractive picture
with its moving and richly decorated façade.
The pilasters in the slightly forward projection taper downward in their lower third, at
which point they are coarsely fluted. It is possible that Hildebrandt was revising one of
Fischer's ideas.

The older Palais Batthyány-Schönborn on
the other side of the Freyung displays this elegant theme (see illustration page 74). On the
upper floor, the window pediments vary playfully between segmental arches and pediments. An ornate balustrade with classical
sculptures on tall pedestals runs surmounts a
mezzanine. Johann Lukas von Hildebrandt's
feel for fine detail comes to the fore inside the
palace. The interwoven bands in the stairway
balustrade merge into leafwork and scrolls or
open out into generous triangular shapes.

ILLUSTRATION OPPOSITE
ABOVE:
Johann Lukas von Hildebrandt
Johann Bernhard Fischer von
Erlach
Palais Schwarzenberg,
formerly Mansfeld-Fondi
1697/1720

BELOW:
Johann Bernhard Fischer von
Erlach
Joseph Fountain on the Hoher
Markt, 1706 and 1732

One of the Raptus groups by
Lorenzo Mattiello in the garden of
the Palais Schwarzenberg

Whereas Fischer chose elevations and
designed decorations which were more to
the taste of the aristocracy, perhaps even
with the Imperial family, Johann Lukas von
Hildebrandt was keener on creating designs
which were elegant and pleasing, but not
quite so resplendent as forms of expression.
He was more interested in subtle decorative
schemes and generously proportioned front
elevations. In addition, he loved to adorn
porticos, staircases, and grand entrances of
all kinds with sculptures which harmonized
with the decor and lent a certain playful element to the architecture.

Fischer, on the other hand, sought
grandiose forms of expression and a decorative style that came close to the monumental. This may well be the reason why the
nobility often preferred Johann Lukas von
Hildebrandt's architectural style. Imperial
buildings, such as the Schönbrunn Palace,
the Court Library, and the Karlskirche were,
however, entrusted to Fischer.

Johann Lukas von Hildebrandt
Johann Bernhard and Joseph
Emanuel Fischer von Erlach
Palais Schwarzenberg, Dome
Room, 1720-28

ILLUSTRATION OPPOSITE:
Johann Bernhard Fischer von Erlach
Palais Trautson, 1710
Facade (above)
Staircase (below left)
Banqueting Hall (below right)

ILLUSTRATION ABOVE:
Palais Trautson, from the garden, 1715
J.A. Delsenbach after a drawing by Johann Bernhard Fischer von Erlach

ILLUSTRATION BELOW:
Bernardo Bellotto (Canaletto)
Vienna from the Belvedere, 1758/61
Oil on canvas,
51 x 84 in (135 x 213 cm)
Kunsthistorisches Museum

Palais Trautson

There were several reasons why Count Trautson chose Johann Bernhard Fischer von Erlach to build his summer palace. To start with, the family had owned valuable property opposite the Hofburg on the edge of Josephstadt, and thus very close to the imperial court, since the seventeenth century. In addition, in 1709, Count Trautson was appointed Senior Controller of the Imperial Court. Occupying this prestigious and lucrative post, he would not necessarily rise to the rank of prince, but it was a strong possibility. The promotion did, in fact, occur two years later. Clearly, these reasons were uppermost in the Count's mind when he entrusted the design of this grand and impressive palace to Fischer (see illustration page 79).

Fischer's plans appear to have fulfilled the count's expectations, as he linked the architectural structure of the grand Winter Palace with the concept of a country house. A similar idea had already occurred to him when designing the Gartenpalais Liechtenstein, a *palazzo in villa* in the Italian style.

The site was ideal for Fischer's plans, as here, away from the narrow lanes and overcrowded squares of the inner city, there was plenty of room to create a truly striking architecture. Fischer brought the central section well forward, thereby emphasizing the central axis, from which a path led over the lawn to the Hofburg gate. The portal, flanked by double columns whose upper pedestals supported allegorical figures, also projected forward. The central section is topped with a pediment, and the recessed wings faced the city with the adjacent building, the Hofburg, turned toward it. This causes the façade to be at right angles to the garden, instead of in line with it as is generally the case.

Visitors who enter the Palace and linger for a while in the spacious vestibule will be able to contemplate the staircase, adorned with monumental figures, and appreciate that these features are designed to underline the high rank of the erstwhile owner (see illustration page 79). Here too, the staircase with landings climbs in a straight line, rather like a *via triumphalis*, from the vestibule to the piano nobile. In the banqueting hall, the gold ornamentation on the pilaster capitals, picture frames, the red marbled doors, and mantelpiece is shown off to advantage by the elegant, off-white decor (see illustration, p. 79).

Access to the garden, now sadly destroyed, was through the Sala Terrena in the right-hand wing. At this point, the magnificent town palace is transformed into a country house.

An engraving, based on a drawing by Fischer, shows the garden forming a unique esthetic whole with the façade (see illustration top left). The middle section determines the width of the central axis, which is traversed by a lateral axis with a circular pond and fountain at the intersection. The parterres are ornamented in the obligatory French style with generous swags and knots.

At the beginning of the eighteenth century, the Viennese aristocracy and the upper middle classes began building with enthusiasm. Against a background of sound economic development, a winter palace and a country house were symbols of increasing prosperity.

The number of manual workers and tradesmen rose sharply in the first thirty years of the century. Naturally, this boosted the state finances to the extent that the Imperial court could now afford to fund grand buildings. Plans to enlarge the Hofburg involved Fischer and later his son Johannes Emanuel. But before that happened, Fischer was to complete his masterpiece, the Karlskirche.

The Karlskirche

Charles VI was crowned emperor in 1711. In 1713, the Plague struck Vienna, and for those citizens who survived, the Emperor vowed to build a church in honor of St Charles Borromeus, the patron saint of plagues. Two years later, the planning work started and the tenders were awarded. Fischer, who in 1705 had been appointed as senior inspector for all the Imperial court buildings and residences, a position confirmed when Charles VI became emperor, was second only to Johann Lukas von Hildebrandt in seniority. The latter had taken over from Giovanni Pietro Tencala in 1700 as Imperial Court Engineer and as such fulfilled the role of court architect.

Fischer nevertheless overcame his fiercest rival for the contract. There was one simple reason for this. The Emperor had been very impressed by the churches which Fischer had designed in Salzburg, namely the Dreifaltigkeitskirche and the Kollegienkirche. Charles clearly rated these more highly than the new Peterskirche near St Stephen's Cathedral, but what was probably even more important was that for this project the planned church was not to be built in the city center but in the suburbs.

In fact, the site was not even strictly speaking suburban, as the plot of land chosen for the church was not even surrounded by houses. Bellotto's painting shows the Karlskirche amid trees and meadows (see illustration page 78, left). The imposing buildings in the picture are the Palais Schwarzenberg to the right and near it the Lower Belvedere with the Salesianerkirche. In the background, against the backdrop of the Wienerwald, lies the city of Vienna, its church towers, and the Hofburg. The site chosen for the new church was a water-meadow close to the Vienna River. Its immediate environment was dominated by splendid palaces belonging to the nobility. If the area to the south of the church, which consisted of Lodovico Burnacini's Neue Favorita—later to become the Theresianum — and the Palais Trautson a little further away, is included in the neighborhood, then it was certainly a challenge to give the new imperial church building the dominance its importance demanded. Only Fischer's project seemed right for achieving this end. Unfortunately the designs of the other contenders, Hildebrandt and Galli-Bibiena, have not survived.

Fischer's plan needs to be viewed in the light of this topography and the town-planning considerations. He wanted to combine the idea of a votive church with that of imperial grandeur, a sacred monument to *pietas Austriaca* (see illustration p. 80 right and page 115). The resulting structure, with its tall drum dome, is a spectacular variation on Salzburg's Dreifaltigkeitskirche and Kollegienkirche. The Karlskirche developed out of local tradition, but differs from its Salzburg counterparts in one important respect, namely the allegorical interpretation on the façade.

Fischer von Erlach designed a unique frontage, almost certainly with the assistance of the court scholars. It paints a complex "picture" of all the imperial allusions of majesty that the House of Habsburg had propagated since it came into existence. This is not some vague reference to classical subjects. What is displayed here is a profound, clearly-defined tableau which legitimizes the God-given domination of the world by the Habsburg Empire. Only the two main themes need to be mentioned here. Firstly, the spiraling columns hark back not only to the Old Testament Temple of Solomon, but also to the rule of the Spanish king and Emperor Charles V. The latter re-interpreted them as the Pillars of Hercules, thus elevating them to symbols of the civilized, i.e. Habsburg, world. Secondly, the similarity with the Columns of Trajan and Marcus Aurelius points to the peaceful years of Eternal Rome. Within the façade of the Karlskirche lies Charles VI's political message. In the light of the Spanish War of Succession, it appears to be a challenging one. Charles VI, a Christian emperor

Johann Bernhard Fischer von Erlach
Karlskirche, begun 1715
View of the interior

in peacetime, is expressing his claim to the Spanish crown, which had just passed into the hands of the Bourbons.

The heavy symbolism of the façade, with its resemblance to an ancient temple, and the triumphal columns reinforces the church's position as an architectural set-piece. It seems as though it has been plucked from an imaginary "architectural catalogue"; a style-book which did not exist. Fischer did, however, produce a book containing a collection of fantasy buildings, architectural themes, and some buildings which had actually been constructed. This was his large-format *Entwurff einer Historischen Architectur* (Plan of Civil and Historical Architecture), mentioned previously. This is a very personalized work, more a magazine of Fischer's architectural ideas and visions than a collection of sketches and theoretical illustrations, relating to column orders and systems of proportion.

The extraordinarily imposing picture created by the Karlskirche is not only created by the interplay between the columned portico, dome, and triumphal arches. For Fischer, the dome was central to his thinking. The oval is the centerpiece of the composition. Above it rises the dome with its tall drum-ring. The nave appears to extend into the remotest corners as well as into the heights (see also illustration page 115). Arranged around the oval are the choir, chapels, and side-rooms. The façade crosses the west-east axis of the nave. A more acute contrast seems barely imaginable. The calm, straight lines of the façade open up in the interior and create a dynamic rigidity. After entering the church, the eyes are drawn upward by the light into the space in which the architecture can reveal its dynamism. The structural and esthetic key to the whole concept is the dome, whether seen from close range or from afar, from within the church or as part of the Viennese skyline.

Fischer died in 1723 and did not live to see the completion of his masterpiece. It was left to his son, Joseph Emanuel, who had worked with his father on the Joseph Fountain in Hoher Markt, to finish the structure. Changes were made to the dome, but there was no significant deviation from the original plan.

The Hofbibliothek (Court Library)

One year before his death, Fischer received another imperial contract, this time to design the Hofbibliothek (Court Library). Just how much the Emperor, Charles VI, involved Fischer in the whole plan for extending the Hofburg it is impossible to say now. It is certain, however, that the background to the library needs to be seen in the context of the Court Chancellery, already under construction, the Court Stables, the Winter Riding School, planned for later, the Imperial Chancellery Wing, and the Michaeler façade (see plan on p. 41).

It seems extraordinary that the emperor should have insisted on basing the position of the library on an earlier building, a riding school, which had been started in 1681. Fischer was thus obliged to retain an older wall structure. Upon its completion in 1737, the Hofbibliothek was clearly distinct from the other wings of the Hofburg and was not even architecturally in keeping with the adjacent building, the Schweizerhof. For the later Hofburg buildings, the library was, as Hellmut Lorenz pointedly observes, "a troublemaker of the first order."

The position and design of the library, following a long, rectangular ground plan, was ideal for the architect. He crowned the center with a tall, oval dome, thus creating a unique building (see illustration left and page 116). The towering hall rises majestically upward, with the light entering through large, round-arched windows.

ILLUSTRATION OPPOSITE:
Johann Bernhard Fischer von Erlach
Vienna, Hofbibliothek (Court Library), 1722

Johann Bernhard Fischer von Erlach
Vienna, Hofbibliothek (Court Library), 1722
View of the oval in the Dome Room

Johann Lukas von Hildebrandt

On June 23, 1699 Emperor Leopold I received an application for the post of court architect. The signatory emphasized that he was the son of German parents and "a country boy born and bred," although he had spent his first twenty-eight years in Italy, mainly in Rome, training as a military and urban architect.

The application was favorably received by the Emperor, probably because the applicant had spent 1695-96 working as a fortress engineer in the army of Prince Eugene and had been involved in three campaigns in Piedmont. It was probably the Prince himself who made sure that his engineer, having left his service and moved to Vienna, soon received the title of Imperial Councillor.

The newly-ennobled German's name was Johann Lukas von Hildebrandt, who, in the same year as his application, was appointed to the position of court architect. The following year, he replaced the elderly and highly-respected Giovanni Pietro Tencala. He took over the post, assuming the title of Imperial Court Engineer at a salary of 600 florins per year and a "grace-and-favor" court

apartment. Now there were two important Baroque architects working in Vienna. Von Hildebrandt managed to create an almost popular architectural style for the town palace and country house. Many of the grand town houses and palaces of the Viennese nobility were built in the Hildebrandt style by other architects, most of them now long-forgotten.

Hildebrandt's speciality was almost certainly the construction of palaces, but he is also responsible for two superb churches. The first is the Peterskirche near the Graben. The original church on the site dated from the time of Charlemagne but was demolished in 1701 and then rebuilt one year later to plans by Gabriele Montani (see illustration above and page 6). The drastic changes made later were probably attributable to Hildebrandt. It is not easy to trace the full history of the building and so be certain which architect designed which part. The church has a Baroque central structure, built to an oval ground plan. Two towers flanking the façade give the whole structure a rather squat appearance, and the central dome is disproportionate to the ornate upper turrets. The church's Hildebrandt-inspired elegance emerges in the curving façade. The concave central projection dates from 1722. The porch, based on plans by Andrea Altomonte, was not added until 1751, long after Hildebrandt's death (1745).

In the case of the second church, the Piaristenkirche Maria Treu in Josephstadt, it is more certain which parts are attributable to Hildebrandt (see illustration right and below). The plans were probably prepared in 1698, two years after he moved to Vienna. However, building work did not start until 1716 and the plans were later changed. Matthias Gerl probably completed the work between 1751 and 1753.

The whole ensemble — the church and the square — create a harmonious impression. The central projection, arcing forward slightly and flanked by double pillars, is framed by narrow towers. The tall façade, with its crowning pediment, lends a very decorative air to the building. In contrast to the cramped location of the Peters-kirche in central Vienna, and because of the broad square and low-rise surrounding buildings, Hildebrandt was able to create a generous and elegant façade. If a direct comparison is made between the two churches, it is hard to believe that the same architect designed them both, even if later changes to the plans are taken into account.

When the architecture of Johann Lukas von Hildebrandt is examined, his two most important designs, the Lower Belvedere and Upper Belvedere, are usually the focal points of the discussion. But these summer palaces, noted

Johann Lukas von Hildebrandt
Palais Schönborn, 1706-11
Street façade (above)
Garden façade (below left)
Picture Room (below right)

particularly for their architectural and landscaping elements, should not really be used as a yard-stick when assessing his architecture as a whole. This would run the risk of not doing justice to his art. The two Belvederes rank as exceptions among Vienna's Baroque buildings, and this is as true today as when they were first constructed.

To measure the wide spectrum of his design skills, visitors should also look at Schönborn Palace in Josephstadt near the Piaristenkirche (see illustration page 86). Friedrich Charles, Count Schönborn, summoned to Vienna by the Emperor and appointed as Imperial Vice-Chancellor, obtained the property and extensive garden area in 1706 and commissioned Hildebrandt to build a palace. The building has two stories, a relatively high roof elevation and a slightly protruding central projection. Above the portal, there is a central, extending balcony with wrought-iron railings. The central window is crowned with the Schönborn coat-of-arms flanked by lions. Incidentally, the theme of the expanded window pediment with a coat-of-arms was one used frequently by Fischer. The pilasters, which span both storeys, give the building a noble and elegant character, while the garden wing, corresponding with the central projection, extends a long way forward, creating the effect of an informal pavilion with curving cornices connecting it to the lateral wings. The avenue through the garden, starting at the central axis, ends in a circular flowerbed with a fountain surrounded by rocks.

Soon after completion in 1725, an extension was added. To what extent the classical reconstruction of 1760 carried out by Isidor Canevale changed Hildebrandt's original plans it is hard to say. The main structure and the ground plan have survived intact.

It is well worth taking a look inside to study Hildebrandt's staircase. The rooms, which house the Österreichisches Museum für Volkskunde (Ethnographic Museum), are also of interest, having retained their original furnishings. The Picture Room is an especially good example. The Palais Daun-Kinsky (see illustration right), which Hildebrandt built between 1713 and 1716, in other words, shortly after completion of the Palais Schönborn, demonstrates the architect's creative breadth and it also clearly illustrates the difference between a winter palace and a summer house. In contrast to the winter palace, a grander and more impressive building, the summer house appeals through its genteel and intimate restraint. The winter palace uses attractive ornaments, fanciful sculptures, and a dynamic façade in order to express the stylishness of urban life and the standing of the owner.

The allegorical figures of the kind found on the broken segmental sections of the pediment at the Palais Daun-Kinsky are frequently encountered in Vienna. They seem to have been a popular theme in the ornamentation of the palaces of the nobility. The Palais Fürstenberg in Grünangergasse adopts the same theme but in an unusual way. Two hunting-dogs are climbing up over the column ends and the scrolls, ornate with leafwork, meet above the keystone (see illustration left). Many other details, such as the sculpted decorations, the variations between segmental and triangular pediments, and the imaginative window treatments on the Fürstenberg Palais, are reminiscent of Hildebrandt's distinctive style. It can be assumed with reasonable certainty that this winter palace was the work of the Italian, Antonio Beduzzi, but the style was Hildebrandt's and one which was extremely popular with the nobility of the day.

Johann Lukas von Hildebrandt
Stadtpalais Daun-Kinsky
1713-16

Antonio Beduzzi
Palais Fürstenberg, Portal around 1720

Johann Lukas von Hildebrandt
Upper Belvedere, 1721-23

The Belvedere

Hildebrandt was kept very busy in Vienna, with most of his commissions from the nobility. As has already been mentioned, he replaced Fischer as the architect in charge of Prince Eugene's Winter Palace. At the same time, he was probably negotiating with the Prince about a planned summer house outside Vienna. In 1693, Prince Eugene acquired several sites outside the city for a palace and a large garden. By 1706, it was probably agreed that a summer house would be built down by the Rennweg; this was to become the Lower Belvedere. Further up, at the end of a long strip of land designated for the garden, there would be a crowning pavilion, a garden belvedere. This was to become the main building, known as the Upper Belvedere.

During the final years of the seventeenth century, Hildebrandt started work on terracing the garden. But it was not until 1714 that he began work on the Lower Belvedere, a long, narrow single-story building, rising up from behind a trapezium-shaped courtyard. Only the central block was to have an upper floor (see

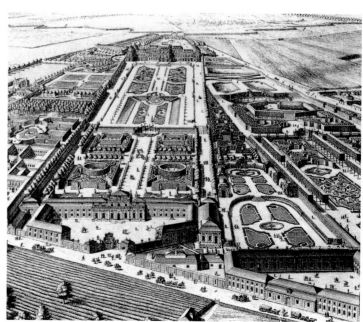

ILLUSTRATION OPPOSITE:
Schloss Belvedere, the whole
complex
Engraving by J.A. Corvinius after
a drawing by Salomon Kleiner,
1740

illustration above). Surprisingly, there are parallels with the Palais Schönborn. The strict pilaster articulation, the only slightly projecting central wing, and the recessed window-frames may well have been ideal for garden architecture, but the fact that the façade was given expressive ornamentation and a balustrade adorned with figures, has to be set in the context of the personality and the dignity of the distinguished prince who commissioned the building. Work on the Belvedere was completed in 1716.

In 1717, Prince Eugene entrusted the Bavarian architect, Dominique Girard, who had been working in Schleissheim and Nymphenburg, with the design of the Belvedere gardens. An embankment forming a lateral axis with steps at each side and a central cascade divides the garden into two terraces, thus overcoming the difference in height between the two palaces (see illustration page 88). On the lower terrace, a knot-garden was laid out with neatly manicured trees. Parterres and fountains were planned for the upper terrace. Comparisons with Versailles are obvious; during this era they

were inevitable. The design of the ornamental shrubbery, which was broken up by a system of diagonal paths, is attributed to the treatise on gardening by Dezaillier d'Argenvilles, which was published in 1709, and was to become the definitive guide to garden landscaping in the eighteenth century.

Shortly after the completion of the first summer palace for Prince Eugene, Hildebrandt received a commission to build the *Geheime Hofkanzlerei* (Court Privy Chancellery) on the site of an old dairy opposite the Amalienburg on Ballhausplatz. Work on this building progressed rapidly. By 1719, only two years after the first plans were produced, the building was completed. The upper floors and mezzanine were broken up by huge pilasters, which served to emphasize the central block. An attic with statuary and a mansard roof rounded off the structure. The building was extended in 1766 by Nicolaus Pacassi.

Not long after, the architect obtained another commission. The brothers Paul and Johann Karl Bartolotti von Patenfeld, were presented with Hildebrandt's plans for a winter palace by

Johann Lukas von Hildebrandt
Lower Belvedere, Gold Cabinet with the sculpture "Apotheosis of Prince Eugene" by
Balthasar Permoser

Johann Lukas von Hildebrandt
Lower Belvedere, Marble Hall with the Mehlmarkt Fountain sculpture
by Georg Raphael Donner

LEFT:
Johann Lukas von Hildebrandt
Lower Belvedere, Marble Gallery with the stature of Maria Theresia
by Franz Xavier Messerschmidt.

the Graben. This was to be more for use by the family than for ceremonial occasions. So not only were the obligatory vestibule and staircase missing, but so was an imposing second floor. The pilasters and window surrounds, so familiar from the Palais Daun-Kinsky, give the main façade, with its four bays, a subdued elegance. The portal's spandrels with two Eros figures riding on scrolls are typical examples of Hildebrandt's style of ornamentation. Franz Jänggls completed the building work in 1720.

In the meantime, Prince Eugene must have decided to build an imposing, crowning structure in the Belvedere instead of a simple garden pavilion. Hildebrandt produced the plans and in 1721 work began on the Upper Belvedere. It was clearly to be much grander and more majestic than the Lower Belvedere (see illustration above and page 88). Behind the staircase and vestibule, crowned by a curving segmental pediment, is the central pavilion with its Marble Hall. At the end of each wing, two

octagonal pavilions both topped with round domes continue and complete the theme of varying levels. The idea is unusual, even novel. The wings are stepped; in other words, the blocks extending either side of the central pavilion, in each case the first five bays, have an additional story which extends above the vestibule pediment. The central pavilion towers above them all, its roof the crowning glory of the whole building. This changing roofscape and the projecting and recessed façades are held together by a unified decorative pattern. Underpinning the dynamic façade is the shared lower floor whose entablature extends right across, even taking in the corner pavilions.

The striking façade of the Upper Belvedere demonstrates more convincingly than any other work by the architect, Hildebrandt's grasp of space and scale. This is also evident in the interior, particularly the staircase. The structure is illustrated clearly by taking a short detour to Upper Franconia.

Johann Lukas von Hildebrandt
Upper Belvedere, 1721-23
Façade (above) and grand staircase (opposite)

In 1711, Hildebrandt was summoned to the Pommersfelden Palace to sort out problems that had arisen in the construction of the staircase. The elector and archbishop, Lothar Franz von Schönborn, who had commissioned the palace, had allowed too much space for the staircase. Hildebrandt solved the problem by building in a three-story gallery, using the lower floor as a staircase.

Hildebrandt must have remembered this relationship between staircase proportions and dimensions when he started on the plans in Vienna. His solution is elegant. It was to create a "sliding" sequence between the Sala Terrena, the entrance hall, and the Marble Hall. The vestibule leads through into the stairwell, where two outer staircases lead up to the Marble Hall and to the apartments at each side.

Baroque Architecture and Johann Lukas von Hildebrandt

The central staircase leads down to the Sala Terrena. Hildebrandt's staircase merges well with the interior architecture and is ideal for displaying scenes painted for Prince Eugene. The staircase is the place in which to experience transcendence. The fact that it manages to fulfill its principal function, namely the linking of the various floors, seems to be of almost minor importance in the light of the allegorical allusions. The ascent refers to the path that the ruler has to complete. His contribution on earth assures him of recognition in heaven, the virtues are the gateways to apotheosis.

Hildebrandt's glittering years as an architect in Vienna ended when work finished on the Belvedere. He was not asked to undertake any more major projects. The court preferred Johann Bernhard Fischer von Erlach. Hildebrandt successfully won the commission to draw up the plans for the conversion and reconstruction of the Vienna Hofburg, but only the work for the three courtyards in the Imperial Chancellery Wing and for part of the façade in the Schauflergasse were completed. Fischer's son, Joseph Emanuel Fischer von Erlach, was preferred for the completion of the inner Burghof wing. The son of Hildebrandt's rival was even appointed to the post of Senior Court Engineer, a position which the older, and no doubt more experienced Hildebrandt, had expected to be offered. Even the Michaeler Wing and the Winter Riding School were completed to plans created by Fischer the younger. His design for the latter was a rather sober and flat façade with huge pilasters and blank areas. However, he transformed the interior into a splendid setting. Some forty-six columns form a gallery and support the guest-boxes. Located beneath them and between the columns are the boxes for the Viennese nobility. At the front, below a temple-style triangular pediment, is the imperial box (see illustration p. 95 below).

In the final years of his life, Hildebrandt was only awarded contracts for building town-houses, but these included the Märkleinsche Haus Am Hof and the Deyblhof in Annagasse. Around 1733, he built something that was at the time very rare in Vienna, a pavilion for the small garden of the Harrach das Salettl town palace. Unfortunately, the pavilion was completely destroyed in World War II.

When Joseph Emanuel Fischer von Erlach died in 1742, Hildebrandt once again glimpsed the prospect of the post of Court Architect. But his time was over. From now on, the French style introduced by the younger Fischer was to dominate the Baroque architectural scene. Empress Maria Theresia's consort, Franz Stephan of Lorraine, later to become Emperor Franz I, chose Nicolas Jadot de Ville-Issey for the post.

ILLUSTRATION OPPOSITE
ABOVE:
Hofburg, Leopold Wing
Pietra Dura Room in the Maria-Theresia Apartment

BELOW:
Joseph Emanuel Fischer von Erlach
Hofburg, Winter Riding School
1729-35

ILLUSTRATION LEFT:
Johann Lukas von Hildebrandt
Upper Belvedere, 1721-23
Detail in the Marble Hall (above)
Sala terrena (below)

Eighteenth-century Baroque Sculpture

Numerous French sculptures served as examples for Viennese sculpture in the eighteenth century, particularly with regard to tomb sculpture. A visit to tombs in Vienna, with their numerous examples of Habsburg burial practice is, therefore, the prime purpose of this section.

When Ferdinand IV, the brother of Leopold I, died in 1654, at the age of only twenty-one, he had already made provisions for his heart to be buried at the feet of Our Lady of Loreto in the principal parish church of St Augustine. The burial, was therefore divided into two parts, the bodily parts and the entrails, a custom that can be explained by baroque piety and the Habsburg understanding of reliquaries.

For the Imperial family, it was a matter of perpetuating the memory of the dead among the living. A religious order which was close to the imperial family was to be honored and the prestige of a particular church increased through its association with princes of the royal blood.

In 1617, the Empress Anna, the consort of Emperor Mathias, founded a church and monastery within the city walls for the Capuchin order so as to provide hereditary burial sites for herself and her spouse. The Capuchin church at the Neuer Markt was thereby elevated to the rank of a court church. The earliest dynastic hereditary burial of the House of Habsburg had been conducted in St Stephen's cathedral. When Frederick, younger brother of Duke Rudolf IV, the founder of the dynasty, died at fifteen years of age in 1362, the Duke had a tomb created under the existing Albertan choir, accessed by a narrow flight of stairs. In the eighteenth century, Maria Theresia had this ducal tomb renovated and extended for the burial of the entrails and hearts of members of the Imperial family.

The Loreto chapel in the principal parish church of St Augustine contains another funerary monument of interest. The Empress Eleonora had the *Herzgrüftl* (little vault of the hearts), as it was affectionately known to the Viennese, erected in 1657 at the request of her stepson, Ferdinand IV, to receive the urns containing the Imperial hearts. The Loreto chapel in the church of St Augustine was endowed by the same Eleonora, second wife of Emperor Ferdinand II, in the wake of the intensified devotion to Mary at the time of the Counter-Reformation.

The cult of Loreto lies in the belief that the home of Mary of Nazareth in the Holy Land, in which the Annunciation was proclaimed to her by the angel Gabriel telling her that she would become the Mother of God, was transported by the. angel Gabriel to Italy, when the Crusades were lost in 1295. The house was deposited in Loreto, near the city of Ancona. Many pilgrims have since worshiped at this shrine at Loreto.

The tradition of separate burials for bodies, hearts, and entrails meant that Vienna acquired three dynastic places of burial which brought about an unusual flowering of baroque tombstone sculpture. Of all the tombs, the Imperial tomb under the Kapuzinerkirche is seen today as a unique monument to art and cultural history. Even a brief inspection reveals to the visitor the wealth of decorative motifs. The artistically embellished coffin handles are frequently adorned with the heads of eagles or lions. In many cases there is an eagle's claw at the foot of the coffin (illustration upper right). Palm fronds, rosettes, laurel wreaths, and arabesques also contribute to animating the seemingly heavy and massive sarcophagus. These decorative motifs are derived, in the majority of cases, from the tombstone sculptures of Antiquity, abstracted and stylized in the late baroque and rococo fashion, and interspersed with plain scrollwork and interlacing.

Skulls are often to be seen in knight's armor or wearing the imperial crown. They are a drastic reminder of the transient nature of earthly power. This aspect is emphasized in ghostly fashion in the so-called "interrogation" in front of a tomb in the Kapuzinerkirche. The Father, begging to be let into the tomb, is asking the corpse for his name. As he always answers by giving his rank with his name, entry is refused. After repeated questioning, the deceased person, using with the voice of his chamberlain, finally has to admit that he is neither emperor nor king but nothing more than a poor sinner who is asking for God's mercy. Now, at last, he may enter his place of rest.

The founder's tomb contains the plain coffins of the Emperor and Empress Mathias and Anna. These are simply worked Late Renaissance caskets with lion's head handles. Maria Theresia commissioned the sculptor Balthasar Moll, to

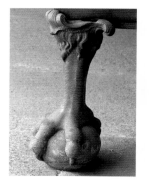

Details of the funerary monument of Queen Anna and the Emperor Matthias, mid-seventeenth century.
Imperial burial site in the Kapuzinerkirche

supply the caskets with powerful eagles' claws as feet so as to add splendor to these important coffins. The tomb of Charles lies beneath the monks' choir stalls and contains the Habsburg's most spectacular sarcophagus. It is assumed that Johann Lukas von Hildebrandt supplied the plans for extension work on the tomb, agreed ca. 1720, and he may also have done so for the sarcophagus of Kaiser Leopold I (illustration p. 96 left). The Emperor, who died in 1705, was buried in a richly decorated sarcophagus on the lid of which there are representations of a crucifix and the imperial eagle with folded wings. The modeling was carried out by Tobias Kracker.

The designs for the coffin of the Emperor Charles VI, who died in 1740, were drawn up by three of the most famous Baroque artists in Vienna, Johann Bernhard Fischer von Erlach, Daniel Gran, and Michael Rottmayr ((illustration right). The Emperor's pewter craftsmen, Johann Georg Pichler and Johann Nikolaus Moll, performed this outstanding work. In contrast to Leopold's sarcophagus, this example unfolds a movement of almost beguiling richness, culminating in an allegory of Austria mourning the Emperor's death. Austria is erecting a monumental portrait medallion of Charles over the globe with clouds above it.

Maria Theresia, who considered her father's coffin to be insufficiently representative and splendid, commissioned Balthasar Moll to execute supplementary work. The loose-limbed rocaille figures on the corners of the coffin were removed and replaced by crowned skulls. In addition cartouche reliefs were added, representing two battles, that of Saragossa in 1710 and the Battle of Belgrade which took place seven years later. According to his daughter's will, they were to highlight the Emperors foreign policy successes.

One year after the death of her mother, in 1751, the Empress Elisabeth Christina, Maria Theresia commissioned an unostentatious coffin by Balthasar Moll which was then placed in the tomb. Whilst the coffin of her father rested on the bodies of lions, the Empress chose an eagle with folded wings as the basis for her mother's coffin. Veiled faces of women, allegories of mourning, grace the corners. As with her father's coffin, here, too, an angel is supported by a putto, holding the portrait of the Empress aloft. A relief, bordered by luxuriant tendrils representing a two-masted barque, was intended to represent the bridal journey of the future Empress from Vienna to Barcelona where, in 1708, she married King Charles III, later the Emperor Charles VI.

When she was just thirty-one years old in 1748, the Empress Maria Theresia gave the order to enlarge the tomb. Five years later, the work was completed by the Lorraine architect, Nicolas Jadot de Ville-Issey, after a number of

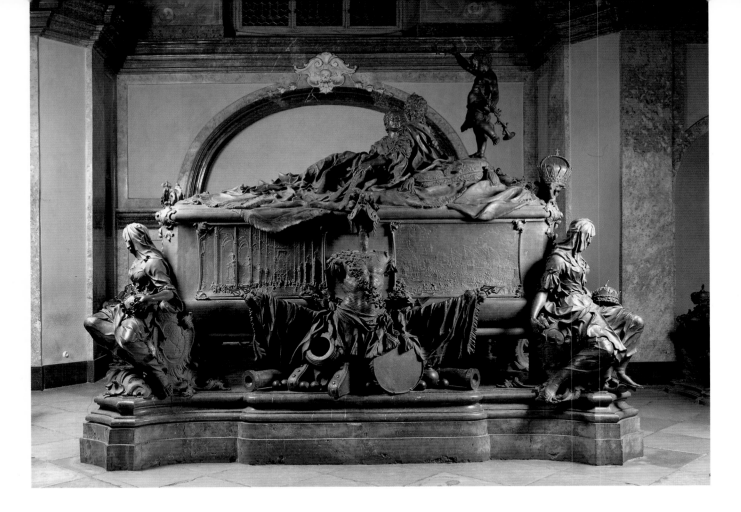

changes to the plans. An oval cupola curves over the central construction which was painted by Ignaz Mildorfer, a pupil of Paul Trogers. It was suggested that Maria Theresia told her consort during the first visit "one day this will provide a good resting place." One year after the work had been completed, in 1754, she commissioned her court sculptor, Balthasar Moll to submit designs for a lavish double sarcophagus. This was the most monumental work in the entire Capuchin tomb (illustration above). The sarcophagus, measuring 190 ft (3 m) in length and 6 ft 8 in (2 m) in breadth stood on six mighty scrolled feet rising out of a richly outlined red marble pediment. The cover of the sarcophagus is decorated with a skull on which the Imperial couple are shown, larger than life, in a semi-reclining position, listening to the last trump played by a guardian spirit calling upon them to face judgment. Large bas-reliefs are set into the sarcophagus, placed between mourning women holding heraldic shields. One of the reliefs portrays the coronation of Maria Theresia as the Queen of Bohemia in St. Vitus cathedral in Prague and the other portrays the entry of Franz Stephen as the Grand Duke of Tuscany in Florence in connection with his coronation procession.

Despite the monumental size of the piece, the sarcophagus has a soft effect as each detail has been executed in gentle folds, outlining, and ornamentation. The heaviness is absorbed by the moderately applied Rococo style. The reliefs on the sides suggest depth of space which is, in particular, expressed in the coronation scene. The delicate architectural structure with pointed lancet windows and airy delicacy of the ribbed vaults and their interplay with the mourners at the corners and the upright figure of the guardian angel gives a rapt quality to the sarcophagus. All the other sarcophagi in this section of the tomb were created by Balthasar Moll and his studio, with the exception of that of Emperor Joseph II with its pronounced classicism.

From the artistic point of view, the tombstones in the Capuchin tomb present a unique high point in their category. The ducal tomb in St Stephen's and the *Herzgrüftl* in the Loreto chapel in the Church of St Augustine are, in this respect, of lesser importance.

Balthasar Moll
Double sarcophagus of Maria Theresia and Franz I. Stephan, 1754
Cast pewter.
Emperor's tomb in the Kapuzinerkirche.

J. E. Fischer von Erlach and B. Permoser

The aristocracy also planned lavish and costly memorials to themselves. The sarcophagus of Leopold Donat Count Trautson in St Michael's church, its design commissioned by the family of the deceased from Joseph Emanuel Fischer von Erlach in 1727, appears to have been closely modeled on the tombstone designed by François Girardons for Cardinal Richelieu in the Sorbonne Church in Paris (1675-94). Dramatic, almost with a little too much pathos, the younger Fischer created a scene of swirling clouds which culminate in a palm frond (illustration right). Embedded therein and held by an angel, the prince contemplates eternity. The difference between the Habsburg and the French feeling for style is expressed dramatically in the weighting between drama and pathos. Whereas Fischer orchestrates a theatrical effect, Girardons restricts his design to a sober, strong ambience with a classical effect. The style of the composition was adopted by Fischer, however, as he discovered that the early classical form used by Girardons had a pathos which he found suitable for his his own arrangement.

French sculpture of the late seventeenth century was at one and the same time the guiding light and esthetic model for Viennese work. In any event, the court artist had to ensure that orientation with the French court did not degenerate into mere copying and even expressed the supposed artistic superiority of the Habsburgs. The maxim was clear: the model, recognizable as such, had to be surpassed. According to this esthetic creed, Prince Eugene had an iconographic plan laid down and transposed into his palaces. There were often cases, however, when a model could not be surpassed, especially where estheticism was placed at the service of power politics.

It is probable that in the terms of his comprehensive program of decoration, Prince Eugene was seeking an artist who was able to portray the political power of the Habsburgs, as concentrated in his person, and transpose it into a complex esthetic form. He found such an artist in Balthasar Permoser, the brilliant sculptor at the court of Saxony in Dresden and the creator of the unique decorative figures at the Zwinger. Prince Eugene wanted a "personified apotheosis" which could physically be walked around and, furthermore, he was to be regarded as the savior of the Fatherland (illustration p. 100 right). The result, from the critical point view, was "overwhelming" and contained altogether "too much virtue" as a secretary remarked, acting on behalf of the Prince. The patron and the artist often seem to have been at odds as regards the concept of the sculpture.

The Prince was mainly concerned with the thematic harmony of the planned paintings in his palaces whereas the artist was more concerned with harmonious composition. Work on the

Joseph Emanuel Fischer von Erlach (design) and Ferdinand M. Brokoff (execution) Tombstone of Leopold Donat Prince Trautson, 1727, Marble, St Michael's church

Balthasar Permoser
Apotheosis of Prince Eugene,
1718-21, marble,
Height: 91 in (230cm)
Österreichische Galerie Belvedere

project did not proceed, because Prince Eugene was frequently forced to drive the sculptor into working more quickly "without hurting his feelings" as it was said.

Perlmoser's sculpture for the town palace showed nothing more than a summary of the iconographic themes of the stairwell. The deeds of Hercules with the Prince's victories were set in tandem. The Herculean hero, equipped with a lion skin and a club, climbs on the back of a vanquished Turk. Fama, cowering behind the Prince, is preparing to trumpet his fame to the world, but the Prince, noble and modest, holds his hand over the funnel of the instrument. The figures are dovetailed and entwined in eccentric contortions, making it impossible to get an overview of the composition and making the work very hard to interpret. Permoser's guest appearance in Vienna was short-lived. The Prince subsequently had no further use for the Saxon artist.

Georg Raphael Donner

Baroque sculpture in Vienna reached its zenith with the work of Georg Raphael Donner. Born in 1693 in Marchfeld, Donner first trained as a goldsmith in Vienna, then moved to Salzburg where he was active in the Archbishop's circle. Inter alia, he created the enchanting sculptures for the large stairwell in the Schloss Mirabell (1726-7). Donner was still quite young when he died in 1741 at the age of forty-eight. The last years of his life were spent in Vienna and it was here that he produced his most important work.

In 1734, Donner received his first commission from the Residenzstadt. The Court requested a design for an apotheosis of the emperor Charles VI. Donner, who had previously studied Permoser's sculptures in Dresden, and who had certainly taken note of the Apotheosis of Prince Eugene, which was criticized by his contemporaries, conceived the memorial in a refreshing

Georg Raphael Donner
Apotheosis Kaiser Charles VI,
1734
Österreichische Galerie Belvedere

ILLUSTRATION OPPOSITE:
Georg Raphael Donner
Providentia or the Mehlmarkt-fountain on the Neuer Markt the former Mehlmarkt, 1737-9
Pewter-lead alloy
The original is currently in the Österreichische Galerie Belvedere

soberness, which to some extent was a counter-point to Permoser's sculpture (illustration p. 100, right). Fama, in the form of an antique angel, flies around the Emperor in order to crown him. Effective and expressively strong, but not nearly so overloaded with symbolism as Permoser's work, Donner knew how to combine the already impending, strong classicism with an almost mannered affectation.

As far as Donner was concerned, the Baroque style had run its course. In no way did it demand that he change the traditional art into the pampered world of the Rococo. On the other hand, it seemed to him that the disillusionment with contemporary French style had become so entrenched that even the noble form of classicism offered him nothing.

The Providentia fountain on the former Mehlmarkt, now known as the Neuer Markt, was created between 1737 and 1739; it was commissioned by the municipal authorities of the city of Vienna. It is Donner's principal work and even today it is still described as the most beautiful fountain in the city (illustration above, p. 102, 103). Providentia, the goddess of welfare, the "good government" of the City of Vienna dominates the center of the fountain. Her shield is emblazoned with the head of Janus and she has snakes in her hands, symbols of changing destiny which is valid for most, and to the eternity to which the city is entrusted. Around her, on the edge of the basin of the fountain, are the personifications of the rivers which flow into the Danube, the Ybbs, Enns, March, and Traun. They are shown as river gods whose attributes point to the history of the Fatherland. Consequently, the Enns river-god holds a rudder, indicating the navigability of the river. The rock beside the goddess March symbolizes the battle of the Marcomannen against the Romans who were driven out of this area. The composure of the figures produces a relaxed effect. Despite the peaceful gestures and seriousness of the facial expressions, there is no pathos. Mobility is not exaggerated. Only the Traun river-god, a young model, seems not to be playing his role in the truest sense of the word. He is climbing down from the edge of the fountain. Donner portrays the figure from a racy back view with spread legs.

Donner's fountain is an impressive example of a work of art on the borderline between Rococo and Classicism. He never loses control of his slender, lissome figures whose mobility is reminiscent of the art of Giovanni da Bologna. What he gives to his figures is not affected movement, but an unusual plasticity. A walk around the fountain opens ever new vistas of each river- god who seems to be engaged in a sort of dance with the other gods.

In the year of his death, Donner was working on another fountain, the Andromeda fountain in

the courtyard of the old Town Hall (illustration below right). Andromeda, chained to the rocks and barely keeping her hold on the steep cliff, is being attacked by the dragon which is rising up behind the young woman and threatening her with its wide-open jaws and widespread wings. Above her, her rescuer Perseus appears as a bas-relief scarcely raised from the flat surface. Water from the fountain gushes forth from the mouth of the monster over the prisoner's thighs and into the basin. This fine piece of work reveals the dimensions between relief and fully plastic form in the finest gradations. The tail of the dragon and parts of the rescuer's winged horse are barely raised or recognizable as a relief. On the other hand, Andromeda is fully sculptured in the round.

Whereas the monumental Providentia fountain shows every aspect of Donner's three-dimensional ability, in the Andromeda fountain the artist shows his artistic talents down to the finest nuances.

In Georg Raphael Donner, Austrian baroque sculpture in Vienna reached its zenith, and also that point at which it changed direction. Whereas the Baroque style was still dominant in other parts of the country during the second half of the eighteenth century — even if only in the refined form of the rococo — after the death of Donner, Vienna understandably took a different route.

The Innsbruck family of sculptors, the Molls, whose work Donner had always praised, to some extent drew closer to the artistic heritage left by the great sculptor. Johann Nikolaus Moll, who is said to have cooperated in the Mehlmarkt fountain and, in particular, his brother Balthasar Ferdinand Moll, placed their talents at the disposal of the Habsburg court in Vienna where they were primarily engaged in sculpting sarcophagi for the ruling house.

Whilst the Moll brother learned some of Donner's concepts of form, they also partially returned to the concepts of the late Baroque style. However, there now appeared in Vienna a sculptor who had, up to that point, broken all the valid esthetic rules. Franz Xavier Messerschmidt hailed from the Swabian Wiesensteig where he was born in 1736. He went to Munich and Graz where he trained as a sculptor. In 1752, he came to Vienna and studied at the academy under Balthasar Ferdinand Moll and Matthias Donner younger brother of Georg Raphael. His travels in pursuit of his art led him to Rome and London. The latter city was said to be of particular importance for his later creations. He arrived in London in 1765, one year after the death of the great William Hogarth. He almost certainly studied Hogarth's drawings of the human face, his caricatures of the human figure, and his biting wit.

While on his travels, Messerschmidt was asked to lecture at the Paris academy. He declined and, instead, returned to Vienna where

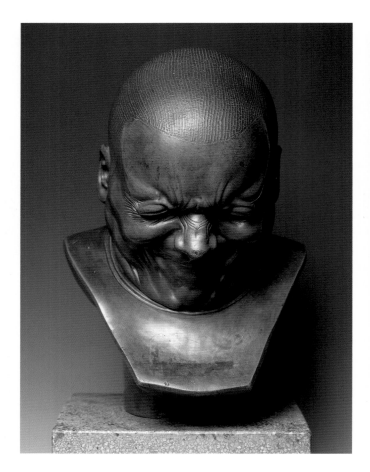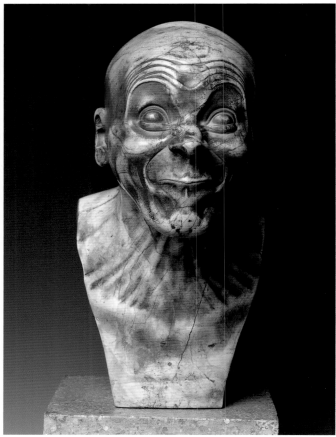

he had justified hopes of attaining the recently vacant chair of the director of the academy. In any event, he was passed over for the position and engaged merely as a lecturer. During his Viennese period, both before and after his travels, Messerschmidt worked for the court.

In 1760, he finished, inter alia, a bronze bust for Maria Theresia and her spouse, Franz Stephan of Lorraine. Later, the court commissioned the larger-than-life lead statue of the Empress and her spouse. We can see here the first signs of an exaggerated individuality (illustration pp. 90-1). The portrait of the director of the Imperial court library, Gerard van Swieten, executed in 1769, is not without a trace of irony which is expressed in the exaggerated dignity of the way in which the head is held and the somewhat ridiculous effect created by the double chin.

Messerschmidt's most important works, or at least those which brought him fame while, at the same time, turning him into an eccentric, were created in Vienna between 1770 and 1775. It was during these years that he created the greater part of his "character heads" such as

the Villain in Metal (illustration above left) the Lusty Fop (illustration above right) or the Head with a Beak (illustration p. 105). There is a rare interplay between the grotesque exaggeration of the features and the mask-like stiffness of the faces, as if the peculiar relationship between mouth, nose, eyes, cheeks, or chin have been stopped in mid-expression. Whether these sculptures were really created for the purpose of scientific study can no longer be established with certainty. The theologian and writer, Johann Kaspar Lavater, a contemporary of the artist, studied Messerschmidt's sculptures for the draft of his *Physiognomischen Fragmente* (Fragments of Physiognomy, 1775-8) which was well regarded at the time. This is shown from his estate.

There has been a much speculation as to whether disappointment over his failure to win academic honors in Vienna led Messerschmidt to his physiognomy studies. This disappointment is said to have turned him into a whimsical eccentric, creating the suspicion that in his grotesque and contorted faces he was, in fact,

portraying himself. Such speculation is futile. What is of greater significance is that Messerschmidt encountered the works of Hogarth and that his strange series of sculpted heads is a continuation of the well-known tradition, dating from the Middle Ages and the Renaissance, of depicting various types and studying human physiognomy. It is conceivable that in this connection he made intensive psychological studies of himself and that these were converted into sculptures showing a range of human types. Lavater's last polemic over the artist's portraits make the last consideration possible.

In 1774, disagreements at the Viennese Academy resurfaced in relation to the new incumbent of the directorship. Once again Messerschmidt had been passed over. Deeply embittered he turned his back on the city and, in 1775, he returned to his home town in the Swabian Alb.

In 1777 he decided to move to Pressburg (Bratislava) where he established a studio and worked on further character studies up until his death in 1783.

18th-century Baroque Sculpture

ILLUSTRATION OPPOSITE AND
BELOW RIGHT:
Franz Xavier Messerschmidt
Four character heads, 1770-83
Austrian Gallery Belvedere

Villain in Metal
Tin lead alloy, H 15 in (38.5 cm)

Lusty Fop
Marble H. 18 in (45 cm)

Second head with a beak
Alabaster H. 17 in (43 cm)

A Hanged Man
Alabaster, H. 15 in(38 cm)

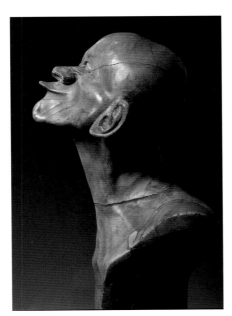

Lower Belvedere, Grotesque room
with the character heads sculpted
by Franz Xavier Messerschmidt.

18th-century Baroque Sculpture

ILLUSTRATION OPPOSITE:
Andreas Pozzo
Jesuit church, false cupola

Charles Georg Merville
The Fall of the Angels, plastic on
the choir walls
in St Michael's church

The high altar, which was created
in 1781, by CharlesGeorg
Merville is no longer entirely
of the Baroque period. Rather, it
is a transitional work in which the
dynamic forms of the fall of the
angels seems to be based on Classicism. This work seems to mark
the end of the Baroque style's use
in the construction of the altar.

Baroque painting

Viennese Baroque painting did not reach its apogee until the late seventeenth century. This is not surprising, in view of its relatively late beginning in the historical context. The defeat of the Turks, the country's increasing strength after the Peace of Karlowitz, and the magnificent victory gained by Prince Eugene all helped Austria to become a great European power.

Absolutism expressed itself even more strongly and awakened a powerful need for courtly representation. The search for symbols of state and power was as strong in the Imperial court as it was among the nobility who gloried in their newfound wealth. The Habsburgs were pleased to call this period their "period of heroism", claiming it was based solely on *Ecclesia triumphans*, the Church triumphant, and thus on the grace of God having been bestowed upon the Emperor. This set down the style and themes of painting — trompe l'oeil and radiant allegory. Without doubt the ceiling paintings must have had priority. At first, Italian painters who had for centuries produced magnificent examples of this genre were summoned to Vienna to practice their art.

Andrea Pozzo, who hailed from the South Tyrol, was one of the first of the great Italian ceiling painters to respond to the call of Emperor Leopold I. Pozzo, who was a lay brother of the Jesuit order, had already made his name as a decorative painter. The fine ceiling frescoes in St Ignazio were famous and were well-known to the Viennese Court. The trompe l'oeil architecture, the differences between architecture that was actually built and what was painted, seemingly disappeared and the result was hailed as an incomparable masterpiece of trompe l'oeil ceiling painting.

In 1704, Pozzo received a commission to paint the arched ceiling of the Jesuit church (illustration right). This presented difficulties, as the ceiling in the main nave had three underpinned transoms and three girders with a strongly protruding arch. The actual architecture could thus scarcely be "trumped up" as trompe l'oeil so that Puzzo was forced to furnish every vault truss with its own separate architectural device. For the central double truss, he chose a trompe l'oeil cupola. He painted the drum on the arch and on the ledges of the side-walls. Immediately on entering the nave the trompe l'oeil cupola was revealed and appeared to advance after only a few steps. The adjoining vault trusses with small pictorial fields built into the gilded stucco work and The Fall of the Angels which takes place inside a trompe l'oeil palace, stand alone and without reference to the dominant central truss. In contrast to St Ignazio in Rome, the light inside the church is bright. The vault is almost illuminated so that changes in the perspective are visible with every step taken.

ILLUSTRATION OPPOSITE:
Andrea Pozzo
Garden Palace in Liechtenstein
Ceiling fresco in the marble hall
depicting the Apotheosis of
Hercules, 1705

Naturally this has a disturbing effect as the "crooked cupola" is omnipresent. By way of contrast in Rome, where the trompe l'oeil cupola joins onto the main nave, and in the diffused light of the inner round, the visitor can experience a more complex and harmonious feeling of space without distortion.

Pozzo's Roman masterpiece also contains references to his work on the Garden Palace of Prince Lichtenstein. The marble hall is one of the most splendid baroque rooms in Vienna. Red-veined marble columns with gilded capitals support a high ledge over which the mirrored vault extends (illustration p. 108). Pozzo had endless opportunity here to put his ability as an illusionist into practice. Beneath the ledge, he painted a palace, the balustrades of which seem to jut out into the room. Above them the palace walls seem to continue upward beyond the architecture of the hall, terminating in triumphal arches with pierced gable segments. In the corners, vestibules are constructed which flow into open circular forms from which cloud banks are emerging, on which by gods, demi-gods, and cupids drift by. The heavenly hosts of Olympus appear to be heading for the central light from which Zeus arises with lightning bolt in his hand.

The iconographic plan is typical and, to some extent, tailor-made for the Viennese aristocracy. The deeds of Hercules represent the Prince, who was in the service of the Emperor, performing his duties. Below and above the painted balustrades, apparently moving into the room-space, the shapes representing the Hercules myth move in individual scenes. The deeds of the Prince are rewarded by the Emperor. Zeus, moving out of the clouds is making for the group containing Rea, Chronos, and their son Poseidon. In their midst Hercules looks up, awaiting his apotheosis.

The allegorical treatment of the Prince and the Emperor, using the genre of trompe l'oeil painting, became a general theme for ceiling painting in Vienna. The theme of heroism, which was adopted in banqueting halls and stairwells, is in many instances connected with the sculptures placed in these rooms. With the exception of the art at the Court of Versailles of Louis XIV, there was nobody who had at his disposal such a decidedly individual iconography as Prince Eugene. In this connection, his personal antipathy to the arch-enemy of the House of Habsburg, Louis XIV, the Sun King, was a factor that decisively contributed to the creation of his plans for the adornment of his palaces.

In 1683, the year of the Turkish siege, the nineteen year old Prince Eugene, who, on his father's side, was descended from the Counts of Soissons, applied to become an officer in the army of Louis XIV. Due to his small stature, he was contemptuously rejected. And that was not all. The sharp-tongued Liselotte von der Pfalz,

spouse of Phillip of Orléans the brother of the Sun King, went so far as to call him a "dirty, very debauched little rascal" and denigrated his looks with the words "… a short turned-up little nose, a somewhat long chin, and such short lips that he kept his mouth slightly open for most of the time…" That was certainly humiliating.

In the same year, the Prince met the Emperor Leopold I, who had fled to Passau due to the threatened danger from the Turks, and repeated his pleas — this time asking to join the other side. In view of the threatened danger there was nothing the Emperor could do but to offer the Prince the likelihood of a command if he should prove himself worthy in the forthcoming battles. Prince Eugene did not let the Emperor down. Quite the contrary; he became the savior of the Fatherland. The "debauched little rascal" turned himself into a noble knight and became the most celebrated commander in Europe.

This is background against which the ceiling paintings in the marble halls of Lower Belvedere palace (illustration above) should be viewed. Psychological factors are not always the reasons for historical facts, yet in this case the fresco relates in a quite special form to the political and private quarrel with the French court. The quadrature painters, Marcantonio Chiarini and Gaetano Fanti, created the trompe l'oeil architecture of a palace, the upper area of which is tinted with gold. A heavenly light streams from the sky, from Apollo's chariot down into the vestibule of the garden palace. The reason why this trompe l'oeil room is tilted at a 45-degree angle to the ground plan of the real room is to emphasize the difference between the heavenly and earthly spheres.

Martino Altomonte
Lower Belvedere
Marble Hall, Ceiling fresco
depicting the Apotheosis of Prince
Eugene, 1716

Martino Altomonte
Lower Belvedere
Principal bedroom, Fresco with
Apollo and Clythia, 1716

The sky, painted by Martino Altomonte, shows Apollo on the upper cloud layer in his sun chariot and, beneath that, the procession of the gods and the Nine Muses, a reference to the prince's inclination to promote the arts and science. Amidst of the company of the gods, a young hero stands on a lower cloud layer. He is being handed a laurel wreath and is escorted by Minerva and Mercury. The youth represents Prince Eugene, of course, and the banner carried by the cupids refers to Mercury; a reference to the objects blessed by Pope Clement XI, the hat and sword which Prince Eugene was awarded after the Battle of Peterwardein in 1716. They are lying at his feet. Shortly before the painting was finished, news of the military victory and the battle honors granted by the Pope became known.

In the context of the Habsburg iconography, Apollo refers to the Emperor who owes his increased prestige to the hero. Leopold-Apollo appears as the true sun, in contrast to the deceitful sun, Louis XIV. For the Frenchman, the gods were, in terms of the corresponding artistic plan, mere protagonists. The Habsburgs regarded this as an example of King Louis' hubris, making himself the darling of the gods and the master of Europe. Prince Eugene, a victim of this hubris, had been chosen by Apollo-Leopold to punish the sinners. The prince received his reward through social and political advancement as well as immortal fame. Thus, the fresco in the Lower Belvedere can be understood as an esthetic correction of Louis XIV's politics.

The mythology symbolizing the Prince's life-story was used in the private and intimate rooms of the palace. The Apollo themes turn up in a skylight fresco by Martino Altomonte in the principal bedroom of the Lower Belvedere (illustration above). Klythia, an Ocean nymph and the mistress of Apollo, accompanied by a cupid, greets the god departing in his chariot and thereby absents herself from daylight. Night falls. On the opposite side Altomonte places a pendant featuring Luna and Endymion.

The Apollo theme, although not with the specifically political function it has in the Lower Belvedere, is also used in the Upper Belvedere. The ceiling of the so-called "Painted Hall" is also adorned with a fresco, executed by Carlo Carlone, *The Triumph of Aurora* (illustration p. 111). The sunrise is suspended proudly in the blue color of the sky, surrounded by swirling clouds. Apollo with his lute accompanies Diana with her bow and the goddesses on the opposite side are greeting them. The painted vestibules, supported by heavy consoles, rise up in a trompe l'oeil effect over the structure of the hall. They open up the ceiling and display the gods' activities in heaven. The marble hall again glorifies the Prince as a hero of Antiquity, surrounded by virtues paying homage to him, and showing how he has vanquished the powers of evil.

112   18th-century Baroque Painting

ILLUSTRATION OPPOSITE:
Louis Dorigny
Town Palace of Prince Eugene
Ceiling frescos in the stairwell
1697

Apollo in his Sun Chariot
(above)
Fama (below left)
The fall of Icarus (below right)

The politically motivated iconography of the Lower Belvedere of Prince Eugene's palace has already been discussed. The passage of the sun, represented by Apollo, and the way of virtuous heroes in the form of Hercules, mark the stations in the entire plan according to motive. The central ceiling paintings in the stairwell, painted by Louis Dorigny (illustration p. 112 above) portray Apollo in the sun chariot. In the accompanying tondi, we see the allegorical Fama, the triumph of the hero, and the fall of Icarus, and the punishment of Hubris, in another trompe l'oeil by Dorigny (illustration p. 112 below). Yet here the hero is still in anticipated glory on earth. Hercules stands with his cudgel on an exposed niche in the stairwell. Close by, Atlantis is propping up the staircase (illustration p. 71). After climbing the stairs and entering the Red Drawing-room, it can be seen that the same theme, the triumph of the heroes, is repeated on the ceiling. Here, Hercules is being received into Olympus. The painter was Marcantonio Chiarine (illustration above).

In the Lobkowitz Palace, the Hercules theme is developed in both sculpture and painting. The entrance hall with its barrel vaulting allows an unimpeded vista of the Hercules fountain. The hero of Antiquity lowers his head modestly whilst the laurel wreath is handed to him. The reference to the Apollo theme is simply hinted at in the same way as the allegories of the arts are represented on the ceiling of the banqueting hall; they are interspersed among the amazing effects of the trompe l'oeil architectural paintings which Marcantonio Chiarini created in cooperation with the Viennese Court painter, Jacob van Schuppen (illustration above).

Chiarini was famous in Vienna for his trompe l'oeil painting and so it is not surprising that many patrons refused figurative representations, in favor of pure trompe l'oeil. These included

Marcantonio Chiarini,
Ceiling fresco in the Red Drawing-room.
Hercules being taken up into Olympus, 1698

Marcantonio Chiarini
Palais Lobkowitz,
banqueting hall
Ceiling fresco with allegories of
the arts ca. 1700

Leopold Donat, Count Trautson, who was able to engage the much sought-after painter to decorate his palace (illustration above right). The four-part architectural elements such as balustrades, consoles, tondi, coffers, and spirals were embellished with candelabra, fruit baskets, laurel wreaths and rocaille. Like an ornamental network in which it is difficult to distinguish between architecture and decoration, the trompe l'oeil paintings on the ceiling and in the window frames as well as in the domes were transformed into a mannered labyrinth which was, however, artistically perfect and a spectacular sight for the viewer.

Johann Michael Rottmayr was able to assert himself as the first Austrian painter to contest the dominance of the Italians and their preference for transforming a relatively flat surface into an impressive trompe l'oeil illusion. Rottmayr, who was born in Bavaria in 1654 and died in 1730 in Vienna, created, inter alia, the vestibule in the Liechtenstein Garden Palace (1711-2). He also created the cupola fresco in the Peterskirche (1715). His greatest work,

however, was probably the painting of the cupola in the Karlskirche (See illustration p.115).

Johann Bernhard Fischer von Erlach already knew the painter from his time in Salzburg when Rottmayr had been employed in the Residenz. It is quite possible that they discussed the relationship between painting and architecture, the obviousness of trompe l'oeil painting and the integration into the painting of groups of figures. Rottmayr regarded it as certain that the architectural structure of the inner cupola of the palace, with its painted cupola cover, had to be painted over in order to incorporate the figures into the context of the cupola itself. Firstly, he chose the color scheme for the drum architecture, a discreet rose with pale blue highlights. He set the architectural elements against these colors not, at any rate, just for framing the cupola, but also to incorporate it as an illusion in the structure of the drum. He decorated the rotunda of the cupola with cloud banks rising upward in ever-decreasing circles to the opening of the lantern. He then set the groups of figures in a rhythmic

Marcantonio Chiarini
Palais Trautson, banqueting hall.
Quadrature painting, ca. 1712

ILLUSTRATION OPPOSITE:
Johann Michael Rottmayr
St Charles' church, cupola fresco
Glory of the Blessed Charles
Borromeus, 1725

Daniel Gran
Court library, Cupola fresco with
the Apotheosis of
the Emperor Charles VI
1730

alternation with the oculi. The scene represents the glorification of Saint Charles Borromeus appearing before God with a plea to save Vienna from the Plague.

Once the cupola fresco in the Karlskirche had been completed, the supremacy of the Italians slowly declined. This might also have had something to do with another Viennese baroque painter, Daniel Gran (1694-1757) who was a generation younger than Rottmayr. Gran quickly gained access to the court and to aristocratic circles as his father held the position of Imperial court chef. Gran, who was strictly opposed to quadrature painting in the manner of Chiarini as well as trompe l'oeil painting in the manner of Pozzo, was unable to gain very many commissions and spent much time in Naples studying the frescos of Solimena. He must also have been deeply influenced by Rottmayr's work, whose paintings in the Karlskirche he was able to view.

One year after the completion of the cupola fresco, Gran received his most important commission which had apparently been obtained through the intervention of Joseph Emanuel

Fischer von Erlach; he was to paint the court library. Here, too, he was required to adorn a cupola (illustration above).

Gran followed a similar concept to that which had been used by Rottmayr and developed a painterly design which was intended to connect the obliquely placed oval space with the cupola architecture. Beneath the oculi, he placed the balustrades which surround the oval and, since they are peopled by figures, they create the impression of a gallery. As the oculi are architecturally framed and linked to each other, the cupola seems at first to be placed above the light openings. It depicts the apotheosis of the patron who commissioned the work, the Emperor Charles VI, surrounded by Virtue and Science. As in the Karlskirche here, too, the groups of figures are placed on cloud banks.

The iconography, which had been devised by the court scholar, Conrad Adolph von Albrecht, was inspired by the Roman Temple of Wisdom, with the Emperor shown in the cupola, with the Emperor a scene symbolizing peace with *Apollo and the Muses* and a war scene with *Cadmus in Vulcan's Smithy*. Gran created these paintings between 1726 and 1729 and then began work on the cupola fresco, which was completed in 1730.

Fischer's architecture to some extent, prepared the way for the carefully and intelligently planned set of paintings. The long gallery, with its view over the central oval, is lined with Corinthian columns. The cupola, the iconographic centerpiece, cannot, as yet, be seen by the visitor. It is only when he has passed through the door of columns with which he is surrounded that he sees the glorification of the Emperor. It stands on the gilded -cross-section of one half of a building. The oval is reserved for the Emperor who is in the cupola as Apollo and the leader of the Muses and, at the same time, as Hercules who has made peace possible by overthrowing the enemy. He is the lord over war and peace. The wings of the library stretch away from him and are dedicated to the science of war and peace.

The strict separation of architecture and the dramatically dynamic groups of people come together in one design created in oils, and very clear in its expression. In 1732, Gran received a commission from Franz Ferdinand, Count Kinsky for a ceiling painting for the hunting lodge in Eckartsau in Lower Austria (illustration above right). The painting was to represent the triumph of Diana and the glorification of the hunt. Once again Gran created a balustrade type of architecture. The gallery is painted with a mixture of mortals and allegorical figures from Olympus. Above them there is a clear blue sky in which a cloud is rising, carrying the assembly of the gods.

This powerful combination of figures, decor, and architecture already relates to the stylistic development of Classicism. It was certainly for this reason that Johann Joachin Winckelmann was so full of praise for the works of this Austrian artist, whom he compared with Peter Paul Rubens.

The ending of the Austrian Baroque period is associated with the painting of Paul Trogers (1698-1762). Troger, who came from Pustertal, was trained in Italy where he studied the style of Solimenas and the Venetian, Piazzetta. As a fresco artist, he was mainly active in Lower Austria and did rather less work in Vienna. In 1750, he was appointed as Rector of the Imperial Academy in Salzburg and was responsible for the training and education of the next generation. His *Christ on the Mount of Olives*, created circa 1750, highlights the breach between the dynamic and dramatic figures favored by the older generation and the restrained color and figuratively quiet composition of the evolving Classical style.

Franz Anton Maulbertsch, a pupil of Troger, took an entirely different path. Maulbertsch was born in 1724 in Langenargen am Bodensee in

ILLUSTRATION
OPPOSITE:
Franz Anton Maulbertsch
Cupola fresco in the
Piaristenkirche showing the
Apotheosis of Mary

Franz Anton Maulbertsch
The Academy with its Attributes
at the Feet of Minerva. 1750
oil on canvas, 28 x 36 in
(72 x 91 cm)
Österreichische Galerie Belvedere

the shadow of Castle Montfort and was appointed to the Academy in Vienna on the recommendation of Count Monfort in 1739. In 1752, Maulbertsch received a commission to paint the Piaristen church (illustration p. 119). The cupola fresco shows the painter's work as innovatively Baroque but not moving in a classical direction and not in the chiaroscuro style of the Italians. The composition bears the hallmark of Troger. Thus the Italianate was discarded.

The illusion of space in the midst of complicated perspective arrangements seemed strange to Maulbertsch. For him color was the only method of creating illusion in a dynamic interplay between painted figures and constructed architecture.

In the principal cupola of the Piaristenkirche, he placed the Virgin Mary who is rising up to the Holy Trinity in a swirling cloud. By means of a positive and easily executed system of different axes, he combined figures from the Old Testament with scenes from the New Testament which are related one to another in that they took place in similar locations. The architectural painting, transposed from palaces, in the sacristy, is no longer seen as an illusionary addition to the church building but is here intertwined with the clouds on which the figures seem to surge up in steep foreshortening.

Given this commission, which was a great honor for an artist aged only twenty-eight, Maulbertsch produced an example of his talents which was definitive for the Piaristen church.

In 1750, a competition was held in the Academy. The text read, "theme for the Painting Prize for 1750. Allegory or allegorical painting of the Empress in the shape of Minerva in a seated position, with her attributes or qualities." Maulbertsch painted the Empress in the figure of Minerva as the goddess of Wisdom and therewith presented her in her protective position as the highest mistress of the arts (illustration above). By these means homage was rendered to the academy on the one hand, and to the character of Maria Theresia on the other. Maulbertsch was awarded the first prize and thereby took pride of place amongst Viennese artists.

The Vienna Treasure Chamber

The Vienna Treasure Chamber

The famous Vienna *Schatzkammer* (Treasure Chamber) is housed in the Swiss Wing of the historic heart of the Vienna Hofburg. It is difficult today to trace the history of all the treasures right back to the Middle Ages, when most of them were first created, partly because not all the Imperial crown jewels have been kept in one place. It is probable that in the sixteenth century, under Emperor Rudolf II, a chamber to house the state treasures was built in the Stallburg. About one hundred years later, during the reign of Emperor Leopold I, the treasure was moved to a wing in the Hofburg., but it did not stay there for long as only a few decades later, this section was demolished in order to make way for the new Imperial Chancellery Wing. In 1723, the treasure was returned to the Swiss Wing.

Even after the treasure was stored in the Swiss Wing, it was not kept together. Between 1871 and 1891, the Habsburg treasures were reorganized. Many of the precious gold objects and small sculptures were transferred to the Kunsthistorisches Museum.

The Treasure Chamber was closed under the Third Reich, and the Imperial crown jewels were officially removed and taken to Nuremberg. After World War II, they were returned to the Austrian government. Ten years later, the old Treasury door, dating from 1712 and emblazoned with the monogram of Emperor Charles VI — two interwoven letter Cs above a cross — was reopened, and the public could once again view the Crown Jewels of Austria.

The importance of any state treasure chamber is not based entirely on the precious works of art it contains but also on what they represent in terms of the power and status of the monarchy. A treasure chamber is a shrine for symbols. The insignia and crowns are worth more in themselves than is their design, however splendid. The Vienna Treasure Chamber only acquired this role during the Renaissance, when it became the home for objects which reflected human advancement through knowledge. Scientific objects and precious objects of special artistic value replaced the medieval collections of coins and weapons. Newly-acquired collections of medieval regalia, which were powerful symbols because of their valuable materials and expression of artistic skills, also found a place there. The Treasure Chamber became more a cabinet of curiosities than a repository for valuables (see illustration above left).

It was not until the transition to the Baroque era that the symbolism of the imperial regalia changed. It was then no longer about the religious role of the ruler, but about his greatness, his status and his splendor, in other words, about worldly values. Miniatures in the Crown of Rudolf II refer not just to the ruler as the

conqueror of the Turks, but also to his coronations as ruler of the Holy Roman Empire, King of Hungary, and King of Bohemia.

The decline in sacred importance in favor of secular prestige resulted in a greater emphasis on the artistic element. Objects in gold, statues, and small bronzes found favor with the emperor. Rare and unusual precious objects without any practical value were very much in demand. Ornately framed natural objects such as corals, emu eggs, and nuts were popular. Esthetic pleasure replaced scientific interest. The skills of the artist and the splendor of the materials gradually came to be more highly regarded than the symbolic content. Such changing attitudes were no doubt reinforced by the remarks of Empress Maria Theresia, who, in a letter to Chancellor Kaunitz, disparagingly described her crown as a "fool's bonnet."

Yet it was under Maria Theresia that the Vienna Treasure Chamber reached its incomparable climax. Between 1747 and 1750, Joseph Angelo de France re-organized the display, placing particular emphasis on the interior design of the rooms. Decorations, furniture, and furnishings were produced in the Rococo style to ensure that the splendid setting matched the gem-studded treasures belonging to the Imperial family. Displayed alongside the world-famous "Florentiner", one of the largest diamonds in the world, were the Imperial couple's diamond crowns, including the notorious "fool's bonnet," which, unfortunately, has since been lost.

The Treasure Chamber can be divided into five sections. The first section contains the regalia and robes of the Imperial family. This includes the previously-mentioned Crown of Rudolf II (see illustration page 120).

The imperial regalia also includes the orb and scepter. These three items gained special

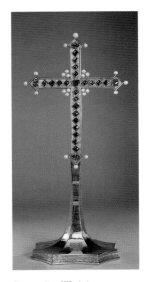

importance at the beginning of the nineteenth century, when between 1804 and 1806 Emperor Franz I unified all the Habsburg territories, whether kingdoms or duchies, into one empire. The crown, together with orb and scepter, which for three hundred years had embodied the elevated status of the Habsburg dynasty, had been designated by Franz as the symbols of sovereignty for the new empire.

Regalia of the Archduchy of Austria can be seen in the second section. The most important piece here is the Archduke's crown, which was awarded posthumously to Duke Rudolf IV, the founder of the dynasty.

In the fourteenth century, Rudolf had tried to secure the *Privilegium Maius*, the status of archduke and elector, from the Holy Roman Emperor, but this was categorically refused. Rudolf's successors continued to fight for this privilege and were finally successful one hundred years later during the reign of Emperor Frederick III. In 1616, Archduke Maximilian III, Grand Master of the Order of the Teutonic Knights, had a new crown made and donated the old one to the Klosterneuburg Abbey, where it is still displayed.

Treasures of the Order of the Golden Fleece can be seen in the third section. Marie of Burgundy, the daughter of the Burgundian duke, Charles the Bold, who lost his territories in the Battle of Nancy in 1477, married Archduke Maximilian of Austria, later to become Habsburg emperor, thereby subsuming large parts of Burgundy into the empire. With the fall of the Burgundian dukes, the Order of the Golden Fleece, founded in 1429 by Philip the Good, passed to the Habsburg family. This Order of Knights, which was committed to the struggle against the infidel and was devoted to the adoration of the Virgin Mary, took its symbols and emblems from the story of the Greek Argonauts, in which Jason and his followers fought monsters, and were eventually rewarded with the prize of the Golden Fleece.

The Cross of the Order, bearing the coat of arms of the Dukes of Burgundy, which had been made in a Burgundian workshop at the time the Order was founded, was probably intended for a member of the royal family (see illustration p. 121 bottom right). The vestment is among the most important pieces in the collection. It was almost certainly made before the Order was founded, as it displays none of its emblems. St John and St Katharine, beside the Virgin Mary, are reproduced in a style typical of the early fifteenth century (see illustration left). The vestment was probably intended for the ducal chapel and it was only later bequeathed to the Order.

The regalia and gems of the Holy Roman Empire are kept in the fourth section. A Western

Rheinish Workshop
Imperial crown, around 950
Gold, jewels, pearls, enamel
Height: 6 in (15 cm)
State Treasure chamber in the
Hofburg

ILLUSTRATION OPPOSITE:
Burgundian Workshop
Centerpiece of the antependium of
the Order of the Golden Fleece
ca. 1410, 132 x 48 in
(330 x 119 cm)
State Treasure chamber in the
Hofburg

prince achieved the highest honors and status when awarded these regalia. According to tradition, such honors can be traced back to the robe of the Byzantine *basileus* or Emperor and thus to that of the Roman emperor. A king, once elected by the empire's princes, received the right to be crowned as emperor by the Pope in Rome. The imperial crown and the holy lance thus embodied the emperor's universal sovereignty (see illustration above).

The imperial crown was probably made in a Rheinish goldsmiths' workshop around the middle of the tenth century, probably for the coronation of Otto the Great in 962. It is interesting to note that the crown was altered on several occasions thereafter. The cross and the arch have been replaced several times. Presumably, each ruler wanted to make the crown into a distinctive, personal symbol of power. The iconography of the crown is concerned with the theme of universal and God-given sovereignty. The

images in cloisonné enamel on the gold plaques include Christ as ruler of the world, King David as the symbol of justice, and King Solomon as the symbol of wisdom.

The coronation ceremony included the handover of the imperial orb and scepter. The orb (illustration above) symbolizes the universe and refers to the duty of the emperor to act within his unlimited sphere of influence on behalf of the Ruler of the World. The orb is thought to have been made at the end of the twelfth century, as research has established links with the Dreikönig shrine in Cologne. Documentary evidence shows that the imperial orb was first used in 1191, when Henry IV of the the Hohenstaufen dynasty was crowned as emperor.

The coronation treasures also include the Imperial swords, of which there are three examples in Vienna. They date from the twelfth and thirteenth centuries, the period of the Hohenstaufen dynasty. As well as the sword of

Cologne Goldsmiths' Workshop
Imperial orb, ca. 1180
Gold, jewels, pearls
Height: 8 1/2 in (21 cm)
State Treasure chamber in the
Hofburg

state, which was worn with the point facing upward, there is also a ceremonial sword, which was used for dubbing knights after the church ceremony. This sword is part of the vestments worn by Frederick II in 1220 during his coronation in Rome. Apart from the crown, which he buried with his wife, Constance, in Palermo, Frederick handed down the robes, shoes, stockings, gloves, and sword for future coronation ceremonies.

The fifth section is where the ruling house accumulated those objects it considered to be of value or of special artistic interest. In ideological terms, they have nothing to do with the sovereignty of the House of Habsburg. They are mainly ceremonial items and memorabilia.

Two of the most unusual exhibits in the State Treasure chamber, generally regarded as heirlooms, are a large bowl carved from a piece of agate and the tusk of a narwhal, described as an *Ainkhürn*. It is almost 8½ ft (2.5 m) long and remains in its original condition. The name "Ainkhürn" refers to the legend of the unicorn (*Einhorn* in German) that, while escaping from

a hunter, found refuge and protection in the arms of a maiden. The legend has been given a Christian gloss. The unicorn represents the Redeemer and his birth as the son of the Virgin Mary. The creature's horn thus becomes a symbol for Christ's victory over death. The religious overtones of this legend are important, as otherwise it is unimaginable that such a curiosity would have been kept in the State Treasure chamber. The agate bowl and the narwhal's tusk date from the sixteenth century. Legend has it that King Sigismund of Poland presented the Ainkhürn to Emperor Ferdinand I. Evidence suggests that the agate bowl probably originates from Burgundy, arriving in Vienna as a result of the unification of the two noble houses.

Jewelry for ceremonial occasions occupies an important part of this section. During the eighteenth century, imperial collectors concentrated on jewels such as sapphires, emeralds, rubies, and, of course, diamonds, whose effect was considerably enhanced if they were skillfully ground and polished. During the Baroque era, such stones were often used in artificial flower displays. One of the finest jeweled bouquets belonged to Empress Maria Theresia (illustration left), and after the death of her husband, Franz Stephan, it was kept in the Treasure chamber, to some extent as a tribute to the Emperor's passion for collecting. Driven by an interest in the natural sciences, he amassed a fine collection of valuable minerals. This last section in the Vienna State Treasure chamber with its curios and jewelry helps to sustain the impression of a "cabinet of curiosities."

The Habsburg Art Collection

A painting hangs in the Kunsthistorisches Museum which perfectly illustrates the Habsburg's passion for collecting (see illustration page 125). It depicts a very significant state event for the imperial house, recorded by the Neapolitan painter, Francesco Solimena, on behalf of the court. The Senior Buildings Inspector, Count Althann, who had been in charge of state buildings since 1716, is kneeling in front of Charles VI and handing over the inventory for the newly-opened painting gallery in the Stallburg. The painting shows both the emperor and his officials looking suitably dignified.

Completed in 1728 and unveiled at a ceremony in the Stallburg, this huge painting is set in a grand frame complete with eagle and imperial insignia. Above the emperor, clad in knight's armor, hover Fama, proclaiming the glory of the House of Habsburg, and a guiding spirit, which holds a crown of laurels above the head of the emperor. The painting clearly reveals the political importance that the Habsburg dynasty placed on this new home for

ILLUSTRATION OPPOSITE:
Francesco Solimena
Emperor Charles VI and Count Grundaker Althann, 1728
Oil on canvas,
122 x 112 in (309 x 284cm)
Kunsthistorisches Museum

Johann Michael Grosser
Jewel bouquet of the Empress Maria Theresia, ca. 1750
Jewels, silver, rock crystal, and paper
Height: 20 in (49 cm)
Museum of Natural History

David Teniers the Younger
Archduke Leopold Wilhelm views
paintings in his gallery in
Brussels, ca. 1660
Oil on canvas,
48 x 48 in (123 x 123 cm)
Kunsthistorisches Museum

their paintings. In the same year, the imperial
art collections in Prague and Innsbruck were
brought to Vienna and incorporated into the
new gallery.

For Emperor Charles VI art was an instrument of power. Solimena's picture portrayed,
in artistic terms, the apotheosis of the House
of Habsburg. Unfortunately, hardly anything
from Charles' collections has survived. However, the legacy of another member of the
Austrian Imperial house is available for inspection. These are the works of art collected by
Archduke Leopold, the younger brother of
Emperor Ferdinand III, bishop and Grand Master of the Order of German Knights, who
between 1647 and 1656 held the office of
Governor of the Spanish Netherlands. Leopold
amassed one of the largest art collections in

Brussels, bringing almost 1,400 paintings
together in his gallery.

On several occasions the Archduke commissioned his court painter, David Teniers the
Younger, to produce a sort of inventory of his
gallery in the style of a large-format painting
(see illustration above). The Archduke himself
can be seen in the center inspecting the work
or listening to the gallery director describing
the new acquisitions. Many of the paintings
shown here are still part of the Austrian collections and can be admired in the Kunsthistorisches Museum.

In the larger of the two gallery pictures, the
collector's preference for sixteenth-century
Venetian paintings is made abundantly clear.
To the left beside the closet there is a portrait
by Titian and *Fratricide* by Simone Cantarini.

ILLUSTRATION OPPOSITE:
Raphael (Raffaelo Santi)
St Margaret, ca. 1520
Oil on wood,
76 x 48 in (192 x 122 cm)
Kunsthistorisches Museum

On the large display walls to the left it is possible to make out the *Three Philosophers* by Giorgione and next to it *The Adoration* by Veronese. On the far right, in the second row from the top, there is another Titian, *Sacra Conversazione* (Madonna with Saints). Below, standing on the floor leaning against a chair, Raphael's *St Margaret* can be identified and beside it Veronese's *Esther before Ahasuerus*, a painting which can now be seen in the Uffizi Gallery in Florence. The Raphael painting must have been acquired soon after 1659, as in that year it was brought from England to the Duke's collection in Brussels (see illustration right). Teniers draped a green cloth over the painting and moved it into the foreground to emphasize that it was a new acquisition.

Leopold's tireless efforts as a collector played a large part in elevating the quality of the Viennese galleries. However, it is important to remember that ca. 1600, Emperor Rudolf laid the basis for those collections that were eventually to be so famous. Rudolf, who had been brought up at the court of Philip II in Spain, had been able to familiarize himself with the art treasures there. He later set up a gallery in his residence in Prague, organizing the accumulated pieces along the lines of the great Art Room in Innsbruck's Schloss Ambras, which Archduke Ferdinand II of the Tyrol, son of Emperor Ferdinand I and a perceptive art connoisseur, had built up.

Rudolf managed to bring many Italian masterpieces to Prague from Spain, including works by Titian, Correggio, and Parmigianino. From the estate of his brother, Ernst, he inherited such famous paintings as the *Return of the Herd*, the *Tower of Babel* (see illustration page 128) and *Children's Games* by Pieter Brueghel the Elder. His principal passion, however, was the work of Albrecht Dürer. Almost all the works by this artist which are on display in the Kunsthistorisches Museum and the Albertina were acquired by Rudolf.

Toward the end of the seventeenth century, Emperor Leopold I, the nephew of the Dutch governor, brought together Rudolf's gallery and the Archduke's collection from Brussels, and housed them with the Spanish Infanta portraits by Diego Velázquez in the Stallburg. But the available space was soon taken up, because his son, Charles, as mentioned earlier, had brought the remaining *objets d'art* from Prague and Innsbruck to Vienna and opened a new gallery of painting there. Fifty years later, the great Rubens' altarpieces were brought to the Habsburg capital from Antwerp.

At the end of the eighteenth century, Emperor Joseph II, who was not fond of the Baroque hangings, looked for a new, imposing residence. He eventually found what he wanted in

Pieter Brueghel the Elder
The Tower of Babel, 1563
Oil on canvas, 46 x 62 in
(114 x 155 cm)
Kunsthistorisches Museum.

Kunsthistorisches Museum
Entrance to the Painting Collection

the gallery of the Upper Belvedere, the former summer palace of Prince Eugene of Savoy. When in 1736, Prince Eugene, himself a patron of the arts and sciences and also a passionate collector, died intestate, Eugene's niece, Victoria, gained possession of the art collection. She auctioned off the majority of the stock, including the valuable antique statuary from Herculaneum and the priceless collection of paintings, most of which were dispersed across the continent.

In 1752, after Maria Theresia had been able to acquire the Belvedere complex, her son, Joseph, urged her to furnish the Upper Belvedere and hang a large part of the Imperial paintings there. Five years later, the gallery opened as the first public art museum. In 1815, the Lower Belvedere was also converted into a museum so that the collection from the Art Room in Innsbruck's Schloss Ambras could be displayed there. However, as part of the imperial collection of antiquities was also housed in the Lower Belvedere, the shortage of space soon led to overcrowding

Relief only came when the Kunsthistorisches Museum was built on the Ringstrasse between 1871 and 1891. The imperial painting collection had at last found a new home, and that is where it remains today. These treasures can now be admired in the spacious rooms on the first floor of the museum (see illustration page 129). The western wing houses paintings from France and Italy, while German, Flemish, and Dutch schools are displayed in the eastern wing.

As well as the many paintings by Dürer, which Rudolf had collected in Prague, there were also about 370 of his drawings, which the emperor had acquired from the estate of the painter's widow and from the inheritance of Cardinal Granvella in Madrid. In the mid-seventeenth century, these drawings found their way into the Treasure Chamber and in 1796, they were bequeathed to Duke Albert von Sachsen-Teschen, the art-loving uncle of Emperor Franz (see illustration page 130 above). The emperor knew what he was doing by giving this treasure to Albert. Married to Archduchess Marie-Christine, the daughter of Maria Theresia, he already had a handsome collection of prints, mainly by Venetian masters. In addition, the Duke, who in 1794

received the title of Imperial Field Marshal, was granted a palace by the emperor which had been built fifty years earlier on the Augustinerbastei.

In 1795, Albert had this building enlarged and converted into an art gallery. The huge collection of drawings and prints finally found a home in the Albertinischer Palast, later known as the Albertina. This is where the important prints of all the main European schools, particularly the German, Italian, French, and Dutch, are represented. The drawings and prints by Dürer, and the drawings by Leonardo, Michelangelo, and Raphael are undoubtedly the highlights.

The collection of sculptures and decorative arts on the upper ground floor of the east wing in the Kunsthistorisches Museum covers the period from the Middle Ages to the Baroque. Of the many priceless pieces, the famous salt cellar (see illustration below left), made for the French king, François I, by Benvenuto Cellini between 1540 and 1543, is one of the most outstanding.

Large parts of the lavish Habsburg Cabinet of Curiosities in Schloss Ambras and Prague were brought to Vienna between the seventeenth and eighteenth centuries and given new homes here. In addition to the Kunsthistorisches Museum and the Treasure Chamber in the Hofburg, the Imperial Tableware and Silver Treasure chamber in the Hofburg contains a large part the Schloss Ambras collection. Also of interest is the nearby Collection of Arms and Armor which contains the largest display of weapons in the world.

It is also well worth taking a look at the Collection of Ancient Musical Instruments. Again, many of the finest examples originated in Schloss Ambras' Art Room.

The Ethnographic Museum in the Neuer Hofburg has a surprisingly rich collection of works of art from both the galleries in Prague and Schloss Ambras. Many of the items originate from southern and central America, particularly Mexico. At the beginning of the sixteenth century, Hernán Cortés, the conqueror of the Aztec empire, presented many precious spoils to Emperor Charles V who, in turn, bequeathed them to Ferdinand II of Tyrol, who added them to his Art Room in Schloss Ambras. These exhibits eventually found their way from Schloss Ambras to Vienna. One particularly splendid piece is the feather head-dress of Montezuma II, the last Aztec emperor, who lost his life in the battle with Cortes' troops.

The desire of the Austrian Habsburgs, such as Philip II, to rule an empire on which the sun never set was unlikely to be realized in a Europe which had been shattered by a succession of wars. The political ambitions of the dynasty are, however, illustrated in an impressive manner by its legacy of rich and varied art collections.

Albrecht Dürer
The Green Sward, 1503
Watercolor,
16 x 12 in (41 x 31 cm)
Print Collection, The Albertina

Benvenuto Cellini
Salt cellar, known as the Saliera,
1540-3
Gold, partly enameled
Ivory base
Height: 10 in (26 cm),
Width: 13 in (33.5 cm)
Kunsthistorisches Museum

Bernardo Bellotto (Il Canaletto)
Schönbrunn Pleasure Palace
View of ceremonial courtyard,
1759-60
Oil on canvas,
54 x 95 in (134 x 238 cm)
Kunsthistorisches Museum

ILLUSTRATION RIGHT:
Johann Georg Hamilton
Partridges in Schönbrunn Park,
1732
Schönbrunn, on loan from the
Kunsthistorisches Museum

The Schönbrunn Gesamtkunstwerk

The term Gesamtkunstwerk or "total work of art" is often misinterpreted. It is not possible to have a totality of all the arts; what is meant, rather, is the interplay between the various art forms in one particular genre.

During the Baroque era, architecture was the dominant art form, painting and sculpture were closely linked, and the performing arts played a part too, offering a formal setting for musical events. Then there was garden landscaping and horticulture, as featured within the narrow context of the Baroque palace or summer house, particularly with regard to the staging of festivals. Apart from spectacular firework displays and processions, ceremonial occasions were unimaginable without theatre, opera, or music

Under the reign of Emperor Charles VI and Empress Maria Theresia, the Baroque *Welttheater* (World Theatre) developed into an important aspect of life at Schönbrunn. Two paintings are indicative of the social function of the palace within the concept of a *Gesamtkunstwerk*. One was the work of Johann Georg Hamilton and shows two partridges and other game birds with the palace as it looked in 1732 in the background (see illustration right). Bernardo Bellotto, the famous Viennese painter of veduta, faithful

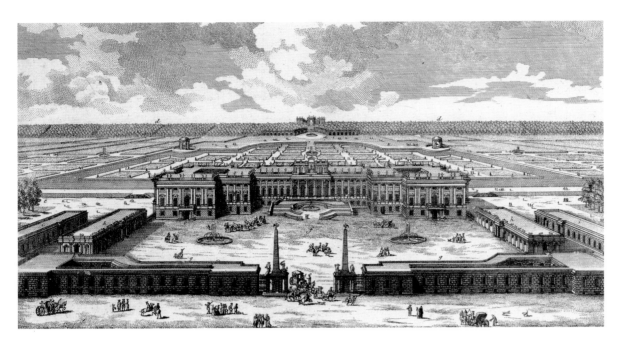

Johann Bernhard Fischer von
Erlach
Second plan for the Pleasure
Palace at Schönbrunn, 1696

representations of an urban setting, is responsible for the other painting, which offers to the observer a magnificent palace complex with a ceremonial courtyard, thronged with people, including clerics, horsemen, and several horse-drawn carriages (see illustration page 131). The scene heralds the arrival of Count Kinsky, bearing news of victory over Frederick II of Prussia at Kunersdorf on August 12, 1759. In this grand veduta-style painting, the palace becomes the symbol of the Habsburg empire as a world power, flaunting its imperial status and political strength. When viewed alongside the game birds, an intimate portrayal of the natural world that alludes to the privacy of the Imperial family, it can be seen how the Schönbrunn Palace occupied a position within a very broad spectrum, as "imperial but private," thus symbolizing the "Habsburg soul."

The pre-Baroque history of Schönbrunn dates back to the sixteenth century, when the mayor of Vienna, Hermann Bayer, enlarged a fortified mill, the Katterburg, into a mansion with a pleasure garden. The origins of the Baroque palace are, however, attributable to Emperor Matthias, who, on one of his hunting expeditions in the area, discovered a water source, which he named *schöner Brunnen* (beautiful spring).

The Emperor built a small palace on the spot, but it was destroyed in 1683 by the retreating Turks. Once the Turkish threat had been banished, Emperor Leopold I commissioned Johann Bernhard Fischer von Erlach to plan a modest, but very elegant, summer house. Building work

began in 1696 and continued well into the following century. It was completed under the regency of Empress Maria Theresia, who put the task of converting and enlarging the palace into the hands of her trusted architect, Nikolaus Pacassi. The complex was finally completed in 1749.

Johann Bernhard Fischer von Erlach's original, visionary design, which would have put Versailles

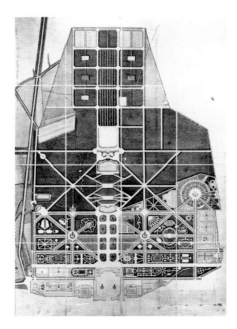

ILLUSTRATION OPPOSITE
ABOVE:
Johann Bernhard and Joseph
Emanuel Fischer von Erlach,
Nikolaus Pacassi
Schönbrunn, 1696
Ceremonial courtyard façade

BELOW:
Theodor Bohacz
View of Schönbrunn shortly
before 1740, engraving ca. 1740

Roman Anton Boos
Plan of the whole palace and
gardens at Schönbrunn
1780.

in the shade (see illustration page 68 above), was surprisingly rejected by the otherwise pomp-loving emperor. He preferred a simpler solution, namely a hunting lodge, which he wanted located in the valley, with a pavilion on the hill.

Upon completion of the central block, the Emperor charged the French garden designer, Jean Trehet, with the task of creating a park. Trehet arranged for the transportation from Paris of a thousand saplings and brought an irrigation device to Vienna. Around 1700, hunts were held in the spacious Schönbrunn grounds and the first festivals were staged.

At that time, after the first phase of building work, Schönbrunn was still a pleasure palace, a center for entertainment used by the Imperial court on only a few days a year, possibly even for only a few hours. Further work was undertaken at the palace during the reign of Emperor Joseph I (1705-11). Wings were built on to the central block, but the roof remained flat. Hamilton's picture proves that work stopped after the reign of Joseph I.

In 1737, after the death of his father, Johann Emanuel Fischer von Erlach took over the

planning work. He had the roof loggia removed and replaced it with steep roofs, but only above the gabled central and corner projections (see illustration page 133 below).

When Maria Theresia became empress in 1740, she contracted her favorite architect, Nikolaus Pacassi, to carry out extensive rebuilding work, as she wanted to use Schönbrunn as her summer residence. For Pacassi, the triangular gables were no longer in tune with the times and did not conform to modern taste, so they were demolished and a continuous cornice line was retained which was only interrupted by the central block. The steep roofs also had to go, in order to highlight Johann Bernhard Fischer von Erlach's original design (see illustration above and page 133 above).

The empress also made changes to the interior of the palace. She wanted smaller and larger cabinets as well as galleries. Pacassi moved the "Great Gallery", the finest room in the building, which was used mainly for state receptions, balls, and banquets, to the courtyard side above

the five-arched entrance to the garden (see illustration page 134). The ceiling fresco by Gregorio Guglielmi describes in allegorical scenes the income and wealth of the Habsburg countries. The iconographic counterpart is to be seen in the adjoining "Small Gallery" which overlooks the garden. The ceiling here, also the work of Guglielmi, portrays in allegorical form the benevolent rule of Empress Maria Theresia.

At the time, some critical voices maintained that Maria Theresia had wasted the opportunity of building a truly impressive palace in the grand European style. Instead, as a Prussian envoy put it, she relegated Schönbrunn to a family palace. Admittedly, Maria Theresia had to find room in the residence for her constantly expanding family, as well as the Austrian court. Most of her sixteen children remained in Vienna. It was obvious that she could not abide by the architectural ground rules for a palace designed purely for the purpose of prestige and status, and nor did she wished to, as it was not in her nature.

Johann Bernhard and Joseph Emanuel Fischer von Erlach, Nikolaus Pacassi
Schönbrunn Palace, 1696/1740
Garden façade

Schönbrunn, Millionen or Vegetin Room with rosewood paneling and Indo-Persian miniatures, ca. 1760

However, the rooms were furnished with great sensitivity, thanks to her initiative. She had a special preference for chinoiserie. In what is now termed called the *Millionen Zimmer* (Millions Room), which in Maria Theresia's time was known as the *Vegetin Zimmer*, the walls are covered with exquisite paneling made from Chinese rosewood. Indo-Persian miniatures, dating from around 1700 (see illustration above), are set into the rocaille-adorned cartouches. The adjacent Gobelin Drawing-room, Maria Theresia's antechamber, which she used specifically as an audience chamber, was probably adorned with Renaissance wall hangings, supplied by a Paris workshop. The tapestries that can be seen in the room today originate from Brussels and were installed in the late nineteenth century.

In the same wing, overlooking the garden, is the *Vieux-Laque-Zimmer* (Old Lacquer Room), an intimate room furnished in Rococo style. It owes its name to the lacquered pictures inset into the

dark brown walnut paneling (see illustration page 137). Maria Theresia was an enthusiastic collector of these panels.

It was the French architect, Isidor Canevale, who produced the plans for this splendid room. He had also been working in other parts of the palace around 1770. The room also contains a painting of the Emperor Franz I, who was the founder of the House of Habsburg-Lorraine, painted in 1772 by the Italian artist, Pompeo Batoni.

The most interesting room in the palace and an important element in the Schönbrunn *Gesamtkunstwerk* is the Porcelain Room, which is also known as the *Kabinett der kaiserlichen Künstler* (The Imperial Artists' Cabinet) (see illustration above). The carved frames are painted in shades of blue and white, imitating the color of the porcelain from which the room receives its name. The walls are covered with a total of 213 small watercolors on a variety of oriental (chinoiserie) themes.

Schönbrunn
Porcelain Room, ca. 1760

ILLUSTRATION OPPOSITE:
Schönbrunn
Vieux-Laque-Room, ca. 1730

Hetzendorf Palace

The central block of the façade at the Hetzendorf Palace, a model of elegant restraint, has all the hallmarks of Johann Lukas von Hildebrandt. Around 1712, the famous Viennese Baroque architect was commissioned by Anton Florian, Prince of Liechtenstein, to produce plans for converting the hunting lodge, which had been built in 1694 for Count Sigismund von Thun south of the grounds of the Schönbrunn Palace, the Schloss-park. The curving pediments above the windows in the piano nobile and the elegant balcony arching out from the central bay, supported by consoles and Doric columns, are fully in line with the architectural style of Hildebrandt and his immediate circle. Lower annexes built on to the main block form a courtyard. It can safely be assumed that Lorenzo Matielli was responsible for the fine sculptured figures on the attic above the courtyard and garden façade.

In the mid-eighteenth century, Empress Maria Theresia took charge of the work and asked Nikolaus Pacassi to convert it for her widowed mother, Elisabeth Christine. Initially, the architect was concerned only with the interior. The ceiling fresco of Aurora in the vestibule was produced by Daniel Gran; the frescoes in the vaulting of the palace chapel, consecrated in 1745, were also Gran's work.

The Japanese Drawing-room (see illustration left) with its Rococo ornamentation and wood paneling is in keeping with the style of Schönbrunn. The ornate steatite reliefs are particularly exotic. Rather more restrained, so as not to detract from the cornices and pilaster-style projecting door and window-frames, are the mirrored galleries, chandeliers, and oval pictures (see illustration page 140).

Johann Lukas von Hildebrandt
Nikolaus Pacassi
Hetzendorf Palace, 1694,
mid-eighteenth century.
Façade (above)
Japanese Drawing-room (left)

LEFT:
View of the Gallery

OPPOSITE:
Banqueting Hall
The famous quadrature painter, Antonio Beduzzi, was commissioned to paint the Banqueting Hall. He opened up the walls and ceiling with imitation balustrades, porticos, and niches ornamented with sculptures. Visitors constantly see new perspectives

The Schönbrunn Park

A comparison of Johann Bernhard Fischer von Erlach's two designs for Schönbrunn (see illustrations page 69 above and page 132 above) makes it clear that the monumental style of architecture for the first project was toned down in order to create space for landscaping. Although the garden complex was not completed until much later, the basis for the initial planning work around 1696 was clearly based on Fischer's second design, of which the central axis has survived.

Fischer's plans included an avenue to lead down to a viewing pavilion on Mount Schönbrunn. A Gloriette, an early classical colonnade (see illustration page 143 above) built as a victory monument to commemorate the Battle of Kolin (1757), now occupies this spot. The fountain basin, envisaged in the plan for the center of the parterre, and two side-pavilions were even taken account of in its final execution. The landscaping work performed by Jean Trehet between 1695 and 1699 has not been restored.

In 1743, Empress Maria Theresia decided to extend Schönbrunn and use it as her summer residence. Shortly thereafter, Josef Hätzel drew up plans for the design of the Great Parterre. This is broken up by a central axis and four transverse avenues, resulting in three pairs of rectangular lawns of various lengths.

The dramatic change to romantic landscaped gardens, so popular in England and elsewhere on the Continent during the latter half of the eighteenth century, occurred at Schönbrunn around 1770. A sketch by the architect, Ferdinand Hetzendorf von Hohenberg, displays an imaginative variation on the Roman Capitol by Piranesi. The Roman Ruins and the Obelisk Cascade (see illustration page 143 below) were built around 1780, at about the same time as the Gloriette. The Neptune Fountain at the foot of Mount Schönbrunn marks the end of the parterre, pointing the way toward the hill crowned by the Gloriette. The fountain, in the form of a vast, rocky landscape populated by mythical figures, constructed to plans by Ferdinand Hetzendorf von Hohenburg, was completed in 1780, the year in which the empress died.

For an idea of what the park looked like around 1780, the plan by Franz Boos, who later became head gardener at Schönbrunn, gives a reliable impression (see illustration page 132). The parterre is divided into eight lawns, of which the four at each corner are curved. At about the spot where Fischer had envisaged the side-pavilions, the plan shows a dovecote and the central pavilion of the maze. The end of the garden complex, accented by the Gloriette, is linked to the parterre by a path with small flights of steps and open spaces.

ILLUSTRATION LEFT:
Schönbrunn Palace
View of the park

ILLUSTRATIONS OPPOSITE
ABOVE:
Ferdinand Hetzendorf von Hohenberg
Schönbrunn Palace, the Gloriette
1775

BELOW:
Laurenz Janscha and Joseph Ziegler
Schönbrunn Palace, the Park:
The Ruins, 1788 (left)
The Obelisk Cascade, ca. 1790 (right)
Historisches Museum der Stadt Wien

Peter Plassmeyer

Architecture in the Nineteenth Century. From Classicism to the Ringstrasse Era

Emperor Joseph II, 1741-90

1780-1848:
From Joseph's Reforms to the Revolution

The decades between the regency of Maria Theresia (1740-80) and the Reign of Emperor Franz Joseph (1848-1916) seem secondary, in terms of architectural history, when compared to the baroque palaces and churches of the seventeenth and early eighteenth century and the architecture of the so called Ringstrasse era that fundamentally shaped the image of the city. It was nevertheless a time of extremely widespread building activity, although hardly apparent. Little concerned with representation, it was administrative architecture in the broadest sense, and by this process, new buildings for such utilitarian projects as hospitals, schools, public administration, universities, the stock exchange, and train stations were developed.

Under Emperor Joseph II, above all, the representation of the divine right of His Majesty the Emperor ceased to be the sole purpose of his activity. Instead, he considered himself the "First Servant" of the state. In 1765, he succeeded his father Franz I Stephan as the German Emperor, originally governing alongside his mother Maria Theresia, who had already performed the official functions on behalf of her husband. He reigned on his own only after her death in 1780, yet his reform work already began while he was at his mother's side. His aim was a tightly organized, centralized state — efficient action being more important than the maintaining of principles. He abolished the serfdom of the peasants, as well as torture, and he significantly relaxed censorship.

Yet the Emperor's aims, that seem so progressive nowadays, did not find undivided support, and various measures were revoked even during his lifetime. The introduction of a general land tax, which affected the aristocracy in particular, naturally caused resistance from that level of society. Joseph also abolished the exclusive right of the aristocracy to become officers in the military and banned the customary pomp and ceremony at funerals. His reform of burial even opened Catholic cemeteries also to non-Catholics (Akatholischen) and strictly forbade any excess expenditure. The corpse was sewn into a linen bag and buried in a mass grave, tombstones were not permitted, although commemorative plaques could be fixed to the walls of the cemetery. These regulations applied to everyone, from peasants to the upper ranks of the nobility.

In a fundamental wave of secularization, Josephs distanced himself from the Catholic Church. This led to the dissolution of numerous monasteries, bringing about land reform. The impending reorganization of the suburban parishes caused the construction of numerous new parish churches, which became small halls with sparse decoration. These churches were built to a similar model on the basis of "standard

plans, a kind of pattern book which regulated decoration, size, and number of church towers based on the expected number of churchgoers. Property owned by the monasteries was used to pay for the parish priest. Joseph's Edict of Toleration of 1781 granted freedom of worship to Protestants, Greek Orthodox, and Jews, albeit in the form of mere toleration rather than equality of rights. These non-Catholics were allowed to practice their religion and to establish their own places of worship, the function of which could not be communicated in the façade, so consequently towers and bells were also forbidden.

The majority of building activity was concentrated on housing, where there was enormous backlog of demand. Within the confines of the circular city wall, land was extremely scarce. Entire districts were therefore developed on the sites of dissolved monasteries. Further land for building was gained through the reclamation of gardens. Today's names like Melkerhof, Trattnerhof, Klosterneuburgerhof, etc. indicate the late-eighteenth-century tenement houses, built on the sites of former monasteries (Höfe) which were repossessed. In the time of Maria Theresia, the monasteries had been asked to donate these Höfe buildings for development purposes, in order to create new housing space.

The new buildings consisted of apartments grouped around inner courtyards. They were elaborately decorated, often with oval staircases. The façades are simple, however, and dispense with adornments like orders of columns and pilasters, continuing the architectural tradition of the late baroque palaces.

The Höfe are different from the Pawlatschenhaus, a second type of urban tenement, so-called after the open, mostly wooden, balconies overlooking the courtyard façade leading to individual apartments. Examples of these Pawlatschenhäuser, as they are called, are still to be found, for example in Blutgasse in Vienna's first district (Vienna consists of 23 separate Bezirke, or districts), and are grouped around a series of interlocking courts are based on rural building forms (see ill. p. 145 bottom right). The enforced building of housing could not keep pace with the increasing population so the number of stories was increased to meet this need.

The Emperor, as commissioner of the buildings, receded into the background. This is certainly the main reason why Viennese architecture of ca. 1800 looks so "plain." The building of castles and palaces no longer played a significant role and was essentially limited to the restructuring and extension of existing complexes.

The collaboration between Joseph II and Isidor Canevale was the last exemplary partnership between an architect and the emperor as patron. Joseph made the Parisian Canevale his court architect in 1775. He had already worked

Isidor Canevale
Summer-house in the Prater,
1782
Façade

ILLUSTRATION LEFT:
Andreas Zach
Empire-style renovation of the
interior of the Starhemberg Palace
1784

OPPOSITE:
Pawlatschenhaus in the Blutgasse
Courtyard

for the Emperor on the ceremonial architecture built for Joseph's marriage with Isabella of Parma in 1760. To begin with, Canevale worked for Cardinal Migazzi, the Cardinal of Vienna, among others, for whom he created the cathedral and a triumphal arch in Vács in Hungary. He was very popular with the nobility and became architect to the Princes of Liechtenstein. In his work for the Emperor, he was in charge of the suburbs, namely, the area between the circular wall surrounding the inner city and the *Linienwall*, the straight rampart, a second line of fortifications. Some of Canevale's buildings from this time, which are still impressive today, are the portal to the imperial Augarten and the Narrenturm in the Allgemeines Krankenhaus complex (General Hospital).

His rise to the position of court architect seemed to go hand-in-hand with a decrease of artistic authenticity. The extent of Canevale's contribution to the Allgemeines Krankenhaus is not certain, although he was in charge of the complex's central planning. Even for the Josephinum on Währingerstrasse, considered to be his main Viennese œuvre, his contribution cannot be quantified clearly since the building was based on plans by the Milanese architect Giuseppe Piermanini.

The centralization of public bureaucracy also affected the Building Administration. In addition to the individual style of the architect, there was now a kind of institutional style which lacked any clear signature. The rigid cubes of his buildings (strongly influenced by French revolutionary architecture), demonstrate in particular, how Canevale used very different stylistic elements from the two other court architects working under Joseph II, Nicolaus Pacassi (inner city) and Ferdinand Hetzendorf von Hohenberg (the suburbs). Both remained closely linked to the Baroque tradition and still harked back to the time of Maria Theresia. Hetzendorf was mainly responsible for Schönbrunn, where he changed the small palace theatre into its current form. Later, he instigated the extension and restructuring of the gardens. His most important work here is certainly the Gloriette which is based on plans by Fischer von Erlach, and which functions as a termination point of the view along the central axis. Additional buildings, an obelisk, and an artificial ruin, create a "view" in the lateral areas of the gardens in the Romantic tradition. Pacassi was in charge of the extension of the Hofburg (the imperial palace), and created its uniform façade on Josephsplatz.

Johann Ferdinand Hetzendorf von Hohenberg was not one of Joseph's favorite architects. However, the Emperor commissioned him to "liberate" the Minoritenkirche and the Augustinerkirche from their baroque decorations and create "Gothic" interiors for them. This return to

Pallavicini Palace (left) opposite the Hofburg
Engraving, ca. 1850, by Würbe
Historisches Museum der Stadt Wien

Carl Schütz
Kohlmarkt, 1786
Historisches Museum der Stadt Wien

Franz Jäger
Theater an der Wien, 1797-1801, Papageno Gate
Mozart's "The Magic Flute" premiered in the Theater an der Wien (in its previous building) in 1791 - hence the name "Papageno Tor."

Gothic style stood in direct opposition to the classicist architecture propagated by the Pope and the Cardinal of Vienna, Migazzi. On the other hand, the purification and elaboration into a minimalist structure fitted in well with Canevale's own architectural rigor, albeit using different forms, which were dictated by the medieval origins of these churches.

Hohenberg gradually became more of an expression of Canevale's taste and thus more in line with the Emperor's own preferences. This is most manifest in the palace Carnevale built in 1783-4 on the Josephsplatz on the site of the former Königinnenkloster, with apartments linked up behind it. The palace had been commissioned by the banker Johann von Fries, for whom Hohenberg had already redesigned the palace and park in Bad Vöslau. Originally, the only structural element for the palace on Josephsplatz was the alignment of the windows. The enormous portal with its caryatids and the triangular pediments of the windows were only added to the "bare" building after fierce criticism from other architects, primarily Gottlieb Nigelli who was also building on the site of the Königinnenkloster.

Hohenberg also deviated from the traditional scheme in the interior, by placing the living quarters in the mezzanine rather than the upper story in order to reduce heating costs by having lower ceilings. The reception rooms were moved into the attic. Hohenberg did not rely on the established pompous style of Viennese Baroque palaces, but chose modern forms in the same sense as Canevale for the town palace of the most important Viennese banker of his day.

It remains unclear whether the adverse criticism was targeted exclusively at the architect, or whether it was also aimed at the patron, who chose his Viennese residence in direct proximity to the Hofburg, traditionally the domain of the highest aristocracy, although he himself had only recently been ennobled.

Joseph II efforts to reduce the privileges of the aristocracy and live as modestly as he could as Emperor, found their echo in the simplified façades of state buildings and by making it possible for commoners to become army officers. The townhouse of the banker Fries was meant to reflect both these imperial desires, the imperial understatement as well as the new prospects which were opening up to other classes as long as they diligently pursued their careers.

The theatre also made use of the new freedoms. Only in such a climate could the play *The Marriage of Figaro* (originally entitled *La folle journée, ou le mariage du figaro*) by Pierre Augustin Caron de Beaumarchais (1732-99), which had been banned in France, be staged in the Hoftheater in Vienna — though not as a drama, but as an opera sung in Italian with music by Wolfgang Amadeus Mozart and a libretto by Lorenzo da Ponte. Count Almaviva's conduct was presented not as a peccadillo, but as an abuse of power.

The enlightened, sometimes radical, Joseph II and the short reign of Leopold II his brother, were followed in 1792 by the "good Emperor Franz." Under the title of Franz II, he was the last emperor of the Holy Roman Empire, and as Franz I, the first Austrian emperor. In reaction to Napoleon's coronation as emperor, Franz introduced the Austrian hereditary imperial status in 1804. He probably suspected that Napoleon's military campaign across Europe might bring about the end of the Holy Roman Empire.

The reign of Franz II (I) was originally overshadowed by wars with Napoleon and a resulting empty treasury. The often hesitant Emperor, proved himself in this duel as a staunch and pragmatic defendant of the imperial crown. In 1810, he even married his daughter Marie Louise to the French parvenu in order to preserve the crown. The inauguration of the Congress of Vienna in 1814 marked the start of a period of peace for Franz. It was also the starting point for the career of Prince Klemens von Metternich, who governed the country in the role of chancellor of state until the turbulent year of 1848.

The political success of the Congress is controversial, yet it undoubtedly marks the beginning of a time of fundamental change. The foundation of the Polytechnic (now the Technical University) gave the necessary impetus for industrialization. The first important continental railway connection, the Kaiser-Ferdinands-Nordbahn, was launched from Vienna, connecting the coal mining regions of Silesia with the capital and the Danube, and thus improving transport capacity.

The invention of the pianoforte and the "Viennese" mechanism changed the role of this instrument in music, making dynamic playing possible and thus increasing its suitability for solo performances. The works of Beethoven and Schubert demonstrate impressively how chamber music changed through its use of the pianoforte as a solo instrument or in partnership with strings. The two other musicians who influenced musical life at least as significantly were Johann Strauss Sr. and Josef Lanner, whose Viennese waltzes were fashionable during the Biedermeier period.

Towards the end of the eighteenth century, the mannered minuet had been replaced by the waltz, which was then still executed in a series of jumps, finding its "floating" form only in the 1830s. During the Biedermeier period, Vienna was considered to be the world capital of music. As the bourgeoisie became more dominant and the influence of the aristocracy waned, numerous musical societies were founded. Concert halls were opened and an academy of music was founded.

Theater was as important as music, again with music occupying a central role. Two court theatres and three suburban theatres were in their heyday during this period. The Burgtheater on Michaelerplatz was the most important German-language theatre of its time, and the Kärntnertheater was the main stage for opera. The suburban theatres served as stages for the *Zauberposse*, a very popular genre in Vienna whose chief proponent was Ferdinand Raimund. Whereas Raimund embodied the conservative Vienna of the Biedermeier period, emerging liberal and revolutionary tendencies was expressed in the sarcasm of Johann Nepomuk Nestroy's farces.

During the reign of Franz II (I), the idea of abolishing the city wall and thus opening up the inner city for development was first considered. In 1809, Napoleon's army had blasted parts of the fortifications of the Hofburg, and this presented an initial opportunity to extend the city.

Rudolf Alt
View from Grabengassse toward Stock-im-Eisen-Platz, 1843
Watercolor 20 x 15 in (51.2 x 37cm)
Historisches Museum der Stadt Wien

TOP ILLUSTRATION:
Emperor Franz II (I), 1768-1835 Franz II was the last emperor of the Holy Roman Empire of German Nation and first Emperor of Austria.
Österreichische National-bibliothek

BOTTOM ILLUSTRATION:
Klemens Wenzel Nepomuk Lothar, then Count von Metternich, 1773-1859, as Austrian foreign minister from 1809.
Österreichische National-bibliothek

ILLUSTRATION FACING PAGE:
Paul Sprenger
Hauptmünzamt on Heumarkt,
1835-38
Central avant-corps of the façade
(left)
Entrance vestibule (right)

Joseph Kornhäusel
Weilburg near Baden, 1820-23,
destroyed in 1945
General view
Historical photograph

Ultimately though, the reconstruction only led to an extension of Burgplatz and the laying out of the *Kaisergarten* (imperial gardens) and *Volksgarten* (people's gardens). In the process, the Theseustempel and the Äusseres Burgtor by Peter Nobile were also constructed. In 1817, the glacis was planted, converted into tree-lined walks, and opened as a promenade.

Demands to open the fortifications for the urgent needs of the city to expand had already been expressed at the end of the eighteenth century. The inner city had not been extended since the final Turkish siege of 1683, yet, in the meantime, Vienna's population had tripled. The aforementioned development of the gardens and apartments built on the sites of monasteris did not provide sufficient relief. New efforts primarily focused on two sites, Kärntnertor and the glacis next to the textile district. The Emperor wished to build a Court Opera Theatre in the vicinity of Kärntnertor, with costs being met by the sale of the adjoining plots of land, to be used solely for the construction of private buildings.

The second section of the circular city wall targeted for the extension was the textile district which lay between Schottentor and the Danube Canal. Here, a whole new district would be created through the development of the glacis. Banking and stockbroking firms such as Rothschild, Gina, Geymüller, Arenstein & Eskeles, Pereira, and Coith had adopted and supported this project since 1838 and it had even won the support of the Court's Council of War. The architect and editor of the *Allgemeine Bauzeitung*, Ludwig Förster, was commissioned to produce a plan and a model.

With the re-introduction of the Austrian Empire, the court's need for representation again

increased. As a first step, Franz had a ceremonial hall built into the Hofburg. The architect was Louis Montoyer who had come to Vienna in 1795, to work for Albert von Sachsen-Teschen and was known for his Palladian, monumental buildings in the southern Netherlands. Montoyer opposed Canevale's rigid classicism preferring a more western European, monumental style. The coffered ceiling of the new hall was supported by colossal, free-standing columns. Shortly thereafter, Montoyer used columns in a façade when building a costly neo-palladian palace for the Russian Ambassador Rasumofsky in 1803, whose reception room was a precursor to the Hall of Ceremonies in the Hofburg. The garden frontage as well as the town frontage of the almost-square palace have temple porticoes right in the center. However, the column used in the façade remained an unusual feature, though it can also be found in Eisenstadt, where Charles Moreau extended the Esterhazy Palace and improved the garden façade with a colonnade.

The most important palace building of the *Vormärz*, the period between the Congress of Vienna and the Revolution of 1848, the Weilburg near Baden (1820-23, destroyed in 1945, ill. above) by Joseph Kornhäusel, shows a wide colonnade in front of a compact main building. The structure is dominated by various twinned elements, clearly differentiated and with separate roofs. Kornhäusel was the most important Viennese architect of the first third of the century; the impressive volumes of his buildings combine the flat design of the walls with elements of monumental classicism. One of his earliest buildings, the Hotel zur Kaiserin von Österreich in Weihburggasse, the interior of which has since undergone significant modifications, was also one of the first hotels in Vienna. Between 1812 and 1818, he succeeded Joseph Hardtmuth as Building Director of Liechtenstein. Later, he erected the Weilburg and converted the interior of the palace of Duke Albert von Sachsen Teschen on the Augustinerbastei — today the Albertin — inherited by Arch-Duke Karl. His ingenious suites of rooms today still guide the visitor to the study hall of the Albertina, conceived by Kornhäusel as a ballroom.

Again and again, Kornhäusel's interiors defy the characterless façades of the first decades of the nineteenth century. The library of the Schottenstift, the completion of the state rooms of the Klosterneuburg, and above all the synagogue in Seitenstettenstrasse, contradict the "understatement" of their façades through the addition of monumental columns and pilasters, coffered ceilings, barrel vaults, calottes, built-in galleries, and the ingenious play of light.

Kornhäusel's façades can be studied on his many apartment buildings which survive, especially those in the Seitenstettengasse. The first of

Beethoven's study in the "Schwarzspanierhaus," Historisches Museum der Stadt Wien

them was designed for the Jewish community, being designed to shield the synagogue from the public, and the expected profits were to cover the building costs. Next door, Kornhäusel built an apartment building for himself, and across the street he created another for the Seitenstetten-kloster. The façades show an even alignment of identical windows, architectural adornment and detailing on the ground floors only, which are the only ones easily visible to passers-by.

On Freyung, the complex of flats supposed to cover the costs of the Schottenstift is designed with a central portico with colossal pilasters, finishing in a triangular pediment. These features relate to the building's position on the square and demonstrate their link to the monastery behind. The size of this building hints at the massive blocks of apartments which were to dominate private building during the second half of the century.

The whole era was characterized by the increasing centralization and bureaucracy of official building policy. Since the days of Maria Theresia, the monarch had gradually withdrawn from being an exemplary patron of architecture. This tendency finally led to the separation of court and state architecture under Franz II (I), making the "civil servant architecture" of the *Vormärz* the true representative of its time. The split had been initiated in 1785 through the establishment of a

public buildings authority and found its high point in the establishment of the *Hofbaurat* (Court Council for Architecture) in 1809. All public buildings had to undergo a technical and financial examination by this authority, which led to the increasing monotony of public architecture in the first half of the century.

The most important architect under the *Hofbauräten* was Paul Sprenger, for many years himself director of the institution. His uninspired buildings made him a much decried figure in the architectural circles of Vienna. The preserved drawings of his unfulfilled projects, however, show a more versatile architect than structures such as the Hauptmünzamt (1835-38, ill. above) and the Finanzlandesdirektion (1840-47) would lead one to believe. These buildings are ultimately comparable with the Tierärztliche Hochschule (1821-3) by Johann Aman in the Bahngasse or the first Nordbahnhof railway station at Praterstern (1838-40), both dominated by the main body of the building and an accentuated central avant-corps. The wall is plastered, and decoration is limited to the fluting in the base and the flat pilasters on the central avant-corps.

Sprenger's design for the Altlerchenfelder Kirche led to the downfall of this minimalist style. This concept again followed the little diversified vocabulary of forms set forth by the Hofbaurat, although Sprenger himself had for a long time

favored a Gothic building. After the foundations for Sprenger's building had already been laid, the recently founded Association of Engineers and Architects insisted on a new competition, which was held in 1848 and was won by the Swiss architect, Johann Georg Müller. The *Hofbaurat* was abolished that very year, although Sprenger did not lose his leading position within the State Buildings Administration. The architects that emerged victorious were those who had never received any public commissions under Sprenger — their time came after the Revolution of 1848.

During the *Vormärz*, Vienna expanded enormously, due to the large-scale building of private housing for the lower nobility and commoners. The demand for homes was huge, brought about by the removal of the Court to Vienna, the general increase in population, and finally a massive surge in numbers caused by the Austrian industrial revolution. Factories and industrialization changed the face of the city forever. Much of this was made possible by the removal of the fortifications which had been an important feature of the city for generations, due to the danger of Turkish invasion.

Another important innovation was the introduction of public street lighting, changing the city's night life completely. This was made possible through a contract entered into between the Municipality of Vienna and the British Imperial Continental Gas Association on May 10, 1841.

Johann Ferdinand Hetzendorf
von Hohenberg
Gothic Revival renovation of the
interior of the Augustinerkirche,
1784-5

The Augustinerkirche and the late eighteenth century Gothic revival

Until 1783, the fourteenth-century Augustinerkirche was the parish church of the Court and played a significant role in the public life of the house of Habsburg. Numerous marriages were solemnized here, and many Habsburgs returned to the church after their death. Until 1878, with the death of Archduke Franz Carl, it was traditional practice to bury individual organs separately in different places. Hearts were buried in a silver bowl in the Vault of Hearts (*Herzgruftl*) in the Augustinerkirche, while the entrails were sealed in a copper urn in the St. Stephan's Cathedral, and only the embalmed bodies were transported to the crypt of the Kapuzinerkirche in a coffin.

One of the most important monuments in the Augustinerkirche was the tomb of the Archduchess Marie-Christine (ill. p. 250), completed by Antonio Canova in 1805. The main façade of the Augustinerkirche fell victim to the homogenous design of Josephsplatz, when it was blocked off by a wing of the Court library.

During the 1780s, Emperor Joseph II gave the order to re-design three church interiors in Gothic style. This was quite surprising, since the Emperor generally favored strict classicism.

In 1781, a Gothic high altar was built into the Michaelerkirche according to plans by L.B. d'Avrange; the overall spatial impression of late Baroque was not entirely abandoned, though. As for the re-design of the Augustinerkirche and Michaelerkirche, no consideration was given to this interesting tension between styles. The court architect Johann Ferdinand Hetzendorf von Hohenberg, of whose work the Emperor was not particularly fond, was commissioned to "liberate" the spaces from their late Baroque chapels and altars and to return the building to a "medieval" state, meaning a uniform Gothic appearance.

In his work on the Augustinerkirche, Hohenberg unified the system of walls and pillars, and the side-altars were given flat niches and a pseudo-Gothic framing. Furthermore, the windows were enlarged and a Gothic pulpit and organ gallery were built in. A multitude of chandeliers soften the impression of the building's extreme height. The high altar, inspired by the Michaelerkirche altar, was replaced later in the nineteenth century and in 1874, the sandstone altar by Andreas Halbig, originally carved for the Votivkirche, was installed.

The asymmetrical layout of the Minoritenkirche made its re-design of more complicated. When the Minorites, a Roman Catholic order of mendicant monks, moved to the Weisspanierkirche in Alsergrund in 1784, the Emperor gave the building to the Italians as their national church. Yet they were told to liberate the church from "everything superfluous" and adapt it to the classicist call for clarity. To achieve this aim, Hohenberg intervened strongly in the substance of the building. He designed a polygonal finish to the side-aisle and adopted the medieval clustered piers on high bases from the southern line of columns, by repeating them throughout the church. On the east wall of the central nave, a monumental pseudo-Gothic altar was introduced into this otherwise uniform space with its three aisles. Emperor Franz II (I) continued the Gothic Revival work in 1802, when he had the Hofburg chapel adapted to the scheme of the Augustinerkirche.

Some of the reasons for Joseph II's campaign for a Gothic Revival certainly lie in his strained relationship with the Roman Catholic Church, which, at the time, favored a pseudo-antique Classicism, in Rome as well as in the lands of the Habsburg Empire. On the other hand, though, the concept also corresponded to his aim for "clear and transparent" architecture. For a medieval building, this could only mean additional work in the same spirit as the original medieval substance of the structure.

L.B. d'Avrange
Michaelerkirche
Nave with Gothic high altar,
1781

Johann Ferdinand Hetzendorf von
Hohenberg
Gothic renovation of the interior of the
Minoritenkirche, 1784-89

Evangelical church buildings

After Emperor Joseph II's Edict of Toleration was introduced in the last third of the eighteenth century, non-Catholic religious communities were given permission to erect their own places of worship. Yet they could have neither tower nor bell, let alone direct access to the street. They were thus merely tolerated and granted only the right to practice their faith in private. Accordingly, the first non-Catholic places of worship were hidden behind the plain façades of residential buildings. Both the Protestant congregations of Vienna, originally called *Akatholischen*, built their places of worship in the Dorotheergasse on the site of the dissolved Königinnenkloster.

The H.B. Protestant Reformed Church (H.B standing for *Helvetisches Bekenntnis* or Helvetic Confession) was built in 1783-84 by the architect Gottlieb Nigelli. He erected a longitudinal space vaulted by two flat domes. The two bays were separated by coffered barrel-arches. The galleries, set back into the lateral recesses of the columns, rest on columns and are topped by coffered barrel- vaults. Artistically, this is the most important ecclesiastical building of its time and, in an ultra-simplified form, has something in common with the spatial design by the architect Germain Soufflot for the Pantheon church in Paris, built in 1757.

The pulpit was originally placed on the side where the entrance now is. When Ignaz Sowinsky redesigned the façade in 1887 and erected the tower, the pulpit had to make room for the new entrance and was therefore placed on the opposite wall.

The A.B. (*Augsburger Bekenntnis* or Augsburg Confession) Lutheran congregation originally made use of the church of the dissolved Königinnenkloster built in 1582-83. In 1846, the Lutherans commissioned the architect Ludwig Förster to build a bigger church on Gumpendorfer Strasse, which had become necessary due to the strong growth of the parish, especially in the western suburbs. In 1849, the foundation stone for the building was laid. The building was built in collaboration with Theophil Hansen in Romantic style

From the outside, the Gustav-Adolf-Kirche appears as a compact block. On the flat wall which has recessed multiple arched windows with an architrave, the elements of decoration seem to have been appliquéd, a familiar element in Catholic churches built at the time. The low ground floor windows and higher first floor windows reflect the interior with its wooden galleries supported on cast iron columns. The head of the Lutheran parish demanded a second gallery floor, suspended within the system of wall columns of the high windows, much to the architect's disgust. This church building shows very clearly how much the situation of the Protestants had improved, since their place of worship now had the right to look like a Church.

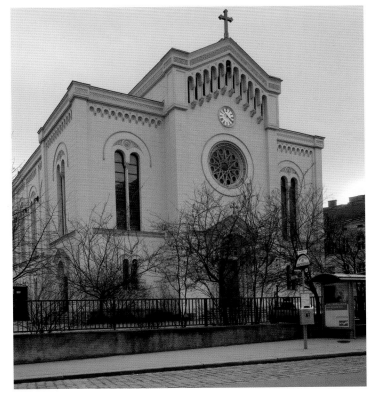

The Augarten Portal

As court architect, Isidor Canevale was in charge of the suburbs and the Augarten and Prater imperial gardens (ill. p.145). The entrance to the Augarten bears the Imperial inscription *Allen Menschen gewidmeter Erlustigungs-Ort von Ihrem Schätzer* (Leisure ground dedicated to all people by their donor) which was added when these formerly private gardens were opened up to the public at large.

More than any other building in Vienna, this formal entrance indicates Canevale's Parisian origins and demonstrates his knowledge of French revolutionary classicism. The central archway of the central portal, enclosed in a semi-circle, ends in a massive attica.Three smaller entrances flank it on each side, at the end of which are janitors' houses with rusticated brickwork. The architecture of gate and triumphal arch is compact, almost uncompromising, and it sets itself apart from the open space of the gardens. Canevale never again achieved such a radical design in his later projects for the imperial gardens.

The Äusseres Burgtor

The outer gate, completed by Peter von Nobile between 1821 and 1824, is part of a whole series of new town gates erected in the early nineteenth century. It had been integrated into the plans for an imperial forum at an early stage and survived the demolition of the walls. In 1817, Johann Aman, Luigi Cagnola, Alois Pichl, Louis Remy and Peter von Nobile entered a competition for the creation of a new gate. Luigi Cagnola, a Milanese architect, won the competition, and the foundations were laid according to his plan in 1821. But Cagnola then left Vienna — most likely irritated by the Emperor's demands for changes — and Peter von Nobile was charged with completing the work, integrating the foundations which had already been laid into his own design. In a certain way, he continued Isidor Canevale's radical classicism and emphasized the link between gate and fortification.

Following the conventional design of city gates, he distinguished between a "best side," facing the city, and a "field side" away from the city. Five arches of equal height open onto the field side; these are flanked by heavy corners on both sides, their walls only containing small segmented, arched windows on floor level. This economical design contrasts with the livelier arrangement of a three-sectioned building decorated with Doric columns on the city-facing side. The central wing has deep receding passageways on this side, the round arch openings in an otherwise closed wall being replaced by an open colonnade.

Nobile presented the field side as a fortification and the side facing the Hofburg as a representative façade, thus inverting the direction of older city gates where the extravagant side faces those approaching the city.

Peter Nobile
Theseustempel, 1820-3

The Theseustempel

Peter von Nobile's Theseustempel (Temple of Theseus), built in 1820-23, is the first building in Vienna exclusively designated for museum purposes. It is inspired by the antique Thesaion in Athens and was erected on the occasion of the purchase of Antonio Canova's marble group Theseus and the Centaur, now displayed in the staircase of the Kunsthistorisches Museum (ill. p. 198 and 251). The group was commissioned by Napoleon in 1805, then purchased in 1821 by Franz II (I) and re-interpreted as the victory over Napoleon. After the reconstruction of the fortifications blown up by Napoleon's troops, the Theseus group was installed in Nobile's temple.

The Theseustempel thus became a national monument of architecture. The very deep foundations, made necessary by the fact that it was built on ground above the bastions, enclose a space where the antique monuments found in Austria are displayed.

Stylistically, Peter von Nobile is second to the court architect Isidor Canevale in being called the most consequential representative of revolutionary classicism in Austria. This can be seen, for example, in his return to the classical Greek Doric order for the design of the columns of the Theseustempel. Ever since the Renaissance, the Tuscan arrangement with smooth shaft and base had prevailed and had been widely circulated in architectural treatises. Nobile copied the Greek original exactly, though, just as he had for the Äusseres Burgtor; he used tapering fluted shafts which emerge straight from the stylobate without a plinth.

The Allgemeines Krankenhaus

The former Allgemeine Krankenhaus (General Hospital), whose rooms are now mainly used by the university, stretches between Alserstrasse and Währingerstrasse. At the time of its completion, it was the most modern hospital complex in Europe. The first buildings were built in 1783-84 on the site of the Grossarmenhaus, built in 1693, and were repeatedly extended until the second half of the nineteenth century. In addition to the actual hospital, the complex included a maternity wing, an asylum (the *Narrenturm*), an infirmary, and a foundling hospital.

The idea of closing small hospitals and concentrating all the patients in one big hospital had come to Emperor Joseph II on a visit to Paris in 1777 where he saw the Central Hospital. Shortly thereafter, he commissioned his court physician, Dr. Joseph Quarin, to design a hospital. The actual work fell to the court architect Isidor Canevale, though his contribution to the buildings cannot be verified. Joseph Gerls was in charge of the supervision of building works.

The various facilities were grouped around several courtyards, creating the impression of a stately cloister or apartment complex. The architecture is austere and lacking in decoration. The work consisted mainly of the rebuilding of the almshouse and the garrison hospital which already existed on the site.

The Josephinum is the building of the surgical and medical faculty and still part of the hospital area, and although built at the same time (1783-85), it is more opulent in style. The three-wing complex is separated from the Währingerstrasse by railings and is considered to be the last Baroque building in Vienna. It is probably based on a design by Milanese architect Giuseppe Piermarini but was heavily reworked by Canevale. In the interiors, Canevale abandons baroque tradition in favor of a purpose-built arrangement of space.

The most interesting part of the hospital is the asylum behind the Josephinum, nicknamed the *Narrenturm* (tower of the insane) by the locals. The insane used to be housed here but it is now the Museum of Medical History. It was the only building in the immediate area of the hospital that was entirely newly constructed

Isidor Canevale created a cylindrical building whose exterior was originally entirely rusticated. The slit-like windows give the building the appearance of a fortification, and similar designs are more commonly to be found in prison architecture than in hospital design. Behind the narrow openings for daylight there are the radially arranged cells, with a walkway connecting with the court. They can only be reached through the guardians' wing which divides the court in two. Through this arrangement, the care and supervision of patients could be maintained with a minimum level of staffing.

Isidor Canevale
Josephinum, 1783-5
Frontage facing Währingerstrasse

Isidor Canevale
Josephinum, 1783-5
Library

Louis Montoyer
Rasumofsky Palace, 1803-7
Garden façade (above)
Festival hall (right)

The Rasumofsky Palace

In 1803-07, Louis Montoyer built a neo-palladian palace for the Russian ambassador Prince Andreas Kyrillovitch Rasumofsky. Rasumofsky was an important patron of Beethoven, who dedicated his three Quartets, Opus 95, to him. Beethoven's Fifth Symphony was first performed in the palace, and during the Congress of Vienna it became a major center for the gatherings of Viennese high society.

The almost square building with its central avant-corps in the form of colonnades was originally surrounded by the English Gardens. The palace itself was rebuilt after a fire in 1814, and reconstructed after the ravages of World War II. Yet the enormous columns of the façade and the magnificent festival hall still demonstrate the original splendor of the building.

Colonnades were exceptional in Viennese architecture around 1800, but were used for the first time on the garden side of the Eisenstadt Palace designed by Charles Moreau. The reception halls of the two-story palace are located on the ground floor. In the banqueting hall, with its monumental Corinthian columns, Montoyer uses from the Hall of Ceremonies he built in the Hofburg, as an architectural symbol of the new Austrian empire. Other impressive features are the central round domed hall with its order of pilasters and the suite of rooms on the garden side.

The Schottenstift after the
renovation of 1826-32 by
Joseph Kornhäusel

Joseph Kornhäusel and Viennese Biedermeier architecture

Although he received hardly any public commissions, Joseph Kornhäusel (1782 - 1860) is among the most significant Viennese architects of the early nineteenth century. Private clients were the first to recognize his talent. These included the Princes of Liechtenstein, whom he worked for as Director of Building from 1812-1818, as well as the Archduke Karl, for whom he built the most important palace of the *Vormärz*, the Weilburg, near Baden, in 1820-23. Later, various monasteries commissioned him with extensive building projects.

The Schottenkloster

Kornhäusel's biggest project in Vienna was the alterations and extension to the Schottenkloster. From 1826-32, he connected church, monastery and tenements to form a unified complex containing various courts. The Schottenhof, positioned in front of the monastery facing Freyung and Schottengasse, anticipates the future apartment buildings which would be erected during the Ringstrasse era.

Like all Kornhäusel's apartments, the five-story building is only sparsely decorated with moldings and architraves around the windows. In contrast to his earlier housing, he designed the long Schottengasse frontage with a flat central avant-corps of pilasters and a finishing pediment. This porticois is repeated on the Freyung side. Directly behind, in the biggest courtyard of the complex, he once more stresses the façade with a portal surrounded by columns, which marks the actual entrance to the building.

The interiors demonstrate Kornhäusel's architectural virtuosity. His special role in the architecture of the Viennese Biedermeier period can be witnessed especially in the luxuriously decorated classicist Prälatensaal (Hall of the Prelates) with its pilasters and library. No other architect, except perhaps Louis Montoyer, used monumental columns so convincingly. Smooth Ionic columns divide the longitudinal space into three aisles and support an enormous entablature on which the coffered barrel-vault rests. The narrow sides end in a straight wall on the entrance side and in an exedra on the opposite wall. The columns support balconies halfway to ceiling height containing shelves of books. The room is lit through a skylight in the apex of the vault.

The Albertina

Kornhäusel also distinguished himself as an interior decorator in his alterations to the Albertina for Archduke Karl (1822-24). The building was

designed as the Taroucca Palace in 1745 and altered for Albert von Sachsen Teschen and his spouse Archduchess Christine, by Louis Montoyer in 1800-4. Part of the Augustinian monastery was incorporated into the building. When Archduke Karl inherited the palace, he commissioned Kornhäusel to redesign the interior. The main project was to improve the design of the long hallway leading to the ballroom-cum-music-room on the second floor.

The sequence of rooms takes its starting point from the oval Minerva Hall on the ground floor. The oval form ingeniously softens the bend in the the corridors leading to the staircase. Kornhäusel ingeniously restructured these corridors by placing Doric columns in front of the wall. At the end of this flight, two sphinxes anticipate the staircase, at the end of which is the ballroom-cum-music- hall. Today, this large room

Joseph Kornhäusel
Albertina
Former ballroom and music room 1822-24 (today reading-room of the print collection)

Louis Montoyer et al
The Albertina (built as Taroucca Palace in 1745-7, altered 1800-4, 1822-4 and 1867)

is used as the reading-room for the Albertina's world-famous collection of prints and drawings.

In contrast to the library of the Schottenstift, the reading-room of the Albertina is structured by means of pilasters dividing the double rows of windows on two stories. The round arches in the lower part of the wall are paired with horizontal rectangular mezzanine windows placed in the upper third of the wall. In front of the pilasters against the yellow and gray walls, stand ten marble figures by Joseph Klieber that represent Apollo and the nine Muses.

In contrast to the marked rigor of the vast halls based on full-length columns, Kornhäusel here aimed at a decorative and colorful solution, similar to that of the Prälatensaal in the Schottstift, which is also structured by means of pilasters.

Synagogue

The community hall and the synagogue of the Jewish community in Seitenstettengasse are the high points of Kornhäusel's œuvre.

Through the new powers of the Edict of Toleration of Emperor Joseph II, Jews, like non-Catholic Christians, were allowed to practice their faith in moderation and to build places of worship, provided the buildings were neither recognizable as such nor directly accessible from the street. Kornhäusel solved this problem by designing the communal hall to look like an apartment building. In the façade, the rusticated ground floor had to counterbalance the steep gradient toward Seitenstettengasse, leaving the basement visible in the left half of the building.

There are four stories above the molding, whose only adornments are the window architraves; triangular pediments are surmounted by straight moldings above, then round-arch windows and finally simple rectangular windows. The lack of decor toward the top took into account the limited visibility of the frontage in the narrow alley as well as a small budget for the building.

The façade belies the interior. This feature is emphasized by the fact that Kornhäusel built his own apartment building next to the Jewish community hall and erected a building for the Seitenstetten Catholic monastery on the opposite side of the street. Kornhäusel designed the temple on the courtyard side as an oval centrally planned structure, as there was no traditional canon of forms for Jewish religious building for him to relate to. Instead, he developed a concept of space that he then adapted for various other functions, such as the library of the Schottenstift, the Roman bath in the Sauerhof in Baden, and the auditorium of the theater in Josephstadt. Full Ionic columns are placed inside an oval space, supporting the women's galleries half-way up and above the capitals. The ceiling is a star-spangled dome, whose lantern skylight in the apex constitutes the only source of natural light.

ILLUSTRATION FACING PAGE:
Joseph Kornhäusel
Synagogue, 1824-6
View of the dome

Joseph Kornhäusel
House of the Jewish community in Seitenstettengasse, 1824-6
Façade

Joseph Kornhäusel
Synagogue, 1824-6
Interior

שויתי יהוה לנגדי תמיד

Railroad stations in Vienna in the Nineteenth Century

Vienna's first railroad station was built near the Praterstern in 1838. The Kaiser-Ferdinand-Nordbahn company had been founded two years previously on an initiative by the Rothschild banking house. Regular train services between Vienna and Lundenburg started the same year and one year later there were trains to Brünn (Brno). At the time, this was the longest railroad link on the continent. The station was a relatively simple classicist building beside the tracks; a terminal building for freight traffic was added at right-angles.

Shortly afterward, the Sina bank founded the Wien-Raaber-Eisenbahngesellschaft, with the aim of running two separate railroad lines, one along the Danube toward Györ (Raab) in Hungary and another via Semmering to Trieste. The station was built close to the Arsenal as a symmetrical complex with separate station buildings for the two lines. It was on the site of these stations, the Südbahnhof and the Staatsbahnhof, also known as Ostbahnhof, were erected in the beginning of the 1870s.

The time of the great Viennese stations began with the construction of the Westbahnhof (1857-59) via the Kaiserin-Elisabeth-Westbahn company. In this instance, there was complete separation between freight and passenger terminals. Like almost all Viennese railroad stations, the terminal consisted of

TOP ILLUSTRATION:
Theodor Hoffmann
Nordbahnhof, 1859-65
General view

BOTTOM ILLUSTRATION:
Wilhelm Flattich
Südbahnhof, 1869-74
Façade with main entrance

Theodor Hoffmann
Nordbahnhof, 1859-65
G. Hofer, Ticket hall and stairways of the Nordbahnhof
Drawing

separate departure and arrival buildings on both sides of the tracks. Entrances and exits were placed along the central axis and emphasized accordingly. A terminal was built in front of the platform hall of the Westbahnhof, which contained waiting-rooms for the Imperial Court and the railway administration offices. The model for the building was the Wittelsbacher Palace in Munich, a reference to the fact that the line also connected with Munich.

Shortly afterward, the Nordbahn renovated and enlarged its station in Vienna (1859-65). It became one of the most splendid stations in Europe, looking like a huge castle, containing splendid grand staircases and waiting-halls and a precinct in a sufficiently grand style. Railroad travel became an almost theatrical production. The staircase alone with its four flights of stairs leading from the station hall, occupied a third of the floor space of the departure building, yet its only purpose was to guide travelers to the waiting-rooms upstairs from which they could reach the tracks.

After this initial railroad enthusiasm, four more stations were built before the World Fair in 1873. The old double station of the Wien-Raaber-Eisenbahn had by then been sold to two separate railroad companies. The private Staatseisenbahngesellschaft connecting Vienna with Prague and Budapest built its Staatsbahnhof on the site (1867-70). Here, the station hall is not hidden behind a terminal building, but is visible in its entire construction. This station building served as a model for the Staatsbahnhof (Westbahnhof) in Budapest, built by Gustave Eiffel for the same railway company.

The Südbahngesellschaft renovated the second station of the old complex. The Südbahnhof (1869-74) was the terminal for Trieste. It is the only Viennese terminal that was also accessed through the terminal building.

Wilhelm Bäumer
Nordwestbahnhof, 1870-3
Entrance polygon on the departure side

Two more railway companies, the Kaiser-Franz-Joseph-Bahn and the Österreichische Nordwestbahngesellschaft were founded in these years of expanding trade and commerce, and they also built their own stations. Both companies made the northwest corner of the Empire accessible via their respective lines. At the time, four companies offered connections to Prague. The Nordwestbahngesellschaft never stood a chance of survival, but its station showed an element rarely found in Viennese architecture, a polygonal wing, designed by the architect Wilhelm Bäumer, as an entrance to the station hall.

All of the railroad stations were destroyed by the bombs of World War II. One by one, they were demolished and replaced by new buildings.

TOP ILLUSTRATION:
Carl Ruppert, Carl Schumann
Staatsbahnhof (Ostbahnhof), 1867-70, entrance side
Historisches Museum der Stadt Wien

BOTTOM ILLUSTRATION:
Moriz Löhr
Westbahnhof, 1857-9
Entrance side
Historisches Museum der Stadt Wien

Emperor Franz Joseph I, 1830-1916
Painting by Franz Xaver Winterhalter
Kunsthistorisches Museum

1848-1890:
From Revolution to the Ringstrasse

On December 25, 1857, the Wiener Zeitung printed a decree by Emperor Franz Joseph I on its front page: "It is my wish that the extension of the inner city of Vienna ... be tackled as soon as possible."

It had taken a long time for an emperor to dare give the go-ahead for the razing of the inner ramparts of the city. There had been various attempts since the late eighteenth century, but the reservations of the military, unable to shake off the trauma of the Turkish sieges, hindered any attempts to rid Vienna of its immense fortifications.

Emperor Ferdinand I ordered the demolition of the walls around the Kärntnertor in 1844, in order to gain space for a new Court Opera Theater, but the events of 1848 put an end to the venture. The revolution forced the resignation of the Chancellor, Prince Metternich, who had been omnipotent for almost half a century, and the abdication of Emperor Ferdinand I. He was succeeded as emperor by his eighteen-year-old nephew Franz Joseph I, who initially pushed ahead once more with the completion of the Fortress Vienna. The huge barracks now being built were no longer intended to deter attacks from the outside, but rather to pre-empt any repetition of a popular uprising from within. Two of these barracks, the Franz-Joseph-Kaserne (1854-57) and the Rossauerkaserne (1865-60), were built along the Danube Canal at both ends of the city ring-wall. The third barracks, the Arsenal, was built between 1849 and 1856 in front of the Belvedere near the Südbahnhof. This complex also contains the first museum building of the monarchy, the Waffenmuseum (Armory), today Heeresgeschichtliches Museum (Military History Museum).

Fortress Vienna had long since ceased to exist in any serious form. The suburbs had continually grown since the second half of the eighteenth century and formed an increasing densely populated protective shield. The second ring of defense, the Linienwall (running mainly along the line of today's Gürtelstrasse), built in 1703 after the last attack by the Turks, and was only ever really used as a tax border. The building of the railway (begun in 1836) and the beginning of regular service on the Danube in the 1830s, ended Vienna's position at the periphery of Europe. The railway, originally financed by private companies, was soon integrated into the defense system of the state,and was used to speed the transport of troops to far-flung regions of the Empire whenever trouble was on the horizon.

Vienna, the third largest capital in Europe, was far behind the others in terms of urban and economic development, in spite of its political importance. A European travel guide dating from

1843 lists two hundred hotels in London, whereas in Vienna, there were only two hotels, the Erzherzog Karl and the Kaiserin von Österreich, and five inns. Vienna was too far away from the route of the Grand Tour, which went up the Rhine via Switzerland down to Italy. Consequently, it was visited by few travelers. This situation changed only with the building of the railroad and connection to an international European railroad network.

There was a great deal of pent-up enthusiasm and high hopes for new buildings once the decision had been made to raze the city walls. The resulting building boom brought in architects, developers and speculators from all over Europe, hoping to make their fortunes from the feverish building activity of the "Ringstrasse Era." Ludwig Förster had already laid the foundations in 1848 with the publication of his Allgemeine Bauzeitung, an architectural journal in which he reported on buildings in and around Vienna from 1836. Förster made early attempts to get international architects to come to Vienna in order to break the supposed stagnation. He was successful, in that he managed to attract the Dane, Theophil Hansen, into his practice, who became one of the most important architects involved in the Ringstrasse.

Building activity and architecture after 1848 were fundamentally different from the situation before that date, when various varieties of classicism had to meet the stringently economical codes of the Hofbaurat. The Revolution introduced the change that had long since taken place in the countryside. Romanesque, Gothic, and Italian Trecento styles now inspired the appearance of so-called Romantic architecture. The buildings became bigger and bigger.

The appointment of Swiss architect Johann Georg Müller (1822-48) was crucial for the shift in Viennese architecture and ultimately for the fall of the Hofbaurat. Müller continued with the building of the Zu den Sieben Zufluchten church in Altlerchenfeld, which had been begun by Hofbaurat (Court Councillor for Architecture) Paul Sprenger. Müller had to incorporate the foundations of Sprenger's design, which had already been laid, into his concept, but even the façade is much closer to Sprenger's design than could be imagined from the complicated history of the building. The main differences are to be found in the digression from the classicist ideal. The driving force for Müller's appointment was the Association of Engineers and Architects, founded in 1847, whose main aim was to deprive the Hofbaurat, Paul Sprenger, of his powers. In fact, the institution of the Hofbaurat fell victim to the Revolution of 1848 and was dissolved in February 1849, to be replaced in early 1850 by the General-Bau-Direktion (General Administration of Building), once again headed by Paul Sprenger, though only until 1854. This at least demonstrated a certain continuity within the state-controlled building bureaucracy.

Initially, only the stylistic appearance of buildings had changed. The exclusivity of classicist rigor was replaced by equally exclusive Romantic round windows, arches with Florentine tracery, and entrances topped with gables and corner towers. Pilasters were replaced by lesenes and entablature by round-arch friezes. Initially, the philosophy of the building block and the flat wall hardly changed. A vivid example is the barracks buildings, with Joseph Sprenger being essentially responsible for the Franz-Joseph-Kaserne. Yet changes can also be discerned beyond the General-Bau-Direktion, such as in the A.B. Lutheran Church on Gumpendorfer Strasse, designed by the practice of Ludwig Förster in 1846. In the history of Viennese architecture, this new style is generally referred to as Romantic historicism, in contrast to the cubic style of the *Vormärz*.

This period is characterized by the interplay of painting and sculpture with architecture, not as pictorial wall frescoes, statues, or reliefs, but mainly through decorative painting and ornamental masonry work (examples are the Altlerchenfelder Kirche and the Hall of Fame and staircase in the Military History Museum). The flat wall was originally a surface to be used for decoration, but it became a relief in its own right with Heinrich Ferstel (Bank and Stock Exchange building in Herrengasse). The Hofoperntheater (Court Opera Theatre, 1861) by Eduard van der Null and August von Sicardsburg, the first building on Ringstrasse, was also built in this tradition. Van der Null had already been involved in the decoration of the church in Altlerchenfeld. For the Ringstrasse, the new Opernhaus, which combined the enormous building masses of the proscenium and auditorium, lobby, and administration offices, was stylistically outdated. According to a popular satire of the time, the architects were completely indifferent as to whether to use Gothic forms or those of the Renaissance.

Sicardsburg and van der Null certainly built the most mature building in the Romantic historicism style. The masterly way in which they dealt with elements of different styles that constituted a style in itself, had nevertheless been superseded by a purer concept of design.

Heinrich von Ferstel, whose Bank and Stock Exchange building was stylistically on the same level as the architecture of the opera, won the tender for the building of the Votivkirche, using a

Colonel Pilhal, Major Karl
Markl
Rossauerkaserne on Schlickplatz,
1865-70, façade

Gothic design. The Votivkirche (1856-79) became the first Ringstrasse building in a "pure style." Other stately buildings followed this ideal of a "rigorous historicism" in the Viennese tradition. Friedrich von Schmidt built the Rathaus (City Hall) (1872-83) in Gothic style, Theophil Hansen the Parliament (1871-83) in Greek-Hellenic style, and the aforementioned Ferstel built the University in Italian Renaissance style. These were not random choices, but established a link between the purpose of the building and the design. For example, the Rathaus (city hall) evoked the bourgeois architecture of Flemish town halls of the late Middle Ages, the Parliament referred to the architecture of the first democracy, and the university design was based on the modern, humanist ideal of education, first developed in Italy. It is again remarkable that architecture alone indicated the purpose of the building.

The different styles of the various stately buildings all relate to the same concept of style. Despite their diversity, they form a uniform bourgeois picture. By the mid-century at the latest, the bourgeoisie had become a crucial factor in the balance of power due to its continual growth and economic importance. This can be seen in Rathaus and Parliament which stand so close to the former center of power, the Hofburg. It is even more obvious in the six stations, all owned and managed by private railroad companies, becoming the driving force behind economic progress.

The wealthy bourgeoisie's struggle for social recognition expressed itself in the desire for recognition by the aristocracy. The manifold stylistic appearance of the architecture, the juxtaposition of Neo-Gothic, Neo-Renaissance, Neo-Classicical, and Neo-Baroque was like a history lesson in architecture. This set the wealthy bourgeoisie in its marked urge for assimilation in opposition to the hereditary concept of power favored by the aristocracy. As a logical consequence, the University of Vienna was one of the first in which art history was treated as an independent department, Rudolf von Eitelberger being appointed as senior lecturer in the subject in 1852.

The development of the Ringstrasse, the opening of the stock exchange, the foundation of the Creditanstalt für Handel und Gewerbe (Bank of Business and Commerce) and ultimately the planning of the first World's Fair in a German-speaking country, set off an unexpected euphoria and an unstoppable feverish speculation. With the opening of the World's Fair in 1873, Vienna presented itself to an astonished international public. The main railroad stations had been completed — much earlier than in most of the other European metropolises — and constituted Vienna's gateway to an international railway network. In essence, the railway made the Fair possible, neither exhibits nor visitors could have reached Vienna in sufficient numbers without it. The site of the World's Fair was bigger than that of all the previous Fairs put together, seemingly trying in one fell swoop to make up for all that had been missed. Vienna revealed itself as a booming, liberal metropolis that had managed to transform itself from a fortress to a modern capital in the shortest possible time.

On May 9, 1873, one week after the opening of the Fair, the house of cards of this economic miracle, built entirely on stock, collapsed. The over-valuation of many companies, which had been looming since 1872, could be kept secret until the opening, but this meant that when it eventually came to light, the collapse was even more dramatic.

ILLUSTRATION FACING PAGE:
Gustav Veith
Panorama of the extended city of
Vienna, ca. 1873
Sepia with pen, 56 x 90 cm
Historisches Museum der Stadt
Wien

The Ringstrasse, celebrated as a *via tri-umphalis*, lent its name to the time of economic euphoria. That is perhaps why it was less a uniform street than a splendid boulevard containing most of the public buildings of the city, such as the Rathaus, the Parliament, the major museums and parts of the Hofburg, alternating with palaces and stately homes. The alternation of free-standing stately buildings with terraced residences, the number of whose floors and roof eves were not of uniform height, offered continuously new impressions. The length of time taken to construct the buildings and changing stylistic preferences indicate that there was no stringent concept for development. Nor were there any stylistic strictures imposed for the façades, as for instance in Munich's Ludwigstrasse and Maximilianstrasse, where urban uniformity was a primary concern.

The urban boulevard enclosed by housing alternated again and again with wide views across open spaces and gardens, particularly around the Volksgarten and the Heldenplatz. The impressive view of Burgtheater, Parliament, and the Rathaus that presents itself on leaving the

Neuer Burg, is only an achievement of the twentieth century. It should be remembered that, in the period under discussion here, the Ringstrasse was, above all, a prospering construction site. Even at the opening of the World's Fair, when it was first presented to the astounded international public, the Ringstrasse was hardly more than a project.

On closer inspection of the design, it becomes evident that it did not serve the better development of the town. Apart from its function as a good place for elegant loiterers, the wide bridle-paths were used for exercising horses and could be convenient for the cavalry when it needed to move fast. These avenues thus formed part of the new concept of defense that had started with the building of the new barracks. When approaching the inner city from the west via the radial streets, one rarely needed to cross the Ring directly in order to access the inner city. Instead, there was a latticework of crossed spears and notices explaining that the ring-wall was merely been replaced by other structures. The city center was thus preserved as testimony to an outdated idea of Empire. The Ringstrasse

Model of the inner city with
Ringstrasse by Erwin Pendl,
1897-8
Historisches Museum der Stadt
Wien

served to combine the suburbs with the inner city only in a limited way. It is the result of both neo-conservatism and economic liberalism and thus the most splendid monument to the long reign of Emperor Franz Joseph I, who ruled from 1848 through 1916.

At the age of eighteen, Franz Joseph succeeded his uncle Ferdinand who had been forced to abdicate due to the Revolution. Ferdinand, who was unable to reign, was allowed to preside over a Council of State, under the presidency of Archduke Ludwig and assisted by Chancellor of State, Metternich, and his internal rival, Count Kolowrat. The tender age of the new emperor heralded a new era. At first, Franz Joseph was under the influence of his mother, the Archduchess Sophie, who was said to be the only man in the Hofburg. Sophie was bitterly opposed to the bourgeois tendencies of the empire that had determined the decades since Joseph II. Her supreme aim was to restore the Divine Right of Kings to the new Austrian Empire.

At the beginning of the century, the building of a new hall of ceremonies in the Hofburg had been enough to provide a dignified framework for the empire, but other architectural manifestations were needed now. Firstly came the barracks, financed by the state, especially the Arsenal, a building of special interest to the Emperor. He did not have the money to build a private palace since he had only inherited office and honors from Ferdinand, but not the private capital of the House of Habsburg. He could therefore only access it after Ferdinand's death in 1875, which explains why the extension of the Hofburg and building of the imperial forum only began in the 1870s.

The first shadow was cast on Sophie's influence over the Emperor when Franz Joseph married his mother's niece, Duchess Elisabeth, in Bavaria. He charged his mother with the education of "Sisi" (short for Elisabeth) who was completely unprepared for her role. In 1855 and 1857, Sisi gave birth to two girls, and the long-awaited successor to the throne, Rudolf, was finally born in 1858. In 1860, having thus fulfilled her duty as the Emperor's wife, the Empress took an outrageus step: she left the children and her husband and spent two years in Madeira. On her return to Vienna, the shy girl had become an independent woman who knew how to use her world-famous beauty in an intelligent and demanding way.

Before the building of the Ringstrasse, the Empress was on the way to becoming "the main attraction of the monarchy," (Brigitte Hamann), lending it the splendor that the Emperor had failed to achieve. Austria had lost the wars of 1860 (Solferino) and 1866 (Königgrätz), had been excluded from the German Confederation, and had even lost Venice. Although Elisabeth did not

Empress Elisabeth (1837-98)
Painting by Franz Xaver
Winterhalter
Kunsthistorisches Museum

ILLUSTRATION FACING PAGE:
Karl Hasenauer
Hermes-Villa, Tiergarten Lainz
1882-6, façade toward the court

Inside the dining room of the
Hofburg: Table of the Court
set for a family dinner

have a strong interest in the court of Vienna, she was responsible for two important upheavals in the policy of the Empire. Firstly, in 1865, she ensured the bourgeois liberal education of her son Rudolf. This was another form of revolution and turned Rudolf into a convinced liberal. Secondly, in 1867, Elisabeth actively engaged in Austrian politics and pushed through the "conciliation" with Hungary, leading to the creation of the double monarchy of Austria-Hungary, and opening the way for the coronation of Franz Joseph as King of Hungary, a title he had been refused by the Hungarians in 1848.

In the 1860s, it was the radiance of the empress that corrected the dull image of her spouse. Even a railway company, the Kaiserin-Elisabeth-Westbahn, asked for permission to use her name as its own. With the coronation as King of Hungary, the now expanding (construction) economy, and the approaching World's Fair, the prestige of the Emperor reached its climax. Elisabeth, on the other hand, withdrew more and more from the court and from her role as empress, and was constantly traveling. The last major public appearance of the imperial couple took place on the occasion of their silver wedding in 1879. The city honored the couple with a procession, decorated by Hans Markart, with ceremonial architecture by Otto Wagner.

Markart, "the prince of painters," was the outstanding artistic personality of the 1870s, though he was already past his prime, whereas Otto Wagner was at the beginning of a career that would make him the most important Viennese architect of the turn of the century. From this point, the year could be seen as a dividing line between another phase.

The end of the Austrian empire began in 1889, with the death of Rudolf, the heir to the throne, in Mayerling, and the assassination of the Empress in Geneva in 1898. Even the silver wedding present from the Emperor, the Hermesvilla in the Tiergarten in Lainz, painted by Makart according to the Emperor's design, failed to create a bond between Elisabeth and Vienna ever again.

The year 1879 also saw the end of a series of liberal governments, and their replacement by the Taaffe conservative government. During the short period of political liberalism, eighty-six directors of various limited companies had been members of parliament; there was even talk of the parliament as a limited company and the Government Department as its executive officers. Banks and stockbrokers maintained their dominant influence on the booming economy, especially the railway companies and the building industry. Families such as the Rothschilds, Todescos and Epsteins, to name but a few, formed the Ringstrasse Association and began to compete with the old-established aristocracy. More than forty savings and

loans companies were active in Vienna during the years of economic boom from 1867 through 1873. Construction was not confined to the Ringstrasse. Countless apartments were built in the suburbs and still form the image of Vienna today. Their façades were inspired by the palaces of the Ringstrasse, yet many of these were tiny one-room apartments with a bathroom.

The railway companies, some of which were only developed in anticipation of the World Fair, built six big stations immediately before the event, partly replacing buildings erected during the *Vormärz*. They contributed massively to the growth of Vienna, bringing many new inhabitants from all over the Empire into the capital. These people settled around the train stations and created new districts.

The suburban churches from Joseph's times had become inadequate for the increasing population and were replaced by new bigger buildings. Traveling along the Gürtel on Underground Line 6 today, along the elevated tracks built by Otto Wagner, one passes many of these new church buildings, for example, the Fünfhauser Pfarrkirche *Maria vom Siege* (1867-69) by Friedrich von Schmidt on Mariahilfer Gürtel.

In addition to the Ringstrasse, Vienna introduced another new cultural trend — the operetta. Numerous theaters were built in the second half of the century. Apart from the Court Opera and Hofburg Theater, they were mainly privately-owned, such as the former Carl Theater on the Praterstrasse, built by August von Sicardsburg and Eduard van der Nüll for theatre director Carl Carl in 1847. Other splendid theatre buildings included the Ringtheater, destroyed by fire in 1881, and the Volkstheater (until 1945, called the Deutsche Volkstheater) by Hermann Helmer and Ferdinand Fellner, who founded forty-eight theatres all over Europe. Another building deserving of mention is today's Volksoper, built in 1898 as the Kaiser-Jubiläumstheater.

The imperial court had lost its dominance through the private theaters. Inspired by Makart's sumptuous fancy-dress balls, historical dramas were staged in which the actors wore sumptuous costumes, though classical drama was also preserved. Theaters hired expensive guest artistes and there were performances by the Meininger company, the most famous theater company at the end of the century, which were as triumphantly successful as Offenbach's operettas had been in Paris in the 1850s and 1860s.

In fact, Offenbach's operettas in particular inspired Viennese composers and conductors who used them to create a new genre. Franz von Suppé's *Die schöne Galathea* (Beautiful Galathea, 1865) and *Boccaccio* (1879), Carl Millöcker's *Der Bettelstudent* (The Poor Student, 1882) and especially the timeless operettas of Johann Strauss such as *Die Fledermaus* (The Bat, 1874), *Eine Nacht in Venedig* (A Night in Venice, 1883) and *Der Zigeunerbaron* (The Gypsy Baron, 1885), conquered first the Viennese public and then the stages of Europe and beyond. The ethnically explosive situation of the Dual Monarchy was drowned out by the sounds of the waltz and veiled by the fantasy world of magnificent scenery and stage sets.

Die Fledermaus in particular became the incarnation of this most Viennese form of musical theater. Self-deception at the stock exchange was now followed by a similar scenario on stage. There is no better description for the atmosphere of fin-de-siècle Vienna than the refrain from one of its songs:" *Glücklich ist, wer vergisst, was doch nicht zu ändern ist.*" (Happy is he who forgets what he could not change anyway).

Johann Georg Müller
Altlerchenfelder Kirche, 1848-61
Façade

Johann Georg Müller
Altlerchenfelder Kirche, 1848-61
Interior decoration by Eduard van
der Null

The Altlerchenfelder Kirche

The building of the Altlerchenfeld church *Zu den sieben Zufluchten* became an architectural testimony to the 1848 Revolution. Hofbaurat Paul Sprenger had been producing various designs since 1846 and finally commissioned the building in 1848. The Association of Engineers and Architects founded in the wake of the revolution, successfully opposed Sprenger's concept, however. The crucial moment was a lecture given to the Association in 1848 by Johann Georg Müller, in which the young Swiss architect criticized classicist church building and Sprenger's concept so harshly, that building work was halted immediately . Müller emerged victorious from the ensuing competition which was open exclusively to the members of the Association.

Nevertheless, Müller had to incorporate Sprenger's foundations into his design. He erected a basilica with three aisles, built in exposed brickwork with a west-facing frontage and two towers, a short transept and an octagonal dome over the crossing. It is interesting to note how extensively Müller's building eventually incorporated Sprenger's ideas in spite of the muddled history of the building. Most of the changes involved the superficial appearance of the church. Pilasters were replaced by lesenes, entablature by round-arch friezes. The individual areas of the building are less compact but the church as a whole seems leaner than the original concept.

In the interior, the two bays of the nave are enclosed by rib-vaults. The transition from nave to side-aisles is achieved through using a triumphal arch in each bay. The flat expanses of wall are covered with polychrome decorations throughout the interior, just as in Sprenger's concept.

After Müller's premature death, the building work was continued by Franz Sitte. In 1853, Eduard van der Null took over the interior decoration work, which was based on the designs of Joseph Führich.

Heinrich Ferstel
Votivkirche, 1856-79
Nave (above)
Historical view of the
façade (right)

Votivkirche

The Votivkirche is the first building to have been designed in a "pure" style on Ringstrasse, as well as being its first ecclesiastical building. It was erected on the occasion of a failed assassination attempt against the young Emperor Franz Joseph I, which took place in February 1853. Only a couple of days later, his brother, Archduke Ferdinand Max, called for the building of a memorial church. Together with the Arsenal, this monument became the second symbol of the Restoration of the monarchy in the post-revolutionary period, when the army and the Roman Catholic Church joined forces to work for the preservation of the Throne.

The design by architect Heinrich Ferstel shows a Gothic basilica with three aisles and a two-tower façade, transept, choir with ambulatory and a ring of chapels. The decision to opt for a Gothic design was a conscious break from the classicism favored by Emperor Joseph that had governed architecture prior to 1848. The building was preceded by a competition that was also open to foreign architects, revealing important changes in Vienna's building industry, since the competition for the building of the Altlerchenfelder Kirche had been restricted to the members of the Association of Engineers and Architects. Seventy-five designs were submitted, some by such famous exponents of the Neo-Gothic as Vincenz Statz, Friedrich Schmidt, and Georg Ungewitter. The foundation stone was laid in 1856 on the wedding day of the imperial couple.

For Ferstel's building, the "national cathedrals" designed by Friedrich Schinkel were less influential than the genuinely Gothic cathedrals of Amiens and Cologne. Ferstel developed a style of his own, which was by no means a carbon copy of the original Gothic.

At first, the status of the church building, flanked by two towers, was subject to some doubt. All that was only clear is that it should not be allowed to compete against St. Stephan's Cathedral. The architecture, which far exceeded the needs of a parish church, required the building to have an extended function. Initially it was planned to use the Votivkirche as the Catholic garrison church (1862), and after completion of the new university building, it replaced the Jesuitenkirche as the university church (from 1878).

The floor plan, with its three aisles, expands to five aisles in the nave, the shallow recesses of the pillars joining up to the bays. The elevation deviates from the classical cathedral scheme by omitting the triforium in the nave and adding galleries in the choir, as in early Gothic style. The bays are covered by a rib-vault. A plinth, suggesting a platform on which the building sits, underlines the character of the Votivkirche as a monument. This contradicts the medieval ideal, but corresponds to the spirit of the age.

The basic form of the pulpit in the Votivkirche is a hexagon, supported by columns of Egyptian marble. The central relief shows Christ teaching

The rectangular building, rigorously structured through symmetrical and main axes, is surrounded by six barracks, a hospital, and the command headquarters, which also contains the main entrance. The various parts of the complex are connected by low-rise storage buildings. The corner buildings serve as barracks and were built in the form of tower-like forts with four wings. There are additional forts on the end points of main and transverse axes, the southernmost fort containing the hospital and the church of Maria vom Siege. A rifle factory, engine workshops, a smithy, a cannon foundry, and engineering works, were erected inside the square. The most typical building is the Waffenmuseum opposite the command headquarters. The buildings were inspired by Italian castles, and finish in a battlement.

All of the important architects active in Vienna at the time had been invited to enter the competition for the work. Eduard van der Nüll and August Sicardsburg, Carl Rösner and Antonius Pius von Rigel, Ludwig Förster and Theophil von Hansen worked in pairs on designs, but none of these satisfied the jury. The individual projects were then split up and distributed among the competing architects. The lion's share went to the architectural practice of van der Nüll and Sicardsburg, who constructed all the barracks and storage buildings, though Carl Rösner designed the hospital and the church. Rösner's collaboration on the project with Rigel ended when Rigel died in 1850, nor did the architectural practice of Hansen and Förster see the completion of the works.

The Waffenmuseum by Theophil Hansen occupied the most representative position. It was originally supposed to replace the arsenal built in the time of Maria Theresia, which had been looted in 1848, and was only converted to a museum during the construction work. This was the first dedicated museum building of the monarch. Hansen's design followed that of Gottfried Semper's gallery of art in Dresden with its broad floor plan and central block covered by a dome. In contrast to Semper, however, Hansen preferred to use exposed brickwork, which he used in different colours. The tracery of the windows, the shape of the dome, and the battlement around the top floor were recognized as Moorish influences.

The main staircase and the hall of fame, which was painted in 1859-71 by Carl Blaas, are accessed through a vestibule containing a "reception committee" of thirty-two marble statues of Austrian generals. Originally, Hansen had intended to include a cycle of frescoes by Carl Rahl, but the latter's "revolutionary tendencies" were too suspicious. The hall of fame is thus to be interpreted as a symbol of national identity and national integration that could only be guaranteed by the military and the Emperor.

Arsenal and Heeresgeschichtliches Museum

The Arsenal, erected 1849-56, claimed to be the biggest building project of the Monarchy. The government had been terrified by the popular uprising of the 1848 Revolution, and undertook the building of a ring of barracks, planned for defense and aimed less at an external enemy than at a renewed uprising by the urban population. Those parts of this enormous military-industrial complex which remain are still impressive. A frontage several hundred yards long faces the Schweizergarten and the Heeresgeschichtliches Museum (Military History Museum), previously called the Waffenmuseum (Armory).

The chosen building plot for the Arsenal was an elevation near the St.-Marxer-Linie, which offered an open field of fire toward the city. Not only was the Arsenal an exceptionally large complex of barracks, it also concentrated the production of weaponry on one site.

Theophil Hansen
Arsenal and Heeresgeschichtliches
Museum, 1852-6
Staircase (left)
Hall of Fame wih frescoes by Carl
Blaas (opposite)

Heinrich Ferstel
Ferstel Palace
(former Austro-Hungarian
National Bank), 1856-60
Herrengasse frontage on the
corner of Strauchgasse

In simplified terms, the building plot consisted of a triangle between the Herrengasse and the Strauchgasse in which Ferstel accommodated the bank and the stock exchange as well as the traditional coffee house. Starting from a central hexagon, a narrow tube-like space linked up to this triangle, allowing for a passage between the Herrengasse and the Freyung in the form of a line of storefronts similar to the type of arcade shopping found in many European capitals.

The largest room in the complex was the floor of the stock exchange, built over two stories from the first floor upward and covered by an open roof framework based on the English style of hammer-beam-roofs. This form of open wooden roof framework can also be found in the booking halls of early British railroad stations. The trading floor of the stock exchange was reached via the court of the stock exchange with its main staircase. This court, as well as the bazaar and the hexagonal area, were covered by a glass roof, demonstrating Ferstel's enthusiasm for architectural innovations.

Whilst the construction of the glass roof and open roof framework establish a link to Great Britain as the mother-country of Europe's Industrial Revolution, the design of the façades borrows from Florentine and Venetian architecture of the Trecento. This is a reminder of the former economic power of these Italian cities, but it was certainly also the result of Ferstel's own study trip through Italy.

The façades of the Ferstel palace are primarily indebted to a rather conservative understanding of architecture. The long wings extending toward the Herrengasse and the Strauchgasse are rhythmically structured through polygonal corner columns, with a balcony on consoles running above the

The Ferstel Palace

The architecture of arcades, symbolizing, with the same intensity as the railroad stations, the changing times that were being experienced in Milan, Naples, and Paris, did not find an echo in Vienna. This is all the more surprising since the *Durchhaus* (through-house) presents an architectural prototype for the passageway. Heinrich Ferstel's Bank and Stock Exchange (the Ferstel Palace), is the only tentative, yet representative variant of a passage. Ferstel's building, which connects the Freyung with the Herrengasse, was not primarily an arcade. It combined many different functions under one roof. It housed the offices of the Austro-Hungarian National Bank, which had commissioned the building, the stock exchange, a coffee house (Café Central), and an arcade of storefronts designed like a bazaar.

For Ferstel, even though he was only 27, this was his second major commission as he had previously worked on the Votivkirche. In using the irregular plot of land between the Freyung, the Herrengasse, and the Strauchgasse, Ferstel created a masterpiece which he was not able to match in his later buildings.

Heinrich Ferstel
Ferstel Palace, 1856-60
Hexagonal courtyard with
Donauweibchen Fountain by
Anton Dominik Fernkorn

ILLUSTRATION FACING PAGE:
Heinrich Ferstel
Ferstel Palace, 1856-60
Hall of the Stock Exchange
(top), heads on the consoles of
the balconies (bottom)

Heinrich Ferstel
Ferstel Palace in Herrengasse,
1856-60, Café Central

ground floor and strengthening the corner and sculptures mediating between the second and third floors. The narrow frontage overlooking the Freyung manages without the polygonal corner columns; the three huge arches of the entrance are reminiscent of the Loggia dei Lanzi in Florence.

Ferstel's choices for the façades stood very much in the tradition established in Vienna since the abolition of the Hofbaurat in 1848. The building materials he used, however, presented a clear break with tradition. The palace was not built in the rendered brickwork customary in Vienna, but rather in freestone.

The public interiors like the passage, the hexagonal court containing the Donauweibchen Fountain by Anton Dominik Fernkorn, and the floor of the stock exchange are basically roofed-in exteriors, their glass roofs and wall elevations in keeping with exterior façades. This can also be seen in the concourses and booking halls of railroad stations. The color scheme of the interior, as in the

Votivkirche, refers to the decoration of the Altlerchenfelder Kirche by Eduard van der Nüll, whilst also demonstrating Ferstel's familiarity with contemporary English interior decoration, such as the work of William Morris or Owen Jones.

The Bank and Stock Exchange building was the last representative building in the inner city before the development of the Ringstrasse. The Café Central is an institution which entered local history as a café frequented by intellectuals, though it only fulfilled this function once the Café Griensteidl closed in 1897. Here, Peter Altenberg, Arthur Schnitzler, Robert Musil, Sigmund Freud, and Karl Kraus, among others, took their daily *Kleinen Braunen* (milky coffee).

Vienna was relatively late in establishing the idea of the coffee house, which became widespread only during the Biedermeier period. The *Wiener Kaffeehaus* reached its heyday in the middle of the nineteenth century but was then copied beyond the borders of the Empire.

Architecture, 1848-1890

Theophil Hansen
Griechisch-Nichtunierte Kirche
on the Fleischmarkt, 1858-61.
Façade

The Griechisch-Nichtunierte Kirche

In 1858-61, Theophil Hansen constructed the building of the parish and school building for the Greek Orthodox community as an addition to the church Zur Heiligen Dreifaltigkeit, closing off the complex in the direction of Fleischmarkt. In the wake of Joseph's Edict of Toleration, the church had been built in 1786-89 by Peter Mollner in the form of an assembly room with three bays, covered by a barrel-arched roof. Due to the fact that the building was being used for non-Catholic worship, no religious symbols could be used on the façade. Mid-nineteenth century liberalism permitted a symmetrical façade with a tower, indicative of the building's function, although the church was still officially still an administrative building.

The church is built along five axes. Hansen chose to use a pseudo-Byzantine style and adorned the brick building with rich surface decoration. In the central axis, a huge round arch spreading over three stories frames a recess containing tracery windows. This tower-like substructure is covered by an octagonal drum, crowned with a dome. Two wings join up to the tower on both sides of it.

The Fünfhauser Pfarrkirche Maria vom Siege

Friedrich von Schmidt was the most important neo-Gothic architect working in Vienna. Apart from the Rathaus, he built a whole series of churches, the Fünfhauser Pfarrkirche being considered as the most important. He erected the brick church, which had originally been planned as an axial building, as a domed central building with two obliquely placed towers. Rising from a square floor plan, they are carefully transformed into octagons, with buttresses connecting them to the dome, whose structure is adapted to the shape of the towers. The number of pediments and pinnacles increases toward the top, with hardly any tracery in the windows.

Inside the church, eight clustered piers form a central space with a gallery and shallow side-chapels, and the choir also has a series of chapels. The nave is arched and covered with a rib-vault. The colored trim along the walls, the murals, and the furnishings provide an exceptionally complete example of neo-Gothic decoration.

Friedrich von Schmidt
Fünfhauser Pfarrkirche Maria
vom Siege on Mariahilfer Gürtel,
1867-9
Façade

ILLUSTRATION FACING PAGE:
Friedrich von Schmidt
Fünfhauser Pfarrkirche Maria
vom Siege on Mariahilfer Gürtel,
1867-9
Interior

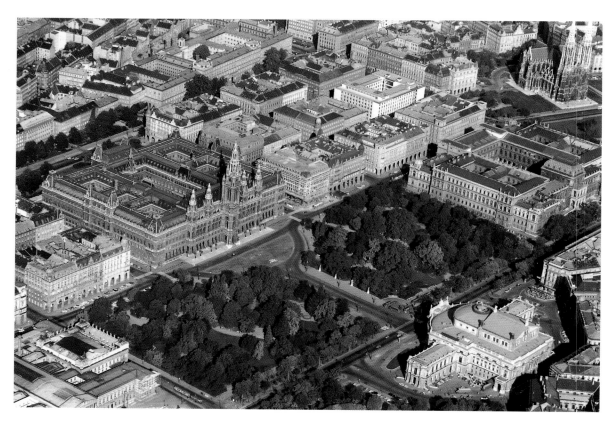

ILLUSTRATION OPPOSITE:
The Ringstrasse
Panorama with Neue Burg, seen
from the roof of the Parliament

The Ringstrasse
View from the Rathausplatz

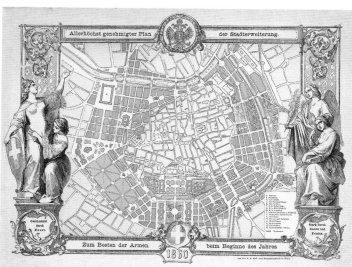

Approved plan for the extension of the city, 1860
Historisches Museum der Stadt Wien

The Ringstrasse shortly after completion with Court museums, the Epstein Palace, and the
Parliament, ca. 1890, Historisches Museum der Stadt Wien

The Ringstrasse

The construction of the Ringstrasse, which in fact meant the development of an entire new district, is one of the outstanding urban achievements of the nineteenth century. Boulevards replaced the ring-walls and their entrenchments as well as the glacis and parade-ground that had previously strangled the inner city and restricted its growth. These walls had long ago lost their strategic function — with the onslaught of Napoleon, at the latest — yet their symbolic power as a bastion, which had been capable of withstanding two sieges by the Turks, was considerable.

Discussions about the destruction of the ring-walls did not cease. The Imperial Family wanted to build a new Court opera house in the area of Kärntnertor, financed by the selling of building land in the former fortifications. In addition to the Imperial Family, it was mainly the wealthy bourgeoisie who aimed at the development of the glacis in the area of the textile district. Ludwig Förster, the architect and editor of the *Allgemeine Bauzeitung*, had already been commissioned to develop a regulation plan during the *Vormärz*, but the suppression of the 1848 Revolution created a backlash against such urban regeneration. During the following decade, the ring-walls were once more reinforced, although this time the fear was not of an external enemy, but of city's own population.

In late December 1857, Emperor Franz Joseph published a letter ordering the walls to be razed. A ring of forts was converted from military to civilian use. Architects and town-planners were now working on schemes for regulatory measures; they included Sicardsburg and van der Nüll, Ferstel, Förster, and Löhr. Since none of the plans was sufficiently convincing, a compromise, mainly modeled on Förster's ideas, was achieved.

The Ringstrasse was designed as a splendid boulevard with various avenues for strolling and horseback riding and with the Lastenstrasse for the transport of goods running parallel to it. Between the two, the land was divided into lots and the building plots were greatly sought after. In only one place was the original aim achieved — the integration of the inner city and suburbs. This was in the square between the Burg and Court stables that crosses the Ringstrasse. All the further line-of-sight open spaces, such as the Rathausplatz and the Schwarzenbergplatz, are based on subsequent alterations to the plans.

The new program for the extension of the city had already been decided with the laying of foundations for the Votivkirche in 1856. The starting point for development was the new Opera building in 1861; most of the work to the great boulevards was only completed in 1870.

The construction of the buildings continued well into the twentieth century. The public buildings are centered around the Burg, and extend into the Neue Burg and the court museums. The parliament, the Rathaus, the university, and the Burgtheater were grouped together around a rectangular square. The main façades did not face the Rathausplatz, as expected, but overlooked the Ringstrasse. Further monumental buildings, including the Musikverein (Musical Association), the Museum für Angewandte Künste (Museum of Applied Arts), the Akademie für Bildende Künste (Academy of Fine Arts) and the Stock Exchange, were situated along the boulevard. The spaces in between were occupied by the mansions of the wealthy bourgeoisie and elegant apartment buildings, accommodating the "Ringstrasse society." As an incentive, members of the Imperial Family were the first to build on the Ring (Deutschmeister Palace, Württemberg Palace, Ludwig Viktor Palace). The industrial and moneyed aristocracy fulfilled their expectations, thus making the *Zinspalais* (rented palace) the main type of building in the last third of the century.

ILLUSTRATIONS OPPOSITE:
August Sicardsburg, Eduard van der Nüll
Staatsoper, 1961-9
Staircase (top)
Tea Room (bottom left)
Foyer (bottom right)

August Sicardsburg, Eduard van der Nüll
Staatsoper, 1861-69
Main façade

The Staatsoper

Vienna's state opera house was constructed by August Sicardsburg and Eduard van der Nüll between 1861 and 1869 as a Court opera theater. It was the first monumental building on the Ringstrasse besides the Votivkirche. There had been plans for a new opera house from the very beginning of the century, and since then the search for a suitable site had concentrated on the area of Kärntnertor, but the military could not be persuaded to give up part of their entrenchment. As soon as the area was converted from military to civilian property, however, the planning began.

Sicardsburg and van der Nüll combined an auditorium and proscenium under one enormous roof. They softened the impact of the huge longitudinal rectangular block by adding two and three story annexes on the sides and facing the

August Sicardsburg, Eduard van der Nüll
Staatsoper, 1961-9
Marble Hall, after 1945

Ring. The building faces the Ring, the frontage consisting of a two-story loggia, the lower floor creating a covered approach with the roof serving as a terrace. The entrances to the grand staircase and the foyers are in this part of the building. The adjoining two-story wings contain the lobbies and run right through to the center of the main block. Here and at the end of the building, three-story "transepts" are offset from the central block. Those at the front again have staircases, the ones at the back and the connecting tracts, which provide space for the administrative offices. The architecture of the interior is complemented by statues and figurative paintings throughout. The frescoes by Moritz von Schwind are the best known.

The opera house building was by no means universally popular after its completion. Sicardsburg and van der Nüll were certainly in great demand as architects throughout Viennese society, the opera house marking the high point of their work. Stylistically though, the building belonged to a former era that had ended as soon as the first spade turned the soil to make the Ringstrasse. This fact had extremely serious consequences for the successful architectural team. Van der Nüll committed suicide in reaction to the harsh criticism and Sicardsburg died shortly after.

The State Opera House was badly damaged by bombing in 1945, although the grand staircase, the foyer facing the Ring, and the tea-room were not destroyed. The interior was completely renovated after World War II.

Architecture, 1848-1990

Theophil Hansen
The Parliament, 1874-83
Façade facing the Ringstrasse

Theophil Hansen
The Parliament, 1874-83
Hall of Columns ("Atrium")

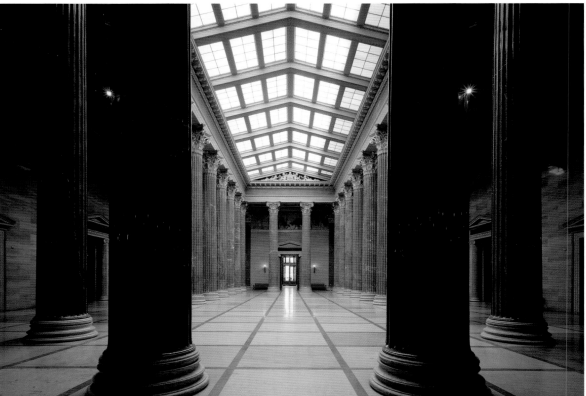

The Parliament

Initially, there was disagreement over a suitable site for the Austrian parliament building that combines the *Herrenhaus* (Upper Chamber) and the *Abgeordnetenhaus* (Lower Chamber). Originally, two separate buildings were planned. The Upper Chamber was to be on the site of today's Justizpalast (Law Courts), the Lower House on Schillerplatz. Finally, the old parade-ground, released for development by the Emperor in 1870, was chosen as the site for the Parliament of the young Austrian government. The Rathaus (town hall, built by Friedrich Schmidt) and the university (by Heinrich Ferstel) were to share the site. In 1865, Theophil Hansen had entered a new design in a competition and in 1869 it was decided to accommodate both Houses in one building for reasons of economy. Hansen was commissioned to work on his design. The final location was decided in collaboration with Schmidt and Ferstel.

Hansen's building shows a transverse rectangular floor plan with an interior division symmetrical to both the transverse and the main axes. Like the Rathaus and the university, which were also built on the former parade-ground, the main façade faces the Ringstrasse rather than the Rathausplatz. The main axis with its enormous hall of columns — the atrium — separates the two Chambers and is the focal point of the building. In the elevation, the compact form of the floor plan is revealed as a masterly interlocking structure of different features.

The restriction to two stories is striking, the ground floor being interpreted as a pedestal, on which the committee rooms and administration offices were accommodated. The main floor, consisting of the plenum and assembly rooms, is reached from a curved access ramp at the front of the building. A grand flight of steps completes the official approach. It is used to conceal the entrances to the administrative areas on the ground floor as well as the central axes of the lateral façades. The whole complex seems a little like an accumulation of various architectural references, combined into a single display area, the ground floor.

Ancient Greece — the first ever democracy — provided the architectural shell for this parliament building, which was then given Palladian detailing. The high point of the majestic façade is the central temple frontage with its monumental colonnade and the triangular pediment above. The temple theme is repeated on a smaller scale at the ends of this section. The extended five-section, two-story complex echoes Palladio's villas in Maser and Emo.

The two building blocks of the Lower and Upper Chambers rise behind this section,

Theophil Hansen
Parliament, 1874-83
Detail of approach

finishing at the top with a balustrade containing sculpted figures. Undeniably, architecture dominates sculpture, pushing it into the background. Figurative sculpture is mainly to be found on the building blocks of the two chambers, crowned by four quadrigas on bases with reliefs. The attica figures, rising freely against the sky, break up the austere and monumental silhouette of the building and soften its impact. Hansen also designed a colored frame for the exterior, although this was never realized.

From the approach and the central colonnade, one enters an enormous hall of columns lit by a skylight. This atrium was not planned in the original brief and was highly controversial at first, but for Hansen it constituted the artistic focus of the building. The cross-section of the atrium is dominated by the enormous temple-style frontage, an allusion to the great achievements of the bourgeoisie in this "temple of parliamentarism." This is equally emphasized in the theme of the gable relief which is supposed to represent the granting of the Constitution by the Emperor.

Theophil Hansen
Parliament, 1874-83
Staircase (top)
Session hall of Lower House
(right)

The two chambers of the parliament are designed as amphitheatres. Here again, there seems to be a reference to one of Palladio's buildings, the Teatro Olimpico in Vicenza, also designed as a theatre-in-the-round, the stage being the permanent architectural construction. In the Viennese parliament, presidency and government are acted out in an architecture consisting of façades formed by half-columns, pilasters, blind windows, massive doors with frontons, and monumental triangular pediments.

Hansen manages to combine painting, sculpture, and architecture, while according overall priority to the architecture. Colossal columns rhythmically structure a smooth, marble-clad wall, punctuated by recesses which are filled with pseudo-antique statuary on high pedestals. Above them, under the architrave, there are murals by Christian Griepenkerl (Herrenhaus) and August Eisenmenger (Abgeordnetenhaus).

The chamber is lit by a skylight, as is the atrium. In the case of the atrium, this is the only natural light, but there are unobtrusive windows in the chamber on three stories.

The Rathaus

Like the Parliament, the Rathaus (City Hall) was also planned originally on a different site, namely the Parkring between Weihburggasse and Johannesgasse. Today's location is a result of the availability of the military parade-ground for development after 1870.

Friedrich Schmidt emerged victorious from the competition. He had already submitted Gothic designs in architectural competitions for town hall buildings in Trier and Berlin. Gothic structures were meant to recall the great bourgeois tradition of Flemish town hall buildings, whose belfries had become an urban landmark in the Middle Ages.

The floor plan of the Rathaus is a slightly transverse rectangle, enclosed by four wings. Two sections parallel to the narrowest side of the main block and four smaller connecting sections structure the area into seven courtyards, the central courtyard being designed as a cloister. From here, there is access to the reception rooms which are aligned along the central axis. From the first floor upward, in the direction of Rathausplatz, the great banqueting hall is several stories high. It is accessed via two monumental staircases, roofed over by rib-vaults, as are all the other arcades. At the back of the Rathaus, on the Lastenstrasse side, the council chamber breaks through the façade in the form of an avant-corps. The polygonal "apse" leading to the arcaded courtyard was originally intended to end in a chapel, but this plan was abandoned due to budgetary constraints.

The central façades of the upper four stories are connected through the clever placing of

Friedrich von Schmidt
Rathaus, 1872-83
Festival hall

windows, the tracery accentuating the first floor. On the upper storey, a triforium window is attributed to each row of windows, the axes being determined by the column arcades of the ground floor. Mouldings and cornices stress the horizontal orientation of the building.

The frontage facing the Rathausplatz is the main façade. It is accentuated by the three towers in the banqueting hall section which protrudes from the façade. The wall is perforated by pointed arches, tracery, moldings, arcades, and galleries, creating a visual screen overlooking the Rathausplatz. This is further emphasized through the lateral displacement of the entrances to the building. The design of the walls as well as the integration of sculpture in the form of column figures, reliefs, and capitals reveal Schmidt's contribution to the rebuilding of the Cologne cathedral. Unlike in Hansen's Parliament, these elements are not additions to the architecture, but constitute an organic element of it.

Friedrich von Schmidt
Rathaus, 1872-83
Staircase

The University

Heinrich Ferstel's second monumental building after the Votivkirche was the new university building, which closes off the former parade-ground (now Rathausplatz) on the north side.

The main façade, with its system of strongly projecting and receding pavilions, as well as an entrance portal, covered by a curving roof, faces toward the Ring, whereas the lateral façades with their essentially compact flat walls, face the Rathausplatz and the Universitätsstrasse. The weighty building mass of this essentially three-story complex is thus softened in the direction of Ringstrasse, creating the appearance of a two- story structure above a monumental, rusticated ground floor.

In some respects, the layout of the building is similar to Hansen's Parliament, with Ferstel referring as much to forms of the Italian Renaissance as to the recently completed new extension of the Louvre in Paris. The building task was of unprecedented complexity since the brief was to accommodate four faculties, the library and lecture halls, reception rooms, and a splendid great hall, the administrative offices, as well as providing living quarters.

The ground plan of the University is based on the courtyard system with a large, cloister-like central court around which the rooms are grouped. In total, there are four smaller court-yards in the lateral wings, surrounded by the lecture rooms. The artistic high point of the elevation is the courtyard. Ferstel here uses elements from the Palazzo Farnese, but has increased the dimensions. On the first two

Heinrich Ferstel
University, 1873-84

Staircase (left)
View of the façade (bottom left)
Late nineteenth-century
painting (bottom right), Historisches Museum der Stadt Wien.

floors, the three-story wall elevation consists of arcades, although the first story is windowed. The upper floor has rectangular windows with straight architraves. Heavy moldings separate the floors, the axes being split by fairly plain, rectangular half-columns.

The façade facing the Ringstrasse presents a very different character. Additional interplay of avant-corps, pavilions, and domes creates a lively frontage, which the eye would have difficulty in taking in all at once, but which requires the spectator to walk slowly past. The façade overlooking the Ringstrasse is bounded on both sides by projecting two-story pavilions, their corners stressed by avant-corps and small domes. The domed central avant-corps projects clearly from the the building, yet remains well behind the line of the pavilions. A two-story loggia topped by a pediment marks the main entrance, which is flanked by two curved approaches. The interior is dominated by the enormous staircases leading to the banqueting halls on the Ringstrasse side and there is a library at the back.

The proximity of the Votivkirche to the university is significant for the choice of building style. In the 1850s, Sicardsburg and van der Nüll had proposed a neo-Gothic design for a new university building on the Josephstadt glacis just behind the Votivkirche. Ferstel had objected to this project, fearing two monumental neo-Gothic buildings so close to each other. Instead, he offered his neo-Renaissance design.

Both designs, however, offered space only for the function rooms and administration offices. All the remaining facilities would have had to be accommodated in separate buildings, in the same way that Ferstel planned the chemistry faculty he had built on Währingerstrasse. When the parade-ground was finally released for development in 1870, a new site was chosen, located in the same area as the Parliament, Rathaus, and Burgtheater, with the aim of uniting all university facilities under one roof.

Heinrich Ferstel
University, 1873-84
Arcades of inner court

The Burgtheater and scenery repository

The Burgtheater was originally built as the Court theater, replacing the existing building on Michaelerplatz which had to make room for the new uniform façade of the Hofburg.

Karl Hasenauer and Gottfried Semper collaborated on the new theater, the main design of which originated with Semper, Hasenauer originally only overseeing the decoration of the building, as well as the flat central avant-corps and the lyre-shaped auditorium.

Semper began his plans in 1869, originally aiming at an independent solution, conceiving the theater in connection with the imperial forum planned by himself and Hasenauer. During the planning, however, a free-standing design prevailed, one which bore strong similarities with other buildings by Semper, namely the second Court Theater in Dresden as well as the design for a Richard Wagner festival hall in Munich, produced in the mid-1860s. The concept of the banqueting hall is emphasized by the widely extending wings containing stairways leading to the boxes. These counterbalance the broad façade of the Vienna Rathaus opposite.

The auditorium, conceived by Hasenauer in courtly tradition as a theater with private boxes, is topped externally with a dome, contrasting with the saddleback roof of the proscenium. The foyers of the theater surround the circular auditorium like a ring on two stories. Both floors are connected by colossal pilasters on high pedestals, topped by a balustrade.

The floor plan, in the form of a lyre, and the exceptional height of the auditorium attracted much criticism, forcing alterations to be carried out as early as 1897 by the architect Emil von Förster.

In 1872, Semper also built the scenery repository for the Hoftheater (Court Theatre) which stands in the Lehargasse. This austere brick building, almost bleak in comparison with the neo-baroque decorative excesses of the Burgtheater, was to be Semper's only utilitarian building in Vienna. It is impressive in the clarity of its four-story façade, structured by the rusticated corners, round-arch windows, and horizontal moldings. Monumentality here is not achieved through luxurious decoration, colossal pilasters, or an exposed site, but rather through the overall proportions of the building.

The irregularly-shaped site also required an ingenious solution for the design of the floor plan. Various walkways for the storage of theater sets branch off from a space. Cast iron was systematically used for the design of the interior, especially the construction of the internal galleries and staircases.

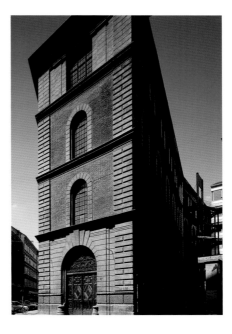

Gottfried Semper
Flats and scenery depot of the Hoftheater, 1872-7
Façade

Gottfried Semper
Flats and scenery depot of the Hoftheater, 1872-7
Interior

Kunsthistorisches Museum and Natural History Museum

Since 1858, when the plan to extend the city was first mooted, the construction of museum and gallery buildings for the various collections belonging to the Imperial Family were an important part of the project. The plans took on a more precise form when in 1864, it was decided to create two identical museum buildings in front of the Hofburg. By 1867, four projects by the architects Heinrich Ferstel, Moritz Löhr, Karl von Hasenauer, and Theophil Hansen had been submitted to the building commission. Ferstel and Hansen's proposal ignored the requirement for two separate buildings and was consequently not considered

further by the commission. The projects by Löhrs and Hasenauer did not find unanimous support either, so both were asked to re-work their plans and resubmit them. Even the subsequent alterations did not lead to a clear-cut result, however, until finally it was agreed to ask the most famous German architect of the day, Gottfried Semper, to examine the projects. In the end, Semper himself was commissioned to plan the Court museums and chose Hasenauer, who was renowned for his decoration, as his collaborator.

In 1869, Semper submitted a proposal which integrated the museums into an extensive enlargement of the Hofburg as a new imperial forum. He planned a building in front of the

Leopoldine building in the Burg, with two wings joining up toward the Ring. The Hofburgtheater was then built overlooking the Volksgarten.

The two museums were to be built on the other side of the Ring in alignment with the new wings of the Hof, and were to be connected through a triumphal arch or buildings pierced by an arch to become a uniform forum. Ultimately, the only features of the original proposal which was adopted were the Neue Burg (1881), the two Court museums and the Burgtheater, though the theater was built on a different site. Permission for the building of the museums was given in 1870, work on the exterior being completed in 1880, but the interior decorations were not finished until 1891. The first halls were opened to the general public two years before completion.

Two rectangular buildings surrounding two courtyards, were built based on Semper's design. Since the complexes are largely identical, only one of them, the Kunsthistorische Museum needs to be discussed here, especially as its interior decoration is renowned.

The elongated façade is structured through a central avant-corps, and this feature is repeated in the corners. The domes over the central avant-corps are the high point, with four small tabernacle-like corner domes surrounding the octagonal central dome. Unusually, Semper did not place the dome over the staircase, but brought it forward onto the main façade, placing it over the entrance hall, making the building seem less deep than it actually is.

The façade is split in two by a frieze running between the ground and second floors. The walls at ground floor level are rusticated and lined with pilasters. There are flat rectangular windows in the ground floor and round-arch windows in the raised ground floor, whereas the upper story is emphasized with round-arch windows (the gallery of paintings) and flat rectangular windows in the mezzanine, thus inverting the design of the ground floor. The axes are divided by three-quarter Ionic columns, and a gallery with a balustrade conceals the roof. In the area of the avant-corps, the roof is raised, and adorned with alternating statues of artists, painters and sculptors, the central dome being crowned by a figure of Pallas Athene.

Semper withdrew from the direction of building work in 1876 after repeated quarrels with the ambitious Hasenauer, leaving Hasenauer free to leave his imprint on the interior design. He commissioned the two brothers Klimt as well as Franz von Matsch, Hans Caron, and Michael Munkácsy to create the painted decorations, and designed the ornamental and figurative sculptures himself.

The halls containing the exhibits on the raised ground floor were decorated with ceiling paintings bearing a direct relation to the items on show in the respective rooms. The directors and curators of the collections, who had been

Gottfried Semper, Karl von Hasenauer
Natural History Museum, 1871-91, exhibition hall

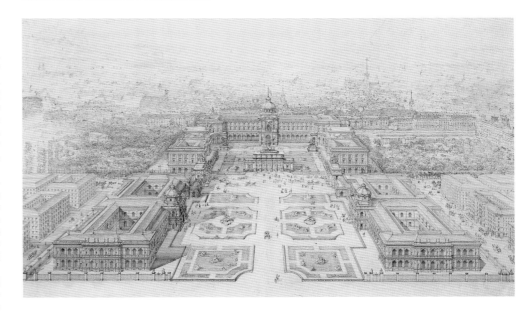

Gottfried Semper, Karl von Hasenauer
Plan for extension of the Hofburg, 1869, Haus-, Hof- und Staatsarchiv Wien

Gottfried Semper, Karl von
Hasenauer
Kunsthistorisches Museum,
1871-91
Staircase with Canova's sculpture
of Theseus (left)
Domed hall (opposite)

Gottfried Semper, Karl von Hasenauer
Kunsthistorisches Museum, 1871-91
View from ground floor into main dome

working on the layout of the rooms since 1885, and the resulting display was exclusively responsible for the historical themes of the images. The raised ground floor contained Egyptian antiquities as well as antiques, weapons, and European arts and crafts from the Middle Ages to modern times.

The gallery of paintings, the nucleus of the collection, was accommodated on the first floor. Here, ceiling paintings were replaced by a system of decoration which was structured by stucco and highlighted with gilding. A direct confrontation between contemporary Viennese historical painting and the historical painting collection was thus avoided.

The high point of architecture and decoration of the Kunsthistorische Museum is the domed hall with an entrance hall below and the monumental

staircase, which was conceived as an apotheosis of Imperial Family and Monarchy. There are obvious parallels to the entrance hall in Hansen's Heeresgeschichtliches Museum in the Arsenal. In both museums, the entrance hall is topped by a circular shallow dome with an opening in the center affording a view into the main dome. From the hall, stairs on the right and the left lead into the exhibition halls. Opposite the entrance, the monumental main staircase of white Carrara marble leads into the domed hall and the painting gallery. It begins as one stairway ascending straight to Canova's sculpture of Theseus, where it divides into two stairways leading to the hall of fame, where, under the prominent dome visible from afar, the most important collectors of the House of Austria are united in an Austrian Pantheon.

Academy of Fine Art

A new academy of fine art became a possibility as soon as the military parade-ground in the Josephstadt was released for development in 1868, enabling the Rathaus, university, and Parliament to be built. Originally, the present site of the Academy had been planned for the Parliament, but the decision to relocate the Parliament to the parade-ground released the plot on the Schillerplatz for the Academy.

Theophil Hansen provided the designs for both Parliament and Academy. Although he had to enter a competition for the design of the Parliament, he was commissioned directly for this second state building. After altering his plans numerous times, in 1872 Hansen settled on an elongated rectangular structure with an inner courtyard. This courtyard is divided in two along the central axis by the mass of the great hall.

The Academy is set back from the Ringstrasse by a small square. The two lower stories of its façades are combined into a base, pierced at floor level by a number of large, round-arch windows and above by as many small mezzanine windows. These are surmounted by two identically designed floors with pilasters and round arches. The round arches are alternately glazed as windows or used as niches in which to display sculptures. The corners are stressed as avant-corps with finishing attica. Through differentiated coloring and the use of judiciously placed gilding, Hansen stressed the strong layering of the wall structure and reproduces his ideas on antique polychrome painting.

The great hall, which originally was also part of the plaster cast museum, is the most splendidly decorated room in the academy. Like the Golden Hall of the Musikverein, it is based on the scheme of a basilica, in which the elevated central hall is separated from

Theophil Hansen
Akademie der Bildenden Künste,
1872-5
Façade toward Schillerplatz

the "side-aisle" running around behind Tuscan columns. The level of the hall is three steps lower than the ambulatory; these steps are interspersed between the bases of the columns.

The central space of the hall was originally intended to be used mainly as a banqueting hall, whilst the ambulatory was considered part of the museum. The architrave carries a frieze with moldings from the frieze in the Parthenon, integrating one of the most precious objects of the museum into the architectural context. The large central painting depicts the Fall of the Titans (ill. p.235) by Anselm Feuerbach, who was appointed lecturer in historical painting at the Viennese Academy in spring, 1873.

ILLUSTRATION OPPOSITE:
Ludwig Förster, Theophil Hansen
Todesco Palace on Kärtnerstrasse, 1861-4
Festival Hall (top)
Dining Room (bottom left)
Detail of coffered ceiling in banqueting hall (bottom right)

Ludwig Förster, Theophil Hansen
Todesco Palace on Kärtnerstrasse, 1861-4
Façade

The Todesco Palace

Between 1861-64, Ludwig Förster and Theophil Hansen built one of the first of the typical "rent palaces" of the Ringstrasse, on Kärtnerstrasse opposite the Opera. The term *Zinspalais* covered the whole spectrum of luxurious living, ranging from apartment blocks containing a multitude of anonymous tenants, to mansions for the wealthy and the nobility.

Todesco, who commissioned the mansion, was one of the "barons"of the Ringstrasse. It is a rectangular building arranged around a central light well, with a five-story façade, divided by moldings free of pilasters or columns. The second floor is defined as a piano nobile by bay windows at each corner. Each of the four central windows is balconied and there is elegant detailing. The building was not entirely the private domain of the Todesco family; there were storefronts on the ground floor and rented apartments on the upper floors, the proceeds from which were to finance the building.

The apartments of the Todesco family occupied the entire second floor. The "public" rooms, including a banqueting-room or ballroom and a dining-room, were located behind the balcony overlooking the Kärntnerstrasse. The dimensions of the rooms were smaller than the respective spaces in traditional palaces, yet emulated them in every possible way. In the private rooms, a careful distinction was made between those used by men and those used by women.

The banqueting-hall, at right-angles to Kärntnergasse, contained dark red pilasters contrasting with the pale walls and window frames. Gilded composite capitals and bas-reliefs against a black background top the walls at ceiling height. The coffered ceiling is filled with ornamental reliefs and mythological paintings by Carl Rahl and Gustav Gaul. An annexe, separated from the main room by two pairs of columns, leads to the dining-room and served as a platform for the orchestra during concerts and for seating spectators when the room was used for dancing.

ILLUSTRATION OPPOSITE:
Josef Langl
Vienna at the time of the World's
Fair 1873 (exhibition building in
the foreground)
Oil on canvas, 37 x 52 in
(92 x 131 cm), Historisches
Museum der Stadt Wien

Visitors to the World's Fair on
the roof of the Rotunda, 1873
Österreichische Nationalbibliothek

John Scott-Russel, Karl von
Hasenauer, Wilhelm Engerth
Rotunda on the site of the
World's Fair 1873, burnt in 1937

Architecture, 1848-1890

The Vienna World's Fair 1873

The first World's Fair to be held in a German-speaking country took place on the site of the Viennese Prater between May 1 and November 2, 1873. It was the fifth World's Fair in total and surpassed the preceding fairs, which had been held in London (1851, 1862) and Paris (1855, 1867) many times in terms of size. The 600-acre (250-hectare) site was bigger than all those of the previous fairs put together.

World's Fairs were gigantic displays of technological, commercial, intellectual, and artistic achievement, and Vienna's included for the first time, representations of the Middle and Far East. Treasures of Islamic art as well as artistic and industrial products from Japan and China triggered off a boom in goods from the Orient.

The exhibition architecture also set new standards. Crystal Palace had been a sensation in London in 1851, and the Eiffel Tower and the engine hall on the Champ de Mars in Paris in 1889 attested to the brilliance of the civil engineers.

The Vienna World's Fair also impressed the world with its architecture, particularly the enormous rotunda in the center of the exhibition park. Unfortunately, this structure, whose unprecedented span caused astonishment, burned down in 1937. The exhibition halls joined up in a herringbone pattern on both sides, over a length of more than 3,000 feet (900 metres). An engine hall, an agricultural hall, an art hall, a World's Fair railroad station, and a multitude of smaller pavilions completed the exhibition park.

The English industrialist and ship engineer John Scott-Russel was appointed to construct the rotunda, yet his calculations proved to be incorrect and this forced the World's Fair architect Karl von Hasenauer and chief engineer Wilhelm Engerth to make extensive alterations. Once it was completed, Vienna was the site of the world's largest domed structure, with a span of over 360 feet (108 metres) and a height of 280 feet (84 meters). The conical building was topped by two superimposed lanterns, each carrying an Austrian imperial crown 60 feet (18 meters) high. In the interior, the main attraction consisted of a hydraulic elevator transporting visitors to a gallery from whence they could ascend onto the roof and walk up to the crown.

However, the World's Fair also made the headlines in a negative sense. A week after the ceremonial opening, the Austrian stock market collapsed, ending the feverish speculation which had spread in anticipation of the Fair and leading to the liquidation of numerous companies. Furthermore, a cholera epidemic caused the expected visitors to avoid Vienna during the first months, and the numbers of visitors did not reach expectations until that September, when the difficulties had been overcome.

Architecture, 1848-1890

The Musikverein

The building of the Musikverein (Musical Association), constructed in 1866-69, contained Vienna's first purpose-built concert halls. There was a small chamber music hall for 500 spectators and a large concert hall for 2,000 spectators and 500 musicians. Previously, large-scale choral and orchestral concerts could only be held in the big Redouten-saal (ballroom) of the Hofburg, in the Winterre-itschule (ill. p. 95) or in the theaters. The building was also designed to accommodate the Academy of Music, which had been founded in 1812.

The Musikverein was built by the Friends of Music of the Austrian Empire Association, who were given the building plot opposite the business school on the Karlsplatz by the Emperor in 1863. The architect Theophil Hansen emerged as the winner in a competition held in 1864. Hansen nevertheless had to significantly re-work and alter his competition project right until the very beginning of the works, which was finally constructed in Greek Revival style.

The floor plan forms a transverse rectangle, broken in the center by the hall section. The large concert hall pierces the main block of the building by its height as well as its protrusion into the façade. The building consequently looks like a basilica. The central avant-corps has three arcade arches, opening onto the entrance on the ground floor and onto a loggia on the first floor.

The concert halls are located on the first floor. The larger Golden Hall occupies three floors over the entire width of the central avant-corps, the lowest of which is divided by caryatids. Above the caryatids, in the central story, there are tall doors with triangular pediments topped by sculptured figures. The top story is dominated by a series of round-arch windows. The building was altered significantly in 1911. For example, the caryatids in the main hall were pushed back against the wall so that the balcony now projects freely into the space, as in the Brahms Hall, improving the view from the boxes, but also distorting the spatial impression intended by Hansen.

Theophil Hansen
Musikverein, 1866-9
Main façade

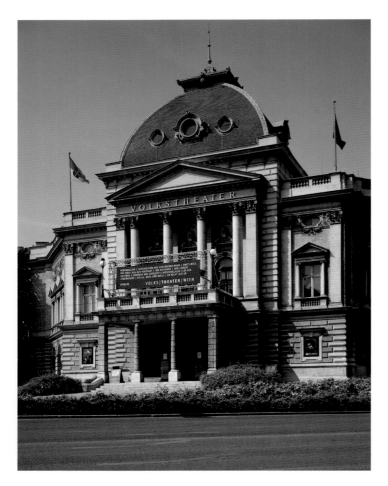

The Architectural Practice of Fellner & Helmer

The architectural practice of Ferdinand Fellner and Hermann Gottlieb Helmer became one of the most significant "theater builders" in Europe in the last quarter of the nineteenth century. Under their direction, nearly fifty theaters and concert halls came into being, from Hamburg to Zürich and from Wiesbaden to Sofia.

In 1888-89, the firm built the Deutsches Volkstheater to replace the Stadttheater, which had been gutted by fire in 1884. Fellner's involvement in this was not only that of an architect; he was also active as a founding member, and later President, of the *Volkstheater Verein* (Pople's Theater Society). This undoubtedly facilitated the rapid expansion of the theater, as by 1911 a new backstage area had been built and a large foyer added. The entrance façade with the pediment and cupola of the old foyer was destroyed in 1944 and replaced by a simpler version.

Throughout the building, which was erected at an angle to the crossroads, each section — front of the house, auditorium and stage — is clearly separated from the other; each has its own over-arching cupola. The vaulted roof of the auditorium is lower than the lofty cupolas of the stage and the foyer. This latter is in the form of a pavilion with a cupola, a columned portico and a passage underneath projecting toward the inner city. Notable features are the diagonal walls which connect this projection to the auditorium; these owe their existence to the fact that the staircases are set at an angle. Inside the auditorium, there is a combination of tiered seats and boxes, the boxes being restricted to the extended proscenium area; at the rear, the two deep circles rise up above the stalls.

Ferdinand Fellner, Hermann Gottlieb Helmer
Volkstheater in the Neustiftgasse
1888-89.
Main façade (left).
Auditorium (opposite).

ILLUSTRATION FAR LEFT:
Ferdinand Fellner, Hermann Gottlieb Helmer
Volkstheater, 1888-89
New foyer, 1907-08

LEFT:
Ferdinand Fellner, Hermann Gottlieb Helmer
Sturany House at the Schottenring
1874, façade

One of the reasons why Helmer and Fellner gained such renonwn as theatrical architects were their alterations to the shape of the auditorium. Departing from the design of the court theater, with its boxes and four tiers in a steeply-raked auditorium, they preferred to have only two tiers extending a long way forward in the direction of the stage. By extending the auditorium into a deep hall in this way, they not only increased seating capacity and improved the view, but also enhanced security. With an audience capacity of 1,900, the Volkstheater is among one of the largest of all the live theaters in the world.

Fellner and Helmer also built houses. One of their most impressive examples of these was begun in 1874, at 21, Schottenring on the Ringstrasse. It was designed for the court architect, Johann Sturany, and his wife Barbara. Seven axial lines can be counted behind the façade, which covers four stories of almost equal height. The emphasis of the central axis, animated by an oriel window supported by two Atlanta figures and extending over two floors, gives the building a consistency seldom encountered in Vienna.

Elsewhere, the linear alignment of the windows, the stringed courses, and moldings are again repeatedly interrupted by the lively outlines of the window-frames. Balustrades and balcony railings mark out the first floor as the piano nobile and give the façade its sweeping Baroque appearance. The pilasters of the upper floor, which mark off the various axial lines, are ironically fractured by the cartouches on which they stand, taking this design element to almost ridiculous lengths.

The Sturany House is a purely residential building, not an apartment house, unlike many other buildings on the Ringstrasse. Inside, sweeping lines and stucco decorations predominate, most impressively in the staircase, whose vaulted ceiling is covered by stucco putti and tendrils. The central room of the piano nobile, facing the courtyard, employs heavily framed doorways and a ceiling with exposed beams, although in both instances, plaster has been substituted for wood. The mirror-frames and fireplaces are inspired by the fantastic and sinuous forms encountered in the window-frames of the façade.

Andreas Streit
Palais Equitable at the Stock-im-
Eisen-Platz, 1890-91
Atrium (right)
Façade (below)

ILLUSTRATION OPPOSITE:
Andreas Streit
Palais Equitable at the
Stock-im-Eisen-Platz, 1890-91
Staircase

The Palais Equitable

In a certain sense, the Palais Equitable, with its late Historicist Neo-Baroque architecture, marks the end of the Ringstrasse style of architecture. This flourished not only along the Ringstrasse itself, but spread throughout the city. Its opulent monumentalism was succeeded by Otto Wagner's Art Nouveau buildings and the purist architecture of Adolf Loos.

At the end of the century, many architects constructed dwellings and commercial premises in the neo-Baroque style, inspired by the construction of the Michaelertrakt of the Hofburg in the 1880s. One such architect was Andreas Streit, who created the opulent headquarters of Equitable, the New York life insurance company, at the Stock-im-Eisen-Platz, with Saint Stephan's Cathedral as its immediate neighbor. The building was erected on an area of land which tapered to a point and comprised several older plots. The main façade is the narrow entrance frontage, the upper floors of which are linked by colossal columns. Above, the narrow front is crowned with a cupola, in front of which three massive bronze eagles spread their wings.

The entrance hall provides access to an imposing open main staircase; adjoining this, separated by three arches of an arcade, there is a square atrium, the walls and floor of which are completely covered with decorative tiles.

The Palm House at Schönbrunn

The glass and iron construction of the "glass palaces" was the innovative building technology of the nineteenth century. Glazed roofs now made it possible to build atria, railroad station concourses and passages lit by brilliant daylight, and — the ultimate expression of the style — greenhouses and exhibition halls.

The development of this type of building is closely associated with the name of the Englishman Joseph Paxton, who erected the Great Conservatory at Chatsworth between 1836 and 1840, and in 1844 began a palm-house for the Royal Botanical Gardens at Kew, near London. When the commission which these two buildings brought him was executed he rose to international fame. He was thus commissioned to build the Crystal Palace, constructed for the first international exhibition at London in 1851. The success of this gigantic glass exhibition hall led to

the construction of a number of glass palaces on the Continent, but few have survived, having met the same fate as the Crystal Palace itself.

The Palm House in the park of the Imperial summer residence of Schönbrunn at Vienna was constructed by Franz von Segenschmid and is one of the greatest glasshouses in the world. Its silhouette resembles those of its models at Chatworth and Kew Gardens, since it also has a long hall and vaulted roofs. In cross-section, the plan is that of a basilica, with a central elevated semicircular arch and two quarter-arches adjoining it laterally. The façade has the appearance of a building in five parts, whose central and corner pavilions are topped with cupolas. An outside gallery runs around the base of each cupola. Unlike its English counterparts, the Schönbrunn Palm House has an external iron supporting structure, the glass wall being suspended under the grid like a membrane from the inside.

Franz Xaver Segenschmid
Palm House at Schönbrunn
1879-82
General view

Gasometer in Simering, 1896-9,
interior.

The gasometer in Simmering

Gasometers count among the most typical architectural monuments of the Industrial Revolution and attest to a fundamental change in the cityscape. Originally, it was not so much the provision of gas to public and private buildings which radically changed daily life in the city, but rather the introduction of public street lighting

The four enormous gasometers, arranged in pairs, are the most striking buildings of Vienna's first municipal gasworks, built in 1896-9. The brickwork of the exterior walls indicates shapes familiar in utilitarian buildings since the mid-nineteenth century. Buttress-like elements divide the axes, which display a different shape of window on each of the four stories. A round-arch frieze and a kind of battlement created the finish below the dome.

The brick walls conceal the actual gas-holder, the so-called bell. This cover could be raised and lowered and the holder could thus contain a maximum of 300,000 cu. ft (90,000 m^3) of gas.

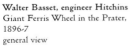
Walter Basset, engineer Hitchins
Giant Ferris Wheel in the Prater,
1896-7
general view

The Giant Ferris Wheel in the Prater

Originally, the Prater was an imperial hunting ground, opened to the general public by Kaiser Joseph II in 1766. Today, the most famous part is the Volksprater (so-called since the eighteenth century), an amusement park with inns, bowling-alleys, swings, and carousels. By far the largest part of the Prater though, is the enormous park, in which the World's Fair was held in 1873 and which later saw the building of race courses for trotting and flat-racing, a stadium, and a swimming pool.

The Prater was the "classical" leisure area of the late nineteenth century, providing entertainment for all strata of society.

The main avenue of the Prater, connecting the Praterstern with Canevale's summer-house built in 1782 (ill. p.145), was the place for strollers and loiterers and Sunday meetings for Vienna's high society, paralleled only by the Ringstrasse. There was an annual flower parade, and the Emperor's birthday was celebrated there as a public festival from August 17 through 28.

A large-scale leisure complex called "Venice in Vienna" was opened next to the Volksprater in 1895. The company, founded by Gabor Stein, offered gondola rides on artificial canals lined with the façades of Venetian palaces. Stein continuously extended the complex with new attractions and had the most prominent building in the Prater, the Giant Ferris Wheel, built in 1897. The wheel has since become a Viennese landmark.

The Giant Ferris Wheel was designed by the English engineer Walter Basset and his collaborator, an engineer named Hitchins. It was modeled on the sensational landmark of the 1883 World's Fair in Chicago. Like a giant bicycle wheel, 120 wire cables act as spokes connecting the axis to the external wheel. There were apparently some doubts about the construction, since it was very reluctantly and suspiciously granted permission to operate.

There are fifteen gondolas on the Giant Ferris Wheel today but originally, there were twice as many. Only every second gondola was replaced after it burned down in a fire in 1945.

Walter Basset, Engineer
Hitchins
Giant Ferris Wheel in the Prater,
1896-7
Construction
(pylon with suspension)

Sabine Grabner

Painting and Sculpture of the nineteenth Century 1780 – 1890

In the closing years of the eighteenth century, artists were increasingly turning away from the voluptuous raptures of form and color of the Baroque and Rococo styles and seeking instead to express themselves using neat, closed contours. Clear arrangement of the composition was the ultimate aim, and man and the human body became the focus of interest. Classical Greek and Roman works of art were revered as the ideal formal model, which is why this new style was labeled "Classicism." The style did not, however, derive purely from imitation or adoption of pre-existing stylistic models. It expressed the thinking of the age – a period of upheaval that sent shockwaves far and wide.

Familiar structures were crumbling. The French Revolution boosted the confidence of the populace and led to the collapse of the *ancien régime*; during the Enlightenment, philosophy — representing worldly wisdom — was hailed as the alternative to religion, and the church saw its influence gradually decline. Classicism was seen as a profane art which held up the world of gods and heroes as a sort of substitute religion and alternative to Christianity. Events which had previously been represented by imaginative allegories, apotheoses, and emblems were now portrayed at face value — historical facts were demanded, and subjects were chosen according to their potential to convey an ethical message.

Scientific and historical issues were favorite subjects of debate at that time. The scientific approach to art adopted by Johann Joachim Winckelmann reflected this preoccupation. This German archaeologist and art historian, who had lived in Rome since 1755, campaigned for the preservation of antiquities and managed to awaken public interest in ancient works of art through his numerous publications. The Eternal City soon became a magnet for artists and art-lovers (the "Italian Journey" by Johann Wolfgang von Goethe is a classic example), and was a major port of call on the Grand Tour, the essential educational tour of important European sights said to turn a callow youth into a man of the world. Winckelmann characterized the essence of Greek and Roman painting and sculpture as, "noble simplicity, quiet greatness," which also defines the esthetic ideal of the Classical period.

Rome was thus the birthplace of the new style. The decision of the Wiener Akademie der bildenden Künste [Viennese Academy of Fine Art] to promote the study of ancient works of art through its so-called Rome Scholarships and to keep the scholars within the institution once they had returned from Rome by employing them as teaching staff brought the institution an excellent reputation and attracted many foreign students to Vienna. However, it should be said that Classicism, in the form that had evolved in

Rome and matured in paintings such as those of the neo-classicist Jacques Louis David in France, was hardly represented in Viennese painting. The Baroque style with its indistinct contours and soft forms continued to prevail here until the turn of the century and beyond. Sculpture, by contrast, was better able to fulfill the Classical aims, as sculptors were able directly to adopt the Classical canons of form. However, having embarked on the path of Classicism, Viennese sculpture proved to be particularly resistant, later on, to the influence of changing styles.

At the dawn of the nineteenth century, Vienna served briefly as the center of the Romantic Movement, but the Movement did not catch on here. In 1809, Friedrich Schlegel — then in the diplomatic service of the emperor — and his circle of artistic acquaintances formed the Brotherhood of St. Luke, which concentrated primarily on religious subjects, but also began to develop a Romantic style of landscape painting. Although both strands had their roots in Vienna, it was in Rome and in the mountains of Salzkammergut and the Berchtesgaden region that they produced their best work.

A few years later, Realism began to make its mark on Viennese painting. Objectivity of representation evidently reflected the mood of the time in the imperial city better than the expression of emotional sensitivities. Since this style reached the height of its popularity during the Biedermeier period, art historians have termed this the age of "Biedermeier Realism." Although the term serves to place the style within a timeframe, it is an unfortunate choice of words since Biedermeier is associated first and foremost with the mentality of the people during that particular political era in Vienna, rather than with a specific style of artistic expression. It is just as inappropriate to apply the Biedermeier label to music, architecture, sculpture, or painting as it is to talk about "Biedermeier literature." These media each have to be considered in their international context. However, Viennese painters in the second quarter of the nineteenth century produced some clearly excellent works of art, especially in the field of landscape painting, which took nature as its one and only true model. In addition, portraits and genre scenes provide a fascinating insight into the life and domestic culture of this age. The focus on the bourgeois middle classes can be seen as a legacy of the French Revolution. Even Emperor Franz I regarded himself as merely the first citizen among many and commissioned a private painting of himself with his family.

The year of the revolution, 1848, marks the historical end of the Biedermeier era. The fundamental changes which led to the political, social, and cultural revolt of the third estate initially elicited little reaction in the art world.

Genre scenes remained extremely popular until well into the second half of the century, despite the superficiality of the subject matter, and portraits and landscapes in the "old style" continued to be in demand.

The decision by Emperor Franz Josef in 1857 to transform the imperial capital into a world-class city by the building of the Ringstrasse changed the whole mood of the city. The plan to build a huge boulevard lined with imposing public and private buildings on the site of the former glacis brought forth a wealth of ideas and inspired all spheres of art to new heights. Given the pronounced historical consciousness of the age, the idea was to bring together different architectural styles which would in each case provide a historical reference to the function of the building. The whole spectrum of artistic styles through the ages was paraded anew: Neo-Classicism, Neo-Gothic, Neo-Renaissance, Neo-Baroque, and Neo-Rococo followed in quick succession.

Historicism was flourishing. Scores of foreign artists including Anton Dominik Fernkorn, Hans Makart, Caspar von Zumbusch, and Anselm Feuerbach followed the call to Vienna to adorn the newly constructed edifices or erect monuments. Hans Canon and Moritz von Schwind were awarded commissions in their birthplace after several years absence in Germany. Domestic artistic

endeavor was given a significant boost by the new influences. In 1861, the Genossenschaft bildender Künstler Wiens – Künstlerhaus, an artists' union and artist's house, was founded as the official body to represent artists' interests. Along with the long-established Akademie der bildenden Künste, it was originally an important promoter of art, organizing prestigious exhibitions and other activities. But it soon began to place constraints on artistic practice by its bureaucratic organization and interfering ways. The required juxtaposition of styles also proved inhibiting. Historicism had reached the end of its days.

At the same time, an astonishing development was making itself felt in landscape painting. This genre, which had remained largely untouched by the various trends which had swept the city, began to model itself on French *plein air* (open air) painting and sought subjects in Hungary, Italy, France, and even the Orient. Many Austrian artists made their way to Paris, the pre-eminent artistic metropolis in the second half of the century, seen as the center of pioneering development in the field of art. Toward the end of the century, a small group of artists rebelled against the stifling traditionalism of Vienna, insisting that art be viewed in an international context. The foundation of the Vereinigung bildender Künstler Österreichs — The Secession, drew a final line under the past.

Hans Makart in historical festive costume.
Historisches Museum der Stadt Wien

Friedrich Heinrich Füger
Death of Germanicus, 1789
Oil on canvas, 62¾ x 88¾ in
(157 x 222 cm)
Österreichische Galerie Belvedere

Painting in the age of Classicism

History had pride of place in Classical painting, whose subjects, drawn mainly from ancient history or mythology, were chosen for their ability to convey the spirit of the Classical style. The intellectual demands of the subject matter of the paintings also lent a sense of importance to this school. However, the link with ancient art posed a particular problem in that the surviving examples were mainly in the form of three-dimensional objects. Artists sought to overcome this problem by turning to the works of the Renaissance for inspiration, and those of Raphael in particular. Anton Raphael Mengs, the first representative of the new style in Rome, who was much admired at the time and provided a reference for future generations of artists in the form of his theoretical writings, fully embraced this approach. Another key figure was Nicolas Poussin, who, as early as the seventeenth century, had developed a proto-Classical style based on mythological motifs.

One of the major works of Austrian Classical history painting is *The Death of Germanicus* by Friedrich Heinrich Füger. Füger was among the first students at the Wiener Akademie who were able, with the aid of travel grants, to spend several years in Rome to complete their general education. In 1783, Füger returned to the institution to take up the post of Professor of Historic Painting, and from 1795 to 1805 he served as director of the Academy, and did much to enhance its reputation.

The *Germanicus* painting, the work which gained him admission to the Academy, follows the compositional conventions which, since Poussin, had been considered compulsory for the portrayal of a dying hero. Germanicus lies bare-breasted on a bed surrounded by his grieving family. The painting depicts the moment when his friends swear to exact revenge for the poisoning to which the hero has succumbed. The picture, which conveys a moralizing message by alluding to ancient state virtues, evokes Jacques Louis David's *Oath of the Horatians* (1785) completed a few years earlier. Like David, Füger drew on a wide repertoire of gestures and facial expressions to reinforce the message of the painting. As far as the interplay of the figures is concerned, however, Füger pays more attention to the requirements of the painted medium than David, whose more statuesque figures remind one of three-dimensional stone sculptures. It was

ILLUSTRATION OPPOSITE
LEFT:
Johann Baptist Lampi the Elder
Countesses Caroline and Zoë
Thomatis, ca. 1790
Oil on canvas, 38½ x 31½ in
(98 x 80 cm)
Österreichische Galerie Belvedere

RIGHT:
Johann Peter Krafft
Franz Wessely, 1810
Oil on canvas, 24 x 18¾ in
(61 x 48 cm)
Österreichische Galerie Belvedere

precisely this aspect which marked the difference between Roman or French, and Austrian Classicism. The break with the past was less radical in Austria, where pictorial composition and technique continued to follow Baroque principles for many years.

The situation was similar in portraiture, where the spirit of innovation manifested itself initially in a change of content. The special interest in the human being that characterized the Enlightenment made it allowable to reproduce man's individuality (take, for example, the *Physiognomic Fragments for the Promotion of Human Understanding and Love* by Johann Kaspar Lavater) and consequently to release the portrayal of facial features and expressions from schematic conventions. Personal symbols and symbolic postures could also be dispensed with. The first portraits of this type had been produced in England by Sir Joshua Reynolds, George Romney, and Thomas Gainsborough and were regarded as epitomizing the tastes of the period. The main standard-bearers of this movement in Austria were Friedrich Heinrich Füger, Johann Baptist Lampi the Elder and the Younger, Barbara Krafft, Josef Grassi, and Josef Kreutzinger. The portrait of the two Polish Countesses, Caroline and Zoë Thomatis, by Johann Baptist Lampi the Elder is one of the most striking examples of Austrian portraiture in the closing stage of the eighteenth century. As the painting remained unfinished, the individual characterization of the women is all the more apparent. The faces are modeled with gentle shading and convey a sense of intelligence and humor. Their attitudes and clothes, by contrast, are only indicated with rapid brushstrokes.

The influence of the French style of portraiture developed by Jacques Louis David and François Gérard only became perceptible in Viennese painting after the turn of the century. The Hessen born painter Johann Peter Krafft can be regarded as an "ambassador" for the style. He had studied under David from 1802 through 1804, before settling in Vienna. His portrait of Franz Wessely, painted in 1810, which captures every minute detail of the face of the 77-year-old (the inscription on the bottom left reveals the age of the subject), anticipates the Realism style which was to emerge a decade later in the works of Ferdinand Georg Waldmüller.

Landscape painting, too, began to shake itself free of its Baroque past and to replace the Arcadian and idealized representations of nature as typified by the works of Claude Lorrain and Joseph Vernet with a realistic depiction of nature. The main impetus behind this new way of viewing nature came from Italy, and was closely associated with Jakob Philipp Hackert. As early as the 1770s, the German painter captured the landscape around Rome and Naples in paintings that attempted to mirror reality, and, as a result, he was highly acclaimed by his contemporaries. Michael Wutky, born in Krems on the Danube, who spent over a third of his life in this part of Italy, his prolonged visits starting in 1772, also showed himself to have been influenced by this new approach. The composition of his pictures still owed much to the Baroque tradition, and his choice of subject matter appears to have been determined by the Baroque desire for decorative effect. The motifs, however, were no longer figures of fantasy, but natural phenomena. In addition to the waterfalls of Tivoli and sea views by night, he liked to paint Vesuvius erupting with glowing lava flows (illustration on p. 220) and the atmospheric play of colors of the Solfatara in the Phlegrian Fields to the north-west of Naples On

Wutky's advice, Josef Rebell set out to establish himself as a landscape painter in Rome. Like many of his contemporaries, he came to appreciate the natural diversity of this part of the country through walks in the Campagna and in the countryside around Naples. Far away from all the academies, he developed a new perception of nature, based solely on observation and painting in situ. Rebell proved his credentials as an outstanding observer of nature in his depiction of the harbor at Granatella near Portici, commissioned by Emperor Franz I in 1819. Although Rebell continued to employ a step-by-step process in the Classical vein for the spatial representation of the scene, the section of landscape is captured in its entirety by the inclusion of human figures, and is superbly presented. The darkened foreground makes the yellow of the royal palace and the gentle blue of the sky appear all the more radiant, beautifully reflecting the strength of the warm sunshine.

The Tyrolean, Josef Anton Koch, took a quite different approach to landscape painting. His depictions of nature were based on a religious view of Creation, which included the belief that the divine is to be found in each and every plant

and stone. Koch spent most of his life in Rome, where he was a central figure in the German artists' colony. One aspect which distinguished him from other landscape painters of the time was his wariness of sunlight. In Koch's view, portraying meadows and mountains bathed in warm light was tantamount to a "secularization" of nature. During his short stay in Vienna from 1812 through 1815, this attitude earned him a leading position among the Romantic landscape painters. The brothers Ferdinand and Friedrich Olivier were disciples of this school of thought, as was the young Ludwig Ferdinand Schnorr von Carolsfeld, who cultivated this approach in his Viennese paintings.

Carolsfeld's respectful attitude toward nature is still evident in the painting of the *Spreading Scots Pine near Mödling*, completed decades later. However, the faithful representation of the landscape, the treatment of light and shade, the lush green of the meadows and trees, the deep blue of the sky, and the fashionable clothing of the couple in the foreground ultimately subvert the generalization of nature in its Romantic sense and bring the scene into the present.

The Nazarenes and Romantic religious painting

In 1809, a small group of mostly German painters expressed their dissatisfaction with academic teaching, strongly focused as it was on the art of antiquity. Led by Friedrich Overbeck and Franz Pforr, they pressed for the inclusion of religious subjects and an emphasis on emotion. This reflected the essence of Romantic philosophy and literature, to which they had been introduced by Friedrich Schlegel. However, their demands went unheeded by the Academy with its inflexible curriculum. This prompted the group to found the Brotherhood of St. Luke and to leave Austria for Rome (in any case, they had only regarded Vienna as their temporary home) in order to put their ideas into practice.

Pre-1500 German and Italian painting served as a constant model for the Brotherhood of St. Luke, or Nazarenes, as they were also known, and formed the basis of their style, the influence of which swept steadily north from Rome. As religious painting, it prescribed a form of representation which has remained valid right up until the twentieth century. It also laid the foundation for "Munich Romanticism," which incorporated not

Nepomuk on the altar wall, and Führich the Stations of the Cross on the side walls). Clarity of composition and the avoidance of complicated spatial arrangements were the prime objectives. A comparison of the works of the two contemporaries shows Führich's to be more powerful, and they therefore fulfilled more of an exemplary role at the time of their creation. Führich had already gained considerable artistic confidence during his time in Rome, where, according to his writings, he undertook a detailed study of the works of the High Renaissance. His paintings *Meeting of Jacob and Rachel at the Well* (1836) and *Mary's Journey over the Mountains* (1841), produced after his return to Vienna, bear witness to this. The name Führich is inseparably linked with the Altlerchenfelder Church (At the Seven Sanctuaries). The church, built between 1848 and 1861 in the style of the northern Italian Quattrocento, was intended to fuse the various art forms into a coherent work of art in keeping with the ideal of

Josef Führich
Deposition of Christ, 1844-46
Johann Nepomuk Church

Johann Evangelist Scheffer von Leonhardshoff
Death of St. Cecilia, 1820-21
Oil on canvas, 60 x 78 in
(149 x 195 cm)
Österreichische Galerie Belvedere

only religious but also medieval themes. However, it is important to note that this was not a coherent stylistic movement, but rather an artistic stance which was adapted by each painter to suit his own personality. The main practitioners, apart from the founding members already mentioned, were Julius Schnorr von Carolsfeld, the brothers Johannes and Philipp Veit, and Peter Cornelius. One of the true masters of Austrian Romanticism was Johann Evangelist Scheffer von Leonhardshoff, who died prematurely. During a trip to northern Italy and Venice in 1812, Scheffer familiarized himself with the works of Raphael, Giovanni Bellini, and Perugino, which were the inspiration for his works full of fine emotion and profound devoutness. His style later crystallized through his contact with the Brotherhood of St. Luke on his trips to Rome. During his last stay in Rome in 1820-21, he created the most acclaimed example of Austrian Romantic painting in the form of his Death of St. Cecilia. The pose of the woman lying dying on the grass bears similarities to the famous marble sculpture by Stefano Maderna in the Church of St. Cecilia in the Trastevere district of Rome. Scheffer's composition includes two grieving angels and is rounded off with a semi-circular upper border, designed to avoid disturbing the calm of the picture, according to the artist's own explanation.

In the 1820s, Leopold Kupelwieser and later Josef Führich, worked for some time in close association with the Brotherhood of St. Luke. The large frescoes produced by them between 1841 and 1844 in the Church of Johann Nepomuk in Praterstrasse, Vienna were based on what they had learned in Rome (Kupelwieser created the Transfiguration of St. Johann

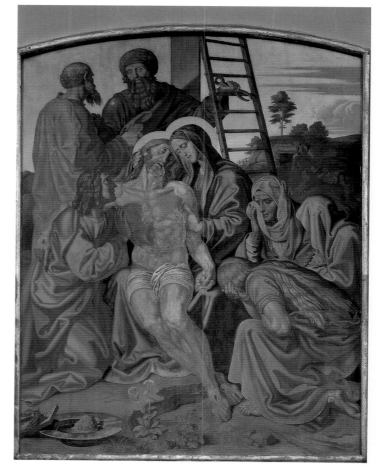

religious Romanticism. Führich was responsible for the design of the frescoes, which were to occupy the entire wall space of the interior. The aim was to illustrate the Bible story from the Creation through the Last Judgement. The project brought together many of the artists painting in the Nazarene style in Vienna at that time. Among the figures of note there were Führich and Kupelwieser, as well as Franz Dobyaschofsky, Eduard Engerth, and Eduard Steinle.

Viennese Biedermeier

The term "Biedermeier" was originally used pejoratively in order to ridicule the attitudes, outlook, and way of life of the people of the time. It was not until the twentieth century that the term was freed of these negative associations. It has now come into general use in German, along with terms such as "pre-March" and "the Metternich era", to designate a particular period in history. Biedermeier denotes the period between 1815 and 1848. It begins with a major political and social occasion—the Congress of Vienna—and ends with a revolution. During this period, Austria had two rulers, the conservative, bourgeois-minded Franz I and the well-meaning, but politically pliable, Ferdinand I. Both were advised by one and the same person, Clemens Wenzel Fürst Metternich. Metternich's prime concern was to maintain law and order and suppress any revolutionary movements. It is he who instigated the setting up of a "Court Police and Censure Body" in 1819 whose role was to censor not only books, newspapers, and speeches, but also the meetings of large organizations. The people, silenced by these restrictions, resigned themselves to the circumstances and withdrew into domestic life. The scenes of the private home-life of the middle classes that are depicted in many paintings are thus the direct result of the political situation, which became increasingly fraught toward the middle of the century and finally escalated into revolution in March 1848. Consequently, these pictures are by no means intended to be a portrayal of the "good old days," as they have often been interpreted.

The large number of painters working in Vienna during this period and the profusion of works produced preclude an in-depth look here at the artistic output of the period. Only Ferdinand Georg Waldmüller, the dominant figure among the Viennese painters of the time, will be considered in detail. Waldmüller's versatility is evidenced by a host of works which have come to be regarded as perfect examples of the painting of Viennese Biedermeier. Throughout his life, Waldmüller spoke out in favor of painting in the open air and the study of nature, which he singled out as the most important method of art teaching in a number of letters of opposition sent to the Academy. "To reflect nature as faithfully as possible" was his ultimate aim, and the landscapes, portraits, still-lifes, and genre paintings produced by him with this in mind rank among the most important in the history of Realism in Europe.

His work created a new freedom in portrait painting, a genre which, during these years, was characterized by a constant balancing of intimacy and representation and, simultaneously, "the striving for trueness to nature on the one hand, and a generalized ideal image on the other." (Frodl). The 1820s saw Waldmüller produce some of his most impressive portraits. They are, for the most part, extremely close-up half-length portraits from which the surroundings are excluded altogether. In each case, greatest attention is paid to the face, which is executed in a fine, smooth style with all its features depicted realistically and accurately down to the last detail. The portrait of the *Mother of Captain Stierle-Holzmeister* (ca. 1819) is the first in a series of paintings mostly portraying elderly women (see illustration, right), and sometimes men, but rarely young women. The patron's wishes, vanity and, to a degree, his sense of daring obviously had a key influence on the outcome, and Waldmüller's oeuvre consequently has a marked tendency toward the artificial pose. However, the facial characterization, based on the artist's early convictions, remains unique among Austrian Realist painters.

Waldmüller's great artistic contribution was in the unified treatment of man and nature. He perfected a portrait style which had its roots in the newly awakened natural sensitivities of the eighteenth century. In his *Self-Portrait as a Young Adult*, painted in 1828, he finally promoted landscape painting from its backstage role into an active conveyor of mood, in that he depicted himself bathed in the same warm sunlight as the trees and meadows behind him. As well as the landscape of the Vienna Woods, which surrounds him in this picture, he also later liked to depict the Salzkammergut region which is where, from the mid 1830s, he produced his most famous outdoor portraits (*Count Demetrius Apraxin*, *The Eltz Family*, *The Kertzmann Family*).

The most prominent portrait painter in Vienna, apart from Waldmüller, was Friedrich Amerling. Amerling was a studio painter who had no ambition to try his hand at depicting natural light. Neither did he cultivate ties with Realism, but he nevertheless endeavored to present an honest likeness of his model. His portraits appeal notably because of their brilliant colors and the tasteful arrangement of drapes and architectural objects in the background—compositional elements to which he was introduced by the English painter Sir Thomas Lawrence during his stay of several months in London. His technical virtuosity and the luminosity and transparency of the colors,

Ferdinand Georg Waldmüller
Rosina Wiser, 1820
Oil on canvas, 19 1/2 x 15 1/2 in (49.9 x 39.9 cm)
Österreichische Galerie Belvedere

Ferdinand Georg Waldmüller
Self-Portrait in Young Adulthood, 1828
Oil on canvas, 37 1/2 in x 29 1/2 in (95.2 cm x 75.2 cm)
Österreichische Galerie Belvedere

Moritz Michael Daffinger
Marie Daffinger, née Smolk von
Smolenitz, wife of the artist, ca.
1830
Oil on ivory, 16.5 x 12 cm
Österreichische Galerie Belvedere

Vienna during the Congress. Daffinger's portraits, despite all their idealism, were in great demand, thanks largely to the lightness of the brushstrokes and their brilliant surface finish. A number of other artists were involved in portrait painting or drawing, including Franz Eybl, Leopold Kupelwieser, Josef Kriehuber, who specialized in lithography, Josef Danhauser, Johann Baptist Reiter, and Michael Neder. However, in the case of the latter three, portraits only accounted for a minor part of their oeuvre; it was through their genre paintings that they made their names.

Genre painting epitomizes Viennese Biedermeier. It conveys a wealth of information about the way of life at that time, family celebrations and public entertainments, excursions to the country, and pilgrimages. Examples can be found in seventeenth-century Dutch painting and French and English works of the eighteenth century. The paintings are generally of a high artistic quality, so the comments that follow will mainly be restricted to the subject matter. Grimschitz described genre painting as a "history of the everyday." However, the intention was rarely merely to illustrate a situation. Painters recognized the propaganda potential of their works and used them, in much the same way as their literary contemporaries, to generate emotions and sympathies. Peter Fendi, for example, did not confine himself to painting small, delicately executed watercolors full of domestic intimacy, but also constantly endeavored to draw attention to the plight of marginal groups in society (*The Poor Officer's Widow*, (1836), *The Impounding* (1840), and *The Freezing Pretzel Boy in front of the Bastion of the Dominicans*, 1828). In *Girl in Front of the Lottery* (illustration on p. 227), on the other hand, he takes an admonishing and moralizing stance, pointing out the risk associated with this game of fortune.

A concise art form within this genre is the "one-figure work," in which a single figure is taken as representative of a trade, a social class, a hobby, or a state of mind. Examples include *Girl Reading* (1850) by Franz Eybl, *Boy Reading* (1849) by Johann Baptist Reiter, and *Girl with a Straw Hat* (1835), *The Lute Player* (1838) and *The Young Widow* (1836) by Friedrich Amerling.

As a visual storyteller, Josef Danhauser was without rival. Many of his paintings portray varying degrees of human weaknesses and works like *Reading the Will* (1839) and *The Widow's Mite* (1839) are designed to hold up a mirror to the population. The message in the pair of paintings entitled *The Wealthy Glutton* and *Soup Time at the Monastery* (illustrations on p. 226) is especially noteworthy. Danhauser has transmuted the New Testament parable of poor Lazarus and the rich man (Luke xvi: 19 – 31) into the present-day and thus demonstrated graphically how, if one lives like a lord, fate may have an unpleasant surprise in store.

ILLUSTRATION OPPOSITE:
Friedrich Amerling
Rudolf von Arthaber with his
Children Rudolf, Emilie and
Gustav, 1837
Oil on canvas, 87 x 61 in
(221 x 155 cm)
Österreichische Galerie Belvedere

even in the most delicate areas of color shading, also owe much to Lawrence's influence. In the mid 1830s, he produced his large family portraits (see illustration opposite), which are remarkable for the informality of the poses of the subjects.

Amerling did not require an invisible framework of compositional lines to ensure the coherence of the picture — as Waldmüller did in the portraits he produced at around the same time — but instead presented the scene as a chance moment. This, of course, perfectly echoed the public taste of the time and the painter thus enjoyed great popularity which lasted until the middle of the century and beyond. The same applies to Moritz Michael Daffinger, who specialized in miniatures and small pictures. His main influences, apart from Lawrence, were the French painters Jean Baptiste Isabey and François Gérard, who worked in

Josef Danhauser
The Wealthy Glutton, 1836
Oil on canvas, 33 1/2 x 54 1/4 in
(84 x 131 cm)
Österreichische Galerie Belvedere

Josef Danhauser
Soup Time at the Monastery,
1838
Oil on wood, 33 3/4 x 51 1/4 in
(85.5 x 130 cm)
Österreichische Galerie Belvedere

Peter Fendi
Girl in Front of the Lottery, 1829
Oil on canvas, (63 x 50 cm)
Österreichische Galerie Belvedere

Danhauser was also fond of portraying scenes from everyday domestic life (*Maternal Love*, (1839), *The Child and his World* (1842)), drawing room entertainments (*The Game of Chess* (1839)) and the excursions to the country which were so popular during the Biedermeier period (*Wine, Women and Song* (1839)). Carl Schindler, in turn, developed the "soldier genre," recording anecdotal scenes from everyday military life, marches and battles. Michael Neder, on the other hand, opted for more lowly subjects. He concerned himself primarily with the working classes (he himself had been trained as a cobbler), the lower middle classes and landless peasants on the outskirts of Vienna, whose daily routine he sketched in an often sober manner. Waldmüller, too, almost invariably chose the farming community as the subject of his genre paintings, but instead of showing the farmer at work, he focused on women of all ages and on children. *Rural Wedding in Lower Austria* (1843), *Morning of the Feast of Corpus Christi* (1857), *Gathering Brushwood in The Vienna Woods* (1855), *The Bride's Farewell* (1860) and *The Worship of St. John* (illustration opposite) span the spectrum from everyday life to special occasions. In these, the painter reveals himself to be an accurate observer of folk customs and dress. In contrast, he adopts a critical stance in *Forced Sale of the Last Calf* (1857) and *The Impounding* (1847), and especially in the painting *Spent Energy* (1854), which visualizes the harshness of the daily fight for survival with uncompromising realism. Genre and landscape painting are usually closely linked in the works of Waldmüller, as was the case with Friedrich Gauermann, whose motifs also tended to be taken from a farming context

Gauermann started out mainly as a landscape painter, and it was only in the late 1830s that he began to add grazing cows, hunting scenes, and animal fights to his repertoire. Initially treated as incidental extras, these motifs became more and more central to the content of the picture. Gauermann, together with Waldmüller, Franz Steinfeld, and Friedrich Loos, belonged to the first generation of realistic landscape painters. In numerous views painted in about 1830 in the countryside around Vienna and Salzburg, they succeeded in reducing the depiction of nature to its essence. This was achieved through the simplicity of the composition, the solemn silence pervading the scene, and the avoidance of any "stage management." This direct approach to nature was adopted and elaborated by Adalbert Stifter, Johann Fischbach, Rudolf Mathias Toma, and Thomas Ender, painter-explorer of the high mountains.

Mastering the art of open-air painting and learning to deal with daylight was one of the great achievements of Viennese landscape

TOP ILLUSTRATION:
Friedrich Gauermann
Landscape near Miesenbach, ca. 1830
Oil on canvas, 12½ x 17¾ in (32 x 45 cm)
Österreichische Galerie Belvedere

BOTTOM ILLUSTRATION:
Ferdinand Georg Waldmüller
Mödling and the Liechtenstein Ruin, 1848
Oil on wood, 21¾ x 27¼ in (55.8 x 69 cm)
Österreichische Galerie Belvedere

Johann Knapp
Homage to Jacquin ("Jacquin's Memorial"), 1821-22
Oil on canvas, 218 x 164 cm
Österreichische Galerie Belvedere

painters from the 1830s onward. Their endeavors to some extent echoed those of the French artists working in the forest of Fontainebleau near Paris at that time. However, unlike the French painters, who wanted to capture on canvas the impression of the subjective perception of nature, the Austrian painters tried for an objective depiction which took no account of the feelings of the artist. From the 1840s onward, Waldmüller, inspired by his almost yearly trips to Italy, attempted to reproduce the effect of shimmering sunlight. However, only in a few works did he succeed in moving away from firm contours and solid forms and applying the paint in dabs, merging the colors together. He more often ended up with over-worked images and sharp contrasts of light and shade. The reason for this heavy-handed treatment of the subject matter can be traced primarily to his painting technique, which was still heavily influenced by Classical conventions. Rudolf von Alt was in a similar situation. Although he had succeeded, early on in his career, in depicting the gleaming, shimmering light of southern Europe in his watercolors, he did not manage to achieve a passable effect in his oil paintings until the 1860s.

Rudolf von Alt had a special place in nineteenth century Austrian painting. He was actively involved in all the developments and changes in painting that took place during his long lifetime. His appointment as Honorary President of the newly formed Secession in 1897 bears witness to how greatly he was valued as an artist right up until the end of his days.

Finally, it is worth saying a word or two about the paintings of flower arrangements and bowls of fruit which saw a revival in popularity during the Biedermeier period. These paintings, modeled on works by Dutch and Flemish masters of the seventeenth and eighteenth centuries, satisfied the public demand for decorative subjects. Skilful arrangement and execution were the ultimate aim, whereas less attention was paid to the laws of botany, with the result that plants of different origins and different flowering seasons can be found depicted in the same bouquet. The foremost representatives of Viennese still-life painting were Josef Nigg, Sebastian Wegmayr, Franz Xaver Gruber, and Franz Xaver Petter.

However, the best-known flower painter was Johann Knapp, who had developed a keen eye and hand for this type of painting while working on hundreds of studies of flowers and fruits commissioned by the imperial family. Knapp's most important work is the painting entitled *Jacquin's Memorial*, also known as *Homage to Jacquin*, dedicated to the pre-eminent botanist Nikolaus Joseph von Jacquin (1727–1817). In this large-format painting, Knapp assembled all twenty-four genera of the plant classification system devised by the Swedish botanist Linnaeus into a single bouquet, along with a large collection of fruits, vegetables, and fauna.

Also worth a mention are Moritz Michael Daffinger, creator of numerous flower watercolors, and Waldmüller, whose still-lifes ranged from complex and colorful arrangements (*Still Life with Fruits, Flowers and Silver Trophy*), to a simple, ephemeral bunch of roses (*Roses in the Window*).

Johann Peter Krafft
Archduke Carl with the Colors of
the Zach Regiment at the Battle
of Aspern, 1812
Oil on canvas, 129 x 112¼ in
(327.5 x 285 cm)
Heeresgeschichtliches Museum

Johann Peter Krafft
The Territorial Soldier's Farewell,
1813
Oil on canvas, 110½ in x 138¼
in (281 x 351 cm)
on loan from the Österreichische
Galerie Belvedere to the Heeresgeschichtliches Museum

History painting as patriotic propaganda

History painting played a very special role in this period. As already mentioned, the Classicists regarded it as a superior form of art which made exceptional demands on both the painter and the viewer. The imperial family soon recognized the effectiveness of this genre as a means of propaganda, and promoted it with numerous commissions. Most of the historical paintings were produced in the first quarter of the century, a time of massive historical upheaval. The numerous wars which had shaken Europe, and the political uncertainty resulting from Napoleon's seizure of power, caused the Roman Emperor Franz II, in 1804, to found an Austrian Empire in opposition to France, which was manifesting new territorial aspirations. Two years later he dissolved the Holy Roman Empire and as Austrian Emperor Franz I, commissioned a number of academics to record the country's history so as to provide a historical foundation for the House of Austria. These writings subsequently provided countless subjects for ballads, plays, and paintings honoring the fatherland. Among the most frequently represented figures at that time were Rudolf von Habsburg, the founder of the dynasty, and Emperor Maximilian I. The interest in early Habsburg history resulted in large part from the fascination with the Middle Ages fostered by Romantic painting, and stands in contrast to the French painting of the era, dominated by such famous names as Jacques Louis David and Eugène Delacroix, who tended to portray the political events of their day.

The link with the present day was also important for Johann Peter Krafft, who, as has been mentioned, had studied under David in Paris. His portrait of the Archduke Carl carrying the colors of the Zach Regiment at the Battle of Aspern, painted in 1811-12, was the first Austrian history painting to refer to a recent event, namely the victory of the Austrian troops over Napoleon in 1809. His portrayal of the flag-waving commander on horseback also provided the prototype for all pictures on this theme.

Among the many works celebrating the victory of the Austrian army in the Napoleonic Wars, *The Territorial Soldier's Farewell* stands out because of the way in which it depicts ordinary working class people. This painting can be viewed as a genre scene set in the farming community. Given that, in 1813, the year in which it was painted, a decisive battle was being fought near Leipzig, it is easy to recognize the original function of history painting, namely, to exert a moral influence over the masses by promoting a sense of patriotism.

The wall paintings in the audience chamber in the Chancellery wing of the Imperial Palace in Vienna, painted by Krafft between 1828 and 1832, can also be interpreted as imperial propaganda. These three episodes from the life of the monarch, occupying the entire wall space, were

Leopold Kupelwieser
The History of Austria from
Marcus Aurelius to the Congress
of Vienna, 1848-50.
Ceiling fresco in the marble room
of the former residence of the
Governor of Lower Austria

intended to demonstrate his popularity and good rapport with the people. These are highly populated scenes in which Krafft skillfully avoided over-emphasizing the main figure. These large-format depictions are among the painter's major works, and can be regarded as the precursors to monumental history painting.

The ceiling frescoes in the Large Meeting Room of the former Imperial and Royal Residence of the Governor of Lower Austria in Herrengasse (illustration above) also mark a significant step forward in the evolution of historic

painting. This is the first work of Austrian history painting to chronicle Austria's past from Marcus Aurelius to the Congress of Vienna in the form of a complete cycle, and is accompanied by a series of secular and religious allegories, designed to illustrate the Divine Right of the Austrian emperor. These frescoes were the work of Leopold Kupelwieser between 1848 and 1850.

The works also served as a model for the Hall of Fame in the Waffenmuseum (today called Heeresgeschichtliches Museum). The paintings, designed to reflect the function of the building, were intended to celebrate the successes of the army and its commanders from the age of the Babenbergs to the battle of Novara in 1849. Carl Blaas was given the commission. Concerned, above all, with historical accuracy, it took him twelve years to complete this, the largest cycle of nineteenth-century paintings, which were only finished in 1878.

Not all painters took such an uncritical view of history as Kupelwieser and Blaas, however. The Year of the Revolution, 1848, saw the creation of a series of works referring to very recent political events, boldly portraying the rebellion of the downtrodden masses. Anton Ziegler painted *The Barricade on Michaelerplatz on the Night of 26 – 27 May*; Johann Baptist Reiter portrayed himself and his wife as *Workers Employed on Emergency Repairs* in a pair of pictures, and Franz Russ the Elder, in a painting entitled *26 May 1848 in Vienna*, shows the revolution symbolically being led by a "Viennese maid"—an obvious allusion to the figure in Eugène Delacroix's *Liberty*, which had been painted in 1830.

August von Pettenkofen's series of paintings depicting the wounded being carried away during the Hungarian War of Liberation of 1849 is of only marginal importance within the historical genre in fine art. These can be seen more as illustrations of a particular situation, designed to reproduce the horrors of war. Anton Romako also sets out to criticize politically motivated killing and bloodshed in a small painting on wood entitled *Dance of the Dead* (ca. 1885), in which the soldiers are merely skeletons in uniform. In his painting *Prince Eugene in the Battle with the Turks at Zenta* (1880-82), the true heroes are the soldiers caught up in the tumult of battle, whereas the army commanders are merely tiny silhouettes in the background. The picture *Tegetthoff in the Naval Battle of Lissa* dating from 1866 was also considered by contemporary critics to be lacking a heroic figure in the conventional mold. The posture of the admiral was considered far too down-to-earth in view of his heroic victory.

Romako deliberately chose not to portray in the picture the instant of triumph following the crucial ramming manoeuvre which brought victory over the Italian fleet, but a moment immediately prior thereto. The action and drama are thus centered on the bridge and at the helm of the Austrian flagship. Portraying the expectant tension on the faces of all involved was Romako's way of acknowledging the magnitude of their achievement. The depiction is much more than a history painting in the conventional sense, which is why it is rated as one of the most important works of this genre in the nineteenth century.

Franz Russ the Elder
26 May 1848 in Vienna, 1848
Oil on canvas, 81 x 67 cm
Privately owned (Kunsthandlung Giese & Schweiger)

Anton Romako
Tegetthoff in the Naval Battle of Lissa (I), ca. 1878-80
Oil on wood,
34 x 19 in (87 x 48 cm)
Österreichische Galerie Belvedere

ILLUSTRATION OPPOSITE:
Anselm Feuerbach
Fall of the Titans, 1874-79
Oil on canvas
Ceiling painting in the hall of the
Akademie der bildenden Künste

Moritz von Schwind
Queen of the Night
Lunette fresco in the loggia of the
State Opera House,
completed 1867

Vienna takes the world stage: the Ringstrasse period and historicism

Developments in Austrian art in the second half of the nineneeth century are generally associated with historicism. This term does not signify a particular style, but instead encompasses the various parallel historical trends of the time. Historicism was a pan-European phenomenon found, to a greater or lesser extent, throughout the nineteenth century (take the preoccupation of the Romantics with the Middle Ages, for example). However, it was in the second half of the century that it reached its culmination in Austria. In painting, it manifests itself most prominently in the monumental paintings adorning the walls and ceilings of various public and private buildings. This historical fascination revealed itself early on in the religious and patriotic works of Kupelwieser and Führich, and found its full expression, from the 1860s onwards, in mythological scenes and allegories. The subject matter was always closely linked to the function of the building, as this was the only way in which to satisfy the desire for an integrated work of art.

In 1868, the first official building on Ringstrasse, the Court Opera House, was completed. Its walls and ceilings bore paintings by Franz Dobyaschofsky, Carl Rahl, Carl Joseph Geiger, and Eduard Engerth depicting musical and allegorical scenes. The paintings in the loggia are particularly noteworthy. They were the work of Moritz von Schwind, whose wall paintings in Munich, Karlsruhe, and at Wartburg, and fairytale illustrations had earned him a solid reputation. Schwind was Viennese by birth, but spent most of his life in Munich, where he figured among the main representatives of Romanticism. The loggia paintings are on the theme of Mozart's "The Magic Flute", a subject which had interested the painter for some time ("The Magic Flute" was his favorite opera) and one which he was particularly keen to paint, especially in his home city. The architectural framework necessitated an illustrative form which suited the painter well. Only the lunettes in the sides of the vaulting and the ceiling sections themselves could be painted, which is why Schwind divided the story into major scenes and minor scenes, the stories of Tamino and Pamina and of Papageno and Papagena. The motif of the inscribed circle in a round arch repeated all over the building is repeated in the lunette paintings in the form of a semi-circular central motif, and the scenes along the longer sides of the room are fitted into round areas enclosed with a semi-circle. In the sections on the transverse walls, this compositional

element is finally incorporated into the ornate scenes as an inherent part of the picture: the Queen of the Night stands against the background of a circular moon, and the place of the fire-and-water trial to which Tamino and Pamino have just been subjected is of the very same form. The graphic style and the muted coloring of the painting, which consists of broken tones only, enable this work to fit in beautifully with its architectural surroundings.

Anselm Feuerbach's ceiling painting in the hall of the Akademie der bildenden Künste (illustration on p. 235), commissioned in 1874, is lavish in comparison. While still a student in Munich, the Speyer-born painter managed to intricately combine subjects taken from ancient times with the vocabulary of form of Antiquity and the Italian Renaissance, making him one of the most important of the Neo-Classicists. The subject chosen for his ceiling paint-

ing was the Fall of the Titans, the "victory of culture over the raw forces of nature," as he put it. However, Feuerbach was not content simply to pander to the public's desire for visual entertainment. It takes an educated mind to understand his works. The depictions on the hall ceiling of the Akademie typically tax the viewer's knowledge. The central motif is surrounded by images from early mythology— Gaea, Uranus, Aphrodite, Prometheus in chains, Eros, Oceanus, Demeter and Prometheus as the giver of fire. The shape of the main picture, an upright oval, adds to the formal unity of the depiction which presents a highly animated scene on three levels. The subtle coloring, dominated by brownish violet and blue-green tones, serves to emphasize the corporeality of the figures in the style of Michelangelo and harmonizes with the architecture of the room.

During the 1870s, historicism tended toward the Neo-Baroque in a new trend led by two painters, Hans Canon and Hans Makart. Canon, who, although born in Vienna, had spent much of his life in southern Germany, was engaged in 1882 to provide the paintings for the stairwell of the Natural History Museum. For the ceiling painting, he chose the theme, The Cycle of Life, while the twelve lunettes in the wall were painted to symbolize the natural sciences. This complex arrangement was the painter's own idea, based on the natural philosophy of the eternal Becoming and Fading which is determined not only by the fight for survival, but more importantly by the striving for power (symbolized by the battling riders in the center of the arch). By toning down the coloring, Canon hoped to bring out the underlying message of the picture, but, in fact, has resulted in a lack of harmony between the painting and the architecture of the room. The painting is striking, nevertheless, due to its dynamic execution, the broad, loose brushwork, and the chairoscuro effect conveyed purely by the use of color.

Meanwhile, Hans Makart had been entrusted with the job of decorating the ceiling of the stairwell of the Kunsthistorisches Museum across the road on the theme of the Victory of Light over Darkness. However, the early death of the artist (1884) meant he was unable to complete the task, and the work was handed over to the Hungarian artist Mihaly Munkácsy. Makart did not receive his first imperial commissions until the 1880s, in other words shortly before his death, although he had been summoned back to Vienna from Munich in 1869 at the emperor's request. Makart's clients were mostly members of the upper classes, whose villas and palaces he embellished with magnificent paintings. As far as the composition and coloring were concerned, he drew his inspiration from the Venetian Cinquecento painters and from Rubens, but he was able to skillfully mask his eclecticism through his masterful handling of color and his swift, sweeping painting style. As Makart explained, "When a painting comes into my mind, at first all I see are a few bright, gleaming spots of color which start to haunt me, and only then do I paint all the rest." The spontaneous appearance of his handiwork is thus attributable more to the paintbrush than to the drawing pencil. His illusionist tricks—placing painted objects next to real, existing ones, providing rooms with splendid garden views, raising the ceiling of a room with the aid of foreshortening and the depiction of motifs from below, or making the ceiling appear to open up skyward—were copied by Julius Berger, Eduard Charlemont, and Julius Schmid, to name but a few, and employed in Viennese painting until well beyond the turn of the century.

In the course of the 1880s, historicism lost much of its spontaneity. The liberal, uninhibited reproduction of widely differing styles gave way to a new, scientific approach, which laid down certain rules and standards to which the iconography and technique had to conform.

In 1882, a collection of prototypes called "Allegories and Emblems" was published, designed as a working manual for the depiction of symbols, concepts, and allegories to represent real life and the imaginary world. Artists involved in producing the set of pictures included Kolo Moser and Franz von Stuck, as well as the brothers Ernst and Gustav Klimt, and Franz Matsch. As the Company of Painters, these latter three launched their careers by decorating a whole host of theatre

buildings in the Makart style during the time of the monarchy. By the 1880s, their style had become less and less turbulent, and their ceiling paintings above the two grand staircases of the Wiener Hofburgtheater on the Ring (the history of theatre from antiquity until the 18th century, started in 1886) and the paintings in the intercolumniation and spandrel spaces in the stairwell of the Kunsthistorisches Museum (for the style study, started in 1890, see illustration on p. 364) displayed perfect unity of composition.

Hans Makart
The Four Parts of the World, ca. 1870/71
Former ceiling painting in the dining room in the palace of Anton Oelzelt Ritter von Newald on the Schottenring
Oil on canvas, 171 1/2 x 113 3/4 in (436 x 284 cm)
Österreichische Galerie Belvedere

ILLUSTRATION OPPOSITE:
Hans Makart
The Triumph of Ariadne, 1873
Oil on canvas,
187 x 309 in (476 x 784 cm)
Österreichische Galerie Belvedere

Gustav Klimt
The Fable, 1883
Original design for the collection of prototypes, "Allegories and Emblems"
Oil on canvas, 331/3 x 46 in (84.5 x 117 cm)
Historisches Museum der Stadt Wien

Historicism in small-format paintings

The description of historicism so far has concentrated on monumental painting, since this best illustrates the wide variety of styles subsumed under this label. By embracing this new trend, Austria was reviving a tradition which had lain dormant since the Baroque period. However, alongside their larger assignments, the painters in question also worked on easel pictures, portraits and paintings with an historical, allegorical, or mythological content, in which the stylistic achievements of the age could be translated into a smaller format. Meanwhile, landscape painting, of course, remained entirely unaffected by the swing towards historicism.

One of the prominent names among painters of small-scale works was again Hans Canon, whose keen skills of observation made him famous principally as a portrait painter. However, Hans Makart was the biggest name on the art scene at that time, although less for his painting than for his extravagant lifestyle and the legendary costume parties he held in his studio. This studio, furnished with items from various periods, including antique carpets, dried plants and drapes, also had an impact on middle-class tastes in home furnishing at the time, and the "Makart style" went down in history. Stage

Anton Romako
Empress Elisabeth, ca. 1883
Oil on wood, 65in x 35in
Österreichische Galerie Belvedere

ILLUSTRATION OPPOSITE:
Anton Romako
Italian Fishing Boy, ca. 1870/75
Oil on canvas, 37in x 29 cm
Österreichische Galerie Belvedere

management in the Baroque sense was all-important to him, which is why he was also entrusted with organizing the procession to mark the Emperor's silver wedding anniversary on April 27, 1879. His elaborate, large-scale oil paintings like *The Triumph of Ariadne* (illustration above), *Venice pays Homage to Catarina Cornaro* (1872-73), *Karl V's Entry into Antwerp* (1878) and *Cleopatra's Journey Down the Nile* (1874-75) were crafted with the same wealth of sensory detail with which he presented himself and his surroundings. Makart was particularly popular as a portrait painter, especially among women, who considered it a great pleasure to be transformed by him into figures from a past age or from another country. In these cases, the person's individual personality was largely disregarded, although this was by mutual arrangement. The chief concern was to present a hint of beauty and eternal youth.

Anton Romako took a more individualistic approach to his models. Superficiality was of no interest to him. He was concerned with the person's individual being, as reflected in his or her external appearance, which would be lost through "corrections."

Romako lived in Rome for nearly thirty years and cultivated his style far away from the frenzy of historicism which had engulfed his home city. This made it all the harder, on his return, for him to gain a foothold in the artistic life of Vienna: the public was used to the paintings of Makart and Canon and did not know what to make of his unconventional portrait style. The portrait of the Empress Elisabeth shows to what extent Romako disregarded the common conventions of society in the matter of prestige commissions to paint the portraits of the nobility. The Empress's eccentricity sets the tone of the picture and is mirrored in her very posture, right down to her fingertips. Romako, unlike Makart, regarded the hands as an important vehicle of characterization. Gustav Klimt was to take a similar approach later on.

By using a lively, open painting style, Romako was able to capture the Italian Fishing Boy in the first light of dawn in such a way that the child seems to be scurrying past the onlooker like some legendary sea creature. In the basket, his catch appears as a shimmer of iridescent colors, whereas the hand holding the basket is captured in great detail. This meticulous emphasis on a particular element of the picture amid a mass of rapid brushwork is a characteristic of the painter which appears again and again in his works. The picture was painted in Rome in the mid 1870s and is one of Romako's most expressive paintings.

Landscape painting in the second half of the century

In 1877, soon after his return to Austria, Romako spent some time in Salzburg and painted several landscapes in the Gasteinertal valley and by the Wolfgangssee lake. The manner in which the paint is applied has much in common with the paintings of William Turner and John Constable. The large, lightly painted expanses are divided only by a quick paint line here and there defining the terrain. However, Romako's use of the serial technique, in which a natural feature is portrayed from the same viewpoint in its various different states throughout the year, is reminiscent of the Impressionists working in France at that time, and represents a novel departure in Austrian landscape painting. In Austrian art, nature tended to be portrayed in a naturalistic manner until well into the second half of the nineteenth century.

August von Pettenkofen
Hungarian Horse-Trough, 1860s
Oil on wood, 15¾ x 10½ in
(40.5 x 27 cm)
Österreichische Galerie Belvedere

The main representatives of this approach were Anton Hansch and Carl Hasch, whose paintings of mountains and lakes were perfectly in tune with contemporary tastes.

Meanwhile, August von Pettenkofen was exploring new paths. In 1851, he came across the town of Szolnok in the Hungarian lowland plains, whose atmospheric mood was to captivate him for the rest of his life. In a series of paintings mostly depicting elaborate natural scenes, he characterized the flat profile of this part of the country with a low horizon, and above it a broad expanse of sky, and added interest to the pictures by portraying the bustle of the marketplace, horses and carts and gypsies. The landscapes were dominated by subdued brown and gray tones, or by a clear, intense luminosity, depending on the weather. However, the paints were always applied in free and easy brushstrokes in an attempt to capture the light, the haze, and the atmosphere. The excellent conditions provided by this region for *plein air* painting (painting in the open air) in the manner of the Barbizon School soon drew other Austrian painters to the region, among them Gualbert Raffalt, Leopold Carl Müller, Tina Blau, Eugen Jettel, and Rudolf Ribarz.

Oriental painting

The search for new subjects, impressions and challenges meant that trips to the Orient, particularly the Eastern Mediterranean and Egypt, became extremely popular among Austrian painters from the 1860s onward. This preoccupation with the Orient — a new trend among French and English artists — was already something of a tradition in Viennese painting. Oriental motifs had first been used in painting in the first half of the century, but these had more in common with the romantic notions associated with *A Thousand and One Nights* and had little to do with reality. Decorative market and street scenes, seraglios, water-carrying women in brightly colored robes, and bizarre buildings were still among the favorite subjects, but were presented in warmer colors. In addition, there was a fascination with the barrenness of the desert and the ruins bearing witness to past civilizations. Alphons Leopold Mielich, Carl Rudolf Huber, Johann Victor Krämer, and Alois Schönn were among those who attempted to capture their impressions in scores of paintings. However, the most significant Austrian Oriental painter was Leopold Carl Müller. On no less than nine lengthy trips to Egypt, he made numerous sketches of the people and made his name as a realistic observer of that country. His *Market in Cairo* (illustration opposite), which portrays the bustle of trade in front of the city walls, avoiding the anecdotal, ranks among the most impressive examples of oriental painting to come out of Europe.

Leopold Carl Müller
A Sphinx Face of Today
Oil on canvas, 26¼ x 15½ in
(66.5 x 40 cm)
Österreichische Galerie Belvedere

TOP AND ADJACENT:
Leopold Carl Müller
The Market in Cairo, 1878
Oil on canvas, 53½ x 85¼ in
(136 x 216.5 cm)
On loan from the Akademie der
bildenden Künste to the Öster-
reichische Galerie Belvedere

ILLUSTRATION OPPOSITE:
Theodor von Hörmann
In the Tuileries, 1888
Oil on canvas, 14¾ x 21½ in
(38 x 55 cm)
Österreichische Galerie Belvedere

Emil Jakob Schindler
February Mood, 1884
Oil on canvas, 47¼ x 37 in
(120 x 94 cm)
Österreichische Galerie Belvedere

"Mood Impressionism"

From the 1870s onward, landscape painting in Austria saw a shift toward a more emotional portrayal of nature, which manifested itself in a growing desire to reproduce subjective impressions. Painters tried to capture a random piece of nature with all its color and atmospheric mood elements, and in so doing, to present it as an example of the whole area. The recognizability of the location was of little importance. What mattered was the exemplary nature of the scene and the individual mood. Art historians have called this Austrian way of presenting reality, based on the personal feeling or "impression" of the painter, "Mood Impressionism," although the Austrian style had little to do with French Impressionism. The only shared aspects were the interest in capturing the moment and the desire to reproduce light in all its nuances. The concern with producing an overall impression of the colors and atmosphere of a place in fact has more in common with the French landscape painting that

preceded the Impressionist period, notably that of the Barbizon School but also that of the Hague School.

The principal representative of "Mood Impressionism" was Emil Jakob Schindler. From an early stage, his pictures revealed his preference for finely tuned atmospheric halftones, which he continued to observe in all their many variations throughout his life, often in depictions of the same motif. Schindler preferred a colour palette in which browns, greens, grays, and blues were mixed to produce an infinite variety of shades. Water and its reflections, water-mills in thick fog, and a summer haze over a quiet backwater of a river awakened his poetic sensibilities and formed the subject matter of numerous paintings.

Schindler soon became a mentor for all those artists who felt drawn to "modern" open-air painting (the main followers included Olga Wisinger-Florian, Marie Egner, the sisters Marie and Louise von Parmentier, Carl Moll, and, for a time, Theodor von Hörmann). Most

of his paintings depicted the scenery of his own part of the country. It was a different story in the case of his one-time fellow students Eugen Jettel and Rudolf Ribarz, who relocated to France early on in their careers and consequently developed a style that was heavily influenced by French and Dutch painting.

Paris exerted an irresistible attraction for many Austrian artists. Tina Blau spent quite some time in the French capital, as did Theodor von Hörmann. Hörmann was a self-taught artist and, in Austrian art circles, was hailed as the champion of modernism. He was the only Austrian to go beyond fine-toned, intricate painting by using bright colors applied to the canvas with broad, sometimes thick, brushstrokes. His experiences and ideas set an example to his contemporaries, and considerably boosted their sense of artistic confidence, enabling them in 1897 to triumph over the conservatism of Austrian art and make the transition to the twentieth century and the modern age with the formation of the Secession.

Classical sculpture

Sculpture, which normally reacts more hesitantly to stylistic changes than painting, was surprisingly quick and willing to adopt Classical techniques. As with any change of style, traditional practices and new methods overlapped for a time, with the new only manifesting itself in small details until it was eventually able to gain the upper hand and displace the old.

Early indications of a Classical approach are most apparent in the works of Georg Raphael Donner, for example in his Providentia Fountain in Neuer Markt, and in the garden figures at Schönbrunn Palace which were created by the pupils of the Akademie, under the supervision of the well-traveled sculptor Wilhelm Beyer of Saxony. Here, Baroque vigor seems to clash with the relaxed, *contrapposto* pose, one which appears relaxed and with subtle gestures. Classicism in its pure form first emerged in Vienna in smaller works, such as porcelain figurines. It was not until the 1780s that this modern trend was adopted in more sizeable works.

The focus on simplicity of form and clear lines demanded a monotone medium. The material which best met this requirement and which "always gives the artist most pleasure, despite all the effort" (Johann Nepomuk Schaller) was marble, preferably Carrara marble. North of the Alps, substitutes for this most noble of stones were found in the marble quarries of Bohemia, Styria, and the Tyrol, and also in the form of sandstone which, despite its brittleness, could be fashioned into the most astonishing forms. Meanwhile, wood began to decline in importance as an illustrative medium, and artistic painting of wooden carvings and decorative gilding began to fall out of favor. Lead, with its softness and malleability—highly prized during the Baroque period—was soon superseded by dense, gleaming bronze. Hard metal and hard stone were needed to satisfy the new preference for sharp contours, corners, and edges.

Franz Anton Zauner and Roman Classicism

The advocate of Roman Classicism in Vienna was Franz Anton Zauner. From 1776, he lived in Rome with Füger the painter, thanks to a grant. The close contact between the foreign artists, discussions of the art theories of the painter Anton Raphael Meng, and of contemporary painting and sculpture supplemented the artists' studies of ancient art treasures and liberated the young Zauner from his Baroque roots. Soon after his return to Vienna (1781), he made his architectural sculpture convey an impression of confidence at the newly-erected city palace of Count Johann Fries (now known as the Pallavicini Palace). The figures personifying Trade and Freedom on the attic story (they were reinterpreted as Apollo and

Franz Anton Zauner
Genius Bornii, ca. 1785
Graphite-coated plaster of Paris,
h.: 31 in (79 cm)
Österreichische Galerie Belvedere

Fama in the 19th century) reveal the influence of Michelangelo's Medici Chapel in Florence. However, Zauner avoided a relaxed pose, opting instead for a casual arrangement, as if this were a chance meeting between the two figures. The gracefulness of the pairs of caryatids flanking the portal is reminiscent of the French art of the era.

The plaster statuette of the Genius Bornii (illustration above) and the sculptural arrangement for the tomb of Count Johann Fries and his son Joseph in the garden of the family's summer residence in Vöslau are based more closely on models from Antiquity. In both cases, Zauner produced a naked male body: the winged genius bears similarities to works by Praxiteles, in the treatment of the bone structure, the slim, elegantly proportioned limbs, and the soft appearance of the skin, while the stocky, sturdy build of the youth in the arrangement for the Fries sepulcher is reminiscent of the works of Polyclitus.

The Equestrian Statue of Emperor Joseph II.

In 1795, Zauner was commissioned to create a memorial to the great eighteenth-century reformer, Emperor Joseph II (illustration opposite). It was to be located in the square in front of the court library, which is also overlooked by the Fries Palace.

Zauner was then at the peak of his artistic development, and his statue of Emperor Joseph II on horseback has been hailed as the most important Classical work in Vienna. The well-balanced proportions and the elements, designed to match the surrounding buildings unified the whole area

ILLUSTRATION OPPOSITE:
Franz Anton Zauner
Monument to Emperor Joseph II,
1795 – 1807, metal casting

Johann Martin Fischer
Hygeia, 1787, metal casting
Hof des Josephinums

and, by creating a sense of harmony and completeness, turned this into the most attractive square in the whole city.

Vienna had no tradition of equestrian statues. The statue of Emperor Franz Stephan of Lorraine produced by Balthasar Moll, shortly before, and now sited in the Burggarten, was an initial, and not altogether successful, attempt. Emperor Joseph, too, was originally to have been portrayed in a standing pose, but of the many designs and models produced, the portrayal of the emperor on horseback eventually became the preferred solution. He sits bolt upright in the saddle in the style of a Roman general and, with his outstretched right arm, commands his imaginary army. The rider's pose and the gait of the horse owe much to the statue of Marcus Aurelius on the Capitol in Rome, although the sense of the animal's overwhelming strength in the Roman sculpture is replaced by imperial calm in the Viennese work. The "life-like modeling of the skin, giving a hint of the play of the muscles" (Burg) reveals the sculptor's close observation of nature. His desire for authenticity is demonstrated by his determination to accurately render the emperor's giant stature — the monarch was 6 ft 4¾ in (192 cm) tall.

A square, granite pedestal completes the monument, and bronze reliefs on its sides illustrate the emperor's achievements in the areas of commerce and agriculture (illustration below).

The wish of the reigning Emperor Franz II (later Franz I) to have the equestrian statue produced in bronze posed an almost insurmountable problem for Zauner. He had no experience in bronze casting, nor were there any trained craftsmen available in Vienna at the time. Cooperation with bronze casters from France, who had the greatest expertise in this field, was ruled out on political grounds.

So, with the aid of relevant literature, Zauner developed his own process, and produced the figure of the emperor in the Imperial and Royal Canon Foundry in 1800. He cast the horse in bronze at the Foundry in 1803. The official unveiling of the statue took place on November 24, 1807 in the presence of crowds of onlookers. Emperor Franz I expressed his appreciation by elevating the sculptor to the nobility. The fact that the very same artist delivered both the model (according to the latest research, the original inspiration for the sculpture came from the painter Friedrich Heinrich Füger) and the bronze casting was a sensation which propelled Zauner to Europe-wide fame.

Johann Martin Fischer and Viennese Classicism

Apart from Zauner, the other major sculptor working in Vienna at the beginning of the nineteenth century was Johann Martin Fischer. Fischer never went to Rome. His knowledge of ancient works of art came from the engravings in the library of the Akademie and the plaster casts that formed part of the teaching materials. Perhaps this was the reason why he was unable to free himself entirely from the Baroque.

The fountain figure of Hygeia (illustration left) can be described as his first — and purest — Classical work, thanks to the steady standing pose and the self-contained form. In the figure of Moses, on the other hand, (illustration opposite), produced eleven years later (in 1798), the spirit of the Baroque shows through once again in the curved pose and the affectation of the outstretched right hand. The solid shape of the torso is enclosed within the parallel lines of the heavy folds of a robe which seems to be no more than a corset designed to restrict movement. This

Franz Anton Zauner
The Work of Emperor Joseph II in Agriculture, 1795 – 1807 Relief panels in cast metal on the Memorial to Emperor Joseph II.

Johann Martin Fischer
Moses Fountain in Franziskanerplatz, 1798, metal casting

intermingling of two intrinsically conflicting styles
now became Fischer's hallmark and gave rise to
the rich vocabulary of gestures of the fountain figures of St. Joseph and St. Leopold in Am Graben,
produced in 1804.

A similar compositional equilibrium was not
achieved until Fischer created his two dual-figure
arrangements in 1812. These were also fountain
sculptures for the Platz am Hof. The narrative
nature of the compositions was the reason for
their rather banal titles, *The Loyalty of the Austrian Nation* and *Farming*. In *Farming*, the farmer's
clothing and especially his muscular arms and
emaciated face convey a sense of realism which
anticipates the developments of much later in the
nineteenth century.

The two works are no longer in their original
locations but can be seen today, relieved of their
original function as waterspouts, as statues in
front of the main entrance of the Historisches
Museum on the Karlsplatz.

Johann Martin Fischer
Allegorical Fountain: Farming,
1812
Metal casting, h.: 104 1/3 in
(265 cm)
Historisches Museum der
Stadt Wien

Franz Kähsmann
Funerary monument to Franz
Edlen von Mack in the parish
church of Kalksburg, 1796,
Carrara marble

square structure. The Berlin-based sculptor Johann Gottfried Schadow, with whom Zauner was in contact, had already used the motif of soldiers in mourning back in 1786, in a frieze forming part of his design for a (never executed) burial monument for Frederick the Great. The emphasis on medieval warrior virtues anticipates the subject matter of Romanticism (the soldier also bears similarities to the Roman tomb guards in medieval depictions of the Resurrection), giving the Laudon burial monument a unique place in Austrian art history.

There is another link with Schadow in the freestanding cenotaph for Emperor Leopold II in the Georg Chapel of the Augustiner church. The relaxed bearing of the deceased and the way in which the figure is slightly turned toward the observer evoke the figure on the tomb of the young Count Alexander von der Mark (1790, National Gallery, Berlin). The Emperor, dressed in the uniform of a cuirassier, appears to rest on the green marble sarcophagus as if asleep. The wistful female figure leaning against it, like the soldier on the Laudon tomb, represents grief personified — the feelings of the bereaved captured in stone. The flaming cross in her hand identifies her as a religious apparition, but her pain is earthly and thus far removed from the Baroque veiling of death with symbols of eternity and the transience of earthly pleasures, and allegorical figures. This figure is in the same tradition as those figures of mourning designed to draw attention to the loss of a loved one, though from the mid eighteenth century onwards they are depicted making extravagant gestures. A more comprehensible, bourgeois variant on this idea is the woman embracing the bust of Lord von Mack (illustration left), a tomb composition erected at about the same time by Zauner's pupil Franz Kähsmann. There is no place for transfiguration or symbolism here; she is simply a mourner weeping at the death of a loved one.

The tomb of Archduchess Marie Christine von Sachsen-Teschen by Antonio Canova

During Canova's stay in Vienna in 1798, Duke Albert von Sachsen-Teschen asked the sculptor to produce a sepulcher for his recently deceased wife, Marie Christine (illustration on p. 250). Canova, one of the most important sculptors and political figures of his time, provided the imperial city with a highly acclaimed work of art that was admired and emulated by many.

The pyramid was a shape that was widely used at the end of the eighteenth century, especially for burial purposes, in keeping with its original function. Canova translated the motif into a two-dimensional form, covering the side-wall of Augustiner church with a pyramid built into the wall. A group of three-dimensional grieving figures bearing the ashes of the deceased is making

Funerary sculpture

On October 9, 1783, Emperor Joseph II issued a burial ordinance which had a significant effect on burial practices in Vienna and caused many members of the nobility to arrange to be buried on their country estates. At the end of the eighteenth century, numerous landscaped gardens were created in the Vienna area based on the English model, which included tombs designed as temple-style buildings. The tombs of Counts Fries in Vöslau and Lord von Mack in Kalksburg near Vienna are good examples. Landscaped gardens reflected the prevailing love of nature and provided scope for further creative expression.

One of the few "park graves" still in its original location is that of Ernst Gideon Freiherr von Laudon (or Loudon), which Zauner erected in the Vienna suburb of Hadersdorf in 1790-91. It is actually based on a design by Füger. The sculpture of a mourning knight sitting on the steps in front of the sarcophagus reveals that the deceased was a staff officer in the high command. Depictions of warriors recur in the bas-relief surrounding the

Franz Anton Zauner
Tomb of Ernst Gideon Freiherr von Laudon,
1790-91
Sandstone, Vienna-Hadersdorf

Franz Anton Zauner
Tomb of Emperor Leopold II in the Georg
Chapel of the Augustiner Church, 1795
Carrara marble, green marble, and lead

Antonio Canova
Tomb of Archduchess Marie
Christine von Sachsen-Teschen in
the Augustiner Church
1800-05, Carrara marble

for the portal-style opening in the center, thus directing the gaze of the onlooker into the dark void. The emotionalism of the scene draws the observer into the action, but would turn him into an unwelcome, albeit unwilling, onlooker, were it not for the winged figure on the right-hand side leaning over the lion and watching what is going on in motionless bewilderment.

For the Marie Christine tomb, Canova used the design for a burial monument to Titian which was never built. He also heeded the wishes of his patron by incorporating a lion as a symbol of the strength of character of the deceased. Although a studio would have been available in Vienna, the monument was created in Rome and it was not until summer 1805 that it was erected in Vienna in the presence of the sculptor.

The fact that he was paid 20,000 ducats illustrates how highly the work was valued, and the esteem in which Canova was held. Even in 1798, Emperor Franz II (I) wanted to persuade him to stay in Vienna, but the Venetian master would only agree to supervise the Viennese scholarship students in Rome. This undertaking was secured largely as a result of the political changes which led to Venice coming under Austrian rule in 1797, making Canova an "Austrian" artist, and thus a subject of the Emperor.

Leopold Kiesling and Johann Nepomuk Schaller

Canova's influence on the next generation of artists is unmistakable. His individualistic, liberal way of treating models drawn from Antiquity was widely accepted and soon displaced the Classical-monumental style of Zauner. It is also thanks to Canova's recommendations to the Imperial court that the Rome-based students were able to demonstrate their artistry by being awarded commissions by the state.

Leopold Kiesling, who had been in Rome since 1801, chose the subject of *Mars and Venus with Cupid* for this purpose. The work bears similarities to Canova's sculpture *Venus and Adonis* created in the early 1790s (Villa La Grange, Geneva), both in Mars's upright posture and arm position, and in the flowing contours of the female figure clinging to the hero. In terms of content, the work in turn bears a resemblance to the group *Venus and Mars* (1816, Buckingham Palace, London), which Kiesling may have known of. In addition, the execution of the hair with the slightly stylized thick curls and the subtle treatment of the skin and fabrics indicate the stylistic influence of the Venetian master.

Schaller, the next imperial scholar, displayed more freedom and independence in his interpretation of the sculptural tradition, and greater sophistication in incorporating contemporary sculptural influences. The young sculptor worked with Canova but also enjoyed regular contact with

Antonio Canova
Theseus fighting the Centaur, 1805-19
Carrara marble
Kunsthistorisches Museum

Johann Nepomuk Schaller
Bellerophon fighting the Chimera, 1821
Carrara marble, h.: 83 in (210 cm)
Österreichische Galerie Belvedere

Leopold Kiesling
Mars and Venus with Cupid, 1810
Carrara marble, h.: 87½ in (222 cm)
Österreichische Galerie Belvedere

Joseph Kähsmann
Jason and Medea, 1829
Carrara marble
Ambassadors' steps, Imperial
Palace

Joseph Klieber and the Baroque Revival

At about the same time, works of art were being produced in Vienna in which Classicism was combined with a softer, almost Baroque touch. This change is largely associated with the sculptor Joseph Klieber. The group, *Flora and Zephyrus*, his principal work, located in Baden near Vienna, is full of overlapping and space-creating elements which make the two figures appear to be spirally intertwined. Bold indents, perforations, and overlaps seem almost to surpass the possibilities afforded by the porous sandstone. In the ten-figure group entitled *Apollo and the Muses* produced shortly thereafter, which graces the former music room in the City Palace of Archduke Carl (now the Albertina Palace), the fabrics of the garments appear to be "lighter," and the folds bunch up at the ends into ornamental ruffles. The faces no longer have a timeless character — instead the faint smiles on their faces give an impression of earthly preoccupations.

Joseph Klieber
Flora and Zephyrus, 1817
Sandstone
Women's pool,
Baden near Vienna

Johann Nepomuk Schaller
Empress Maria Ludovica, 1814
Marble, h.: 28 in (71 cm)
Österreichische Galerie Belvedere

the Danish sculptor Bertel Thorvaldsen, whose cool brand of Classicism is evident in the early Roman works. He also took an interest in German Renaissance art and the works of the Italian early Renaissance, to which he was introduced by the Brotherhood of St. Luke. Commissioned by the Imperial court to produce "a life-size statue of a young male," Schaller went as far as to create a complete group entitled *Bellerophon fighting the Chimera* (illustration on p. 251). Schaller purposely designed the sculpture to be viewed from different angles, thus enabling the viewer to gain a constantly changing impression of the dramatic fight. By doing this, Schaller went against the prevailing tradition in Rome of designing a sculpture to have one main aspect. A comparison of this work with Canova's monumental group, *Theseus fighting the Centaur*, produced in Rome at about the same time and bought by Franz I for the city of Vienna, shows the Austrian to be in confident form at the peak of his artistic maturity.

When Canova died in 1822, the Danish sculptor Bertel Thorvaldsen became a valuable contact for foreign students staying in Rome. However, his remote, "idealized" style found little favor among Austrian artists, although his influence is recognizable in particular in the works of Joseph Kähsmann, who followed Schaller to Rome as a scholar. His group, *Jason and Medea*, produced for the imperial residence in 1829, is similar to Thorvaldsen's *Jason* in the way the figure of the warrior is executed, but without achieving the same proportional balance. There is only one work by Thorvaldsen himself in Vienna, *Amor triumphans*, which stands beside the grand staircase in the City Hall. The two commissions which he was awarded during his short stay in the Imperial city in 1820 were never realized.

It was undoubtedly Klieber who ensured the continued development of the Canova style in Vienna. Klieber, who had never been to Rome, learned the principles of Classicism from Zauner and Fischer at the Viennese Academy and refined his skills while working for a respectable firm of sculptors. Works in many towns around Austria testify to the artist's versatility. In the capital, as well as the group of muses already mentioned, he also produced the sculptures of *Minerva* and of *Mars at Rest*, a pair of sphinxes, and a series of reliefs for the palace of Archduke Carl. For the library of the Abbey of the Scots (*Schottenstift*) he created an allegory of the arts and sciences in the form of a relief. He was also responsible for the façade of the main building of the Technical University and adorned "The Blue Carp" house (Annagasse 14) with a frieze of frolicking cherubs. In addition, he demonstrated his sensitivity as a portraitist in the bust of Archduke Carl and in the statue of Franz I, both of which are to be seen in the hall of the Technical University.

An Import from Lombardy: the Franz monument in the Inner Palace Courtyard

After the completion of the equestrian statue of Joseph II, there were no more official commissions for large sculptures in Vienna for several decades. The Napoleonic Wars, followed by the Congress of Vienna, put considerable strain on state finances, and a phase of regeneration followed. In 1903, the art historian Ludwig von Hevesi accurately described the situation when he wrote: "First, people had no time for art, and then they had no money." When a competition was finally held in 1838 for a bronze memorial in honor of Emperor Franz I, it became a tempting challenge for the majority of Austrian sculptors.

However, before the competition was even over, Ferdinand I awarded the contract to the Milanese sculptor Pompeo Marchesi. The Emperor was not unfamiliar with his work, since shortly before, Marchesi had erected a monument to Emperor Franz in the city of Graz and enjoyed an enviable reputation at the time, even outside Lombardy. However, this decision meant that Austrian artists missed out on the only large commission to be awarded in Vienna in the first half of the nineteenth century. Klieber's statue at the Technical University, mentioned above, was only small consolation. Schaller, on the other hand, produced his main work for the town of Innsbruck (the monument to the freedom fighter Andreas Hofer) and for the town Stanislav (monument to Franz I) in Galicia (now in Poland and called Ivano-Frankivsk).

The Franz monument was to be sited in the Inner Palace Courtyard. Marchesi portrayed the Emperor in a standing pose, resembling a Roman emperor, on a massive granite pedestal. The straightforward iconographic depictions are limited to the monarch's contributions to trade, agriculture, art, and science (relief panels on the pedestal) and the three-dimensional personifications of Justice, Strength, Peace, and Religion at the feet of the main figure. The actual statue of the emperor is huge and, despite the emphasis on the body forms, only crudely executed. The allegories are also stiff and reserved. Only the architectural division of the base and the sequence of movements in the relief panels offer any sense of fluidity. The figures and reliefs were cast in Milan and transported to Vienna in several stages. The unveiling of the monument took place on June 16, 1846. Contemporary critics rightly expressed their regret at the lack of a "modern" solution in the style of Christian Daniel Rauch in Berlin or Johann Nepomuk Schaller, whose design for the monument was in narrative epic form.

Religious subjects and Romanticism

Following the reforms of Joseph II, there was a massive decline in commissions for sacred buildings, and sacred art in Austria entered a period of stagnation. Religious subjects became less and less popular and increasingly had to make way for Classical subjects from Antiquity until, eventually, religious motifs went completely out of fashion, except for the occasional fountain decoration. Regrettably, one of the rare works of Classicism on a religious theme, the high altar in the Augustinerkirche, is no longer in its original place. It was in the early 1780s that Franz Anton Zauner was asked to produce the angels for the altar, but just a century later, the altar was sold to the parish church of Sarasdorf in Lower Austria. All other church decorations created around this time were predominantly Baroque in style, and this continued to be the case well into the next century.

It was only in the second quarter of the nineteenth century that a change of style became perceptible. The angels by Johann Nepomuk Schaller (1840) in the Dominikanerkirche, his *Black Madonna* for the Abbey of the Scots in Vienna and his *St. Margaret* on Margarethenplatz show how Classicism was already being "diluted" and supplanted by a more Romantic, Nazarene-influenced approach. The figures give an impression of sincerity and spirituality, thus portraying emotions that had previously been neglected. Schaller's approach was emulated by many of his contemporaries, such as Joseph Kähsmann, who created *The Madonna and Child on the Globe* and the *Crucifixion Group* in the Schottenfeldkirche, Adam Rammelmayr, creator of the *Rebecca Fountain* and his stepson Joseph Preleuthner, who sculpted the *Guardian Angel Fountain* on Rilkeplatz. In terms of their structure and sparse movement, the figures undoubtedly retain something of the Classical style, but the poses and facial features herald a new sense of gracefulness reminiscent of the works of Raphael.

The historical and political path of Romanticism, on the other hand, was shaped by patriotic thinking, and expressed itself in art as a whole primarily through the use of medieval or "German Renaissance" forms. An important

Johann Nepomuk Schaller
St. Margaret on the Margaret Fountain, 1836, metal casting. Margarethenplatz

Adam Rammelmayr
The figure of Rebecca from the Rebecca Fountain on Franziskanerplatz, ca. 1846, metal casting

Franz Bauer
High altar figures in the Church
of Maria am Gestade, ca. 1846
Gilded and painted wood

best artists he had come across on his travels in Italy to help revitalize his royal capital. A tendency emerged which combined Romanticism with patriotism, based on the thinking of the Romantics and the Nazarenes, which exchanged Classical mythology for the home-grown Nibelung legends and subjects from German history.

This approach also forms the basis for the design of the fountain on the Freyung, which was meant to symbolize Austria as a world power. The river deities Danube, Po, Vistula, and Elbe represent the geographical scope of the country, which is symbolized by an allegorical female figure — Austria — on the upper level. The wall coping, spear, and shield are the traditional symbols used to depict a city or country, whereas her Valkyrie-like armor, the heavy heraldic cloak over her shoulders, and her partially loose, flowing hair hark back to the medieval age of chivalry. There is also a medieval note in the trunk of the oak tree which links the two levels, and the stylized oakleaves. The personified rivers, on the other hand, give the impression of a soft, smooth physical presence; their genders are based on their German names.

What strikes the onlooker is the lack of overlap within the group. There are no links between the levels, making the fountain appear to be divided into two distinct parts.

Hans Gasser and Munich Romanticism

Hans Gasser of Carinthia must be viewed in the context of his association with the German sculptor Ludwig Schwanthaler. After studying at the Viennese Academy, Gasser obtained a scholarship to go to Munich to broaden his skills. In the course of his five-year stay in the city (1842-47), he acquainted himself with Munich Romanticism, particularly through his friendship with the painter Julius Schnorr von Carolsfeld and his close contact with Schwanthaler. This constituted the basis for his artistic endeavors.

Upon his return to Vienna, Gasser immediately produced the small statuette *Heartache* (illustration on p. 257). The work, full of quiet intimacy, portrays a girl saying goodbye to her two sisters. The narrative-style treatment of the subject was unique in the history of Austrian sculpture, and, indeed, in the œuvre of the master himself, many of whose works—particularly large sculptures— are to be found in Vienna. A short-term teaching post at the Viennese Academy enabled Gasser to apply the methods of the Romantics to Austrian art, and thereby to mediate between Munich and Vienna. However, despite being extremely popular with his students, he was soon relieved of his post because of his political activities.

example of this tendency is the Franzensburg Palace in Laxenburg near Vienna, started in 1798, whose architecture, sculptures, and interior design echo the Gothic style. An early example in Vienna itself is the Church of Maria am Gestade, one of the city's oldest places of worship, destroyed in 1809 by French occupying forces and rebuilt in the original Gothic style in 1820 on the instructions of Franz I.

The use of historic styles still lacked scientific accuracy, and so the high altar erected in 1845-46 by the Bohemian sculptor Thomas Marik combined a Baroque canopied altar with Gothic ornamentation. In contrast, the figures by Franz Bauer, and especially those of God the Father and the two angels in the composition (illustration above), are reminiscent of the paintings and drawings of the Nazarenes.

An Import from Munich:
The Austria Fountain on the Freyung

The first "patriotic" monument on Viennese soil must have been the *Austria Fountain* on the Freyung, completed in 1846 (illustration on p. 257). It was commissioned by the then Mayor of Vienna, Ignaz Czapka, and conceived and executed by the Munich-based court sculptor Ludwig Schwanthaler. In the years leading up to 1850, Munich had started to supersede Rome as the center of artistic activity. The art-loving Regent Ludwig I managed to engage the

Nineteenth Century Sculpture

Hans Gasser
Heartache (The Three Daughters
of Julius Schnorr von Carolsfeld),
1851, plaster of Paris,
h.: 14 1/4 in (36 cm)
Österreichische Galerie Belvedere

Ludwig Schwanthaler
Austria Fountain in the Freyung
Completed 1846, metal casting

The vast amount of construction in Vienna in the second half of the century meant Gasser was able to leave his mark on many public buildings and squares. His works include the portrait statue of Empress Elisabeth in the hall of the Western Railway Station (fortunately the statue was saved when the building was destroyed in 1945) and the statue of Baron von Sonnenfels in front of the City Hall. However, his most famous work is *The Danube Woman*, erected in 1865 as a fountain statue in the Municipal Park (now replaced by a copy). Water nymphs were one of the key motifs of Romanticism, but the figure in Gasser's interpretation has lost her status as a mythical creature. The pose of the female figure exudes feminine confidence, while the leg placed slightly forward and the raised arm invite the onlooker to observe the naked body.

By creating such an active presence, Gasser avoided the introverted narrative style that sometimes occurs in Romantic historicism, for example in the *Goose-Girl Fountain* by Anton Paul Wagner (at the corner of Mariahilferstrasse and Rahlstiege), produced around the same time. The figures on the two basin fountains by the State Opera House, dedicated to music and the Lorelei, display a similar dynamism — the former through the personification of dance, joy, and carefreeness, and the latter through the personification of grief, love, and revenge. The design is similar to that of the Austria Fountain, but Gasser managed to link the different levels to rhythmic effect.

Like Gasser, Anton Dominik Fernkorn also studied under Schwanthaler before settling in Vienna in 1840. While in Munich, the two artists formed a close friendship. Their mutual influence is evident in many of their works, such as Fernkorn's *Danube Woman Fountain* (1861) in the Austro-Hungarian Bank, now the Ferstl Palace. However, Romantic depictions of nymphs and woodland scenes were of no interest to Fernkorn. Instead, he found his artistic expression in heroic monumental sculpture.

Hans Gasser
Danube Woman, 1865
Marble
Historisches Museum der
Stadt Wien

Anton Dominik Fernkorn
The Lion of Aspern, 1850
Sandstone
Asperner Heldenplatz, Aspern

Anton Dominik Fernkorn

The first monuments to be commissioned during the reign of Franz Joseph were intended to illustrate Austria's "military might" and draw attention to the empire's military glory. The erection of a military monument to strengthen morale in the army also seems to be an act of political calculation in this context. The monument was erected at Aspern, and was intended to commemorate the battle against Napoleon which had taken place there on May 21-22, 1809.

Fernkorn was entrusted with the creation of the memorial in 1855. In the resulting *Lion of Aspern* (illustration above), he uses the metaphor — one that had been commonly employed since Antiquity — of the dying lion to represent fading strength. The motif had been used not long previously in Classical works such as Thorvaldsen's sculpture in Lucerne, Rauch's work in the Invaliden cemetery in Berlin, Zauner's relief on the Laudon tomb and the tomb sculpted by Canova in the Augustinerkirche in Vienna.

However, Fernkorn does not repeat the usual passive posture of the animal. Despite being fatally wounded from the spear-tip in his side, the lion crushes the French trophies with his powerful front paws, almost as a final act in the death throes. Despite the heroic treatment of the subject, the animal's pain is expressed in a vivid, human way in the pose and the face.

What made Feldkorn's name, however, are the two equestrian statues on the Heldenplatz. These works earned the sculptor a definite place in the history of art. It should not be forgotten that, at the time these two monuments were being planned, the city of Vienna consisted only of the Inner District, and that vehicular access to the Imperial Palace was via what is now the Heldenplatz. The two monuments to Archduke Carl and Prince Eugene thus assumed

Anton Dominik Fernkorn
Monument to Archduke Carl on
Heldenplatz, 1860, metal casting

the function of "gatekeepers" (Krause), which
was considered to be perfectly in keeping with
Romantic ideals.

The two statues were not planned simultaneously. The design for the monument to Archduke Carl (illustration on pp. 258-259) was completed by 1848, but because of the turmoil of
the revolution, the actual monument was not
commissioned until 1853. Fernkorn based his
portrayal of the victor of Aspern on a legend
according to which the army commander
spurred on his troops by raising the regimental
colors high in the air, thereby securing victory
over the forces of Napoleon. Fernkorn's sculpture was modeled on the painting *Archduke Carl
with the Colors of the Zach Regiment in the Battle of Aspern* by Johann Peter Krafft.

The translation of the image into a monumental, three-dimensional bronze figure constitutes an enormous achievement on the part of
the sculptor. The rider and horse are portrayed
at the height of the action and only the horse's
two rear hooves are on the ground, so that the

weight is transferred to the baseplate at only
two points. The ease with which the horse and
rider appear to hover over the pedestal is thus
based on a well-calculated distribution of masses and proportions. In this bronze statue of
Archduke Carl, Fernkorn fulfilled the centuries-
old sculptors' dream last accomplished by
Leonardo in his equestrian monument to
Francesco Sforza in Milan.

It was only through Fernkorn that artistic casting was made possible in Vienna. He had
acquired the requisite technical knowledge
about the casting process while studying at the
Munich Academy. Back in Vienna, he set up his
studio and workshop in the Royal and Imperial
Canon Foundry, which had not been used for
artistic purposes since the production of the
memorial to Joseph II, and changed its name to
"The Royal and Imperial Art Foundry." As well as
his own works, many of the other bronze sculptures of the period were produced there.

Much as this monument is appreciated today,
it received a poor reception upon its completion

from critics at the time. The art historian Rudolf von Eitelberger, for example, likened it to a "statuette enlarged to colossal proportions," in which the "first law of monumental sculpture, namely the maintenance of a spiritual balance between movement and stillness" had been ignored. This condemnation may have been a factor in the decision to portray the horse and rider moving at a gentle trot in the next military sculpture, namely the monument to Field Marshall Schwarzenberg on Schwarzenbergplatz, created by Ernst Julius Hähnel in 1860.

The commission for the second equestrian statue on today's Heldenplatz, to honor Prince Eugene's victory over the Turks, was eventually also awarded to Fernkorn. However, this time, the Monuments Committee had a much greater say in the design. The first design proposed by the sculptor, which portrayed horse and rider with the same dynamism as the Archduke Carl Memorial, was rejected on the grounds that this depiction did not match any known episode in the prince's life. Eventually, a compromise solution was reached. The horse rears up, with the army commander greeting his soldiers below. However, the figure did not share the same effortless appearance as its earlier counterpart. The monument was unveiled in 1865.

History in stone:
The Hall of Commanders in the Arsenal and the figures on the Elisabeth Bridge

The first major commission during the reign of Franz Joseph was the Arsenal. In the Waffenmuseum (now the Heeresgeschichtliches Museum), in particular, the idea was to create harmony between the architecture, painting, and sculpture. Many of Vienna's sculptors worked here together. On the ground floor hall of this, the first museum building on Viennese soil, called the "Hall of Commanders", fifty-six famous commanders were commemorated with life-size statues (illustration opposite.) Many of the sculptors who worked on these figures were also working on some of the most important buildings which were being erected at the time. These sculptors included Joseph Preleuthner, Anton Paul Wagner, Vincenz Pilz, Joseph Gasser, Johann Meixner, and Karl Kundmann. However, because they had to follow a set scheme, their creative style was very much cramped. They were asked to produce standing figures which could be placed around a pillar in groups of four. The figures also had to bear a strong likeness to their subject and be presented in historical dress. Thus the impression of grandeur is due mainly to the quantity of sculptures, rather than any outstanding artistic merit.

The creation of the Waffenmuseum, an armory museum, marked the zenith and the apotheosis of the demonstration of military might. The figures commissioned in the 1860s already show signs of a more liberal approach, in that great thinkers and even artists were considered worthy of a monument. An early example of this change of outlook is in the eight figures on the former Elisabeth Bridge, which now line the square between the City Hall and the Burgtheater. The theme was originally meant to be a military one, but the works eventually focused on the history of Vienna and those who had rendered outstanding service to the city. These were Heinrich II Jasomirgott (illustration left), Leopold VI the Glorious, Rudolf IV the Founder, Niklas Graf Salm, Rüdiger Graf Starhemberg, Bishop Leopold Graf Kollonitsch, Johann Bernhard Fischer von Erlach and Joseph Sonnenfels. The execution of the statues was entrusted to eight different sculptors who went about their task independently of each other and without any restrictive brief (with the exception that the figures had to appear in contemporary dress). This may explain the lack of schematic unity within the ensemble.

Unfortunately, it is impossible to overlook the unimaginative reworking of existing forms in the modeling of the figures. Poch-Kalous was right when he called his era an artistic low-point, despite the large number of working artists and the high level of output. However, the confident pose and facial expression of Bishop Kollonitsch by Vincenz Pilz are worth a mention, as is the figure of Heinrich Jasomirgott by Franz Melnitzky, whose statue is the most convincingly modeled of the eight, thanks to the way in which the cloak is draped naturally over the figure's back.

Architectural sculpture on the Ringstrasse

As already mentioned, the cityscape was transformed by the emperor's decision to enlarge the Imperial capital. After the architects, it was the sculptors who made the largest contribution, both in the creation of free-standing monuments,

Johannes Benk
Jamb figures on the main portal of Votivkirche, 1870, marble

Franz Melnitzky
Heinrich Jasomirgott, 1867
Marble, Rathausplatz

Access ramp at the Parliament
with rich sculptural decoration

Testament wall figures (illustration on p. 261) were the first work produced by the young Benk on his return from Italy, so it is not surprising that traces of Italian flair are detectable in the modeling of the body — particularly in the sculpture of Isaac on the far right — in the rhythm of movement and in the confident presence of the figures. Above these, in the tympanum, Joseph Gasser's figures of the saints and reliefs depicting the Sermon on the Mount, the Birth of Christ, and the Crucifixion, on the other hand, hardly protrude from the surface and are stereotypical in their movements. Together with Christ the Saviour on the trumeau pillar, they are more clearly subordinated to the overall concept and thus to the medieval building principles adopted than are the figures by Johannes Benk.

The Parliament

The individual most concerned with presenting a unified architectural and sculptural style was Theophil Hansen, architect of the Imperial Council building (now the Parliament, illustration left). Here, every sculpture was tied into the architectural concept in terms of both form and content, with the aim of creating an integrated work of art. The construction spanned several decades. It was started in 1878 and only finished in 1902 with the completion of the fountain in front of the ramp. The main figure in this fountain was originally supposed to be Austria personified — it may have been due to political considerations that a "masterful solution" was eventually decided on in the form of a figure of Pallas Athene. "Masterful" in that the actual plan of the fountain was not altered. The river deities would still symbolize the rivers of Austria but would now simply have a politically neutral figure, the goddess of wisdom, standing over them. The statue was produced by Karl Kundmann, and modeled on the Athena Parthenos.

The architect had to make artistic concessions with regard to the design of the center gable, however, since it was the intended site for the scene to be entitled Emperor *Franz Joseph grants the Crown Lands their Constitution* (illustration opposite). The Monuments Committee awarded the commission to Edmund Heller, against Hansen's will. Hansen thought Heller's painterly style of sculpture, which at that time was Baroque-orientated, would jeopardize the neo-Classical principles of the building, which is why there was considerable friction while the work was in progress.

This conflict between the Classically-inspired and the Baroque-inspired manifests itself in the way movements, gestures and drapes are dispensed with wherever possible. All the figures are arranged in relation to the central point, and the individual groups are positioned strictly in relation to the portico below, and never overlap. In the

ILLUSTRATION OPPOSITE
TOP:

Edmund Hellmer
Emperor Franz gives the Crown
Lands their Constitution, ca.
1880
Tympanum relief on the main
portico of the Parliament
Marble

BOTTOM:
Vincenz Pilz
Chariot, ca. 1880
Crowning figure on the roof of the
Parliament, metal casting

fountain sculptures, and architectural sculptures, and in the ornamentation of ceilings, walls, and even light fittings. The large number of objects produced rules out a detailed examination of the sculptural achievements of the time, so only a few examples can be discussed here. Unfortunately, as in the case of the Arsenal, the sculptor's artistic freedom was usually restricted by having to adhere to the architect's set scheme, which brought results of varying quality.

The Votivkirche

A discrepancy between the plan and the end result can also be observed in the Votivkirche, the first building to be constructed on the Ringstrasse, founded even before the demolition of the city walls. It was intended as a monument to recall the foiled assassination attempt on the young Emperor Franz Joseph in 1853. Although the Neo-Gothic edifice was constructed strictly according to the medieval principles of the association of church builders and craftsmen, and despite the close cooperation between the architect, Heinrich von Ferstl and the chief sculptor, Joseph Gasser (unrelated to Hans Gasser) the result did not produce the desired harmony of style. French, German, and Italian elements of High Gothic and the early Renaissance co-exist here, prompting a comparison with a "source book of designs of medieval art forms" (Poch-Kalous). The juxtaposition of the conflicting styles of Joseph Gasser and Johannes Benk on the main portal, however, is particularly endearing. The Old

each drawn by four horses, produced by Vincenz Pilz, starting in 1882, tower over the square building (illustration on p. 263). They are the best and most original works on the parliament building. Despite their varied movements, the impetuous surging of the horses and the gestures of the winged Victory figures urging them on, the groups each form an integral, self-contained whole. The chariots are positioned facing each other in pairs, so that the whirl of movement is confined to the square of the roof area. Thanks to their sheer size and their exposed position, they give the building a powerful finishing touch. Whereas the other figures are modeled in pale-colored stone, the dark metal of the chariots creates the perfect connection to the bronze horseriders at the foot of the ramp of the building.

The Tegetthoff Monument by Karl Kundmann and Carl von Hasenauer

The monument to the victor of the naval battle of Lissa (1866), Admiral Wilhelm von Tegetthoff, at the Praterstern (illustration left) was also produced with the sculptor and architect working closely together. It is an unusual monument which portrays the hero standing on a tall pillar. His pose is that of a naval officer on the bridge of a ship, who pays no attention to his immediate surroundings but instead is taking a closer look through his binoculars at something he has spotted in the distance. The allusion to Nelson's Column in Trafalgar Square, London (William Railton, 1839-49) is evident, but here the concept is taken a step further by the architect, Carl von Hasenauer. He interrupts the shaft of the column with pairs of ships' bows, whose stylized rams play on the idea of the ramming tactic which Tegetthoff employed when he led the Austrian fleet to victory over the Italian enemy in 1866. Allegorical figures such as Bellona and Victoria, Neptune escorted by seahorses, and a trophy on the base of the monument, glorify the military achievements of the hero in the traditional Baroque manner.

Rudolf Weyr, Theodor Friedl, and Victor Tilgner

At the same time as architects were imposing strict historical contexts on sculptors, a more liberal style of sculptural modeling had begun to emerge in the course of the 1870s. It lent sculpture a painterly feel and eventually gave rise to works in the neo-Baroque and neo-Rococo styles. This release from inhibiting stylistic constraints finally enabled sculptors to confidently leave their own personal signature on their works. The Vienna World Exhibition in 1873, and the works of the French sculptor, Gustave Deloye, in particular, had a huge impact on artistic development in this period. But the real forerunner of the Neo-Baroque in Vienna was the painter, Hans Makart. His lifestyle, his studio, and his pictures paved

Karl Kundmann and Carl von Hasenauer
Monument to Admiral Wilhelm von Tegetthoff at the Praterstern 1879, metal casting and stone

centre of the tympanum, in front of the throne, stands the most crudely worked figure of the ensemble, Emperor Franz Joseph. His engaged leg and free leg are uninspired, and his cloak hangs like a sheet around his naked body. However, what is interesting about the tympanum sculpture is the treatment of the subject: here, on the Imperial Council building, the reigning ruler of the Austrian Empire is assigned a god-like position — he is raised up on Mount Olympus in the style of a deity in Ancient Greek art.

The lower part of the parliament building bears no sculptural ornamentation apart from the caryatids on the side-ramps, and the only architectural partitions are the pillars and pilasters. This simplicity contrasts with the mass of ornamental and scenic reliefs and statues in the roof area of the two recessed side-rooms, the work of Werner David, Victor Tilgner, Anton Paul Wagner, Rudolf Weyr, and others. Eight bronze chariots,

Theodor Friedl
Cupid and Psyche
Marble, h.: 76 in (193 cm)

the way for painterly, animated depictions of great sensory appeal.

It was one of Makart's paintings, *The Triumph of Ariadne*, which, soon after its creation, prompted the sculptor Rudolf Weyr to rework this subject as a wedding procession, executed in the form of a relief. It was completed in 1882 and since then has adorned the attic frieze of the Burgtheater (illustration above). Ariadne and Bacchus are portrayed on their chariot, surrounded by scenes of music and dancing and flirting nymphs, centaurs, and cupids. Weyr based the detailed execution on relevant models in painting and sculpture, and made free use of motifs from Rubens, Coreggio, and others, and from various depictions of abduction scenes.

Weyr was one of the most powerful representatives of the Neo-Baroque and Neo-Rococo in Vienna. As well as the reliefs on the Grillparzer memorial, the fountain outside the Michael Wing of the imperial palace, produced in 1895 which was intended to symbolize *Austria's Power at Sea* (illustration right) is especially worthy of mention. It was produced as the counterpart to *Austria's Power on Land* by Edmund Hellmer, but the structure is more organic, with a more narrative style. Weyr, too, makes reference to Tegettshoff's ramming maneuver. The ship seems to be breaking out of the building with great force, surprising the figures lying on the strand and drawing the evil powers down into the watery depths. Although Hellmer's composition is animated and full of detail, the layered structure and the static pose of the crowning figure detract from the drama of the overall effect.

Rudolf Weyr
Austria's Power at Sea, 1895,
marble
Michaelerplatz, Imperial Palace

Theodor Friedl, creator of the two Horseriders on Maria Theresien-Platz, proved to be an artist of many talents. However, only a direct comparison with the group *Cupid and Psyche* (illustration on p. 265) in the Östereichische Galerie of the Oberes Belvedere, which imitates the style of Antonio Canova in terms of its delicate and animated appearance, and the lamp-bearing cherubs in the stairwell of the same building, whose Baroque forms and gestures fit harmoniously into the architectural context, gives a full picture of Friedl's flexibility and adaptability.

Viktor Tilgner was the most confident of the sculptors of that time. His six portrait busts which he exhibited at the Vienna World Exhibition — including one of the famous actress Charlotte Wolter — had already brought him widespread recognition. However, the works of Gustave Deloyes had a crucial influence on his development. They confirmed to him that he was on the right path and at the same time spurred him on to use animated lines where appropriate, to work with light and shade, and thereby liven up the monotone material with a variety of "color shades." Tigner went on to produce the highly animated but — for niche figures — extremely independent sculptures on the ground floor of the façade of Vienna's Burgtheater and some of the figures in the window spandrels.

In the case of the fountain ensemble in the Volksgarten depicting the Theft of a Naiad by Triton (illustration left), the sensuous appeal of the surface is massively heightened by the dynamic subject-matter. The powerful grabbing action of the male sea-creature is depicted alongside the equally intense self-defensive action of the woman, a motif which is mirrored by the composition itself in the two opposing lines of vision. Krause interprets this as mimicking a detail in Makart's painting *The Triumph of Ariadne*.

Depictions of abduction scenes were generally very popular in Vienna — the Baroque groups in the garden of Schwarzenberg Palace are a good example. Tilgner had his idea for the fountain group during or soon after his trip to Italy with Hans Makart in 1874. It was thanks to a coincidence that it came to be implemented. Emperor Franz Joseph saw the model in 1875 on a visit to Makart's studio and immediately commissioned the sculptor to produce it. After being exhibited at the World Exhibition in Paris in 1878, the fountain was re-erected in the Volksgarten in 1879. Tilgner's œuvre includes fountains of all descriptions in Vienna, Bratislava (Pressburg), Bad Ischl, and many other cities of the Austro-Hungarian Empire. But it was the Mozart monument, now in the Burggarten, which made him famous.

Meanwhile, Tilgner also continued to work on portrait sculptures, increasingly turning his great talent to the challenge of achieving a life-like surface treatment. He also made use of "psychological

ILLUSTRATION OPPOSITE:
Viktor Tilgner
Triton and Naiad Fountain in the
Volksgarten, 1875-77, marble

insight" and "the gift of intuitive comprehension and penetration of the individuality of the subject" attributed to him by his contemporary, Berggruen. This judgement is confirmed by the portrait bust of Anton Bruckner—to which Franz Zerritsch added an adoring female genius—erected as a memorial in the Municipal Park three years after Tilgner's death in 1899. The plaster model is even more interesting than the finished work (illustration right). The head of the composer, which Tilgner reproduced from his own observation—Bruckner had died in 1896—is realistically modeled, and in no way disguises the facts. However, real beauty is visible in the old face through the sense of inspiration conveyed by the slightly raised hand and the distant focus of the eyes.

Memorials to musicians and poets
As already indicated, there was a radical change in the type of subject chosen for monuments in the course of these decades. From the 1860s onward, the cult of monuments was no longer led solely by the Court; the bourgeoisie were now also able to play an active role. The first memorial to a commoner from a non-military background was

Viktor Tilgner
Anton Bruckner, 1891-92
Plaster of Paris
Historisches Museum der
Stadt Wien

Karl Kundmann
Monument to Franz Schubert
Marble, municipal park

dedicated to the composer Franz Schubert (illustration left). The initiative for this came from the Vienna Male Choral Society, which entrusted the sculptor Karl Kundmann with the task of producing a "portrait statue of Schubert in the strictest sense of the word." Kundmann showed the composer sitting in an armchair while composing. He is portrayed in contemporary dress and appears to be listening to an inner voice, a new melody, his eyes gazing into the distance. The strong facial likeness was achieved courtesy of the painter Moritz von Schwind, a friend of Schubert, who made a quick sketch of his face in plaster on one of Schubert's visits to his studio.

The Schubert memorial set the precedent for the simple monument whose attractiveness depended on the artistic quality of the portrait sculpture. This also applied to the memorial to Joseph Haydn by Heinrich Natter in front of the Mariahilfer Church. Reliefs or inscriptions on the base — in Schubert's case they symbolize musical creativity, instrumental, and vocal music—were sometimes added to round off the composition.

At the same time, there was a growing trend toward portraying the artist with accompanying figures and allegories, in the manner of the monuments to Austria's rulers. The Schiller memorial by the Dresden-based sculptor Johannes Schilling (1876) was the first civic monument of this kind to be erected on Viennese soil. However, Schiller is not accompanied by allegories in the conventional sense, but by representatives of various groups of society who found moral inspiration in the works of the poet.

The Beethoven and Maria Theresia Memorials by Caspar von Zumbusch

The memorial to Ludwig van Beethoven by Caspar von Zumbusch, unveiled in 1880 (top illustrations), is regarded as the greatest artistic monument in Vienna. This Westphalian artist was commissioned to produce the monument in the year in which the World Exhibition was held, but soon after the design was completed, Vienna was hit by an economic crisis, which made production of the memorial impossible for the time being. It was the helpful intervention of Franz Liszt, who had made his last public appearance on the fiftieth anniversary of Beethoven's death (March 16, 1877) and donated the proceeds from this concert to the memorial fund, which provided the necessary finance.

Beethoven, sitting on a high pedestal, has enormous presence thanks to the oversized dimensions and the realistic portrayal. The confident pose and the brash expression on his face (in keeping with his portraits) reflect the sense of genius which flows from his compositions. The winged Victory with the laurel wreath at the base of the pedestal and Prometheus, embodying the heroic element of his musical compositions, although subordinated to the overall grouping, are perfectly modeled.

The painfully distorted body of Prometheus with the eagle at his chest is particularly impressive. The circle of nine dancing children, repre-

Detail of the Beethoven memorial: Prometheus

ADJACENT:
Caspar von Zumbusch
Memorial to Ludwig van Beethoven, 1880, metal casting

senting the nine symphonies, completes the ensemble and unites the figures on both levels to form an integrated whole. In fact, the main figure alone would have been quite sufficient for an accurate characterization of the composer.

Zumbusch's reputation spread further following the production of the memorial to the Empress Maria Theresia which stands between the Kunsthistorisches Museum and the Naturhistorisches Museum (illustrations left and opposite). The statue was conceived in 1874, in other words at exactly the same time as the Beethoven monument. This memorial which, presumably following the example of the monument to Friedrich the Great by Christian Daniel Rauch in Berlin, brings together many of the important figures of the age, was designed with reference to the ten-volume biography of Maria Theresia by Alfred Ritter von Arneth. According to contemporary reports, Zumbusch originally planned to present the monarch accompanied by powerful, galloping horses.

The figures on horseback in the actual work accentuate the cornerless form of the monument. They depict the Empress's four great commanders, Daun and Laudon, the heroes of the Seven Years War, and Khevenhüller and Traun, but the movement is controlled, with the horses appearing to move at a steady walk. This variant was obviously more appealing to imperial tastes in Vienna, as borne out by the equestrian statues of Joseph II and Schwarzenberg, as well as those of Archduke Albrecht (1888-89) and Radetzky (unveiled in 1892), the latter two by Zumbusch.

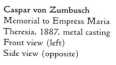

Caspar von Zumbusch
Memorial to Empress Maria Theresia, 1887, metal casting
Front view (left)
Side view (opposite)

Monument to Franz Grillparzer
in the Volksgarten, 1889, detail

The Grillparzer Memorial in the Volksgarten

The monument to Franz Grillparzer (illustrations top left and below), erected in 1889, represented a new type of memorial for Vienna. It is located in the Volksgarten, off the Ringstrasse, where it occupies one side of the rose garden. With its imposing architectural structure, it honors the poet in epic style. It is the work of the architect Carl Hasenauer and the two sculptors Carl Kundmann (Grillparzer) and Rudolf Weyr (reliefs). This joint project came about because of the Monuments Committee's inability to agree on who should carry out the work. Unlike the monuments described so far, which show the subject either standing or sitting on a high or low, square or curved, pedestal decorated with reliefs or allegories, here the main figure sits centrally between two flat-topped side-wings that curve forward into a semi-circle. The architectural form resembles the apse of a church, and the position of the poet in the cathedra is similar to that of a sacred adoration scene, which can only be interpreted as illustrating the high status of the poet in the nineteenth century.

The monarch (illustrations on pp. 268-69) sits atop a high, partitioned pedestal. In her left hand, she holds the Pragmatic Sanction, the agreement negotiated by her father Karl VI, which secured her place as successor to the throne. The sides of the pedestal, the corners of which are accentuated with double pillars, show famous figures of the time from the worlds of politics, science, and the arts, some as free-standing sculptures and some in high relief. According to the original plans, the memorial, conceived on a monumental scale, was meant to occupy a central position on the so-called "Emperors' Forum," the giant square planned by Gottfried Semper which was to link the court stables with the imperial palace, but which was never built.

Scenes from the poet's works are carved in stone on the side walls (left: *Die Ahnfrau* (The Female Ancestor), *Der Traum ein Leben* (Dream is Life), *König Ottokars Glück und Ende* (King Ottokar's Good Fortune and End); right: *Sappho, Medea, Des Meeres und der Liebe Wellen*

ILLUSTRATION OPPOSITE:
Edmund Hellmer
Monument to Johann Wolfgang
von Goethe on the Opernring,
1900
Metal casting

**Karl Kundmann, Rudolf Weyr,
Carl von Hasenauer**
Monument to Franz Grillparzer
in the Volksgarten, 1889, marble

(Waves of the Sea and of Love)) are outstanding works by Rudolf Weyr. He manages to disguise the transition from the almost three-dimensional figures in strong relief on the surface to the area of bas-relief, where additional space is created through the perfect foreshortening accomplished with the aid of calligraphic engravings.

The breadth of content exhibited by the Grillparzer memorial remains a unique phenomenon among Vienna's monuments. However, the architectural form set a precedent for future works, such as the monument to Strauss and Lanner in Vienna's Rathauspark (F. Seifert, R. Oerley, 1905) and the monument to the Empress Elisabeth in the Volksgarten (H. Bitterlich, F. Ohmann, 1907), which, with its adjacent rose hedges and pond, has even been described as a "monumental grove" (Krause). The choice of location, on the edge of a green space, is particularly interesting, since it gives the memorial an intimate, quiet character.

The Goethe Memorial by Edmund Hellmer

These observations on the development of sculpture in the nineteenth century must end with a final mention of Edmund Hellmer, the sculptor whose works on the Parliament building and whose fountain on Michaelerplatz have already been discussed. He should stand as an example of the versatility of the artist in the second half of the century. Yet at the same time, he also stands for craftsmanship and high artistic quality, which, particularly during these decades of enormous stylistic diversity, necessitated an extraordinarily high degree of adaptability or even acquiescence on the part of the sculptor. His Goethe monument (illustration right), located on the Ringstrasse, was unveiled in 1900, and represented a confident step forward into the new century.

Goethe sits in an armchair on top of a moderately high, minimally profiled pedestal. However, the poet is not portrayed in a grandiose pose. Instead, he rests comfortably, as if chatting with friends. The rug on which he is sitting, which is pushed slightly to one side, and the comfortable frock-coat also convey a sense of domesticity. The statue therefore highlights the human side of the man. There were, of course, some vehement opponents to Hellmer's design, who accused it of "banal mediocrity," and favored the proposed monument in the Neo-Baroque style. The artist's naturalistic characterization of Goethe was also said to be lacking in respect.

In the end, the chorus of approval after the unveiling confirmed the wisdom of this naturalistic approach, one which was to shape the way in which the human figure was portrayed in sculpture for years to come.

Barbara Borngässer

Architecture from the Late Nineteenth Century to the Present Day

From the Late Nineteenth Century to the End of the Monarchy

"Let me sing to you, O Vienna of the future." These are the opening lyrics of *Gross Wien* (Greater Vienna), a waltz Johann Strauss presented to an enthusiastic audience in 1891. His composition honored "Greater Vienna", which had come into being a little earlier, on December 19, 1890, when Emperor Franz Joseph I signed a decree to confirm the incorporation of the suburbs and establish the administrative status of the city on the Danube. Vienna's population now numbered just under 1.5 million people and it covered an area of 70 sq. miles (178 km²). The increase in the city's size was accompanied by profound changes in its social structure, and these provided a breeding-ground for the resurgence and cultural innovation of the city on the Danube. Vienna, seat of the imperial residence, set about competing with Paris, Berlin, and London, and the frictions that went along with this process created the myth that was fin-de-siècle Vienna.

In fact, the period between 1900 and the outbreak of World War I which ended in the abolition the monarchy was more a period of contradictions than of light-hearted festivities. The harmonies of the waltz were intermingled with less harmonious sounds. Every stratum of society was gripped by a deep sense of insecurity, fueled by uncertainty about the future of the dual monarchy, by discontent over social problems, and conflicts over the issues of religion and nationality. The "good old days" and their ethos were over and unlikely to return, and the present offered no security.

Characteristically, the tensions that dominated everyday life in the melting pot of Vienna discharged themselves in a kind of "artistic thunderstorm," an explosive mixture of elegiac otherworldliness and a great lust for knowledge, melancholic decadence alternating with bursts of high energy, sensuality, and materialism — all of which merged into an undreamed-of momentum of creative excitement.

The political situation

The euphoric mood of the industrial boom, when the Imperial city had become a haven of liberal thought, had long gone. The workers in the rapidly expanding suburbs were living in appalling conditions. The influx of Slav families from the Eastern provinces of the empire alarmed the "Germanic" population; the 1897 language decrees of Prime Minister Count Badeni resulted in severe unrest. Nascent anti-Semitism proved a time-bomb. Most of Vienna's Jewish population originated from the Sudetenland and Hungary. New arrivals soon took key positions in the commercial and cultural spheres, and were accused of capitalist machinations. The Austrian nobility, on the other hand, resisted all attempts at innovation. They shut themselves away from the rising tide of the bourgeoisie who strove to emulate their values and lifestyles.

As a result, various groups in society, who were disempowered in many different ways, sought to gain influence by creating political mass movements. The concomitant confrontations associated with this polarization became increasingly radical. Intense rancor was caused by the election to the mayoralty of the anti-Semitic Roman Catholic Karl Lueger (Illustration opposite). Initially, the Emperor refused to confirm Lueger in

Wilhelm Gause
Vienna City Ball, 1904, watercolour
Vienna Historical Museum

Sigmund Freud in 1912

A. Mayerhofer
Karl Lueger, Mayor of Vienna
1897–1910
Painted in 1902
Vienna Historical Museum

office, but eventually even he had to give way to pressure from the masses. Lueger's Christian-Socialist conservatism had the support of the petty bourgeoisie who saw him as its charismatic defender against "(Jewish) capitalism." On the positive side, Lueger made numerous improvements to the city's infrastructure, though these were a great strain on the city's coffers.

On October 31, 1899 Lueger opened the Central Gasworks at Simmering, a plant that provided street lighting for the city. Electricity for an extensive tram network followed a little later at the same location. The new mayor also founded social and charitable institutions, and he created one of the first urban "green belts" to give the population the opportunity for rest and relaxation.

However, these measures hardly changed the situation of the working population, and Lueger's anti-Semitism and clericalism proved fatal for the intellectual climate of the city. Many intellectuals and artists, including Sigmund Freud, Arthur Schnitzler, Arnold Schoenberg, and Ludwig Wittgenstein, were Jews who were completely assimilated into Viennese culture, and, through their education and entrepreneurial spirit, had gained access to the upper echelons of society. Having long felt that they "belonged" and having contributed greatly to the reputation of Vienna, these men now became disillusioned. One of the consequences of the malaise which gripped Viennese Jewry was Theodore Herzl's quest for the establishment of a Jewish state, manifested in the pamphlet, *Der Judenstaat*, published in 1896 which laid the foundations for the modern Jewish state. Attitudes were hardening in other areas too. There could be no doubt that the liberal era had finally come to an end.

The period between 1910 and 1918 saw the apocalyptic end of the Habsburg monarchy. Mass demonstrations, ending in bloodshed, against price rises and housing shortages were the order of the day; assassination attempts and scandals undermined democratic reforms. When the heir to the throne and his wife were murdered in Sarajevo on June 28, 1914, any remaining hopes for stability were shattered. One month later, Emperor Franz Joseph, urged on by a frenetic population, signed the declaration of war against Serbia. As yet, no one realized that his action would precipitate World War I and that Austro-Hungary stood on the brink of ruin. When the Emperor died on November 21, 1916, his son Charles I took over the state's affairs, but even he was unable to save the monarchy. The non-German-speaking nations broke away from Habsburg rule and the Republic of German Austria was declared on November 12, 1918.

"Art as a surrogate for action"

The turn of the century not only set the tone for the following decades in terms of social policy; but produced equally profound changes in the

realms of art and culture. Whilst the bourgeoisie felt secure during Lueger's term of office, liberals and intellectuals responded strongly to the all-pervasive mood changes. Whilst some retreated into a melancholic, moralistic, and self-pitying state, others saw the universal answer in an "estheticization" of life and dedication to art. As far as culture was concerned, the haute bourgeoisie was able to emulate aristocratic values and lifestyle." The life of the arts became a surrogate for action. The more futile political action proved to be, the more art became a religion, a source of meaning, and nourishment for the soul" (Carl E. Schorske). From this point it is no a great leap to Sigmund Freud (pictured left), who has already been mentioned and whose work provides the backdrop to an understanding of the era. Freud's *The Interpretation of Dreams* was first published in 1900, at a time when the avant-garde was finally able to banish traditional structures.

Esthetics and philosophy, architecture and town-planning, music, fine art, literature and theatre—during this period all the arts were gripped by a sense of creative unrest. In 1897, the Secession group went public with its demand for art to pervade every aspect of life, for a union of the pure and applied arts. Only three years later, the movement was to represent Austria at the Paris World's Fair. The year 1897 also saw the publication of *Ver Sacrum*, a luxuriously "stylistic" periodical which advocated the idea of the total work of art. However, because it was so lavishly produced, the journal only reached a small readership and was forced to stop publication as early as 1903. The *Wiener Werkstätten* (Viennese Workshops), launched in the same year, enjoyed greater success, and the functional yet elegant style of the publication influenced graphic design well into the 1930s and beyond.

Reinhold Völkel
In the Griensteidl Café, 1896
Watercolor, Vienna Historical
Museum
Around the turn of the century the Griensteidl Café in Michaelerplatz became a popular meeting-place for literati and politicians. The eclectic and highbrow nature of the discussions that took place there, caused the establishment to be nicknamed "Café Megalomania".

The literary arts

More immediate manifestations of the search for new values were to be found in other media, for example in the popular theatre, which had always been a barometer of Vienna's prevailing mood, and in the literary scene, which — thanks to the institution of the coffee house — was very lively indeed. The café, which had replaced the drawing rooms of earlier times, served as a meeting place for the literati, and was a hothouse of ideas, a stage, and a vanity fair — the Griensteidl Café (illustration p. 273) was aptly nicknamed "Café Megalomania." It was here that new trends first saw the light of day, new work was reviewed, people talked shop, and tore each other's work to shreds. Many publications focusing on cultural issues were launched from 1890 onward and these constituted another means of communication. Apart from *Ver Sacrum*, mentioned above, there was *Moderne Dichtung* (Modern Poetry), the voice of the *Jung Wien* (Young Vienna) writers' group, and from 1899 *Die Fackel* (The Flame), in which the critic Karl Kraus provided a biting commentary on Viennese life and literature.

Turn-of-the-century poetry oscillated between the influence of Nietzsche, symbolism, and naturalism. Titles such as *Der Tod des Tizian* (The Death of Titian, 1892) and *Der Tor und der Tod* (Death and the Fool, 1899) by Hugo von Hofmannsthal, *Der Garten der Erkenntnis* (The Garden of Knowledge, 1895) by Leopold von Andrian, *Der Ruf des Lebens* (Life's Call, 1905) and *Der Weg ins Freie* (The Lonely Road, 1908) by Arthur Schnitzler, are indicative of the themes which preoccupied and concerned the younger generation of literati. Estheticism and hedonism, a longing for death and ostentatious decadence were part of the values and lifestyle of the "esthete."

Hugo von Hofmannsthal and Arthur Schnitzler described this emotional, self-centered society in all its variations. Both writers shared an awareness of the fragmentation of the old order and a realization that human beings are governed by impulses and emotions, yet they drew completely different conclusions from this knowledge. While Hofmannsthal, "the young narcissist," helped his characters to discover themselves and thus move onto a higher plane, the more sociologically oriented Schnitzler was an ironic observer and dissector of tragic fates. However, unlike Freud, whom he resembled in many ways, Schnitzler found no satisfaction in self-knowledge.

If the Viennese Decadence movement, with all its focus on superficialities, had dominated the literary scene until the turn of the century, the new generation turned in on itself, with self-examination, the inner monologue, analysis of personal crises, and their sociological roots. Robert Musil's *Mann ohne Eigenschaften* (The Man Without Qualities) and Stefan Zweig's *Jeremiah* (1917 and 1918 respectively) are indications of this changed sense of reality.

Music

The changing times had a profound impact on the established music scene. If opinions had been divided about Bruckner and Brahms, the genius of Gustav Mahler with his sense of mission caused an even greater stir. His ten years as artistic director of the Vienna Imperial Opera —a period that was not altogether uncontroversial—began at the very moment of Bruckner's and Brahms' deaths, 1896 and 1897 respectively. As a composer of symphonic poems and an interpreter of Wagner, Mahler paved the way for a musical vocabulary that focused on expressiveness.

The real "innovators," however, were Arnold Schoenberg and his pupils Alban Berg and Anton von Webern who started the transition to twentieth century music. Schoenberg's twelve-tone compositions, Berg's compressed orchestral pieces — some of them only seconds long — such as the dramatic *Wozzeck*, shocked audiences and only gained the recognition they deserved at a much later date, and generally outside Austria.

Viennese audiences, on the other hand, were captivated by Johann Strauss' operettas *Die Fledermaus* and *Der Zigeunerbaron* (1874 and 1885) or by Franz Lehar's *The Merry Widow* (1905). The style known as *moderne* did not enter the repertoire of the Vienna Imperial Opera until later, with Richard Strauss' compositions *Salome* and *Der Rosenkavalier* (1905 and 1911). In subsequent years, the co-operation between Hugo von Hofmannsthal, Richard Strauss, and Max Reinhardt achieved legendary heights.

The era ended with another waltz, Ravel's *La Valse*, which symbolically begins harmoniously but ends in wild cacophony. This was the theme music for the outbreak of World War I and the end of the Austrian monarchy.

Architecture and town-planning

The many-faceted personality of Otto Wagner (illustration opposite) marks the turning point between historicism and the *Moderne* movement. Born in 1841, Wagner was growing up as the Ringstrasse was being developed. He studied in Vienna and at the Bauakademie in Berlin, where he became familiar with Schinkel's architecture. At the age of only 23, Wagner began his career by designing residential buildings, banks, and town houses, including his own "Rose House", built in the late Romantic style. These early buildings, designed in a "free interpretation" of the Renaissance style, may well have made him feel "sick to his stomach" later, as he claimed, but they were already characterized by a strong desire for clear, abstract shapes.

In 1892–93, Wagner was tasked with the implementation of the "General Regulation Plan", which covered the development of a public transport system with over 30 stations, as well as major engineering works on the Danube canal and its attendant infrastructure. These huge projects and Wagner's own ideas on town-planning broke new ground in terms of artistic and development work, and they helped him to make his name in a Viennese architectural scene that was already deeply rooted in eclecticism. In the following years, Wagner's firm became the driving force of architectural innovation. His seventy employees included chief designer Joseph Maria Olbrich, as well as Josef Hoffmann, Josef Plecnik, and Max Fabiani — artists who would take their place in the history of early twentieth century architecture

Egon Schiele
Portrait of Otto Wagner, 1910,
Watercolor, Vienna Historical
Museum

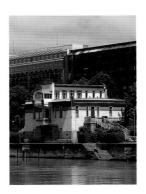

Otto Wagner
Kaiserbad lock, 1906–07

ILLUSTRATION ABOVE:
Otto Wagner
Wienzeilebrücke, 1893–98

BELOW:
Otto Wagner
Nussdorf weir and lock, 1894

OPPOSITE:
Franz von Bayros
An evening with Johann Strauss
Vienna, Bank of Austria AG
Art Collection

historic, context. It is no accident that his public transport designs create the feeling of transition through a gateway, or that — like the lock at Nussdorf — they give the impression that they are signaling to the user.

As a result of his success, Wagner was appointed director of the Vienna Academy of Architecture in 1894. In 1896, he set down his architectural and town-planning philosophy in his book *Moderne Architektur*. The work he did from 1897 through 1899 shows the influence of the Secession group, whose anti-academic attitude initially met with his sympathy and later his support. It is by no means certain whether the rich decorative detail with which classical structures now began to be encrusted arose out of Wagner's own desire to adorn or from the input of Joseph Maria Olbrich. In any case, at the time, the Hofpavillon station, which today seems a strange mish-mash (a steel dome with an idiosyncratic combination of Imperial and Secessionist motifs), caused such a furore that a whole issue of the *Secession* review was dedicated to it.

The design of the Secession building itself would be left to Joseph Maria Olbrich, but the Wienzeile buildings, two adjacent residential and commercial properties, seem to point the way toward the new style, and not only because of the design of their elevators. As for the Majolika House, decorative floral detail adorns the entire facade, and the visual separation of the stories by framing or gabling the windows, a device which had been in use for centuries, was abandoned. At No. 38 Wienzeile, the house on the corner, the classical focus on the first story, the "piano nobile" gave way to an emphasis on the whole of the ground and second floors which were designed to be storefronts. This was a decisive step toward modern commercial developments.

Otto Wagner's most important design was for the Post Office Savings Bank and it won him the design competition for this building in 1903. The project was completed in two stages, 1904–07 and 1910–12, and it gave him the opportunity to put his ideas for functional architecture into practice. The result is a revolutionary building of reinforced concrete whose visibly attached marble cladding is an almost ironic persiflage of Semper's theme of "the outer skin." The interior is dominated by the purely functional fixtures of the main hall with its counters, an area flooded with light. There are glass-doored offices, austere light fittings, and warm air vents. Nothing could have come closer to Wagner's motto "*Artis sola domina necessitas*" ("art's only mistress is necessity") than this building, erected as part of the Ringstrasse development. Wagner applied similar rigor to the design of the Steinhofkirche, a church attached to an institution for people with mental illnesses, which he had been commissioned to build by the Christian-Socialist mayor Karl Lueger.

under the name"The Wagner School." Projects such as the Ringbahn stations, the lock at Nussdorf, and the bridge over the Wienzeile (illustration opposite) reflect Wagner's main interest, a striving for a clear, functional, and progressive architectural style, combining technical innovation with esthetic design and contemporary decorative detail. Built around a steel or iron frame, these structures disguise neither their function nor their construction, although the structural framework may be shrouded in a symbolic "shroud." With regard to this dissonance between basic structure and outer layer, between reality and meaning, Wagner's earlier work still followed the tradition of Gottfried Semper. Wagner placed great importance on the location of a building, and the way in which it fitted within its urban, and even its

Here he used plain cubic shapes over a Greek cross, alongside neo-Byzantine tendencies which appealed to Lueger's conservative Roman catholicism. Wagner broke new ground, however, with the interior, which was wholly oriented to the needs of the patients, as well as its overall design which included stained-glass windows by Koloman Moser and mosaics by Remegius Geibeling. All the furnishings and decorative details served the demands of practical and spiritual therapy. After 1910, Wagner's interest shifted to the design of ideal municipal parks, but his massively uniform project in this area lacks his otherwise vibrant connection with reality.

The Secession building — erected in 1898 as an exhibition hall for the group by Wagner's younger colleague Joseph Maria Olbrich (1876–1908) — became even more of a symbol for the new architectural style than did Wagner's rational style of architecture. This "temple of the arts", inspired by a drawing by Gustav Klimt, is an archaic-looking cube topped by a dome of gilded laurel leaves. "*Der Zeit ihre Kunst – Der Kunst ihre Freiheit*" (To every age its Art, to Art its freedom) reads the inscription in gold lettering above the portal. The religious symbolism continues in the cruciform entrance hall and in the "bright and chaste" walls of the interior which provided a flexible space for displaying artwork. In contrast with Wagner, however, Olbrich focused not on the building's function; his intention was to give the artwork an aura that would stimulate the visitors' sensibilities. Although the building received a lot of attention and successfully captured the spirit of the age, Olbrich was unable to secure further work in Vienna. In Darmstadt, however, he created the Mathildenhöhe artists' colony, a unique artistic environment that was to influence every aspect of modern art.

Wagner's most important pupil, who gained international renown, was Josef Hoffmann (1870–1956, pictured left). Alongside Olbrich, was a founder member of the Vienna Secession group. He was initially known as a designer of furniture and interiors, and taught at the Arts and Crafts School from 1899. His later style, elegant and with classically pure lines, was profoundly inspired by an exhibition of work by the Scotsman Charles Rennie Mackintosh which was held in the group's exhibition hall in 1900. The Arts and Crafts movement also provided inspiration for his holistic approach to art. The establishment of the artists' colony at the Hohe Warte, as well as the setting up of the Wiener Werkstätten in 1903 were largely due to his initiative. Hoffmann's first significant architectural design, a pair of semi-detached houses for Carl Moll and Koloman Moser (1900–01) is a homage to the English country house style. It also tries to reduce the opulently "masked" architecture of the turn of the century to an artistically more sophisticated, elegant simplicity.

The architect and designer Josef Hoffmann (1870–1956)

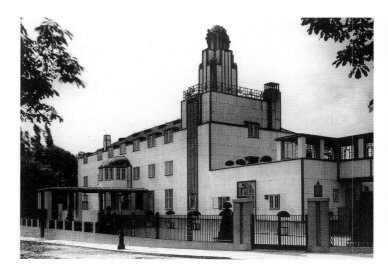

The Purkersdorf Sanatorium (1904–06) is considered to be the first outstanding example of a new esthetic in Vienna and the wider world. Recently renovated in an exemplary manner, this complex is a model of perfect craftsmanship and "honest" clarity. Hoffmann and his friend and colleague Koloman Moser designed every detail, from the facade even down to the cutlery, in a desire to "bring an (artistic) dimension to all elements of life." The building itself was a manifestation of ultra-modern structural esthetics. Reinforced concrete elements support and self-consciously clad the geometric building; the exterior is clothed in whitewashed nakedness, broken up only by a narrow strip of blue-and-white tiling by way of ornamentation. Balanced proportions, smooth lines, and black-and-white decor are the theme of the austere interior, which was originally given an air of spontaneity only through carefully selected flower arrangements. The control Hoffmann and Moser sought to exert with this groundbreaking design approach stemmed from their belief in the positive influence art could have on society. Thus, it was no accident that the most rigorous application of this belief was applied to a sanatorium.

A few years later, Hoffmann, working with Klimt, created the Palais Stoclet in Brussels (1906–11, pictured above), a project commissioned by a young Belgian patron. This commission gave the artists free reign to put their ideas into practice. Although the Palais Stoclet is located such a long way away from Vienna, it may well be the most perfect architectural expression of what the Wiener Werkstätten sought to achieve. However, by contrast with Purkersdorf, the architecture appears far less radically abstract; the design of the facade, with its marble cladding and copper inlays, is very delicate and intricate.

Josef Hoffmann
Brussels, Palais Stoclet, 1906–11
Hoffmann's most important commission was created away from Vienna. The Belgian banker, Adolphe Stoclet, asked Hoffmann, along with the painter Gustav Klimt and the furniture designer Koloman Moser, to design his town residence. Together, they created a convincing total work of art, perhaps the most characteristic Art Nouveau building ever erected

Adolf Loos
Café-Museum, 1899
Albertina, print collection.
The café had an interior that
was "cold" for its time, as were the
attitudes of its patrons—hence its
nickname "Café Nihilism".

Adolf Loos and the poet Peter
Altenberg
Historical Museum Vienna

Adolf Loos (1870–1933, illustration opposite), was the same age to the very day as Hoffmann and was driven by the same rationalistic values, but arrived at completely different solutions. Loos was the son of a stonemason, who studied in Vienna and Dresden and then went to the United States, where he made contact with the newly emerging Chicago School. He was particularly attracted to Louis Sullivan's functional style. After his return to Vienna in 1896, Loos wrote numerous polemics attacking the art of the Secession and Jugendstil (Art Nouveau). He dubbed the Ringstrasse project "a sham," and the tastes of the turn of the century seemed to him to be degenerate and uncultured. Loos preached a brand of purism which recognized only the plainest engineering and craftsmanship as architecture, and he allowed artistic (i.e., sentimental) ornamentation only for religious buildings. Unlike Olbrich and Hoffmann, he did not strive to "estheticize" everyday life but sought a clear differentiation between function and creative externals. In 1903, Loos launched a short-lived journal entitled *Das Andere. Ein Blatt zur Einführung abendländischer Kultur in Österreich* (The Other. A Paper to Introduce Western Culture into Austria), and in 1906 he set up an independent school of architecture. In 1908 he published a pamphlet entitled *Ornament und Verbrechen* (Ornament and Crime), in which he set out his revolutionary ideas.

It is little wonder that the uncompromising Adolf Loos was neither the most popular nor the busiest architect of his time! However, his designs — reduced down to their basic structural elements — represent a decisive step toward modern architecture. Even his first project, the Goldman und Salatsch menswear store (1898), was characterized by an absence of any kind of ornamentation and achieved its effect only through high-quality

materials and pure lines. The cool, sober interior of the Café-Museum (1899, pictured above) challenged the Viennese taste to such an extent that it was dubbed "Café Nihilism." His own house, built in 1903, has a certain degree of intimacy, tending more toward the English and American country house tradition. Similarly, the elegant Kärntner (or American) Bar, completed in 1907, using the finest materials, once again bears witness to Loos' affinity with the Anglo-Saxon tradition.

Whilst these projects remained a fulfillment — however radical— of the Arts and Crafts tradition, Loos completely broke with tradition around 1910. The exterior of the menswear store in the Michaelerplatz caused a scandal in Viennese society. Within sight of the Hofburg, Loos dared to abandon all surface ornamentation of the facade, to negate any division into stories or along axes, and to allow the vast proportions of the massive white walls and unframed window bays to speak for themselves. In the face of this austerity, Loos' contemporaries paid little attention to the fact that, despite its radical simplification, the building is divided along almost classical lines — pediment, cornice and roof — and that the entrance hall in particular, rendered in veined marble, toys with classical elements. Despite its functionality, the interior was also anything but plain. When compared with the Palais Stoclet in Brussels, the complex, total work of art of the Wiener Werkstätten, it is clear why the Michaeler House triggered the most violent resistance and the most acerbic mockery. "The verbosity of the exteriors of the late-industrial boom period" were confronted by "Loos' taciturnity"(Achleitner).

Two town houses designed by Loos in 1910 and 1912 respectively were to prove even more architecturally important. The Steiner House and the Scheu House, the first reinforced concrete structures of their kind, took formal reductionism to the extreme. They even abandon the articulation of base and roof — unadorned white cubes are piled high and low. There is no attempt at "concealment" or hierarchy in the exterior. Loos remained faithful to this style until the end of the decade, thus laying the foundations for the Bauhaus architecture.

Alongside Loos' avant-garde forays, the "Wagner School" continued to flourish until the outbreak of World War I. Apart from Olbrich and Hoffmann, Josef Plecnik (1872–1957) and Max Fabiani (1865–1962), in particular, developed their own style and designed important buildings in Vienna. Max Fabiani worked with Otto Wagner from 1894 and, like his employer, sought to combine functional clarity and esthetics. In the Portois & Fix House (1898–1900) the ornamental tiling of the exterior replaces a three-dimensional subdivision, and the apartments on the upper floors are strictly separated from the storefronts at ground level. On

Max Fabiani
Urania, 1909–10
The shape of the building is
reminiscent of a ship; the exterior
experiments with Baroque
ornamentation

Karl Ehn
Karl-Marx-Hof, 1926–30

the Artaria House (1900–01) a continuous iron architrave emphasizes the division. The Urania (1909–10, illustrated on p.277, right) is an unusual pastiche of historical building styles combined with functional planning. Plecnik also started out with his own distinctive style but, like Olbrich, he failed to gain recognition in Vienna. On his Zacherl House (1903–05), an office building designed as a metal frame covered with sheets of granite cladding, the iron and metal reinforcements determine the rhythm of the external structure; the base of the roof is aptly supported by telamones. Plecnik was also the first architect in Vienna to use reinforced concrete structures for religious buildings. In the "mushroom capitals" of the crypt of the Church of the Holy Spirit on the Schmelz" the possibilities offered by the new techniques are rigorously translated into new forms of expression.

Friedrich Ohmann (1858–1927) chose a completely different approach. As a pupil of the Ringstrasse architect Heinrich von Ferstel, Ohmann started out as a passionate disciple of the Secession, but soon turned to romantic neo-historicism. Like Wagner, he was commissioned to work on the Danube canalization and Vienna River embankment design in Vienna (1898), and he designed the landscaping scheme along the Danube at the point where it runs through the city park. Late Baroque architectural backdrops and Art Nouveau elements create a scene that integrates perfectly into the landscape.

Ohmann proved wholly retrospective in his projects for the Hofburg, which eventually failed, and with his plans for converting the Votive Church (1916), which drew on the "artistic" urban building style of Camillo Sittes.

The Karl Lueger Memorial Church, built by Max Hegele in 1908–10, shows how quickly the

pendulum can swing back from avant-garde to historicism. Patently influenced by Wagner's church at the Steinhof, this church is once again built using traditional techniques, and its cool mass and simplified shapes express a greater degree of pathos. This change of mood is most apparent in the competition to design the War Ministry. The projects designed by Wagner and Loos were swept aside by Ludwig Baumann's design for a grandiose, neo-Baroque palace.

Thus, as in many other European countries, traditional and progressive tendencies intermingled in Austria in the period just before the outbreak of World War I. Rationalistic and functionalistic tendencies, truly implemented only by Adolf Loos, stood isolated within a mass of conservative, historicizing — even nostalgic — edifices. It would be wrong, however, to ascribe this ambivalence, or rather the pluralism of Viennese architecture, to social stratification, typology, or any individual mentality. The rift went deeper, permeating almost all artistic expression at the time. The monumentalism of Wagner's town-planning schemes of 1911, which were deeply rationalistic, surpassed that of the Ringstrasse; awakened by the Arts and Crafts movement. The once "modern" call for traditional craftsmanship easily co-existed with charming elements of folklore, and even Hoffmann's purist architecture gradually began to incorporate classical elements once again. Wagner's functional architecture, Loos' radicalism and Hoffmann's estheticism initially had to capitulate in the face of the reality of a metropolis shaken by crisis; their messages were only adopted and developed later, in the "new building style" or — in the late twentieth century — in the work of Hollein.

"Red Vienna" and the architecture of the inter-war years

After the collapse of the Austro-Hungarian Empire, the Social Democratic Party took over the government of the Vienna city-state. Its primary aim was to combat the housing shortage and to improve the appalling living conditions in the city. At that time 73 percent of the population lived in tiny, overcrowded tenements with little or no sanitation. As early as 1919, the course was set for a comprehensive housing and social policy program which included the staggered introduction of rent controls, redistribution of living space, and eventually the creation of workers' project housing at the edge of the inner city. Through these measures, the Social Democratic Party hoped to give Austria's capital a new image as a workers' stronghold and to secure the support of the proletariat at the same time. Initially they had to put in place the administrative structures to implement this program; Vienna was given federal status and was thus able to raise its own taxes — a vital prerequisite to achieve the comprehensive social policy program. More than

Opposite:
André Lurçat
Blocks in the Werkbundsiedlung, 1930–32

André Lurçat
Main building of the Werkbundsiedlung, 1930–32

60,000 new housing units, kindergartens, laundromats, libraries, and hospitals were built between 1922 and 1934. These were spread over smaller projects with green spaces, or located in "hyper-projects" which accommodated up to 5000 residents. The latter were built in the traditional Viennese "courtyard" style, a semi-open or closed grouping of residential blocks, open spaces as well as social and communication facilities. Hygiene conditions and layouts were in accordance with the latest findings, and the rent for the standard flats, measuring between 110 and 150 sq. ft (33 and 45 m^2), amounted to only a few percentage points of the average wage.

The design concept of the courtyard buildings — which have such inspiring names such as Karl-Marx-Hof, Bebelhof, Matteottihof etc.— was seen as an interpretation of socialist ideals. Functionality was their prime aim, a vocabulary of form reduced to essentials, as well as a striving for "democratic" standardization of living space. Yet even during the planning of these projects, it became clear that an architectural equivalent to the socialist workers' town had not yet been achieved. The projects on the edge of town all follow traditional structures, either by echoing the organization of feudal palaces, or in reflecting Camillo Sittes' late Romantic style of urban building. Whilst overall the urban developments of Vienna are comparable with the housing projects of the "Amsterdam School", for instance with Michel de Klerk's *Eigen Haard* or Piet Kramer's *De Dageraad* (both dating from ca. 1921), they are markedly more traditional, almost ambivalent. The progressive ideas on which they were based were only rarely complemented by modern building styles or innovative typologies. There was a conscious adherence to traditional exterior ornamentation. The expressionistic elements in Karl Ehn's Karl-Marx-Hof (1926–30) or the comparatively sober structure of the exteriors of Josef Frank's Leopoldine-Glöckel-Hof (1931–32) are exceptions rather than the rule. Adolf Loos failed in his attempt to build an estate in a terraced style.

The public housing projects built thus oscillate between "proletarian monument" and "residential palaces for ordinary people." Proudly juxtaposed to the Ringstrasse as workers' palaces, they end up utilizing the very same pathos. Their structural repertoire is drawn from Baroque castles, monumental, symmetrical, and axial, with a hierarchy of structural elements, the inclusion of ceremonial courtyards, and particularly in the way they are shut off against the outside world. Josef Frank alone noticed this strange coincidence of architectural features; to him the urge for representation seemed a symptom of "a petty bourgeoisie that has lost its way."

Almost all the architects who implemented the "Red Vienna" building program were pupils of Otto Wagner. They included Schmid & Aichinger, Rudolf Perco, Robert Oerley, Hubert Gessner, and

Karl Ehn. Adolf Loos, who headed the public housing office for the period 1920–22, later withdrew, having become disillusioned. Josef Frank, the central figure of the *Wiener Werkbund* (Vienna Work Union), had a special position from which he could viciously and violently mock and criticize his peers. Thus, the Wagner School dominated the architectural scene, and whilst this was likely to be one of the reasons for the traditional approach discussed above, it was also guaranteed to ensure a professional and artistically sophisticated execution of the projects. Familiar with complex urban development tasks and used to a symbolic codification of architecture, they were easily able to apply their experience to achieve new goals.

This might be the reason why Wagner's visionary *Artibus* concept of 1880 had a far more profound influence on the urban development of Vienna than, for example, the modern "garden cities" by Bruno Taut or Otto Haesler. A revolutionary architectural language was apparently not required, an esthetic program did not exist or at least was not considered opportune. The only "voice of dissent" came from Margarete Schütte-Lihotzky, who was involved in designing the interiors of the "subsistence level" tenements, or from Josef Frank himself. He countered dogmatic triviality and hollow pathos with individualistic, "seemingly accidental" elements.

Of course, even in Vienna, there were moves toward an expressionistic vocabulary of form. Long before Karl Ehn used the characteristic gate-tower motifs for the Karl-Marx-Hof, Clemens Holzmeister had created the crematorium in Vienna's main cemetery, an idiosyncratic building which interpreted the characteristics of the *genius loci*. The medieval-looking complex with its area of funerary urns was commissioned by the Workers'

Funeral Association. The *Moderne* arrived in Austria with Ernst Plischke's labor exchange in Liesing (1930), with its echoes of Le Corbusier. The buildings are probably Vienna's most important example of the "international style."

The Werkbundsiedlung, built in 1930–32, became a benchmark for the "new building style." Paradoxically, this was at the time when totalitarian forces increasingly dominated the Austrian scene, both politically and in the classic vocabulary of form. Austrian and foreign architects, such as Gerrit Rietveld, Josef Hoffmann, Adolf Loos, Hugo Häring, and André Lurçat, assembled under the leadership of Josef Frank. In the model estate in Hietzing they put into practice their ideas about living in small houses and seemingly "organically grown" projects. These architects deliberately sought to create a "humanistic" alternative to the courtyard housing of "Red Vienna". The outstanding achievements of the Vienna Werkbund Exhibition include Lurçat's row houses, designed in Le Corbusier's style, with their cylindrical staircases, as well as Rietveld's geometric terraces, Loos' and Kulka's "nutshells", Oskar Strnad's idiosyncratic "twin" houses and Josef Frank's and Hans Vetter's detached houses.

The exhibition was widely acclaimed, although the local press spoke of the "battle of geometry run amok amid the mild landscape of Vienna." However, the compact manifestation of the Modern Movement in Vienna was basically obsolete; conservative forces had long gained the upper hand. The "spirit of the age" called for "simple monumentality" (Friedrich Achleitner). Under emergent Austrian fascism there was no future for the white, minimally dimensioned cubes with unadorned, uncluttered exteriors. They remained what they had been built for — an exhibition.

Otto Wagner
Former Länderbank, 1882–84
View of the main lobby

Otto Wagner and the former Länderbank

Otto Wagner and his buildings mark the watershed between historicism and *Moderne*, a conflict which has characterized and stimulated Viennese architecture until the present time.

Wagner's early work shows how deeply rooted architecture was in the academic tradition of the nineteenth century. A witness of the Ringstrasse development and a student at the Schinkel-influenced Berlin Building Academy, Wagner was a master of all facets of "style architecture." His technical knowledge

was excellent and later influenced his own rationalistic architecture as well as the work of his many pupils.

The building at 3 Hohenstaufengasse, formerly the Länderbank, created between 1882 and 1884, is an exciting modern office building, although it is hidden behind a conservative exterior, influenced by the town palaces of Renaissance Tuscany. The tall "lower stories" (which are actually the public rooms of the banking establishment) are lined with continuous rustica friezes, while the two upper stories are brought together by a monumental pilastered structure. An attic story with oval windows runs below the huge circular cornice. However, Wagner's pragmatism soon becomes apparent in relation to the courtyard. It is enclosed and thus remains hidden from public view but it is completely bare. The plain stone structure with windows in between seems to anticipate the architectural style of the following century.

Wagner's design for the interior of the bank was a stroke of genius. Not only did he shift the axis to compensate for the wedge-shape of the site, but the whole interior is dominated by clarity and functionality. "There is no searching, no fumbling, no losing one's way; one feels that one will always be able to reach the counters by the most direct, easiest, and simplest route" wrote Joseph Lux in 1914.

Compared with the magnificent interiors of many of the Ringstrasse buildings, the staircases and counter hall are almost plain, though captivatingly elegant and functionally unambiguous. Wagner created this impression by using classical shapes. The main lobby, an elongated semicircle, is reminiscent of the domed halls of antiquity; high-based double columns carry the tambour, opened up by arches, and smaller double pillars in between support the architrave. However, in place of the expected dome there is a huge glass window whose panes are surrounded by bare metal frames. The brightly lit lobby is adjoined by the counters themselves, running radially away from it.

Although the Länderbank is still wholly rooted in historicism, it pre-empts important elements of Wagner's later work; the counter hall is a precursor of the grandiose counter hall of the Postsparkasse.

BELOW AND TOP RIGHT:
Otto Wagner
"First" Villa Wagner, 1886–88
Staircase and portico as
refashioned by Ernst Fuchs

The "First" Villa Wagner

Between 1886 and 1888 Wagner designed and built the "First Villa Wagner", at 26 Hüttelbergstrasse in the Fourteenth District. Here, he reinterpreted the Renaissance style, freely translating its stylistic elements. The work of the Italian architect Andrea Palladio, emulated by whole generations of architects, also provided the inspiration for the artist's summer house on the outskirts of Vienna. This cubic building, flanked by pergolas, opens out into a three-axis Ionic order colonnade, the sculpture-filled recesses emphasizing the massive lateral axes. The protruding cornice, which harmoniously completes the upper section of the house, was to become Wagner's hallmark. The left wing of the pergola was enclosed in 1889 and used as a studio. A glass window designed by Adolf Böhm suggests a view over a fall landscape.

The Hütteldorf house evokes a Roman villa, an idealized retreat into cultivated nature and into a life dedicated to esthetics. Parallels with Adalbert Stifter's novel *Der Nachsommer* (Indian Summer), and the "Rose House" it describes in detail, are surely no coincidence, for the fostering of culture and a backward-looking educational ideal were guiding principles of the Viennese bourgeoisie. But Wagner's ideas were to change. A quarter of a century later he built his second summer house, the neighboring Villa Wagner II, this time in a strictly functional style.

Villa Wagner I was later owned by the painter Ernst Fuchs, who remodeled the building to his own taste, so it no longer looks exactly as it did in Wagner's time.

ILLUSTRATION OPPOSITE:
Otto Wagner
Imperial Pavilion of the
Metropolitan Railway, 1898
The Emperor's waiting room

Otto Wagner
Imperial Pavilion of the
Metropolitan Railway, 1898
Exterior (top)
Detail of the radiator covers
(below)

Otto Wagner and the Imperial Pavilion of the Metropolitan Railway

Wagner's artistic breakthrough came with two engineering projects, the retaining works on the Danube Canal and the construction of the Vienna Metropolitan Railway, for which he had won a competition in 1892-93. Between 1894 and 1901, working together with his large consulting engineering firm, he designed and built the local transport network, with its more than 30 stations, track system, bridges, and tunnels. The system was designed in accordance with Wagner's ideas about "meaningful art", based on functionality, appropriate use of materials, and technical clarity.

However, the Imperial Pavilion in Hietzing (1894-98) seems anachronistic from a modern point of view, especially in relation to its purpose.

As the private station for the Emperor and his family, it was built in a particularly stylized manner which clearly set it apart from the other stations. The square white base of the building is crowned by a "baroque" cupola — clearly a reference to the status of the building and its proximity to the Palace at Schönbrunn. The decor shows the influence of the fledgling "Secession" movement. The entrance is sheltered by a glazed porch, whose iron framework is adorned with lavish depictions of fruit and vegetables. However, the most splendid decoration is reserved for the main central waiting-room. The walls are draped with embroidered silk tapestries and an ornamental carpet covers the floor. The panels inside the octagonal cupola are decorated with classical friezes and flowing, stylized philodendron leaves. The main wall contains a bird's eye view of the Metropolitan Railway system, illustrating "his" transport design for the benefit of the Emperor.

The combination of classical proportions and extravagant fruit and vegetable motifs caused much excitement, as did the interplay of the materials. In 1899, a whole issue of *Secession* was devoted to Wagner's Imperial Pavilion. The Emperor himself used his station only once, in 1901, on the occasion of the opening of the Metropolitan Railway.

Otto Wagner and the
Karlsplatz Metropolitan Railway Station

The Vienna Metropolitan Railway system became the setting for experiments in a modern, functional style of building. Moving on from historic styliized" architecture, Wagner and his design bureau developed a techno-esthetic principle which paved the way for the functionalism of the twentieth century.

The two pavilions on the Karlsplatz were built between 1898 and 1899 in collaboration with Max Fabiani; they were to set new standards. The construction and materials of the building dominated its exterior to an unprecedented extent. The structural iron girders are not only clearly visible, but at the same time create an esthetically pleasing framework, in which the metal structure clearly defines the horizontal and vertical composition of the wings and the curve of the arch over the entrance hall. The girders are interspersed with white marble panels, reminiscent of half-timbering, making a charming contrast between the framework and the cladding. A characteristic feature of the matching buildings is the "transparency" of the architecture. The cladding over the framework does not conceal the functionality of the structural elements.

Once again, Wagner found inspiration for his design in Renaissance architecture; however the combination of different materials and elegant superficial decoration lend additional charm and novelty. Wagner was nevertheless taking a fundamentally different route from his fellow-architect, Hector Guimard, who at the same time was decorating Paris Metro stations with flowing shapes.

The two pavilions, along with the Karlskirche, were to have been pulled down during the building of Vienna's subway; only a sit-in by students at the Technical University which prevented the loss of these revolutionary works by Wagner.

Otto Wagner
Karlsplatz Metropolitan Railway
Station 1898, facade

**Otto Wagner and
Joseph Maria Olbrich**
Houses on the Wienzeile,
1898-99
(Left): the so-called Majolica
House (40 Wienzeile)
(Right): the corner-house, 38
Wienzeile (medallions by
Koloman Moser)

Otto Wagner, houses on the Wienzeile

In the houses on the Wienzeile, (above left, 40 Wienzeile, above right, 38 Wienzeile and 3 Köstlergasse round the corner) the Secession style was even successfully used on apartment buildings. As part of the plan to prevent the Danube from flooding, they were planned as part of a boulevard which was to link the center of the city with Schönbrunn.

Acting as his own project manager, Otto Wagner and his students erected the neighboring structures in 1898-99, thus revolutionizing residential and commercial building in Vienna. Unlike the traditional "Renaissance palace" style (such as Wagner himself had created for the Länderbank), he now developed a near-timeless genre which anticipated the megalithic constructions of the future. The focus is no longer only on the piano nobile, the second floor, but rather the whole of the floor is characterized architecturally as a separate, commercial area, separated by iron railings.

The residential floors above also break with tradition and have none of the standard structural features or classical window surrounds. The strongly three-dimensional overall effect of the facades of the *Gründerjahre* (years of rapid industrial growth from 1871) has given way to a relatively "flat" frontage. Instead, Wagner had the frontage of the Majolica House (40 Wienzeile) clad in weather-resistant tiles, and did so at his own

expense. The rows of tiles blend together to create a floral pattern. Free-standing balcony sections decorated with leaf motifs frame the flattened frontage overlooking the street.

The neighboring house (38 Wienzeile) is even more lavishly decorated. Tall arrangements of gilded palm leaves and stylized peacock feathers are "draped" between the rows of windows on the upper floors. The horizontal lines are emphasized by a broad band which appears to continue behind the openings and is covered with relief medallions by Koloman Moser, showing women's faces in profile. The *guttae* beneath the window-sills are taken from classical architecture. Wagner shaped the corner of the building in a particularly striking way. While in the lower two stories—the storefronts — the corner forms a sharp angle, the residential stories are curved in an elegant sweep and open to the outside with a loggia surmounted by statues. This was another step toward modernity; rounded corners and flowing lines of facades were to become favorite features of twentieth century architecture.

Joseph Maria Olbrich was responsible for a significant part of the imaginative decoration of the Wienzeile houses. Unlike the rationalist Wagner, who had his roots in classicism, his younger colleague tended toward a more extravagant, symbolic form of expression, more in tune with the principles of Art Nouveau. On the Majolica

House, the otherwise plain frontage is festooned with ornamental, symbolic depictions of the Tree of Life and bunches of roses; they create a unique flower-arrangement which causes the absence of traditional three-dimensional decoration on the facade to go unnoticed. The delicate red and turquoise of the flowers contrasts artistically with the rich green of the foliage. In addition to the unusual esthetic effect of the street frontage, Wagner and Olbrich always bore in mind the functional nature of the materials. The ceramic cladding is weather-resistant and thus economical in the long-term. It is a matter for debate whether the ambivalence between structural functionality and decorative extravagance is a source of productive tension or merely a contradiction. Loos condemned the Majolica House as "architecture with tattoos!" In any case, the Wienzeile houses broke with tradition and created a new definition of the nature of facades. Inside the buildings, the concept of the "synthesis of the arts" lives on. The lift shaft in the center of the stair-well is swathed in cast-iron lattice-work and railings.

Otto Wagner
Spiral staircase in the apartment building at 40 Wienzeile, 1898-99

Othmar Schimkowitz
Decorative aluminum bolts and winged Victory on the roof of the Austrian Post Office Savings Bank, 1904-06 and 1910-12

Otto Wagner and the Austrian Post Office Savings Bank

No other work by Otto Wagner better illustrates his architectural ideals than the main building of the Austrian Post Office Savings Bank. After a competition for which tenders were invited, and from which Wagner's design emerged triumphant, the building was begun in 1904 on the Georg Coch Platz. Construction was in two stages; the front section was completed in 1906 while the rear was only finished between 1910 and 1912. The Post Office Savings bank is Wagner's greatest achievement and a milestone in the history of architecture. Despite being clearly rooted in Imperial Vienna, it pointed the way forward for the whole European Modern Movement.

Paradoxically for one of the last projects on the Ringstrasse, the building embodies to a previously unprecedented extent the interplay of functional architecture and modern esthetics. Unlike in the Wienzeile houses, where the decoration was still developed independently of the structural framework, in the Post Office Savings Bank Wagner displayed the rationalism of a technocrat. As long ago as 1895, in his book *Modern Architecture*, he had demanded the rejection of everything "impractical"; materials should be selected for their cost and durability, and any artistic refinements were superfluous. "Uniformity elevated to the monumental" should be the style for the modern age and its faceless society.

Bearing in mind these radical theories, it is thus surprising to find a "temple of Mammon" which makes use of traditional features and is even topped with figures symbolizing Victory

(Othmar Schimkowitz). Wagner's architectural revolution lay not in rejecting tradition but in making visible the art of the engineer, in the "transparency" of materials and techniques.

Thus, the facade of the building, as in the Wienzeile houses, is divided into two floors forming the base and four upper stories, topped with a "triumphant" cornice. Unlike the Wienzeile houses whose facades were draped in fruit and vegetables, the frontage of the Savings Bank is clad in thin sheets of marble, attached to the reinforced concrete frame by clearly visible but highly decorative aluminum bolts. The flower motifs, which until recently had symbolized romantic communion with nature, had now given way to an equally aesthetically pleasing tribute to structural technology.

The Post Office Savings Bank is almost trapezoid in shape. The main facade on the Georg Coch Platz has a two-storey vestibule concealing a simple but extremely elegant staircase; the offices are on the periphery of the building, while the center opens out into a monumental hall, surrounded by annexes and commercial areas.

The hall is the heart of the building and Wagner's undisputed masterpiece. Glass, iron and aluminum define the character of the well-lit room, where the technical boldness and almost provocative esthetics win over every visitor. Gone is the classical row of pillars, used to add status to a public building, to be replaced by the "transparency" of the construction, the delicacy of the glass,

Otto Wagner
Austrian Post Office Savings bank, 1904-06 and 1910-12
Façade (below)
View of the hall (opposite)
Warm air vent in the hall (top)

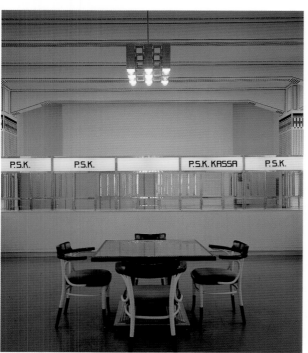

the strength of the iron girders and the gentle sheen of the aluminum, heralding a brave new world of architecture. "Remarkable how well people fit in there", commented the Emperor.

Even the minutest details obey the principles of creative "honesty." The metal wall-lights which are essentially purpose-made lamp-holders, the chairs made of aluminum-strengthened slats, the strikingly plain counter design or the famous warm air vents, which look like futuristic sculptures. Wagner's motto "*artis sola domina necessitas*"(necessity alone dominates art) is here embodied in the most aesthetically pleasing, complete way possible.

The management offices of the Post Office Savings Bank have also survived almost unchanged, or have been authentically restored. Unlike the bright and gleaming hall, these are decorated in stronger colors and furnished with tasteful elegance.

The furniture however, is just as practical as the structural design of the building. Hardwoods,

such as mahogany or beech, generally reinforced with metal, contrast with the red, green, or yellow wall coverings which suggest a certain intimacy. The chairs in the meeting-rooms were the subject of much criticism:"Good light-weight chair, definitely more suitable for sitting in than for sleeping" (Ludwig Hevesi, 1909).

Otto Wagner's interior design was the precursor of modern style. The level of perfection which he achieved was a result of his all-embracing architectural concept. Just as he considered a piece of furniture as a"structure", so he saw all fittings in functional and technological terms as part of the structural whole. His clear, functional treatment of stairwells, service areas, and facilities, and the elegant practicality of the furnishings, were by no means incidental, but constituted essential components playing their part in the function of the building.

Wagner's concept of "beauty" was linked to a belief in unlimited progress, in which the citizens of Vienna—despite some all-too-public disagreements—seemed to support him.

Otto Wagner
Austrian Post Office Savings
bank, 1904-06 and 1910-12
Large meeting-room

Otto Wagner
Steinhof Church, 1902-07

of a domed, cross-shaped church. The church was built between 1905 and 1907. The influence of Byzantine models, such as St. Mark's in Venice or the Hagia Sophia in Constantinople, is clearly felt. Wagner and his students adopted this style in countless studies. However, he deviates from the classic style in one important respect, namely, the solemn darkness and ponderous might of Byzantine domed churches are replaced by cheerful brightness and light, effects which the architect believed to be therapeutically beneficial.

Wagner's countless sketches for the design, interior, and construction of the Steinhof Church show how pragmatically he approached the planning of a project. The functionality of even the smallest detail was at least as important to him as the artistic and sacred effect of the building. It is said that he calculated that for every schilling spent on building his church, more people would be able to attend Mass and be able to see the high altar than in any other comparable church.

Like the Post Office Savings Bank before it, the building is constructed on a metal framework, to which the marble blocks of the facade are simply attached to form a screen. The splendid interior is in perfect, dazzling white with delicate gold lines marking out a paneled ceiling. The work was performed in amicable collaboration with Koloman Moser, who designed the stained-glass windows, Remigius Geyler, who made the mosaic decoration, and Carl Ederer and Othmar Schimkowitz, who created the high altar and the sculptures. Sumptuous materials and simple, icon-based imagery have a calming effect on the observer.

The design therefore also met its therapeutic aims. The beauty and brightness of the synthesis of arts were intended to be stimulating and instructive for the patients. The furnishings complied fully with the practical requirements. Sharp edges were avoided, the tiled floor was hardwearing, since the floor is slightly sloping, it is easy to clean. Circulating air, central heating, and even running water in the font guaranteed the best possible standards of hygiene.

Outside, however, the Steinhof Church had another, no less important function. Standing as it did in solitary splendor at the center of an arrangement of terraces, the church was a sacred "crown of the city" easily visible from afar. The emphasis on religion was in keeping with the times. The building represented the revival of Catholicism, which was gaining ground under the auspices of the Christian-Socialist Mayor Karl Lueger. Despite this conservative setting, Wagner succeeded in creating a modern building which was clearly distinguished from the eclecticism of the period when the Ringstrasse was built. Admittedly here, too, there are stylistic elements from earlier times, but they are subordinated to the new, rationalist way of thinking.

Otto Wagner and the Steinhof Church

Wagner's second major work is — perhaps not entirely by chance — a sacred building, St. Leopold's, known as the Steinhof Church (*Kirche am Steinhof*). It represented a most unusual challenge. As the chapel for the Vienna Central Sanatorium for the Mentally III, it had to satisfy particular pastoral concerns, yet also needed to be functional in special ways, to meet the needs and weaknesses of the patients.

The Steinhof Church was part of a psychiatric nursing home which still stands on the edge of the Vienna Woods. As early as 1902, Wagner had designed a system of pavilions for the sloping site. This idea, which was ahead of its time, influenced the final design of the complex. However, Wagner himself was only involved in building the chapel. The design had again been the subject of a competition, which Wagner won, using the idea

ILLUSTRATIONS OPPOSITE:
TOP:
Otto Wagner
Am Steinhof Kirche, 1902-07,
view of the interior

BELOW LEFT:
Carl Ederer and Remigius Geyler
High altar and mosaic decoration

BELOW RIGHT:
Koloman Moser
Stained-glass window

Otto Wagner and Carl Ederer
Steinhof Church, 1902-07
Pulpit and details of the high altar by Carl Ederer

Otto Wagner
Projects to redesign the Karls-
platz and erect the Emperor Franz
Joseph City Museum

TOP:
Bird's eye view of the Karlsplatz,
1909

MIDDLE AND BELOW:
View of the City Museum

Otto Wagner, museum projects

Throughout his career, Otto Wagner showed a keen interest in town-planning and planners' utopias. Like his 'spiritual father" Gottfried Semper and his contemporary Camillo Sitte, who opted for highly controversial approaches, he was fascinated by the idea of designing a modern, growing city, for which Vienna was to be the paradigm. At the heart of his vision — and incidentally for Sitte as well — was the museum as a monument to civilization and a seat of learning.

However, whereas Sitte envisaged a retrospective, romantic national museum, Wagner's concept was of a space for ideals, where the art of the present and the future would be displayed. Around 1880, he designed a gigantic set of museums for this purpose, which he called *Artibus*, meaning "dedicated to the arts." Long colonnades with a triumphal gateway link the gallery and library wings, while at the heart of the arrangement there is a pantheon beside an artificial lake. This idealistic design, quite clearly not intended to be realized, reveals many similarities with the academic style of the Beaux-Arts planners, despite its visionary content.

In 1898, Wagner submitted plans for the Academy of Fine Arts, and in 1900 plans for a Modernist gallery. The first study for the Emperor Franz Joseph Museum dates from the same year, and this was to lead to lively controversy between the architect and his employer, the City Council of Vienna, for nearly a decade. Intended as the crowning glory of the Karlsplatz, which would bring it to perfection, his architecture was designed to contribute to creating "an artistic image for the City" and "one of the most beautiful squares in the world."

Plans for the various stages of the ambitious undertaking were drawn up and annotated by Wagner himself in minute detail. At first, they were less favorably regarded than a design by Friedrich Schachner, but the large dome of the latter's building would have detracted from the effect of the Karlskirche. After much debating, the building committee under Karl Lueger re-opened the planning process in 1907; Wagner submitted new plans, but their simple lines and restrained decoration could not compete with the building by Fischer from Erlachs. Yet even this project was never built, after a less-than-convincing model of the square was created in 1910.

Yet another, no less megalomaniac project of Wagner's came to nought. This was the extension of Vienna's twelfth district. Influenced by American town planning, in 1911 he developed an idea for the "infinitely extendible city," this being his urban vision. The architect deliberately emphasized the idea of "uniformity into monumentality", but failed precisely because of this egalitarian utopian approach to planning.

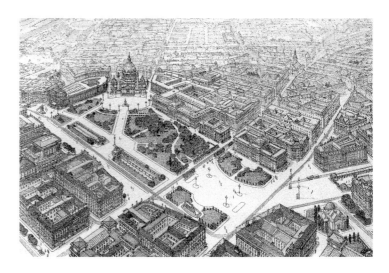

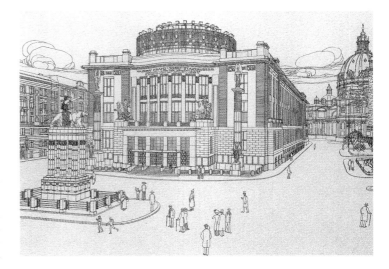

Otto Wagner
Villa Wagner II, 1912/13
frontage

Otto Wagner and the Villa Wagner II

Like town-planning, the building of villas is a continuous thread running through all Wagner's
work. While his later urban projects represented
a step backward into traditionalism, possibly on
account of their monumental character, on a
more intimate scale Wagner succeeded in pre-
serving the avant-garde approach he had adopted
from the turn of the century.

Compared with his first home, Palladian Villa
Wagner, built in 1886-88, the second Villa
Wagner, constructed quite nearby in 1912-13, has
radically simplified lines. Decoration on the building is restricted to a few areas between the windows of the ground floor and the surround of the
doorway, with the glass mosaic designed by

Leopold Forstner depicting Athene with her
Gorgon's head shield. The upper story of the villa
is completely "bare." It is dominated only by the
geometric white plastered blockwork, built on a
reinforced concrete framework. The building is
subtly proportioned so that the dimensions of the
rooms inside can be seen from the exterior. As so
often with Wagner, a paneled cornice extends
outward over the facades.

Important features in the basic layout of the
"simple detached house for use in summer"
were the lighting of the interior and the use of the
latest materials. Thus, reinforced concrete,
asphalt, Eternit, and aluminum were used alongside more traditional construction materials such
as marble and glass.

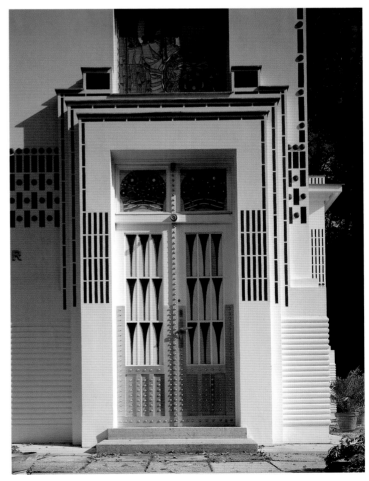

Joseph Maria Olbrich, Secession building

It fell to Joseph Maria Olbrich, Otto Wagner's creative young colleague, to provide the Secession with an appropriate architectural environment. This association of artists which was founded in 1897 with the aim of countering traditional academic restraints with a "modern" attitude to life, free of all historical baggage, required a building for the exhibitions which it staged at regular intervals, a "temple of art," shrouded in "solemn dignity," the walls "white and shining, holy and chaste," as Olbrich himself later described it. Olbrich was inspired by a design of Gustav Klimt, the real mover behind the Secession movement. Klimt envisaged a Cubist building, dominated by a temple-like gabled frontage. Olbrich's own creation was far less dramatic, a standard design such as was used for dozens of pavilions at world exhibitions.

The sacred character of Klimt's design was preserved, above all, in the dominant entrance hall. The Secession building clearly breaks with the museum tradition of "enlightening the people. "it is enveloped in a hieratic, mystic aura, access to this shrine to Art only granted to the initiated. This effect is heightened by the massive blocks of the facade, reminiscent of the pylons of Egyptian temples, which flank the entrance. Except for the shaping of the pedestal and cornice, these are windowless, completely bare and free of decoration. The visitor is magically drawn toward the opening of the entrance which is recessed and at the top of a flight of steps. This is where the eye encounters the most lavish decoration, a broad frieze of golden leaves forming the background to the cone-shaped frame around the doorway, on which embossed female heads represent the arts of painting, architecture, and sculpture. The flawless white pedestal is topped with a sort of cornice, on which the motto of Secession "To every age its Art, to Art its freedom" is emblazoned in gilded letters.

The masiveness of the construction and the symbolism are relieved, however, by one outstandingly poetic feature. Over the vestibule, there "floats" a filigree cupola consisting of thousands of intertwined gilded laurel leaves. These represent dedication to Apollo, chief of the Muses, from whom the younger generation

Joseph Maria Olbrich
Secession building, 1898

DER·ZEIT·IHRE·KVNST·
DER·KVNST·IHRE·FREIHEIT·

of artists awaited inspiration. This dome became the real symbol of the Secession movement, although the Viennese public took a more prosaic view of it, so that it soon became known colloquially as "the cabbage-head!"

The interior of the Secession building satisfied practical requirements to a surprising extent. The entrance-hall with its administrative areas leads into a large, cruciform exhibition hall, which was not sub-divided and remained virtually free of decoration. The exhibition hall is lit by four overhead lights and windows on the north side. The bright, well-lit space was intended to be adaptable for any kind of display, a concept which, in view of the "static" museum design which was then current, was in itself truly revolutionary.

This adaptability was also seen as a metaphor for the haste of modern life, in which

only art can offer moments of reflection. Incidentally the present building does not create quite the original effect. The original Secession building was burned down in 1945 and was rebuilt in 1964. In 1982-86 it was adapted to meet the technical requirements of a modern museum by Adolf Krischanitz. At the same time, a room was added in the basement to house Klimt's famous "Beethoven frieze", which he had drawn here in 1902 on the occasion of the seventy-fifth anniversary of the composer's death, as part of the Fourteenth Secession Exhibition.

The Secession building made Olbrich's name as an architect. Just one year after the building was finished, he was summoned to Darmstadt by the Grand Duke Ernst Ludwig von Hessen, where, with Peter Behrens, he established the artists' colony on the Mathildenhöhe.

Joseph Maria Olbrich
Secession building, 1898
Detail of the cupola made of
gilded laurel leaves (top)
Ornamental leaf frieze (left)

Façade decoration in the Art
Nouveau (Jugendstil) style is to
be found everywhere in Vienna:

LEFT:
Franz von Matsch
Anchor clock at the Hohen
Markt, 1911

ILLUSTRATION BELOW LEFT:
Otto Schönthal
Villa Vojcsik, 1901

Architecture 1890-1938

Max Fabiani
Business premises of Portois &
Fix, 1898-1900

Max Fabiani, Portois & Fix Building

The "Wagner School", which had grown up in connection with the Metropolitan Railway building works, defined Viennese architecture until the outbreak of World War I. Its adherents were remarkable for their outstanding technical and organizational skills, which they had developed while working with Wagner on this huge project, but at the same time they also guaranteed high artistic standards. Among the personalities who clearly emerged from the shadow of Otto Wagner was the Slovene Max Fabiani, who interpreted the functional art of his master in his own way.

As early as 1898-1900, and thus at about the same time as Wagner's Majolica House, Fabiani built the business premises for Portois & Fix at 51 Ungargasse. This went further than the Wienzeile buildings in its consistent separation of the residential from the commercial area. The lower part, which was destined to be used for commercial purposes, is even more clearly differentiated; between the bare supporting walls, which are reduced to a framework, there are huge windows giving the impression of plate-glass display windows. Fabiani also experimented with cladding the facade, this time with pyrogranite tiles, their decoration reduced to a geometric pattern of colors. Only a few other features still betray the influence of the Secession movement. These consist of the prominent lamps, which light up the street as well as the store windows, the railing along on the attic story with its elegant tracery, and the chimney pots.

Josef Plecnik, Zacherlhaus

Josef Plecnik was another gifted student of Otto Wagner though he, like Olbrich, after a promising start to his career, turned his back on Vienna.

Plecnik was also involved in the field of residential and commercial building, to which he probably contributed the most interesting product of the time, the Zacherlhaus in the Wildpretmarkt. Plecnik built a technically bold and unusually esthetically-pleasing building, constructed entirely on a metal framework for Johann Evangelist Zacherl, a factory owner, between 1903 and 1905 The frame was clad with sheets of granite, with clearly visible iron girders running between them, embracing the stories in a double row and thus producing a lively, dynamic feeling. Compared with Wagner's and Fabiani's buildings, the ground floor is less accentuated; instead the windows of the second floor are slightly protruding. The facade itself sweeps in a bold curve round the corner, a design which seems to anticipate the streamlined buildings of Erich Mendelsohn. One surprising motif is the row of telamons which appear to bear the weight of the principal cornice and give the impression of sharing the burden with the iron girders.

The lens-shaped stairwell is splendidly elegant. It contains a centerpiece: an ornate, sculpted candelabra in the shape of an indeterminate insect with a long proboscis, an allusion to the owner's source of income, the production of insecticide!

Josef Plecnik
Zacherlhaus, 1903-05,
façade (top)

View of the staircase showing
candelabra with insect motif
(opposite)

Ferdinand Andri, Archangel
Michael on the Zacherlhaus.

echoes of early Christian churches. The walls of the nave were to be decorated with hangings in the style of medieval Lenten vestments.

Plecnik also experimented with the potential of concrete and iron for the crypt. Trapezoid columns support to the metal roof girders which in turn carry the steel-reinforced concrete roof. The load-bearing strength of the structural supports is deliberately emphasized. To relieve the monotonous grayness, the floors are colored with crushed brick dust; smooth and rough surfaces add extra interest to the walls.

The carefully-planned interior fixtures and fittings were a long time coming. Plecnik, who was on the point of moving to Prague, drew up plans for the design of the nave, free of charge. However, they were not popular with the heir to the throne who described them as "A cross between a Russian bath-house and a stable (instead of stable one could say barn) plus a temple of Venus". Franz Ferdinand suggested instead that the building be converted into a traditional columned basilica. In the end, a cheap compromise was reached but one from which Plecnik vehemently detached himself. In 1912, all further work stopped.

Plecnik's expressive building has only been fully appreciated in recent times. Parallels with the work of the well-known steel-reinforced concrete pioneer Auguste Perret were noted. Plecnik himself gained popularity after he abandoned Vienna for Prague and is considered one of the founders of the so-called "Czech Cubist" movement.

Josef Plecnik
Church of the Holy Ghost on the Schmelz, started 1910
View of the crypt (top)
Facade (right)

Josef Plecnik, Church of the Holy Ghost

In the Parish and Mission Church of the Holy Ghost "on the Schmelz" in Ottakring, Josef Plecnik experimented with new materials and appropriate design as applied to sacred architecture. The building, erected between 1910 and 1913 in a run-down, working-class district, and constructed of reinforced concrete, does not disguise its rigidity. Nevertheless, or maybe because of it, it is strictly classical in style.

The new techniques had rarely been used before in a more public place. The pebble-dash frontage, designed in the style of a Greco-Roman temple, uses strictly Tuscan proportions to display the qualities of the material. In fact according to the original plans, it was to have been three-dimensional and decorated in bright colors. However, this did not come about, due to a shortage of money. A surrounding courtyard and "Venetian campanile" were abandoned for the same reason.

The interior also reveals new esthetic principles. The two unsupported iron beams, with a span of over 82 feet (25 m), which separate the nave from the side-aisles are inconspicuous, but clearly draw the eye to the focal point of the room, the Eucharist altar. In the elevation of the choir stalls and their mosaic decoration, there are

Max Hegele
Karl Lueger Memorial Church,
1907-10
Interior by Leopold Forstner,
Hans Zatzka, Othmar
Schimkowitz et al.
Stained-glass window (top left)
Exterior (top right)
View of the apse (bottom right)

Max Hegele and the Karl Lueger Memorial Church

Not all Viennese architects were involved to the same extent in the quest for a contemporary style. A second group of artists, the Hagenbund, founded in 1876, was of some importance in opposition to Secession. Having originally been avant-garde, it now represented more conservative tendencies. One follower was Max Hegele, whose most remarkable building was the memorial church for the reactionary mayor Karl Lueger.

The Karl Lueger Memorial Church at the Central Cemetery (1907-10) was, in fact, inspired by Otto Wagner's Steinhof Church but, unlike the latter, it represents a marked step backward into the era of historicism. The main building, crowned with a high dome, is built along traditional lines, a monumental memorial constructed over the sarcophagus of the Christian-Socialist mayor which lies in a vault. Despite being closely related in their essential structure, the Steinhof Church and the Karl Lueger Memorial Church are worlds apart. Hegele's dramatic architecture has no touch of lightness and no hint of utilitarianism. The solemn, dignified appearance of the exterior conforms to traditional rules, while the interior of the dome is decorated with extravagant religious symbolism.

Friedrich Ohmann
Palm-house in the garden of the
Vienna Hofburg, 1901-07

Friedrich Ohmann and the new Winter Garden at the Hofburg

Friedrich Ohmann was also no innovator, but an architect and town-planner to whom Vienna owes many charming landscapes. As a pupil of Karl König and the Ringstrasse architect Heinrich von Ferstel, he was initially a member of the Secession movement.

Ohmann was an expert on Austrian baroque architecture and in 1899 was appointed works manager of the Hofburg. However, his designs for alterations to the Hofburg met with little approval, so in 1907 he felt obliged to resign.

However, Ohmann found success elsewhere. With his romantic sensitivity to the environment, he became an impressive creator of

architecture to suit particular landscapes. The few projects for the Hofburg which Ohmann realized include the the New Wintergarden, "The Palm House", which he built between 1901 and 1907.

This structure demonstrates the extremely sensitive and poetic way in which Ohmann could transform a functional iron framework into a dream castle. The greenhouses, of varying heights, are decorated down to the tiniest detail with architectural motifs which nevertheless do not detract from the structural framework of the buildings. The interplay between the classical support elements, borrowed from masonry, and the filigree iron structure of the glass palace is particularly attractive.

Friedrich Ohmann, Vienna River project

Since the eighteenth century, there were plans to contain the Vienna River, a tributary of the Danube, within retaining walls since it was prone to flooding. The plan was re-adopted when the Metropolitan Railway was built, and Friedrich Ohmann was approached. In 1898, he was commissioned by the city to enclose the Vienna from where it rose in Weidlingau to where it flowed into the Danube Canal, and to landscape the banks. The bridges which were rendered unnecessary were removed; gardens were built on the covering structure and, in 1916, over the western section of the river bed, the Naschmarkt.

One characteristic feature of Ohmann's embankment landscaping remains in the City Park, the original design of which dates from the time of the planning of the Ringstrasse. Pavilions, sculptures, and reliefs in fin-de-siècle style line the course of the river, now enclosed, and make walking along its banks a pleasant experience. The river landscape, like a stage backdrop, is in the baroque tradition of a "synthesis of the arts." Engineering works, architectural window-dressing, statues, water-sports, and vegetation all come together in perfect symbiosis. Technology, in the form of the iron and steel framework of the bridges, harmoniously combines with Nature. The duct through which the Vienna River canal flows is turned into a romantic grotto and the bridges into varied features of interest.

Water is the overriding theme of the symbolist design. A room in which the waters can

Relief from the Wien river enclosure project

be taken is evidence of the healing power of this element. Fountains, waterfalls, and curtains of water express its freshness and vitality. The iconography of the sculptures uses the stock themes of Art Nouveau, the fluid female figures, surrounded with flowers, allegories, masks, and floral motifs are woven into the river landscape.

In this neo-romantic park design, Friedrich Ohmann's work contrasted sharply with that of Otto Wagner, who preferred a strictly technical style in his work on the Metropolitan Railway. However, Ohmann, too, must be counted among the important engineering artists of the turn-of-the-century. Between 1898 and 1901, the worked with Josef Hackhofer to build a series of new bridges along the course of the Vienna River, pioneering iron structures which were nevertheless still decorated with eclectic Art Nouveau motifs. The simplest, but technically most advanced of these is the Zollamtsbrücke; its elegant parabolic curve served as the model for the construction of the City Park footbridge, which was created much later by Hermann Czech between 1985 and 1987.

Friedrich Ohmann,
Josef Hackhofer
Vienna River project, 1898-1901

Embankment with pavilion:
General view (left)
Detail (top right)

Josef Hoffmann
Purkersdorf Sanatorium
1904-1905

Josef Hoffmann, Purkershof Sanatorium

This functional building on the outskirts of Vienna revolutionized esthetics. The "Westend" sanatorium symbolized the end of historical tradition and enabled Josef Hoffmann to pave the way for the modern age. The sanatorium, in which Vienna's upper class took health cures, was commissioned by Viktor Zuckerkandl who, like his sister-in-law, Berta, supported the work of the Wiener Werkstätten. Construction work was started in 1904 and finished in 1905.

After having been ignored for years, this pioneering steel construction was recently renovated and has been restored to its former condition. Once the extensions added in the 1920s were demolished, the radical reduction to pure cubist forms and the renunciation of every unnecessary detail can be clearly seen again. For the first time,

a building was almost totally structured by its plastic forms, such as those of the broadly spaced main section, the projection, the portico and the recessed top floor. Whereas Wagner still clearly stressed the surmounting element, it is now restricted to projecting flat roofs that further underline the horizontal element of the building.

The white façade had a stark appearance for those days, and is not divided by horizontal or vertical architectural features. The windows are the only structural elements but in many ways they give rhythm to the surface, as do the very narrow bands of blue-and-white tiles that instead of attenuating the "frigidity" of the functional building, actually emphasize it. The façade of the building is, in fact, determined by its function. Its very elegance likes in the resulting harmony between shape and content.

Josef Hoffmann
Sanatorium Purkersdorf,
1904-1905
View of the dining hall (top)

Entrance hall seating with
armchair by Koloman
Moser, 1903 (below)

Not only should the building be conceived as a whole, but the interior design and that of the fixtures and fittings should harmonize with the functional and esthetic requirements: "To create a harmonious entity out of a building, its surroundings and its interior furnishings need to subordinate themselves to the main purpose. Whether it serves artistic or practical purposes, the building as an entity must absorb them and it is the architect's task to bring them into line with the true nature of the building." This is an extract from a manifesto by the American architect Frank Lloyd Wright and sounds like an eyewitness account of a visit to Purkersdorf.

Hoffmann and Koloman Moser set a precedent by harmonizing the design of the interior structure as far as they could with the specially-styled furnishings. The geometric lines of the chairs, and even tableware and vases correspond to the gridlines of the exposed reinforced concrete beam construction. The artists took care that nothing interfered with the layout.

Naturally, the concept of "*Gesamtdesign*" (entire design) was not to everyone's taste. Hoffmann was nicknamed *Quadratl-Hoffmann* ("Squarist Hoffman") while Moser was the butt of waspish suggestions for "geometric menus". "Two parallel strands of macaroni can only be cut in an infinite space..In order to carve beef correctly, you will need a ruler and a pair of compasses; the dumplings should then be carved by a craftsman and the only stylistically pure pasta is the black-and-white poppyseed pasta improved upon by Koloman Moser; here insanity goes hand-in-land with geometry." Armin Friedmann's comment in the *Neues Wiener Tageblatt* newspaper culminates with the sentence: "*Wuensche wohl liniert zu haben.*" ("Enjoy your line!", instead of "Enjoy your meal!").

Despite the mocking of their contemporaries, it must be said that Hoffmann and Moser put the principles of the Wiener Werkstätten into practice, the principles of the investigation of all manifestations of existence through design and the spiritual unity of art and life.

The brilliance of the Purkersdorf Sanatorium was only surpassed by one other building, the Palais Stoclet in Brussels. This mansion was erected between 1906 and 1911 as a commission from a young banker. It was the result of sympathetic cooperation between the client and the artists he commissioned who included Hoffmann and Moser, as well as Gustav Klimt who created the Stoclet Frieze. Yet it is just outside Vienna that the most important manifestations of the Wiener Werkstätten are to be found and the most significant works of contemporary art were created.

Josef Hoffmann, Moser-Moll House

Hoffmann fullfilled one of his dreams with the semi-detached house that he designed for the painter Carl Moll and the designer Koloman Moser. He gave the villa on the Hohe Warte in Döbling the atmosphere of an English country house. The romantic, but nevertheless spacious building with its half-timbering, hipped roof, chimneys, and little gables represented the longing for the simple life in the delightful countryside.

The semi-detached house, which was begun in 1900, was intended to become part of an artists' colony, like many others which then existed in Europe. It was mainly the English Arts and Crafts movement and its protagonists William Morris, and Charles and Margaret Mackintosh that provided the ideas for a communal life, imbued with art. The "Anglo-Saxon" cottage design had become well-known in buildings by Charles F.A. Voysey. Two Viennese patrons, Hugo Henneberg and Victor Spitzer, were prepared to finance the project.

Initially, Josef Olbrich had been in charge of the planning. However, when Olbrich left for Darmstadt, Hoffmann took over the project. First, the Moser-Moll House (left) was built in 1901. By 1909, several artists' homes had been constructed. However, neither the rural surroundings, nor the farmhouse style of the buildings could hide the fact that the furnishings were rather upper-class and elaborate. The villas on the Hohe Warte set a precedent for several other villas in Vienna that even today are called by the English name "cottages."

Josef Hoffmann, Knips House

In 1924-1925, what was probably the last Viennese villa was built in the classic English style. It seems that the Biedermeier style of the old neighbourhood influenced the decoration of the façades, considering that ornament and linear decoration play an unusually important role for the time. Despite the fact that at the time a house did not mean anything more to Josef Hoffmann than "four walls which define a ground," he was probably carried away by co-operation with the artist Dagobert Peche into yet again designing a functional building on artistic lines.

The rather rigorously square block is decorated with a line of ornamental features, metal frames, lozenge-shaped decals and even umbels shaped like clusters of grapes below the unusual window treatments. The main section, as well as the connecting flat side wing, are crowned by massive hip roofs that on their part are decorated with shingles.

The building was commissioned by Sonja Knips, born baroness Poitier des Echelles, who sympathized with the Wiener Werkstätten and their ideas.

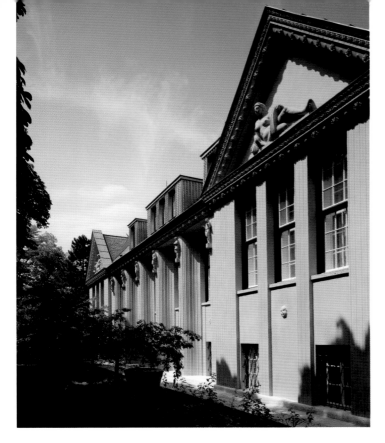

ILLUSTRATION OPPOSITE
TOP:
Josef Hoffmann
Semi-detached house for
Koloman Moser and Carl Moll,
1900-01

BELOW:
Josef Hoffmann
Knips House, 1924-25

Villa Skywa-Primavesi
View of the stairwell

Josef Hoffmann, Villa Skywa-Primavesi

In a short period of time, Hoffmann's architecture went through several stages that were influenced by the state of his order-book and the spirit of the time. After the purism of the Purkersdorf Sana-torium and the elegant symbolism of Palais Stoclet in Brussels, in around 1910 Hoffmann acquired a decorative classical style that was also to be found among other architects of the period. It was a sign of his final rejection of Art Nouveau.

In 1913-14 Robert Primavesi, a sophisticated landowner, commissioned the villa Skywa-Pri-mavesi as a townhouse for his longtime compan-ion Josefine Skywa and himself. Hoffmann's building set new standards for interior design for the Viennese upper classes that could hardly be surpassed. The lavish concept and decoration is more suited to a palace than a residential building. There are eleven rows of windows, framed by fluted pillars and recessed external walls on this monumental building where it overlooks the street, while the recessed middle section is flanked by projecting triangular cornices. The lat-ter are topped by triangular gables whose tympa-na are filled with recumbent figures by the sculp-tor Anton Hanak. They are supposed to represent the client's tideal of a classical education.

On the whole, the façade of the villa Skywa-Primavesi is richly decorated with elements such as classical egg-and-dart motifs and stylized leaf ornaments form the entablature and the gable framework. In the central section, small statues stand in front of the outer walls. Even if the dif-ferent functions of the two buildings are taken into consideration, the contrast between the bare façade of the Purkersdorf Sanatorium and the elaborate frontage of the villa Skywa-Primavesi could not be greater.

The interior represents a masterpiece of orga-nization of the available space. The various areas, such as the entrace hall and stairwells, liv-ing-rooms and dining rooms, the library, the win-ter- garden and terraces that lead into the gar-den, are all organized in compact units. Each room has an individual character, suited to its function, and designed on a differently shaped ground plan, into squares, rectangles, ovals, and curves. The extensive basement with its large kitchens and store rooms point to a household that took food seriously. The lavish villa was completed by outhouses, a teahouse with an arbor, a separate apartment for the gardener and a greenhouse.

The interior furnishings have mostly been pre-served and are decorated in a neo-classical style for which Hoffmann and young Oskar Strnad are responsible: Robert Primavesi was in close con-tact with the Wiener Werkstätten through his brother-in-law, Otto Primavesi. In 1914 he even became a Wiener Werkstätten shareholder.

TOP LEFT AND RIGHT:
Josef Hoffmann
Villa Skywa-Primavesi, 1913/14
Façade and exedra

Adolf Loos
Fireplace in the artist's flat, 1903
Reconstruction in the Historische
Museum of the city of Vienna

Adolf Loos, apartment and Kärntner Bar.

Adolf Loos was heavily influenced in his thinking
and work by his experience in the United States.
Between 1893 and 1896 he took the opportunity of familiarizing himself with the ideas of the
young Chicago School and to reflect both
its constructive and esthetic guidelines. His
later radical position against ornamentation and
in favor of functionalism had its roots in his
American period.

Loos' predilection for American architectural
style is particularly noticeable in his interior
design which first attracted attention after his
return to Vienna. Unfortunately, only few of the
original designs have been preserved. In 1898,
Loos decorated the Goldmann & Salatsch
menswear store in a purist, though very sophisticated, style. In the 1899 café-museum, he put his
ideas into practice in such a radical way that the
favorite meeting-place of the literati soon
became known as Café Nihilism.

Loos' own house at 3 Bösendorfer Strasse
was simple and tasteful, with a strong American
influence. This was in great contrast to the bom-
bastic interior of the Ringstrasse period. There
is a huge, eye-catching chimney in the dining-
room which gives the room an aristocratic feel
with the intimacy of an English country house.
Loos almost considered it his mission to familiarize Austria with the culture of the English-
speaking world. He published a magazine which
he called *Das Andere. Ein Blatt zur Einführung
der abendlandischen Kultur in Oesterreich*

(Other. A periodical for the introduction of western culture into Austria").

Naturally, Loos' arrogant behavior was not to
everyone's taste. The public responded in a more
positive way to the introduction of the bar-room,
known as a *Stehbar* that so far had been
unknown in Vienna. Loos' American bar in the
Kärntner Durchgang (1907) is a classic English-
style "menswear club" only 14 ft 10 in x 20 ft 6
in (4.45 x 6.15 m), and is a classic example of
space-saving interior design. A glittering sign
showing the American flag runs the length of the
facade of the cube-shaped building, with the
promise of New World atmosphere. Onyx panels
allow a milky light to penetrate the interior which
thanks to its overstuffed furnishings appears to
be almost monumental. Mirrors create the optical
illusion of a much larger interior, enhanced by
mahogany and marble which produce delightful
contrasts of materials and colors.

Adolf Loos loved to play with classical design
features. The strictly geometrically structured
room is completed with a coffered marble ceiling. This was not only daring in static terms, but
also constituted something of an esthetic challenge. It is an example of how Loos' used elements of the art of Antiquity. However, he did
not use such classical elements merely within
the context of a scheme based on historical decoration. As a "modern" architect he would
employ the art and craftmanship of the ancient
world within a clearly defined structure and as
part of the functional rhetoric.

ILLUSTRATION TOP AND
OPPOSITE:
Adolf Loos
American Bar, 1907
Façade and view of the inside

Adolf Loos: House at the Michaeler-Platz

The house at the Michaeler-Platz, built by Adolf Loos built between 1909 and 1911, unleashed what was probably the greatest scandal in the architectural history of the new century. Constructed within sight of the Vienna Hofburg, although some way away from it, the most striking feature of the flagship of the Goldman & Salatsch menswear store is, at first glance, the total lack of any decoration on the façade. The upper four stories are completely bare, merely rendered in white; no moldings or pilasters articulate the construction, neither are there any window-frames or pediments above the windows. This was Loos' material expression of the statements in his famous essay *Ornament und Verbrechnis* (Ornament and Crime), written in 1908. Here was an honest building created to expose the lies of the sham architecture of Historicism. It was this that caused the Viennese authorities to intervene; on several occasions during the construction they contrived to have the work stopped. Only when Loos agreed to allow window-boxes was the building completed!

Loos did not set out to provoke. On the contrary, he claimed he had attempted "to bring the house into harmony with the Imperial palace, the Platz, and the city." In fact, a second glance reveals the Michaelerhaus to be wedded to tradition to an astonishing degree; the articulation into storefront at ground level and residential floors above, the cornice and the relatively shallow pitch of the roof are thoroughly Viennese. The elegant design of the commercial premises again reveals the classically-influenced esthete in Loos. Costly Cippolin marble with pronounced veining clads the lower floors. As the visitor enters, he or she encounters monumental classical columns; the office floor has elegant English-style oriel window bays. The obvious break between the heavily decorated lower part of the building and the radically simplified upper floors was intentional.

The interior is also kept effectively cool in a design understatement. Its beauty and the "authenticity" of the materials—mahogany and Cippolin marble, now reconstructed from original photographs— are presented in almost exemplary fashion. Structural clarity underlines the functionality of the interior. Loos formulated these fundamental principles of his designs as early as 1898-1903 in the first commercial premises for the menswear firm (these have not been preserved).

The Viennese public received this epoch-making building with savage mockery and incomprehension; it was hotly debated in the coffee-houses, and caricatured in every newspaper. Rumors circulated that the Crown Prince had drawn the curtains of his room at the Hofburg to avoid seeing Loos's "abomination."

Adolf Loos
House on the Michaeler Platz
1909-11
General view (above left)
View of the staircase (below left)

ILLUSTRATION OPPOSITE:
View of the mezzanine floor
(furniture partially reconstructed)

Adolf Loos: the Scheu House

In 1910 Adolf Loos was given the opportunity to apply the architectural purism he had advocated for the Michaelerhaus, to a private residential building. In the Steiner House of 1910, with its clear three-dimensional articulation throughout and almost total absence of ornament, and the Horner *Waggonhaus* (Covered Wagon House), with its barrel-shaped roof (1912), he had already mapped out new lines for designing the traditional Viennese detached home, thus determining its development over the succeeding years. The Scheu House at 3 Larochegasse, built between 1912 and 1913, introduces a further novel element which he later also applied to rented houses and apartment buildings, namely the gradation and terracing of the various volumes. The complex, which is now unfortunately marred by extensions, is staggered over three floors above a low basement. Here again, the horizontal window-sills and differentiated subdivisions of the windows are more deeply recessed than before. The three-dimensional white cubes seem to anticipate the "international style," in that they form modules that can be combined in various ways, and are emphasized by the manner in which the windows are set, like the component parts of a kit. The building authorities objected to the bare façade of the Scheu House and demanded that the surroundings should be landscaped with vegetation in order to conceal it.

Adolf Loos: the Moller House

The Moller House in Pötzleinsdorf is the most consistent and radical of all the Viennese villas designed by Adolf Loos. It is a white cube, only sparingly relieved by geometrically-placed glazing bars in the windows and a block-like oriel window; moreover, the building's only decoration is in the equilibrium of the masses, the play of volumes which appear to be fitted together like a set of child's bricks. No superfluous detail, still less any ornamentation, disturbs the purity of the minimalist, square masonry.

The interior is also based on a grid pattern; the ground-plan and elevation are developed from underlying geometric forms, with freely added variations according to their function, "parcels of space," as Friedrich Achleiter fittingly terms them. Thus, the interior becomes a well-judged presentation of different living areas: the private, "intimate" rooms are not the same height as the imposing "public" rooms, such as the hall or music room.

The building, erected in 1927-28, is in a sense a summary and culmination of the views which Adolf Loos had developed during his most creative years. Here, his experiments in building Viennese private houses were influenced from his still fresh impressions from his stay in Paris, during which he had come into contact with the work of Le Corbusier.

Adolf Loos
Moller House, 1927-28

ILLUSTRATION OPPOSITE, TOP:
Paul Engelmann and
Ludwig Wittgenstein
Wittgenstein House, 1926

BELOW:
Josef Frank and Oskar Wlach
Beer House, 1929-30

Paul Engelmann: the Wittgenstein House

In 1931, Ludwig Wittgenstein described "working on philosophy" as being "in many ways like working in architecture — actually more work on oneself. On one's own outlook. On how one sees things. (And what one demands from them)."

The house of the philosopher Ludwig Wittgenstein could be interpreted as a manifest to logic and pragmatism in the form of a building. The momentum for its construction in 1926 came from Margarethe Stonborough's belief that this project would pull her brother out of a profound psychological crisis. Paul Engelmann developed the initial plans, but the unique clarity and precision of the proportions and the resolution of detail derive from Wittgenstein's own interventions over a two-year period. The purity of the total concept is matched by the materials and the way they are used, for example the metal doors with unframed keyholes and the exposed light bulbs, which are even inserted naked into their fittings.

Unlike the almost contemporaneous Moller House, the interior is designed in traditional fashion. It would be pointless to search for the free ground-plan and consistent application of the block grid which make Adolf Loos' constructions so avant-garde. Even the original fittings tended to reflect the taste of the haute bourgeoisie.

Today, the Wittgenstein House is occupied by the Bulgarian Cultural Association.

Josef Frank and Oskar Wlach, The Beer House

Josef Frank and Oskar Wlach belonged to the younger generation of architects who had grown up as modernism became established. Frank, the driving force of the *Wiener Werkbund* (Vienna Work Association) was at once a theoretician and a pragmatis. His critical, ideological outlook enabled him to combine Utopian attitudes with the demands of everyday life. His view that dwellings should be understood as a cultural expression left its stamp on decades of housing projects in Vienna.

The Beer House in the Wenzgasse (1929-30) illustrates the views of its architects that buildings should be in touch with life. It does not impose strict rules on those who live in it, as, for example, the houses built by Hoffmann or Loos do; despite the consistent modernism of its design. it allows individuals areas of freedom in order to enable them to decide their own surroundings.

It is characteristic of Frank's emphasis on the "random" and natural that the tree in front of the asymmetrically articulated façade was retained. A similar absence of constraint dominates the interior; upholstered armchairs and Persian carpets create an easygoing, welcoming and comfortable atmosphere, which is difficult to imagine in the interiors of Hoffmann and Loos.

Clemens Holzmeister, Crematorium

One of the few testimonies to Expressionist architecture in Vienna is the Zentralfriedhof Crematorium on the Simmeringer Hauptstrasse. Clemens Holzmeister built it in 1921 through 1923 for the *Arbeiterbestattungsverein* (Workers' Burial Society), which had adopted the following original motto: "A proletarian life, a proletarian death, and culturally-progressive cremation!"

In his competitive design entry, which secured him the commission, Holzmeister made conscious use of "medieval" motifs. For example, the fortress-like elevation and the battlements of the curtain wall are reminiscent of the nearby Imperial summer-palace, the so-called "Neugebäude" (newly-built); they give this functional structure an exhalted and ecclesiastical character. At the same time, these elements also fulfil entirely prosaic functions. The added towers concealed the chimneys necessary for operating the crematorium, while the arcades in the surrounding urn grove conceal the incinerating furnaces from the view of the mourners.

The interior of the crematorium is determined by the high, square chapel of rest. Here again, "medieval" elements predominate, giving the austere room an aura of sanctity: arcades of broad pointed arches carry a steep dome-like arch; the only ornament is the triforium-like windows and small vertical connecting pieces running like joints.

The conflict between tradition and progress characterizes Holzmeister's life's work, as it does the whole of Austrian architecture. In the 1930s, at times working for the National Socialists, he produced churches in a restrained modern style, and on occasion rationalistic functional buildings, some of them on a monumental scale. In 1938, he emigrated to Turkey, where he designed important government buildings. After 1954 he taught at the Vienna Academy of Visual Arts and counted Hollein, Holzbauer, and Peichl amongst his pupils. Their freer approach to historical models, which can be seen almost to anticipate Post-Modernism, probably derives from Holzmeister's pictorial traditionalism.

Clemens Holzmeister
Crematorium at the Central
Cemetery, 1921-23

ILLUSTRATION OPPOSITE:
View of the chapel of rest

Otto Nadel and Karl Schmalhofer
Amalienbad

Among the improvements to the infrastructure of
'Red Vienna" was the construction of a modern
indoor swimming-pool. In 1923 Otto Nadel and
Karl Schmalhofer started to construct the
"Amalienbad," designed to hold 1,300 people,
which at that time made it the largest indoor
swimming-baths in Europe. The extensive complex was outstanding in its technical innovations,
its many facilities for sports and relaxation, and
the elegance of its styling. The glass roof, with its
100 ft (30 m) span, could be retracted when the
sun shone; a 33 ft (10 m) tower and steam baths
in the inner courtyards added to the attractions of
the baths. The sitz or "droplet" baths, available
for hire, enjoyed the same sort of popularity as
whirlpool baths do today. The Amalienbad baths
were recently renovated and re-opened to the
public; the interior design and fittings have been
largely preserved in their original condition.

The building's exterior gives little hint that an
extensive leisure and relaxation center is concealed behind its walls. The soaring, fortress-like
complex, constructed from a variety of superimposed cubes, gives the effect of having been put
together almost arbitrarily from small parts. Nothing betrays its real function; no view of the interi-
or is permitted from the outside. Small windows
and an unpretentious entrance, and finally the signal-like clock tower, are more suggestive of one of
the contemporary residential blocks — the "workers' palaces" of "Red Vienna" — than of a swimming pool. The baths are named for the Social
Democratic city councillor Amalie Pölzer.

Otto Nadel and
Karl Schmalhofer
Amalienbad, 1923
(reconstructed in 1946 after war
damage, re-opened after renovation
in 1986)
Detail of façade (above)
Reception hall (left)

The municipal buildings of "Red Vienna"

When the Social Democratic Party took over the government of the City of Vienna in 1919 its prime concern was to overcome the housing shortage and alleviate the catastrophic living conditions of the proletariat. Within the space of a few months, firm plans had been made for a comprehensive housing and welfare program, providing for controlled rents, redistributed dwelling-space, and the creation of workers' project housing at the edge of the Inner City.

The Karl-Marx Hof's name was not the only reason why it was one of the showcases of the period of new beginnings which later became famously known as "Red Vienna." Karl Ehn, a disciple of Otto Wagner, constructed it in the Viennese tradition of the *Wohnhof* or "courtyard dwellings" between 1926 and 1930. The "workers' castle", as this fortress-like building soon became known, contains five-floor apartment blocks, which cover an area of over 500,000 sq. ft (150,000 m^2) and are over half a mile (1 km) in length. Broad arched gateways, which recall the architecture of Clemens Holzmeister's crematorium, articulate the main façade. Projections create a lively, three-dimensional surface. Gables and towers, reduced to their essential forms, underline the defensive appearance of the exterior.

Within the walls of the Karl-Marx Hof there are 1,325 apartments, nurseries, offices, stores, green open spaces, and a library, expressing the striving for a "democratic" simplification of living-space. It was this that made it the target for state-directed right-wing incursions in the 1930s.

The Karl-Seitz-Hof (Hubertus Gessner, 1926) is an example of the effort put into the creation of a new formal language to accompany the new content. Elements of Italian palazzos are added like set pieces, which are at once an allusion to the might of the Tuscan communes and a traditional expression of dominance.

As an alternative to the monolithic housing blocks, a series of housing projects were built on green field sites. Typical of these is the Sandleiten-Hof, which was erected by Emil Hoppe and his colleagues in the years 1924-28. He also presented it as a type of "city within a city". The total area of 322,000 sq. ft (96,502 m^2) contains 1,587 homes, 76 stores, 58 craft workshops, three schools, nurseries, library, and a concert hall. Unlike the Karl-Marx-Hof, the dominant element is not the concentrated, compact dwelling area of the urban "courtyard", but a looser, more rustic complex. A rich variety of constructional forms, "more intimate" structures and parkland predominate in this huge complex on the outskirts of the city. For all its modernism, the design is based on Romantic concepts, as in Camillo Sitte's work "City Planning According to Artistic Principles."

ILLUSTRATION TOP LELT:
Karl Ehn
Karl-Marx-Hof, 1926-30

BELOW:
Hubert Gessner
Karl-Seitz-Hof, 1926

ILLUSTRATION OPPOSITE, TOP LEFT AND RIGHT
Emil Hoppe
Sandleiten-Hof, 1924-28

ILLUSTRATION OPPOSITE, RIGHT CENTER AND BELOW:
Werkbund project 1930-32
Gerrit Rietveld
Apartment block (centre)
Hans A. Vetter
Detached house (below)

The Werkbund Housing Project

Model housing projects enjoyed great popularity throughout Europe in the late 1920s and early 1930s. In the charged and tense atmosphere of the years following World War I they served as an artistic and political manifesto, indicating escape routes from housing shortages and social injustice. Thanks in no small measure to the cohesive force of the CIAM (Congrès Internationaux d'Architecture Moderne), the most renowned architects in the world met on a more or less regular basis, in order to expound their views on modern housing and "the new building." The exhibitions, which were generally dedicated to an all-embracing theme, thus became the trend-setters of modern architecture. On the other hand, it must also be admitted that they generally failed to achieve their socio-political aims.

The Viennese Werkbund housing project, which was carried out between 1930 and 1932 under the auspices of the GESIBA (Municipal Housing Project and Building Materials Institute), is one of the last of its kind before the outbreak of World War II. It was based on the model of the Stuttgart Weissenhof estate, whose project manager, Josef Frank, had been the only Austrian to participate, in 1927. Frank's design represented a counter-demonstration in two senses; on the one hand he wanted to display a "human" alternative to the monumental housing projects of Red Vienna, while on the other he called upon the very architects who had been passed over due to internecine strife at Stuttgart. Therefore, in addition to the Viennese Clemens Hofmeister, Joseph Hoffmann, Adolf Loos, Ernst Plischke, Richard Neutra, Oskar Strnad, Ernst Lichtblau (among others) Gerrit Rietveld, Hugo Häring, André Lurçat, Margarete Schütte-Lihotzky were taken on board for the project.

The general complex which took shape at Lainz on the south-western edge of Vienna was free of

dogmantism and fitted Frank's ideas of "planned randomness," in their crooked pathways, small squares, and a multiplicity of housing styles. This gave the impression of a mature complex, with detached, semi-detached, and row houses alternating in a loose sequence. The interiors of the homes, which were generally small, were designed with maximum flexibility. Since Frank rejected "ascetic" white architecture, he commissioned the painter Laslo Gabor to design a palette which would further emphasise the individuality of the seventy buildings.

The outstanding achievements of the Vienna Werkbund exhibition include Lurçat's row houses with their spiral staircases, which are constructed in the manner of Le Corbusier. The geometric apartment buildings of Rietveld, the "nutshells" of Loos and Kulka, the original style of the semi-detached houses of Oskar Strnad, and the free-standing detached houses of Joseph Frank and Hans Vetter are also worthy of note.

The exhibition, which opened from June 4 through August 7, before the homes were rented or sold, had a generally favorable reception. Approximately 10,000 Viennese visited the model complex. The international trade press also responded positively. The local newspapers, on the other hand, described it provocatively as a fiasco, a "battle between geometry run wild and the placid Viennese landscape." However, the compact constructions of the Viennese moderns had long since become obsolete. Conservative forces had long since gained the upper hand; the "spirit of the age" demanded "austere monumentality" (Friedrich Achleitner). Thus, the Werkbund exhibition remained what it had originally been planned to be — just an exhibition.

During the war years the Werkbund estate was forgotten; it was not until the 1950s that it was "re-discovered." In 1983-85 it was renovated by Adolf Krischanitz and Otto Kapfinger.

Eugen Kastner and Fritz Waage Substation

Eugen Kastner and Fritz Waage's electricity substation in the Favoriten district of Vienna was built in 1928-31 and is an outstanding testimonial to industrial architecture. The architects' task, no easy one, was to install elaborate electrical plant and administrative offices on a difficult plot of land which tapered to a point. The whole of the building work also needed to be integrated into the surrounding urban landscape and carefully separated from the nearby housing estates. A further problem was the accessibility of the switching gear, and the need to ensure that it functioned optimally.

Kastner and Waage decided on a varied complex of buildings, which owes much to the esthetics of steamship travel and is thus entirely in keeping with contemporary trends. Like the bows of a ship, the ground floor building plouws into the crossroads; the tower-ladded soars above it, like the captain's bridge. The alternating current and direct current buildings, like the two-phase building, are accommodated in visually distinct wings; the control center stands at right angles to the main block. Despite the clear differentiation of the various parts of the building, the substation is linked together by its organic and fluid forms. The elegant curve of the expanses of wall and the window moldings pull the complex together and define its outline.

Friedrich Tamms, Anti-Aircraft Towers

The six anti-aircraft towers of Vienna symbolize, in as way that practically no other monument does, the horrors of war in the 1940s. The builder was Friedrich Tamms; between 1942 and 1944 he constructed the twin anti-aircraft defense command posts which were used as observation posts, to light up the sky, and as anti-aircraft gun posts.

The towers, which form a triangle around the city, could be completely self-sufficient in an emergency. They could hold up to 30,000 people and contained a hospital, their own power supply, springs for drinking water, and air filters in case of a poison gas attack. Their reinforced-concrete walls, which are up to 16 ft (5 m) thick, withstood all enemy action, and also resisted subsequent attempts to blow them up. They therefore continue to dominate the Vienna skyline. Two are located in the Arenberg Park and two in the Augarten; the other two are in the Esterházy Park and in the courtyard of the Stiftskaserne.

After the war, the Romanesque-style defensive towers were to be marble-clad as victory monuments. Since then, it has been decided that they should be preserved as memorials. Only the tower in the Esterházy Park has been converted into a museum and now contains the Haus des Meeres [(House of the Ocean)].

Clemens Holzmeister in collaboration with the architectural practice of Schmid and Aichinger
Broadcasting Center, 1935
After it was damaged in World War II, the building was remodeled in 1979-83 by Gustav Peichl, particularly in the courtyard area

Architecture from the Start of World War II to the Present Day.
Austrian Fascism

The ground had been prepared for fascism in Austria long before the Anschluss (the annexation to Hitler's Germany) which occurred on March 12, 1938. A nation ruined by economic catastrophe and plagued by unemployment and violence welcomed promises of salvation from any quarter. Daily life and the cultural scene became increasingly dominated by the Habsburg myth, the *Heimatschutz* (the right-wing militia), conservative Roman Catholicism, and a deeply-rooted hatred of modernism, which was viewed as both immoral and threatening. The novels of Joseph Roth and Franz Werfel are moving testimonies to this inexorable process.

Under the Christian-Socialist Chancellor Engelbert Dollfuss, democratic structures were dismantled step by step. In 1934, the struggle against "Marxist" forces erupted into civil war and open terror. The battles were centered around the "Red Vienna" project housing which was engulfed in bitter fighting and bloodshed. On May 1, 1934, Dollfuss proclaimed his "corporative state on a Christian basis", banning the Social Democratic party. But even this development was too slow for Austria's National Socialists; on July 25, 1934, at Hitler's instigation, they organized a *putsch* which failed but nevertheless cost Dollfuss his life. His successor, Kurt Schussnigg, could not long ensure Austria's independence "in reconciliation with the Nazis"; on March 12, 1938, the German army marched into Vienna, to wild cheering and mass enthusiasm. Soon afterward, the open terror against the Jewish population began. About 50,000 people left the country in the ensuing months, including almost all the intellectual and artistic elite.

The first deportations, which marked the start of the Holocaust, began in October 1939 and ultimately cost the lives of 65,000 Austrian Jews. There were also many victims among the Gentile population, and when War broke out, it also took its toll. The bombardment of Vienna began in March 1944, although the worst destruction occurred in the very last days of the war, during the "Battle of Vienna" which began on April 6, 1945 and concluded with the entry of the Russians on April 13.

Austrian Fascism drove almost all of the Austrian avant-garde into exile or even death; a few of the many architects in this category who deserve a mention here were Josef Frank, Ernst A. Plischke, Grete Schütte-Lihotzky, Oskar Wlach, and Otto Breuer. Those who remained were undoubtedly less progressive and compromised with the architectural views of the Third Reich, which shared their own reservations about functionalism.

The buildings of the years 1934-38 tend either toward emphatically traditionalist and regional forms, or to monumentalism as expressed in such prestige state buildings as Clemens Holzmeister's RAVAG building, the headquarters of ORF, the Austrian broadcasting corporation. Its blend of moderate modernism and emotion has strong parallels with Italy, where *razionalismo* became a state art, expressed as a Classicism emerging from the Utopian Futurist movement translated into monumental form.

Few residential buildings were constructed, but several asylums were built, as well as many churches, which reflected the process of re-Christianizing society. They are variations on an austere, undecorated style which could be reproduced ad infinitum. As in Germany, road-building was accelerated as part of the "work creation program." The panoramic mountain roads and the Viennese Höhenstrasse were intended to be manifestations of the glory and success of the dictatorship.

There was no precisely defined esthetic underlying the Fascist architecture in Austria, since its ideological function was much less important than that of Germany. However, the gulf separating it from the progressive forces of the early decades of the century proved fateful later in the post-war period, and the gap was not bridged again until well into the 1960s.

Utopia and Memories;
Vienna after World War II

The Battle of Vienna in April 1945 left its mark on the metropolis. 11,000 people had lost their lives in the air-raids, 35,000 were homeless, and a third of the city was a pile of rubble and ashes. The destruction of homes and almost all the bridges which connected with the areas on the other side of the Danube severed the city's lifeline. The rubble in the historic center, the ruins of St. Stephen's Cathedral, the Opera House, the Burgtheater, and the Albertina, left no doubt that the "old days"—not by any means always the "good old days"—were buried for ever. But Vienna would not have been Vienna if it had not immediately begun to dispel the shadows of the past and return to the normal daily routine. Only fourteen days after the entry of the Russians, on April 27, the Vienna Philharmonic Orchestra once again played in the city, which was now divided into four zones of occupation. The Opera and the Burgtheater also opened again for business in makeshift quarters. In November 1945, the first free elections took place, from which the Socialists and the Austrian Volkspartei (the People's Party, the former Christian Socialists) emerged victorious.

While the political situation stabilized relatively early, economic recovery was sluggish, gathering momentum only with the currency reform and the

Marshall plan. Nevertheless, at least the worst wounds the city had sustained were soon healed. In 1948, Mass was once again held within the walls of St. Stephen's Cathedral. The reconstruction of such symbolic buildings as the Opera and the Burgtheater was begun. However, city planning was the main preoccupation of the years between 1945 and 1955; the aim being to establish, and also reorganize the focal points of the inner city. However, in most cases the planning directors, Karl Brunner (1945-53) and Josef Schimka (1952-58), were forced to capitulate in the face of technical and economic difficulties. Ambitious solutions remained the exception, it was more a case of "make do and mend," but with the aid of Franz Schuster's "quick-build program" approximately 5,000 new homes were completed every year.

Under Vienna's Socialist city government, the cultural climate was open-minded and tolerant, and this favored a new beginning. Gradually some, although by no means all, of the artists who had been driven out by Fascism returned to the Danube. However, in only a few instances were there any open conflicts with the past. These included Heimito von Doderer's literary comedy of manners *Die Strudlhofstiege oder Melzer und die Tiefe des Jahres* (The Strudlhof Stairway or Melzer and the Abyss of the Years), 1951; Friedrich Torberg's *Tante Jolesch* (Aunt Jolesch), a depiction of Jewish Vienna; and Herbert Zand's novel *Die Wolfshaut* (The Wolfskin), 1960.

The cabaret performances of the 1950s and early 1960s, which pitilessly held up a mirror to the "Viennese heart of gold," had a stronger impact. Helmut Qualtinger and Carl Merz's sketch "Herr Karl" touched a raw nerve among the petty bourgeoisie; the programs and songs of Gerhard Bronner, Peter Wehle, and Georg Kreisler celebrated decisive moments of popular cabaret. There was a more avant-garde approach in the "literary cabaret" of the Vienna Group, which centered around Friedrich Achleitner and which strove toward a fundamental revival of literature.

Films were widely discussed, not least for the histrionic talents of Hans Moser and of Romy Schneider in her legendary role as *Sissy*. International successes, such as *Der Vier im Jeep* (Four Men in a Jeep) and Orson Welles' *The Third Man* created a powerful impression of Vienna in the immediate post-war period.

With the Austrian State Treaty of May 25, 1955 Vienna once again became the capital of a free nation, even though its territory was now situated at the edge of the Western world, and the Iron Curtain cut it off from its hinterland and its culturally related neighboring states.

The next two decades were marked by a slow but continuous improvement, supported by a general though superficial consensus. Outwardly much remained the same, but below the calm surface seethed an urge to break free of the fetters of social convention and bigoted religiosity.

In 1955, the Burgtheater re-opened its doors; at the Opera, Viennese society gathered for the Opera Ball, just as it had done in former times. In Herbert von Karajan, the Opera House gained a charismatic director. Famous performers returned to the Viennese stage and a number of outstanding orchestras revived the great tradition of classical music.

In the same year, various United Nations institutions moved their headquarters to the Danube. They helped the city to gain a reputation as a conference venue, one which was enhanced by the meeting of Nikita Kruschev and John F. Kennedy in 1961. Vienna once more presented itself as a hub between East and West, despite being somewhat hampered by the presence of the Iron Curtain. The increasingly stable political and economic situation once again made the city a place of sanctuary for East European refugees; socially, this was highly explosive, but in many ways acted as powerful cultural stimulus.

The clearance of bomb sites and the planning and building of new structures continued apace under the guidance of Roland Rainer. Only in a few "model housing projects" did Rainer's concept of a "loosely-articulated city," a functionalist version of the garden city, become a reality, and it encountered growing criticism. There was no question of continuing the large-scale and uniform housing developments of "Red Vienna." At the same time, Roland Rainer and his colleague Karl Schwanzer managed to ally themselves to International Modernism.

Meanwhile, the architectural avant-garde aligned on various sides and took up new stances which were experimental and sometimes Utopian. In 1962, Werner Hofmann opened the Museum of the Twentieth Century, which, like its New York counterpart which inspired it, was designed to represent the entire spectrum of modern art. Monsignore Maurer directed the fortunes of the Gallery by St. Stephen's until his death in 1973. As before, the works displays tended toward informal abstraction but increasingly also tended to favor architectural Utopias. The affinities between various artistic genres became the theme of various works such as Frederick Kiesler's *Endless House* and Friedensreich Hundertwasser's *Endlose Spirale* (Infinite Spirals), both created in 1959; Arnulf Rainer's *Übermalungen* (Overpaintings) on paper were an alienated version of the buildings which symbolize Vienna. The interplay of the arts culminated in the sculptural *Kirche zur Hl. Dreifältigkeit* (Holy Trinity Church) which Fritz Wotruba designed and installed in 1965.

The theme of the age was boundary-crossing. Whether this meant removing the tidy demarcation lines between the various arts, or in breaking social taboos, the now legendary Vienna Action of

Karl Schwanzer
The Philips House, 1962

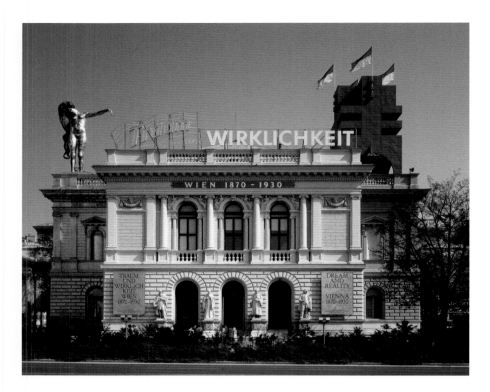

Hans Hollein, Traum und Wirklichkeit (Dream and Reality), exhibition design for the Artists' House at the Karlsplatz, 1985

the 1960s did its utmost to destroy the old-established order. With their shock "happenings," their "breaking tests" — both emotional and physical — which took both spectator and artist to the brink of endurance, they were seeking an escape from the confines of society as much as from the restrictions of the traditional concept of art.

Boundary-crossing was typical of even the less aggressive artists. Friedrich Achleitner, architect, architectural critic, and man of letters, published his *Quadratroman* (Square Novel); Gerhard Rühm, writer, graphic artist, and musician entered the public arena with his ironic *W.I.E.N.* (V. I.E.N.N.A.) project; Peter Handke alarmed the theatrical world by making actors and audience exchange places; and Thomas Bernhard, Ernst Jandl, and Ingeborg Bachmann produced further proof of the vitality of the new generation of Austrian literature.

Cabaret and film felt satisfied with the appealing irony and charm of Peter Alexander. At the same time, Viennese songwriters disseminated their black humor and self-pity; the representatives of "magic realism" did full justice to their exquisite, dark visions. Friedensreich Hundertwasser and André Heller staged a presentation on a long-familiar Viennese theme — the Ego.

During the mid-70s, the Viennese idyll was convulsed by several seismic shocks. The oil crisis and the after-pangs of the Europe-wide student revolts put an end to the post-war faith in technological progress. In the wake of the general crisis in confidence, there was a resurgence of anti-Semitism and racism. This limitation of outlook was something which could not be overcome even by the many international meetings and congresses held in Vienna during Chancellor Bruno Kreisky's long term of office. A series of acts of terrorism appalled the city. These included the attack on the OPEC building in 1975, and attacks on Jewish citizens and the synagogue in the 1980s. This melancholy list has continued to grow; subsequent examples are the letter-bombs which have been sent to prominent liberals, including the mayor of Vienna, Helmut Zilk.

The way in which the little people came to terms with their "Brownshirt" past is demonstrated by the affair of Kurt Waldheim, former General Secretary of the United Nations and President of Austria. The way in which right-wing attitudes continue to be entrenched is proved by the political success of the FPÖ, the extreme right-wing party whose leader is Jörg Haider.

Despite all this, Vienna's balance-sheet remains relatively clean since the Second Republic was first founded after World War II. Since the disintegration of the Iron Curtain and Austria

became a full member of the European Union, the Danube Republic has regained its place at the heart of Europe.

Art and culture have made no small contribution to Vienna's new renown. Although the experimental "departures" of the 1960s and 1970s were directed mainly at an avant-garde public, the discovery of the 1980s was that art could appeal to the masses and also enjoy economic success. Painting, especially, made a dazzling comeback. A flood of galleries and art journals followed the trend; large-scale exhibitions and festivals drew crowds. These included *Der Hang zum Gesamtkunstwerk* (The Trend to a Complete Work of Art), 1983, *Traum und Wirklichkeit* (Dream and Reality), 1985, and *Zauber der Medusa — Europäische Manierismen* (Magic of Medusa — European Mannerisms), 1987.

State-sponsored projects fared less well. The Museum of Modern Art, opened in 1979, was not the success that had been hoped; the plans to build a museum quarter around the old royal stables were delayed and watered down by more than a decade of political wrangling. One of the failed plans was EXPO, the World Exhibition of 1995, a potentially prestige project which was defeated in a referendum. The future of the planned Guggenheim Museum, which was to be erected within the area set aside for the World Exhibition on the other side of the Danube, is still unclear at the time of writing. Beside the private galleries, then, the most important contribution to the Viennese art scene is from exhibitions sponsored by private investors and associations.

Meanwhile, the agitators of the post-war period have come of age, and have since acquired some of the trappings of academic art. The cult of stardom and ignorance of new media and modern trends have allowed the *Akademie die bildenden Kunst* (Academy of Fine Art) to fade into obscurity. The avant-garde has migrated to the rival *Hochschule von Angewandte Kunst* (School of Applied Arts) whose director is Oswald Oberhuber, and the gallery scene is the result. Artists of the middle and younger generation, such as Franz West, Gerwald Rockenschaub, Brigitte Kowanz, Heimo Zobernig, Lois Weinberger, and Heinrich Georg Pichler, who are Viennese by birth or by choice, have used private galleries as a launching-pad for their international careers.

The most successful of the post-war arts in Vienna has undoubtedly been architecture, especially in export terms. In Gustav Peichl, Hans Hollein, and the COOP Sky-Blue architectural co-operative, it boasts personalities whose creativity will enrich the international scene for years to come. Viennese public housing projects have consistently hit the headlines in the international architectural press.

This phenomenon and its pre-history will be examined in the ensuing pages.

Is architecture pointless? An overview of building in the post-war era

The history of post-war architecture in Vienna began with painful memories, namely the symbolically important restoration and reconstruction of "cultural icons" (Friedrich Achleitner) such as St. Stephen's cathedral, the Burgtheater, the Opera, and the Parliament buildings. Housing, which posed a more urgent problem, was designed along traditional lines, not those of the progressive workers' settlements of "Red Vienna" but rather of the conservative estates built in the wake of the National Defense movement. Designers such as Roland Rainer and Karl Schwanzer, who worked along functionalist lines, were the exception. With the Stadthalle, which Roland Rainer finished in 1958 (and which incidentally he himself extended in 1994 in the same style), he sent a clear signal that Austria had reconnected to the International Modernist movement. In the same year Karl Schwanzer represented his country at the Brussels Expo, in the form of a purist edifice of steel and Eternit.

The initial momentum for the rebirth of Austrian architecture came from the Academy of Fine Arts on the Schillerplatz. Here, some of the students of Clemens Holzmeister and Lois Weizenbacher formed "Working Group 4" (Wilhelm Holzbauer, Friedrich Kurrent, and Johannes Spalt), which to the modern eye seems to have represented a synthesis between the International and Austrian Moderne styles. Gustav Peichl and Hans Hollein also began their work against this background. In the early 1960s, Karl Schwanzer created two buildings which were perfectly in keeping with the time, his Museum of the Twentieth Century and the Philipshaus (illustration on P.327).

Surprisingly, it was ecclesiastical architecture which produced the most progressive results. Two buildings in Salzburg paved the way, the parish church in Parsch and St. Josef's College, (1953-56 and 1961-64, both by Working Group 4), but Rudolf Schwarz's St. Florian's in Vienna (1961) also helped to set the pace. These buildings are distinguished by their use of modern materials, steel, and concrete, and clear, esthetically pleasing design, which in its austerity creates a meditative impression. The social and "moral" implications of these works are unmistakable.

As previously mentioned, the Catholic church was trying to show solidarity with contemporary art; it found the ideal advocate in the person of Monsignore Otto Maurer, who dominated the Vienna art scene in the post-war years. Maurer's influence probably also played a decisive role in the construction of what could be the most spectacular building from the Austrian post-war years, the Dreifaltigkeitskirche (Holy Trinity Church) on the Georgenberg on the outskirts of Vienna (1965-76). The sculptor, Fritz Wotruba, a close friend of Maurer's, designed a vast sculpture for it of

primeval strength. Asymmetric cubes of concrete are piled, apparently at random, into a rock-like formation, a sculpture which can be walked inside, that is penetrated by countless shafts of gentle light. Only Gottfried Böhm was able to work in such an organically expressive way when he designed the pilgrimage church at Neviges.

By the late 1950s another group had emerged, one which was primarily united in its criticism of functionalism. "Architecture has no purpose. Purposeless in the sense of pre-determined material application." This was the provocative theory which Hans Hollein expounded in 1962, immediately after his return from the United States. Like his colleague, Walter Pichler, Hollein called for universal architecture, architecture for its own sake, without purpose and unconfined by structural constraints. "Its function should be purely spiritual, magical." After decades of rationalism, cult worship, mythology, symbolism, and ritual were once again considered to have the right to exist. The *BAU* magazine, whose editors included Gustav Peichl, Hans Hollein, and Walter Pichler, became the mouthpiece for the opponents of functionalism. Provocative ideas were given form at the "Club seminars" organized by Günther Feuerstein. These gave rise to such utopian groups as the Haus-Rucker Co., Coop Himmelblau, Zünd-up, and Missing Link, whose imaginative ideas were to

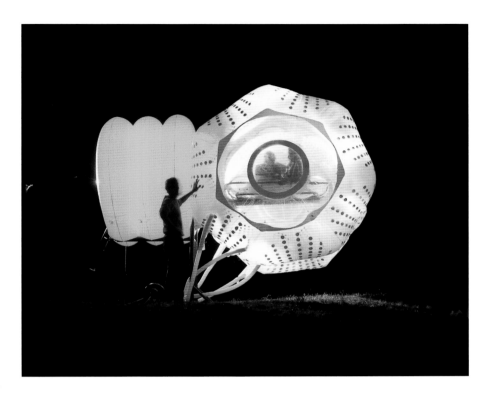

Haus-Rucker Co.
Gelbes Herz (Yellow Heart), 1968

enrich architecture for decades. There was a similar trend in Graz, which was becoming the second center for avant-garde architecture after Vienna. Unfortunately, this is not the place to discuss the "Graz school" and its influences.

To return to Vienna, in the mid-1960s, the Haus-Rucker Co. took up the archaic-seeming cudgels of Hollein and Pichler and endowed them with futuristic variations. Projects such as the *Gelbe Herz* (Yellow Heart) (1968) and *Ballon für zwei* (Balloon for two) (1969) were influenced by space science and technology, and represented an attempt to tear down the barriers between architecture, space, and life. By deliberately overstepping the genre boundaries, their work came to resemble Viennese Actionism, and also to Pop-Art with its cult of basic commodities. Reality and fiction became blurred, as when the Haus-Rucker Co. suggested filling the city of Braunschweig with imitation rocks, crevasses, and cliffs, to transplant the felicity of nature into urban drabness. "Everything is architecture" was the slogan; huge billiard tables and footballs stunned the Viennese public. In 1968, the Himmelblau Coop (Wolf D. Prix and Helmut Swiczinsky) formed a "Bureau for experimental architecture." They too saw their task primarily as the development of

Hans Hollein
Mönchengladbach, Abteiberg
Museum (1972-82)

Haus-Rucker Co.
(Klaus Pinter, Zamp Kelp and
Laurids Ortner) wearing
"Environment Transformers,"
1968

visionary ideas. It is no surprise that for a long time these groups — including Hans Hollein — were not allowed to execute their concepts. Nevertheless their ephemeral ideas, like those of the London group Archigramm, fundamentally changed the international architecture scene and made a major contribution to the conversion from Modern to Post-Modern. The Post-Modern movement, with its representational character took much of its inspiration from them, as did High-Tech architecture with its techno-esthetics.

In the mid 1960s, Hans Hollein received his first commissions to redesign Viennese stores and boutiques. Within the limitations of the four walls, he showed himself to be not only a skillful interior decorator but also an imaginative and elegant designer. Examples of his work include the Retti candle store (1964), the CM boutique (1966-67), and especially the Schullin I jewelry store (1972-74) and later Schullin II (1981), with their exquisite fittings, their "expressive facades," and by no means least, their individuality, were to become milestones of modern design. The idea of having a vein of gold passing through the front window of a jeweler's store, which, in fact, houses the air-conditioning ducts, must surely be unique in its intrinsic and functional refinement: Hollein reveals just enough to be provoking, to make the spectator dream of the delights which lie behind the glittering facade. These store windows in Vienna formed the basis of Hollein's international fame. They were followed by commissions from the United States, and especially in Germany, where in the Abteiberg Museum in Mönchengladbach (1972-82), Hollein created a building in which the architecture was in harmony with the exhibits.

Coop Himmelblau also enjoyed its first successes with small-scale architecture. Examples

are the Reiss Bar (1977) which is divided by a 20-in (48-cm) wide rift; for the "Hot Flat" project (1978-79) they installed a flame-shaped glass roof.

Unlike Hollein and Coop Himmelblau, Gustav Peichl, a pupil of Clemens Holzmeister and Arnulf Rainer, won major commissions in Vienna early on in his career. He achieved international acclaim with his six regional studios for ORF (the Austrian Broadcasting Corporation), all designed on the same principles and completed between 1969 and 1982. Here, Peichl employs a variation on a style of architecture which is based on functional and production processes, making use of the esthetics of ship-building. The buildings, which consist of pre-fabricated concrete components, become machines themselves, in which flashing "instrument panels" produce a delightful, sometimes playful, touch. There are little towers, cones, gables, and bridges. Peichl, who worked for years as a caricaturist (penname: *Ironismus*) alongside his architectural and academic activities, is taking a swipe at the set-pieces of Post-Modernism.

Yet there are other aspects to Viennese architecture of the 1970s. Following the establishment of United Nations headquarters just outside the city, the local government had decided to develop the surrounding area on the far side of the Danube, with administrative and conference buildings which were to give a new look to the metropolis. Unfortunately, they decided not to build the award-winning design of the American firm of Cesar Pelli & Partners, and opted instead for Johann Staber's Y-shaped plate-glass skyscrapers, with the intention of giving Vienna, albeit rather late in the day, monuments in the International Style. On the other hand, Günther Domenig from Graz went his own way by placing a pièce de résistance in a previously unremarkable

Gustav Peichl
Bonn, National Art Gallery
"Gateway" and entrance hall,
1986-92

shopping street in the Favoriten district—though this was by no means uncontroversial. His Central Savings Bank is a glittering biomorph with aggressive gestures and exuberant internal life, plainly struggling to force its way into the lifeless postwar architecture.

Friedensreich Hundertwasser had also called for creativity and individuality in his *Verschimmelungsmanifest* (Moldering Manifesto) of 1958: "The straight line is a betrayal of human individuality. As soon as you let the windows dance by making each one different, you give the whole building a chance to recover." His buildings (Hundertwasserhaus 1985, the *Erlebnis* (Experience) shopping mall, and the district heating works in Spittelau, 1990) were unable to live up to these ambitious words, since they are neither technically, ecologically, nor structurally "alternative". Nevertheless, the decoration and "greening" of their facades draw sightseers from all over the world. Hundertwasser's original avant-garde ideas have long since been realized more coherently by others; he himself has repeatedly turned against contemporary art, which he has branded "un-art" (in a speech at the Grand Austrian State Prize award ceremony in 1981). His cult following and the astute marketing of his creations are nevertheless part of the contemporary Viennese art scene.

The Viennese avant-garde architects, who in the meantime had been causing a stir beyond the bounds of Vienna or Austria, were given the opportunity by Mayor Helmut Zilk (1984-94) to produce large-scale work at home. Apart from Peichl — who was already in the public eye on account of the ORF studios, and who had since achieved world-wide recognition with his design for a phosphate elimination plant in Berlin — this was particularly important for Coop Himmelblau, who were able to produce several sensational buildings. In 1988, at about the same time as their first major industrial building in Funder in Carinthia, they completed the alterations to the roof of a building occupied by a firm of lawyers in the Falkestrasse, which was immediately featured on the front pages of architectural journals. The diagonals, steep gradients, and angles defy the laws of gravity; a parabola which overarches and supports the structure lends wings to the rules of statics. The historic nature of building is "in upheaval" and the spectator is tricked out of long-held ways of looking at things in terms of poetry and humor.

In the same year, an exhibition in New York coined a term for the new "disorder" in architecture: "deconstructivist architecture", the name being a reference to a concept introduced by the French philosopher Jacques Derrida.

Deconstructivism struck the post-modern architectural scene like a bolt of lightning. Although Coop Himmelblau was credited with playing a decisive role in formulating the trend,

the Viennese could not bring themselves to award the advocates of deconstructivism a major project. The deconstructivist design for renovating the Ronacher Theatre failed for financial reasons.

Hans Hollein was luckier, for he had won a difficult and extremely important commission to rebuild the Haas House next to St. Stephan's Cathedral. Hollein, who had become a leading architect in the popular mind following his museum buildings in Mönchengladbach and Frankfurt, and his designs for Salzburg, proposed a plan for this area, which offered little scope for development, in the heart of the city; it was controversial at first but since its completion it has gradually won acceptance.

Hollein places different building sections beside and inside one another as in a collage, so that they can blend easily with the very varied buildings nearby. For the detail, he draws on all levels of post-modernism. As in his earlier, already

ILLUSTRATION ABOVE:
Coop Himmelblau
UFA Cinema Complex, Dresden, 1998

ILLUSTRATION BELOW:
Coop Himmelblau
Ronacher Theatre renovation project, model, 1987

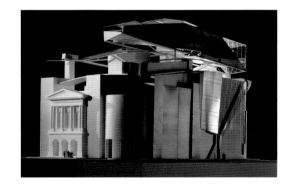

ILLUSTRATIONS LEFT:
Carl Pruscha
Traviatagasse housing project,
1991
Hamam (Turkish Bath) -
exterior and interior

legendary (but unfortunately largely destroyed) Vienna Travel Agency, the interior is an explosion of stimuli to the senses, of allusions and fictions, which are ultimately subordinated to commerce and suggest a world of pure illusion.

By the early 1990s, the furor over post-modern and deconstructivist seminal buildings had largely died down. When the Iron Curtain was demolished, residential building once again became important due to an expected influx of people from Eastern Bloc countries. Word spread of a new *Gründerzeit* (period of rapid industrial expansion), with the focus on ecological and social factors.

Against this background, a number of functional buildings were built, mostly schools and housing projects, in which Viennese architects demonstrated their talents on a wider stage. Among many significant creations were Helmut Richter's school on the Kinkplatz (1992-95), the public housing project in the Pilotengasse by Jacques Herzog & Pierre de Meuron, Otto Steidle, and Adolf Krischanitz (1989-92), and the housing project in the Traviatagasse, controversial on account of its metaphoric isolation (master-plan by Raimund Abraham, built by Carl Pruscha et al., 1991). Boris Podressa, Elsa and Rudolf Prohazka, and Heinz Tesar are also worthy of mention here. These architects, all born in the 1940s and early 1950s, can scarcely be pigeonholed but they are united by a critical, often ironic, approach to Modernism and, at least in most cases, an undogmatic, sensitive approach to the urban and social setting.

The plans to develop and link up the area across the Danube, the so-called *Transdanubiens* turned into a farce in terms of the media and architectural politics. Many fine plans burst like bubbles when the World Exhibition, EXPO 95, on the theme of "Vienna-Budapest" was canceled by popular demand. However, it must be admitted that historical events had overtaken and defused the controversial nature of the twinning project. Nevertheless, a sense of anticlimax gained a hold, causing ambitious undertakings to be implemented in an attempt to bridge the gap. When the city released the land on the Wagramer Strasse which had originally been set aside for the EXPO, Hans Hollein/Coop Himmelblau drew up the land usage plan and Adolf Krischanitz/Heinz Neumann the master-plan for "Danube City." This was to be a new, second focal point in the structure of Vienna, and was supposed to put an end to the old "one-sidedness" of the metropolis. At the same time, it was an attempt to improve the image of Vienna as a city of architecture, by using leading international architects, such as Jean Nouvel, Zaha Hadid, and Arata Isozaki, as well as the Austrian ones. A Viennese subsidiary of the Guggenheim Museum was to cater for the Fine Arts.

For reasons which cannot be entered into here, the majority of the designs have remained on

Boris Podrecca
School in the Dirmhirngasse,
1990 - exterior and view of the
entrance hall

paper. By 1998, the following projects had been completed: the elliptical Andromeda skyscraper, a glass outpost of United Nations City with apartments and offices for diplomats, and the tower-blocks on the Wagramer Strasse, which were built by Gustav Peichl, Coop Himmelblau and NFOG (Nigst, Fogatti, Ostertag, Gaisrucker).The three tower-blocks, which do indeed give Danube City a skyline and its own identity, are designed and built in very different ways. The Coop Himmelblau's cone-shaped sky-scraper with its glass-houses and air-conditioned facades, is the most technically and ecologically advanced. NFOG equipped their tower with extremely attractive metal sun-screens. Gustav Peichl's cylinder-shaped building has been called "Obelix" because of its pale blue-and-white stripes. NFOG have built a school not far from the residential complex.

The acid test for Vienna's drive toward innovation is centered on discussions about the museum district, which, at the time of writing, remain unresolved. It was decided at the beginning of the 1980s that the Hofstallungen, which had scarcely been developed, and which had been used since about 1920 as a fairground site, should be developed as an "island of museums." The competition, which finally took place after much debate, was won in 1990 by the brothers Laurids and Manfred Ortner, whose design cleverly bridged the gap between the "imperial structure" of the Hofburg and the Biedermeyer quarters of the neighboring seventh district. Various institutions were to be brought together in the

complex, including the Museum of Tobacco, the Museum of the Media, the Museum of Modern Art, the Art Gallery, and the Museum of Austrian Modernism. The area was also to have conference and function halls and a media forum with a striking, transparent "reading tower." However, before building could begin, the tabloid press instigated a vicious campaign against the insertion of modern buildings "amid the baroque ensemble," which incidentally was never completed here. A controversy had been instigated around the issue of the museum quarter which tarred all modern architecture with the same brush. Modern architecture was to be viewed as experimental, not as *Kultur*. Since then, the die has been cast. What has been built is a version of the original Ortner & Ortner design modified almost beyond recognition, ultimately banishing all "contemporary material" (the media center, the cultural information center in the reading tower, and the film and photography sections). Instead the Leopold Museum—a collection of late nineteenth and early twentieth century Austrian Art — now enjoys pride of place. It is as yet unclear how the two cultural initiatives left in the wilderness, the Museum of Childhood and the Vienna Center of Architecture, will fit into the scheme of things.

Of course, Vienna will survive with this compromise solution. However, the opportunity to have a serious architectural dialogue between old and new in the Danube metropolis appears to have been missed for the time being.

Rudolf Schwarz
St. Florian's Parish Church,
1961-63

Church building in the post-war era

The main stimulus to architecture in the post-war era, in Vienna as elsewhere in Austria, came from a rather surprising genre, that of the design of ecclesiastical buildings. It was thanks to liberal clerics such as Monsignor Otto Maurer and the Jesuit father Dr. Herbert Muck that the Catholic church sought a closer relationship with modern art and thus affected the course of architectural development. Thus, in the 1960s and 1970s religious building, rather than housing, became the setting for experimentation. The architectural avant-garde encompassed a broad spectrum which oscillated between traditionalist-romantic tendencies, functionalism, and utopianism.

Rudolf Schwarz, star pupil of Hans Poelzig in Berlin and Professor of Urban Development at the Düsseldorf Academy, was one of the protagonists of church-building in the post-war era. However, St. Florian's on the Wiedner Hauptstrasse (1961-63) was bitterly attacked, because Schwarz had the earlier Baroque building demolished, and then replaced it with a box-like container, which is nonetheless decorated quite sensitively. Narrow concrete girders form criss-cross and zigzag patterns, creating a filigree effect despite the severity of the structure.

Fritz Wotruba used a different concept for his Holy Trinity Church, built between 1965 and 1976 in collaboration with Fritz G. Mayr. Wotruba, who had been top of the sculpture class at the Academy of Fine Arts, produced a building on the Georgenberg which was in a class of its own in its near-unlimited creative freedom. The building consists of a walk-in sculpture, an apparently random pile of chunks of concrete which are combined into an extremely artistic shape. "Harmony by overcoming differences" was the aim of its creator, who as a socialist and an atheist was expressing his own almost chthonic esthetics. The shapes were initially made by hand in plaster, to be subsequently converted into concrete. The sacred purpose of the building is expressed only in the interior, in which a huge cross made by the artist signals the Christian context. The area for silent worship, despite the wall of compact, asymmetrical concrete blocks, is simple and atmospheric; daylight enters through the slits and glazed windows offer a view of nature.

Unfortunately, Wotruba never lived to see his work completed; he died in 1975 and had to leave most of the decoration of the interior of Holy Trinity Church to his colleagues.

Fritz Wotruba
Holy Trinity Church, 1965-76

ILLUSTRATIONS OPPOSITE:
TOP:
Karl Schwanzer
Museum of the 20th Century,
1959-62

BOTTOM:
Roland Rainer
Stadthalle, 1952-58

Architecture from 1939 to the Present Day

Karl Schwanzer, Museum of the Twentieth Century

This purist, steel-framed structure in the Schweizergarten, and Roland Rainer's Stadthalle, are among the few buildings with which Austria attempted to connect to the international scene in post-war architecture. Originally designed as a contribution to the Brussels Expo in 1958, the almost square, box-like structure, built on pylons, was taken down at the end of the event and re-built in Vienna between 1959 and 1962. In so doing, the open-plan areas — the ground floor and the atrium — were enclosed or roofed over, enabling the complex to be used as a museum.

Today, three sculpture gardens surround the functional building. The former Expo building was built using technology that was pioneering in its day. The clearly visible steel skeleton made of DIN standard sections was clad with sheets of Eternit, a material which was invented in Austria and which was soon to spread triumphantly around the world.

Under the egis of Karl Schwanzer, the architecture department of the Technischen Hochschule, which had hitherto been rather conservative, experienced radical reform. Schwanzer himself produced other buildings in Vienna, but was noted principally for the BMW building in Munich and the Austrian Embassy in Brasilia.

Roland Rainer, Stadthalle

The Stadthalle, a versatile location for events, sports, and training in Wien-Rudolfsheim, became the showpiece of the Viennese Moderne style in the second half of the century. The designer, who was principal of the Master School of Architecture at the Vienna Academy, Roland Rainer, was linked to the pioneering building throughout his life. In 1952-58, he built the splendid main hall with its characteristic asymmetrical roof design, made of reinforced concrete and sloping down to the middle. Not only was this esthetically ahead of its time, but it also provided excellent acoustics, good thermal insulation, and a good view of the stage. There was room for 15-20,000 people in an area of 33 x 33 ft (100 x 100 m). In 1971-74, a swimming pool and sauna were added, and in 1994 the foyer and main hall were modernized and the new, smaller performance hall E built. Here, too, freestanding steel girders and ventilation pipes, air-bricks, and glass panels define the classical modern look.

Roland Rainer, who was in charge of the work on the Stadthalle over four decades, remains true to his functionalist style to this day. Functionality and economy of design, absolute sincerity, and "transparency" of construction are his trademarks.

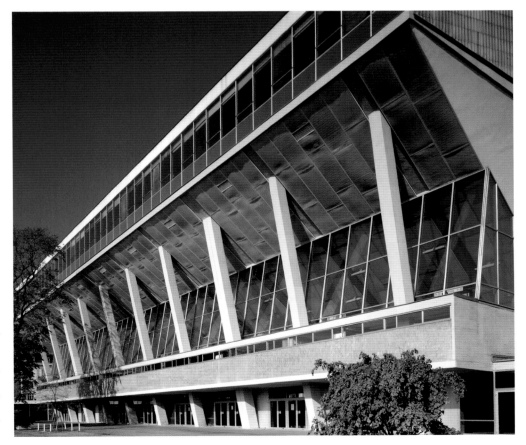

Gustav Peichl's buildings in Vienna

A feeling of joy imbues the work of Gustav Peichl more than that of almost any other architect. Since studying under Clemens Holzmeister at the Academy of Fine Arts in Vienna, Peichl has maintained a sensitive, emotional, and sometimes even ironic approach to his profession. It is not for nothing that he has entertained the professional world for years as a caricaturist using the pen-name of *Ironismus*. Despite the playful levity which distinguishes his sketches, Peichl is a rationalist through and through. Like his predecessor and mentor Otto Wagner, the usefulness of a building, and its technical clarity and form are the essential pre-conditions for the success of its architecture and also ultimately for its esthetic effect.

Peichl's first commissions in Vienna and the surrounding area were residential and functional, which showed his roots to be firmly planted in the "Classical Modern" movement. His own house in Döbling (1960-62) is an elongated white cube, broken up only by a single narrow band of windows overlooking the street; however, it opens on to the garden with huge plate-glass windows. The Atrium School in the Crimea (1961-64) should be mentioned as an example of his early school-building style. The clearly constructed complex, built of "economical" materials (exposed concrete, plaster, and wood), is grouped around an open courtyard; so that each of the classrooms spaced, as it were, around a cloister, has an additional outdoor area in front of it. In the 1960s, Peichl also made a name for himself together with Oswald Oberhuber, Walter Pichler, and Hans Hollein as publishers of the journal BAU, a strong advocate of modern architecture.

Peichl's breakthrough came with the serial design of six regional studios for Austrian Radio (Dornbirn, Innsbruck, Salzburg, Linz, Graz, and Eisenstadt, 1969-81). Each of these complexes, developed from a basic plan, characteristically and unmistakably mirrors the functional operation of the broadcasting station and projects it outward onto the structure and the appearance of the building. Different sections of the radio building are arranged in a circle around a two-story round hall, the distances between them thus being reduced to a minimum. The whole complex is conceived as a giant machine, with the mechanisms interlocking smoothly inside. The decoration underlines this metaphor. The concrete surfaces are painted metallic silver, and structural elements and technical installations such as the ventilation pipes are artistically incorporated.

Gustav Peichl
Peichl House, 1960-62

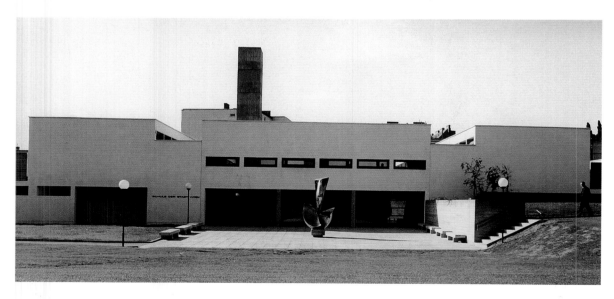

Gustav Peichl
Primary school in the Crimea,
1961-64

The ground radio station in Aflenz (1976-80) was designed in a similar way. Here, however, there were different pre-existing conditions from those which applied in the regional studios. Since the best location for the satellite station lay in a nature reserve, the buildings had to be dug out of the ground. Even in these circumstances, new standards in functional architecture were set. The complex, which is circular like the antenna, is elegantly "immersed" in the green mound of earth.

Aflenz and the radio studios, the "silver shrines of communication," earned Peichl architecture prizes and international acclaim. Large contracts from abroad followed, notably from Germany and Italy. These included the building of the phosphate elimination plant in Berlin-Tegel (1979-85), which was in the shape of a ship's bow, the National Arts Hall in Bonn (1986-92), and the extension to the Städelsch Institute of Arts in Frankfurt-am Main (1987-90).

Peichl was also involved with designing exhibition buildings in Vienna. In 1989, he designed a new Fine Arts Hall for the Austrian Regional Bank's Arts Forum, a building which had been built in 1916. The most famous feature is the Freyung gateway, which adds a new and exquisite touch to the historic ensemble. A gilded ball 6 ft 8 in (2 m) in diameter, the "pearl of Freyung," crowns the narrow entrance, which is reminiscent of the way into an arcanum. Two free-standing pillars of natural stone emphasize the dignified atmosphere and lead the visitor on into the showrooms, which are decorated with sumptuous materials. Peichl's designs constitute yet another homage to the art of the Secession with its "inclinations toward synthesis of arts," as well as to its protagonists, Josef Hoffmann and Joseph Maria Olbrich.

Gustav Peichl
Stage complex of the Vienna Burgtheater, 1990

In his design for the stage complex of the Vienna Burgtheater (1990), Peichl once again took up the idea of the atrium which he had formulated in the 1960s. Here, three rehearsal stages (two for the Burgtheater and one for the Academy Theater) are grouped around a sunken inner courtyard containing lawns and trees. The halls, each measuring 100 x 70 ft (30 x 21 m) are covered with flat roofing sections, while a transverse section topped with pyramids protects the atrium from the elements.

The latest work by this Viennese architect is the residential tower-block on the Wagramer Strasse on the Danube Island. Alongside the structurally and technically advanced towers created by the Himmelblau Coop and NFOG, Peichl has placed a simple cylinder, the "round Wagramer," which soon became a new landmark for the area. Its shining, pale, blue-and-white vertical stripes have earned it the nickname "Obelix."

Gustav Peichl
Residential tower-block on the Wagramer Strasse, 1994

Johann Staber
UNO City, 1973
Left in foreground: Wilhelm
Holzbauer, Andromeda Tower,
1993

UNO City and the Andromeda Tower

A controversial chapter in the history of Viennese architecture was that which involved the International Center of the UNO City, the massive administrative complex, located near the Danube Park which has been growing ever since the first plans were drawn up in 1970. Built in the traditions of the International Style, it was to make Vienna, according to the then Chancellor Bruno Kreisky, the third United Nations headquarters city (alongside New York and Geneva). Between 1983-87 the office complex was extended by the addition of a conference center and at about the same time plans began for EXPO 95, the World Exhibition on the Danube Island site.

When the World Exhibition plans were abandoned, the associated plans for a Danube City were also thrown into uncertainty. Thus UNO City has never been fully integrated into the cityscape. Only the Andromeda Tower, an elliptical glass

cylinder built in 1993 by Wilhelm Holzbauer to contain residential and office accommodation for diplomats, was a step forward in urban development. From the start, the planning of UNO City presented problems. Although the first prize in an international competition was won by an American design firm, Cesar Pelli & Partners, the city and state decided to opt for a design by the Austrian Johann Staber. This was an attempt to find a national solution which would at the same time signal a link to the international, markedly rationalist, architectural scene. Staber's design is conventional, though the curve of the plate-glass tower blocks, built in a Y-shaped layout, lends it some elegance and dynamism; the pylons and windows are in the style of Mies van der Rohe. The problems of UNO City are functional and urban. Since it is a purely administrative center with a necessarily high level of security, there is little scope for life to develop within its walls.

RIGHT AND FAR RIGHT:
Wilhelm Holzbauer
Lasallestrasse office complex,
1989

BOTTOM RIGHT:
Wilhelm Holzbauer et al.
Ringstrasse Galleries, 1993

Wilhelm Holzbauer, Lasallestrasse office complex, and the Ringstrasse galleries

In the late 1980s, the team of architects who worked with Wilhelm Holzbauer was presented with some extraordinary challenges in urban development, which they met with bravura. In 1989, as part of the renovation of the area around the Nordbahnhof (northern railway station), they were to make a mark with the Lasallestrasse office complex. They achieved a perfect balance between compact construction and urban open areas (atria and internal areas several floors high).

The second commission was less prestigious. The Ringstrasse Galleries were to be built on the site of the burnt-out administrative headquarters of the Steyr motor plant on the Kärntner Ring. The problem lay in respecting the historic integrity of the magnificent avenue while at the same time placing a contemporary building next to the magnificent Gründerzeit facades

As a first step, the frontage of the former Palais Corso was rebuilt and a luxury hotel erected behind it. A steel bridge connects this with the next site, that of a burnt-out building transformed by Holzbauer which now houses offices and penthouse suites as well as shopping malls. His facades fit in with the surrounding houses in type of stone and structure. An interesting feature is the framework effect on the facade, which permits a fleeting glimpse of the interior. The bold metal structures, bright glass, and polished marble have been used to create atria and galleries, attractive areas in which to shop and browse.

Architecture from 1939 to the Present Day

Günther Domenig, Favoriten Central Bank

Günther Domenig has certainly placed an alien object in the previously rather boring Favoritenstrasse. It is a glittering, scaly nose, the lower part pouting like the mouth of a fish, which has been confidently inserted among the unexciting, post-war architecture. The metal surface is contorted, causing interesting reflections which change as the light falls on it. The "thing," as it was rather unimaginatively called, seems to breathe, to be alive, even to threaten to swallow up people who enter, were it not for the reassuring sign "Central Bank" ensuring a certain degree of security.

This branch of the bank, built between 1975 and 1979 and intended to be a cultural center, breaks all the conventions of Viennese architecture. It disregards its surroundings, makes no historical references, is not trying to be popular, is not even functional. Instead, it radiates vitality and creativity, something which, in this monotonous pedestrian precinct, cannot be rated too highly.

Perhaps it is no coincidence that its creator, Günther Domenig, is not from Vienna. He was born in 1934 in Klagenfurt and studied in the 1950s at the Technical High School in Graz, where he witnessed the rise of the so-called "Graz school." The Styrian architects had set themselves the aim of countering the rationalist architecture of the post-war era with expressive, emotional forms; imagination was once again allowed a freer rein. Nowadays, Günther Domenig is regarded as one of the driving forces of the group.

Domenig's work is strongly influenced by the requirement for his buildings to be viewed more as over-sized sculptures which can be walked in than as functional buildings. The idea of a "synthesis of the arts" emerges once again here, and this impression is certainly reinforced on entering the Central Bank. The visitor is stunned by the vitality of its exuberant, high-tech, futuristic interior. He is surrounded by a morass of girders, trusses, pipes, and metal bars, making him wonder if he has blundered into a machine-room or even a jungle. He may glance uneasily at the huge hands and other anthropomorphic sculptures which loom spectrally between the hi-tech components. Then he will realize that this gruesome, yet beautiful, artificial world does function and serves as a surreal setting for exhibitions.

Since 1980, Domenig has been Professor at the Technical High School in Graz. He has created many different structures in his unique expressive-fantastic style, including a pavilion at the site of the Munich Olympics.

Günther Domenig
Favoriten Central Bank 1975-79
Interior (opposite) and
Frontage on to Favoritenstrasse
(right)

Architecture from 1939 to the Present Day

The Himmelblau Coop and its buildings

Wolf D. Prix and Helmut Swiczinsky, known as the Himmelblau Coop, are today, along with Georg Peichl and Hans Hollein, Austria's leading architects on the international stage. Having graduated from the Vienna Technical High School, initially, like Haus Rucker Co. and Hans Hollein, they represented Viennese architecture of the postwar period, which was militantly opposed to conventional traditions and old-fashioned structures.

"As Viennese, we have a rapport with Freud, who taught us that suppressing emotions uses up a lot of energy. We apply this to our projects. The unscathed world of architecture no longer exists. It will never return." For a long time they had no major contracts. They used their time in their "Bureau for experimental architecture," founded in 1968, to develop primarily utopian projects, which generally remained theoretical. Criticism of the Post-Modernist movement, which had become stale, helped the Himmelblau Coop to achieve their own breakthrough. Their creativity, based on unselfconscious creative processes, led to them becoming co-founders of Deconstructivism, which was to define the architecture of the late 1980s.

Like Hans Hollein, Prix and Swiczinsky began with small-scale projects, mostly with theme bars. Their declaration of structural war on traditional architecture is characterized by imaginative displacements and aggressively fractured lines. An unconventional project to renovate the Ronacher Theater failed, partly at the hands of those who called for a more pleasing reconstruction of the original Variety theater.

ILLUSTRATIONS OPPOSITE AND BELOW:
Coop Himmelblau
Roof extension, Falkestrasse 6, 1987

Coop Himmelblau
Wagramer Strasse tower-block, 1994

The Coop achieved world-wide notoriety as well as recognition with the roof extension to a lawyer's office in the Falkestrasse. The static concept of the glazed conference room is indeed bewildering, rising as it does above a cornice dating from the *Gründerzeit* cornice in the heart of the city. An arch like a bird's wing rises over the L-shaped room, intersected by many diagonal lines, angles, and sloping surfaces. The laws of gravity appear to have been disregarded, the only constant is the dynamic of lines and surfaces. Stability and implied instability, unity and staged "chaos" are arranged in poetic juxtaposition.

The Himmelblau Coop's latest coup is the tower-block on the Wagramer Strasse on the Danube Island. The skyscraper, right next to the blocks by Peichl and the NFOG Architectural Association is striking for its high-tech design (air-conditioned frontage, heat accumulator, winter gardens), but, above all, for its strikingly elegant appearance.

Hans Hollein, retail premises

In the 1960s and early 1970s, three rather modest business premises which gave architecture a whole new impetus, and created a new star in the architectural firmament — Hans Hollein. Born in Vienna and returning to his home town after a long stay in the United States, Hollein first created a stir with his utopian projects. With the Retti candle store-front in 1964, he won his first real contract.

In a move away from the trend at the time, Hollein did not build the usual plate-glass frontage. Instead he isolated the façade with a glittering aluminum wall, with only a candle-like slit for an entrance and narrow rounded windows. Lavish materials and effective lighting reinforce the impression that one is about to enter an arcanum, a sanctuary, the world of business. The cult style of the store is also emphasized in its interior. The entrance opens out onto an octagonal display area, almost as in an ecclesiastical building; although the confines are narrow, they give the illusion of spaciousness thanks to the use of mirrors. Behind this is the rectangular store and sales floor area.

The most outstanding of these exquisite shop fittings were the Schullin I and Schullin II jewelry stores, built by Hollein in 1972-74 and 1981. On the façade of the earlier building, a golden-brass fissure breaks through the brown polished granite and extends over the doorway to a crevasse-like opening. The entrance to Schullin II is covered by a gently curving metal arch which anticipates the jewels on offer within.

In the three travel agents' offices which Hollein built in Vienna in the late 1970s and early 80s, the associative character of his architecture was even more pronounced. Metal palm trees suggest tropical lands; fragments of pillars and pyramids hint at the world of classical antiquity and Egypt, while in between are stylized references to ships, aeroplanes, and trains, and even a radiator grill, to symbolize voyages of adventure. Trompe l'oeil paintings complete the illusion of faraway places. Yet Hollein's interiors are no panoptic vision, seeking to replace real life; the motifs in Hollein's scenes point calculatedly, even ironically to their purpose and meaning — whether it be sale of package tours or ventilation; in their imagery, they appeal to the observer to remember or recognize, and to let his imagination run wild — while at the same time he is the victim of visual mockery.

Hollein's semiotic architecture was in contrast to the frigidity of functionalism, which had defined architecture for decades. In 1979, Hollein expressed the situation as follows: "Architecture is a cult, a ritual, a medium of communication. Architecture is a means of maintaining bodily warmth."

Hans Hollein
Jewelry store Schullin I, 1972-74

Hans Hollein, Haas House

If Vienna had been struck with another architectural thunderbolt after the Michaeler House, then it was the Haas House. "Consumers' rocket", "a cross between a soda fountain and a barrel-organ", "the tombstone of Post-Modernism" — critics strove to outdo one another in their pithy epithets and hasty judgements.

Indeed Hans Hollein's office and retail building, completed in 1990, does present a challenge to Viennese traditionalism. For one thing, it is located close to St. Stephan's cathedral, on a prominent corner between the Graben and Stock-im-Eisen Platz, an aggressive glass and marble structure which forces its way, brashly and boldly, into the heart of Vienna. Laws actually had to be changed on its account and it even dares to offer a reflection of the noble cathedral itself.

Hans Hollein
Jeweller's shop Schullin II, 1981

Hans Hollein
New Haas-House, 1985
Façade on to St. Stephen's Square

The vociferous protests have died down since then and Hollein's work — the first monumental work by the internationally acclaimed architect in his home-town — is judged in a more considered way. The Viennese master did indeed succeed in boldly redefining a tricky point in the city's image: since the first Haas House, built in the Gründerzeit by architects Edouard van der Nüll and August Sicardsburg, was pulled down, no-one since the war had managed to find an appropriate structure for this site in the shadow of St. Stephen's, which was so hard to exploit; the building of the Underground had added to the problems, imposing considerable engineering limitations.

Hans Hollein found an extravagant solution to the problem, unusually effective in the context of the town as a whole, by building the exterior in several layers, with some sections appearing to be cut out of one another. Thus the marble side façade with its geometric windows echoes the structure of the shops in the Graben. With the corner cut off in a quadrant (recalling the layout of a Roman camp), it is a glittering glass edifice which is magically attractive, especially at night. The cylinder has a glazed oriel facing toward the cathedral, which extends upward like a telescope and is then topped with a roof reaching up like a springboard ("a landing strip for the Christ child," as one of the workers put it). On the top floor, there is a bar from which there is a breath-taking view of St. Stephan's, the avant-garde department store paying its respects to the mediaeval cathedral.

Hollein used a collage technique to relate to the various structures in the vicinity of the new Haas House. He contrasted the delicacy and verticality of St. Stephen's with the towering oriel, which also reflects and refracts the image of the cathedral. The stepped wall on to Goldschmiedegasse is described by the architect himself as "gothic." The geometrically divided surfaces of the marble façade key in with the Graben, while the architectonic "chaos" visually enlivens the junction between Stock-im-Eisen Platz and the Graben. The marble outer skin opens up with a magnanimous gesture here to reveal the glittering world of the interior. Lights on St. Stephen's Square act as reflections of the sparkling temple of consumerism. Despite all the criticism, there can be no doubt that the pompous monstrosity has an enlivening effect on the dreary post-war buildings nearby.

Inside the Haas House there awaits an explosion of motifs; it is not without reason that some say it is overdone. The design is based on a central room extending upward, lit by a flat glass dome. Architecturally this is no novelty, but the stairs and escalators, galleries and terraces, create a unique "experience," extending horizontally and vertically over five floors and including both stores and bars.

Everywhere, there are fixtures and fittings which are reminders of the situation and function of the building, but Hollein's postmodern metaphors are not always as happy as those in the Austrian Travel Agent's. However, the over-riding maxim of the Haas House, which functions both as a store and a public arena, is to see and be seen. It was spawned from the atrium in American skyscrapers where the open squares of a town are transplanted into a tower-block. There of course it is mostly determined by the climate. Movement, represented by the sliding escalators and the constant comings and goings in the stores and bars, becomes a metaphor of modern life.

Hundertwasser as "architecture's doctor"

Fritz Stowasser, alias Friedensreich Hundertwasser, the Viennese painter and activist, was
always good at surprises. Back in 1958, he presented his ideas about humane building and living in his "Moldering Manifesto." This controversial document was an appeal for imaginative building which was close to nature, and at
the same time constituted a vehement attack
on rationalist architecture, condemning its
straight lines as "ungodly." Subsequently,
Hundertwasser presented ever new suggestions for architecture in harmony with nature to
the public at large. With his demands for natural materials, for diversity instead of monotony, for organic and irregular forms, and for the
"greening" of roofs and façades he was the
forerunner of "alternative architecture."

However, it was to be twenty years before
Hundertwasser had the opportunity to fulfill his
dreams himself. In 1979, the city of Vienna
commissioned him to design a residential
building in the third district, on the corner of
Löwengasse and Kegelgasse. Here, he built fifty-
two homes over a three-year period, using reinforced concrete, bricks, ceramics, and timber.
The attractive exterior has become a tourist
attraction over which architectural critics and
Hundertwasser fans disagree. The terrace house
on an L-shaped foundation was given a colorfully
designed façade. Its organic lines conceal the
structural framework; its onion domes, gables,
and concrete figures suggest a romantic atmosphere. According to Hundertwasser, Fensterrecht (window right) and Baumpflicht (tree duty)

are a must for an ecological house. Fensterrecht means the freedom of the inhabitants to creatively shape the residential space they are allotted, especially the exterior walls of their apartments: "A person must be able to lean out of the window and paint everything within arm's reach pink, so that it can be seen from afar, and from the street, that "somebody lives there." Baumpflicht means the re-establishment of the dialog with nature, the installation of nests of green plants (Baummieter), roof planting and the "greening" of the façade. In keeping with the character of the district, Hundertwasser built a piece of imitation Gründerzeit façade on the Kegelgasse. Opposite it, he built a "shopping-mall experience."

The interior decorations with mosaics of broken tiles are a trademark of Hundertwasser's, the bright fragments constantly assembled to form new patterns. Incidentally, this idea is not new. it comes from Antoni Gaudì, who popularized this unusual form of decoration in Barcelona at the turn of the century. Hundertwasser also takes after the Catalan architect in his striving for "organic" architecture.

At the beginning of the 1990s, Hundertwasser built his own museum in the Untere Weissger-berstrasse, in his own imaginative style. This Kunst-Haus-Wien (Art House Vienna), to which two building of the former Thonet furniture factory were converted, displays his own works and presents exhibitions of other internationally-renowned artists.

A further project in Vienna was the architectural conversion of the Spittelau district heating plant in the city's Alsergrund district (1992). He has transformed a sober monstrosity of industrial architecture into a mosque-like cult building.

Other artists and non-architects such as Arik Brauer and Ernst Fuchs, both co-founders of the "Vienna School of Fantastic Realism", were given the opportunity in the time of Mayor Zilk to create their ideas for an "artists' house," with considerable financial support from the city fathers.

ILLUSTRATION OPPOSITE:
Friedensreich Hundertwasser
District heating plant, Spittelau,
1988-1992

Arik Brauer
Vienna Council housing, Brauer
House, 1988-95

New Viennese housing projects

In the 1980s and 1990s, Viennese housing schemes achieved world-wide acclaim. After the fall of the Iron Curtain, the city again became the destination for a wave of immigrants, creating a considerable demand for living space. The town, which had already taken impressive steps to meet the need for housing with the workers' projects of "Red Vienna" and even with the worthy apartment blocks of the post-war era, again became the scene of experimentation in the politics of construction. With contributions by well-known domestic and foreign architects, exemplary solutions were found, especially for "living in the outer city." Two of these will be described below.

Radical isolation from the outside world, the consequence of an inhospitable suburban wilderness, was the basic concept behind the design of the Traviatagasse settlement in the Liesing district, completed in 1991. Raimund Abraham, who drew up the master plan, along with four other firms of architects, including Carl Pruscha (see illustration on page 332), tried to create an ordered, geometric alternative to the faceless environment. The layout itself is based on a strictly square grid, with only a touch of randomness achieved by shifting the inner axis. The elevations are also dominated, while allowing for characteristic differences between the four firms of architects involved, by unified block-like forms, giving the settlement the effect of a Moroccan casbah. Whether living in a split-level house, a family house with several floors or a row-house, the resident here is guaranteed privacy, undisturbed by the outside world, but also programmatically prescribed. The narrow, shady atrium-style courtyards measuring only 8 ft 4 in x 8 ft 4 in (5 x 5 m), leave no room for socializing; the cool passages between the crystalline, hard-edged house walls do not invite one to linger.

The Pilotengasse project, built in 1989-92 according to the plans of Adolf Krischanitz, Herzog & de Meuron and Otto Steidle, is also defined by fundamental geometric principles. However its character is quite different, more open and lively. The two hundred homes are divided into cube-shaped or L-shaped detached and semi-detached houses, put together in slightly curved rows. They each have small patches of garden, which clearly express the many different ways in which their owners use them. The Cubist severity of the architecture is countered by the very lively colors of the façades (Oskar Putz) and the various window arrangements.

Particular attention was paid to the buildings at the heads of the eight line. These are open on the ground floor and deliberately jut out into the surrounding landscapes, acting as monumental signposts for the project and its architects.

Helmut Richter, School on the Kinkplatz

"I wanted to build a school in which the unpleasant features which are always so striking in schools were not so immediately obvious." Helmut Richter did not only succeed in this aim; with the school on the Kinkplatz, he created an internationally esteemed masterpiece, which set new esthetic and technical standards in Vienna.

Transparency, brightness, and friendliness are the values which one sub-consciously perceives on approaching this elegant building, which is set on a hill. Sloping and curving glass surfaces, supported by matchstick-thin struts, offer an uninterrupted view of the reception and communal areas. The fixtures and fittings are painted in bold colors, brilliant yellows, reds and blues, so that they too are visible and cheerfully incorporated into the scene.

The layout is original and functional: three wings of unequal length are attached to a broad cross-piece like the fingers of a hand; these accommodate the classrooms. The wedge-shaped hall of the main section, with its picture windows, covers the vestibule, the staircases, and a three-part gymnasium. Corridors and landings are incorporated appropriately and logically into the layout.

It is only on closer inspection that it becomes clear what engineering skill lies behind this airy and functional design. As concrete elements are reduced to a minimum, steel structures spanning up to 84 ft (25 m) have to support the huge glass surfaces; but despite their burden they, too, remain amazingly delicate. Even the air-conditioning, always a problem in glass buildings, is excellently designed. The triple-insulated glass with a reflective outer layer prevents the building from becoming over-heated.

Helmut Richter had already caused a stir in 1984 with his elegantly practical Kiang Chinese Restaurant, and in 1986-91 this was followed by a housing complex in the Brunnenstrasse in Liesing, where he was already experimenting with high-tech glazing and extensive sound insulation. The transparency and lightness combined with best use of space were features which would be repeated in the school on the Kinkplatz.

Helmut Richter
School on the Kinkplatz, 1992-95
Exterior and view in the glazed hall

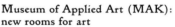

Museum of Applied Art (MAK):
new rooms for art

For a long time, Vienna struggled for an appropriate, contemporary way in which to display its
art treasures. It is principally the works of the
avant-garde and the "new media" which have
still not yet found a permanent home. However,
in recent years, some projects have managed
to bring a breath of fresh air into the Vienna
museum scene.

Under the directorship of Peter Noever, the
Austrian Museum of Applied Art was extended
and renovated between 1986 and 1993. Famous
artists and architects, including Günther Förg,
Donald Judd, Jenny Holzer, Heimo Zobernigg,
SITE, and Herrmann Czech were invited to decorate the rooms of the Kunstgewerbemuseum,
founded in 1864, and to create unusual features
with their own works.

Few, but bold changes were made to the
exterior of the splendid neo-Renaissance brick
palace, dating from 1871; they were to "allude
to" the historical context. The SITE group of
artists made the spectacular archway into a ring,
Walter Pichler created the theatrical "Gateway
into the Garden," and Peter Noever built an
impressive terrace in the garden of the museum.

A walk through the collection shows how differently the various artists approached the task
they had been set.

Museum quarter and Exhibition Hall

A battle has been raging since the 1980s about the Museum quarter which was to be built in the architecturally virtually unexploited area of the Hofstallungen. In 1990, the first competition was won by the brothers Laurids and Manfred Ortner, for their design which brought together various cultural institutions — the Museum of Tobacco, Museum of the Media, Museum of Modern Art, an Exhibition Hall, and the Museum of Austrian Modernism — a long-felt want. The area was also to have performance halls and a media forum with a striking transparent "reading tower". A popular initiative spurred on by the tabloid press raged against modern buildings amid the "Baroque ensemble," and a noisy debate began about all modern architecture.

Subsequently the Ortner & Ortner project was altered almost beyond recognition and all "contemporary material" (including the media center, the cultural information center in the reading tower and the film and photography sections) was banished. Instead the Leopold Museum, a collection of works of Austrian art from the turn-of-the-century, took pride of place.

To serve as a temporary site for displaying contemporary art and new media, an Exhibition Hall was built on the Karlsplatz by Adolf Krischanitz in 1992. The yellow cube, suspended on sixteen sky-blue steel legs, conceals about 3333 sq. ft (1000 m²) of exhibition space. A turquoise tubular bridge connects the unpopular temporary building with the Girardi-park. However, thanks to cavalier policy on exhibitions, it has become a permanent feature of the Vienna art scene.

Laurids and Manfred Ortner
Design for a museum quarter, model 1994

Viennese bars

One of the strengths of Viennese architects had always been avant-garde interior design. The American Bar by Adolf Loos (1908, see pages 312-13), a tiny area decorated with unusual style and impact, became the progenitor of Viennese interior design. Its re-discovery in the late 1960s — it had been neglected for years and fallen into disrepair — also led to the revitalization of interior design.

The "Little Café" by Herrmann Czech, the "miniature building site," on which he worked from 1970 to 1985, is an example of the compactness and quality of the new Viennese interior design. "Architecture is the background" and "Architecture should not get in the way... it could have always been like that" are Czech's maxims, which he expresses effectively yet apparently effortlessly in his work.

Hans Hollein, Luigi Blau, Wolf. D. Prix, and Helmut Swiczinsky, the latter two as the Himmelblau Coop who would create a stir in the world of mainstream architecture, had also been involved in interior design in their earlier years. In 1977, the Himmelblau Coop had created an "expressive" atmosphere in the Reiss Bar, in which there is an actual structural cleft through the interior. In 1979, they built the first of a total of three versions of the "Red Angel" music bar. Its landmark sign is an abstract angel made of strips of stainless steel which hangs from the ceiling and is echoed on the façade with a sort of wing-like structure.

"Ron con Soda" is one of the latest attractions on the Viennese bar scene. It is on the Rabensteig, right beside the Himmelblau Coop's "Red Angel." The Eichinger or Knechtl team (Gregor Eichinger and Christian Knechtl), which in addition to its architectural projects has also designed the cover of *Falter*, the local newspaper for many years, and now also stages techno-parties, came up with an original solution. The terraced interior is decorated simply with inexpensive materials; salsa and rum immediately conjure up associations with the improvised interiors of Cuban clubs. As an interesting gimmick, the chair and table legs are sawn off on one side so that they can still stand straight on the floors of different heights. If you cross the "Ron con Soda" floor, you can go up a flight of stairs to the top floor, the "second floor," the second bar fitted out by Eichlinger or Knechtl. Here you enter a tunnel-like room, whose light-source is principally from two large aquariums. The narrow room is furnished with fittings from the legendary Mounier Bar of the 1930s, which was demolished in the early 1990s. This retro decor, combined with the modern detailing, creates a stylish and atmospheric setting.

Eichinger oder Knechtl
Ron-con-Soda-Bar, 1994

Eichinger oder Knechtl
First-Flor-Bar, 1994

Gabriele Bösch, Silvie Steiner

Painting and Sculpture in the late Nineteenth and Twentieth Centuries

Koloman Moser
Title page for Ver Sacrum
Ver Sacrum II, 1899, Vol. 4

Paths toward modernism:
From Secessionism to Expressionism
The struggle for freedom in art

When, in 1897, nineteen Viennese artists combined to form the *Vereinigung bildender Künstler Österreiches — Wiener Secession* (Artists' Union of Austria — Vienna Secession), an era in the fine arts began in the capital of the Austro-Hungarian Empire which was distinguished by exceptionally creative and intellectual power. Two decades before the fall of the Empire, artists, sculptors, architects, composers, writers, and intellectuals joined forces, presenting themselves as a *Gesamtkunstwerk* — a total art work of Vienna.

The Old World values and orders were discarded, and new maxims were devised. The replacement of "Ringstrasse architecture" by the buildings of Otto Wagner, Joseph Maria Olbrich, and Adolf Loos, the triumph of the composers Gustav Mahler, Arnold Schönberg, and Alban Berg, were all part of this revolutionary movement, as was the expressive literature of Karl Kraus, Oskar Kokoschka, and Robert Musil. The part played by the psychoanalysis of Sigmund Freud as one of the innovations of the turn of the century should not be underestimated. His insight into the deepest recesses of the human psyche brought to the surface what had hitherto been concealed. The visible world, with its repressive superficiality, no longer seemed bearable, and the threat of suffocation by the old made the cry for renewal all the louder. At a time which has been described with some justification as "the End of the World Experiment," the Secessionists declared art to be a substitute religion which would improve humanity and the world, and whose esthetics would drive away all that was bad and ugly.

Yet it was not long before the founders of the Wiener Werkstätte saw the next evil in this very concept, for only the few could participate in this beautiful illusion. They once again tried to divest art of its sacred quality, and to break through the barriers between art and the commonplace. Yet even the craftsmen failed in their belief that life in its entirety could be subjected to a new esthetic; they too created their products only for a small, well-to-do circle of clients. The Expressionists, finally, radically exposed human imperfection, holding a mirror up to the insincerity of the Secessionist esthetic.

The most vehement demands of the generation of artists born around 1860 were for liberation and modernization. With the foundation of the Vienna Secession, a small group of painters took a decisive step toward the revitalization of an ossified art world. Admittedly, the Secession had had to struggle against great resistance before it came into full flower. Ten years before the turn of the century, the reactionary upper middle classes, together with the tradition-bound

imperial house, set the tone in all things cultural. With the death of its leading artists, Hans Makart, Hans Canon, and Jakob Emil Schindler, art in Vienna had lost all innovative power. The generation that succeeded Makart and his contemporaries was not in a position to live up to the great heritage of its predecessors, remaining faithful instead to the generally favored "atmospheric Impressionism." With the help of the "Austrian Artists' Cooperative" founded in 1861, artistic activity became established as a profitable occupation. Almost every painter and sculptor was a member of the cooperative, whose committee determined the success or failure of each individual. Artistic tendencies which developed outside Austria were deliberately withheld from the public; artists, such as Theodor von Hörmann, who had spent some years in France, who wanted to enrich the art scene through their experiences abroad, were rejected. The works of all those whom the committee deemed to be "too modern" were deliberately hung in disadvantageous positions in the cooperative's exhibitions.

Since the early 1880s, modern-minded artists had been meeting in two cafés, frequented by, among others, Gustav Klimt, Josef Hoffmann, and Koloman Moser. At these convivial gatherings, the idea took root of founding a Secession in Vienna, taking as its model the movement which had been founded in Munich as early as 1892. The first official revolt occurred in 1895, when the so-called "Young Ones" — in the face of resistance from the management of the cooperative — organized an exhibition of the works of Theodor von Hörmann, who had died that year. A crucial factor for those who eventually resigned from the cooperative was the ban it imposed on the participation of certain young artists in an exhibition in Dresden in the spring of 1897. As a result of this authoritarian attitude, some members dissociated themselves from the cooperative, founding the "Artists Union of Austria – Vienna Secession." At its inaugural meeting on April 3, 1897, Gustav Klimt was elected its first President.

Since the *Künstlerhaus* (Artists' House) used by the cooperative, which today is still their base and exhibition hall, was the only independent arts center in Vienna, the Secessionists' decision to split away from the artists' cooperative was a very risky one. As a first step toward independence, the artists rented the rooms of the Horticultural Association for their inaugural exhibition. While traditional art continued to dominate the Vienna art scene unhindered, the Secessionists demonstrated great self-confidence from the very start. They promoted clearly defined concepts for the liberation and renewal of art, and their progressive ideas were successful in gaining the support of the liberal and intellectual elite of the financially strong bourgeoisie, whose help, both moral and material, was essential to the fulfillment of the

Joseph Maria Olbrich
Poster for the Second Exhibition
of the Secession, 1898
lithograph, 34 x 20 in
(86 x 51 cm)
Private collection

Secessionists' aims. The most prominent of their patrons, the forward-thinking industrialist and art collector Kurt Wittgenstein, supported the group of young artists in several ways, including a munificent donation which enabled the Secession building, designed by Josef Maria Olbrich, to be built. This new exhibition hall, which was used by the Union of Secessionists from fall, 1898, still serves as a meeting-place and exhibition center. The hall consolidated the activity of the group.

Among the most committed champions of Secessionist ideas were the art critics Ludwig Hevesi and Hermann Bahr. Hevesi, who eagerly awaited new developments, had become the chronicler of the Secessionists even months before the group's formation. His reviews and essays, collected in 1906 in a book entitled *Acht Jahre Secession* (Eight Years of the Secession), provide evidence of the most important years of Austrian Secessionism. Bahr created the guiding motto for the Union, which was affixed to the facade of the Secession building in golden lettering, which was visible from far away: *Der Zeit ihre Kunst, der Kunst ihre Freiheit* (Art for the times, freedom for art).

At first, the Union was less concerned about stylistic innovation in the spirit of *Art Nouveau* (Jugendstil) than about a universal liberation of art and the creators of art from outside pressures. Thus its members initially concentrated on programmatic ideas, which were dominated by social reform and demagogic demands on the model of the British Arts and Crafts movement.

The Secessionists started from the assumption that the estheticization of life would naturally lead to an automatic improvement in the ethics of the human race. They saw art as a religion, themselves as its priests, and the Secession building as a Temple of Art.

The "Sacred Spring" in Vienna

The Secession journal *Ver Sacrum* (Sacred Spring), which was published between 1898 and 1903, represented the group's attempt to convey its ideas to a wider public. At the same time, however, *Ver Sacrum* represents a building block in the *Gesamtkunstwerk*, the Total Work of Art, toward which the artists strove as their highest aim. In addition to explaining the movement's agenda, the journal offered a forum for essays from the modern intellectual world of Vienna. Poems by Rainer Maria Rilke and Hugo von Hofmannsthal, as well as contributions by Adolf Loos, are evidence of the close contact fostered by the Secessionists with representatives of the related arts. Issues of *Ver Sacrum* included the work of various artists who liked to experiment with graphic design. The stylistic development from arabesque forms to bold lines and squares, whose use as an esthetic form was one of the most creative devices used by the Secessionists, can be traced particularly clearly in the formal changes that took place in their art journal. However, after a relatively short time it had to be admitted that the journal was only reaching a small, elite group. After fruitless discussions about an increase in circulation, the journal was closed down in 1903.

The Secessionists saw the preconditions for the fulfillment of their artistic and idealistic aims not only in a democratic organization of exhibitions based on purely artistic criteria, but rather, at the same time, they sought commitment to new norms and standards. This involved confrontation with current international trends in art. Since the Vienna Secession, compared with its counterparts in other European countries, had been founded comparatively late in the day, its members were in a position to incorporate into their work the experiences of the modern German, French, and British movements. In the same way, they confronted Art Nouveau, Impressionism, Naturalism and Symbolism. However, most of the Secessionists failed throughout the course of their lives to free themselves from these models.

The development of the characteristic Austrian Secession style is to be credited to the creative activity of a few individuals. Thus, for example, Klimt combined the decorative language of forms of Art Nouveau with the expressive force of Symbolism in such a manner that the Austrian yearning for the estheticization of life was taken into account as much as the desire for profound artistic statements. The Vienna of the turn of the century, intellectual and with a tendency toward the morbid, was preoccupied, more than all other centers of art, with the most elemental experiences of mankind — birth, death, and desire. Among the international artists, therefore, whose works

Koloman Moser
Poster for the 13th Exhibition of
the Secession, 1902
lithograph, 70 x 24 in
(177 x 60 cm)
Private collection

Members of the Vienna Secession
at the Beethoven exhibition
Left to right: Anton Stark, Gustav
Klimt, Kolo Moser (in front of
Klimt, wearing hat), Adolf Böhm,
Maximilian Lenz (recumbent),
Ernst Stöhr (with hat), Wilhelm
List, Emil Orlik (seated),
Maximilian Kurzweil (with cap),
Leopold Stolba, Carl Moll
(semi-recumbent), Rudolf Bacher

Anton Hanak
The Last Man (Ecce Homo)
1919-1924
Bronze
The sculpture stands in front of
the Historisches Museum der
Stadt Wien.

Anton Strasser
Marcus Aurelius, 1895-1900
Bronze
Property of the Municipality of
Vienna; since 1901, placed next to
the Secession building

were repeatedly shown in the Secessionists' exhibitions, were the Symbolists Fernand Khnopff, Jan Toorop, Giovanni Segantini, Arnold Böcklin, and Ferdinand Hodler. A number of works by these artists were acquired by the Austrian State Gallery (today the Österreichische Galerie Belvedere). At the instigation of the Secessionists, the gallery had been founded with the task of establishing a collection of modern art. Today, it owns works by Monet, Klinger, Böcklin, Rodin, Segantini, as well as by all the Austrian Secessionists and Expressionists. Further major works of the time are to be found in the Historisches Museum der Stadt Wien and the Ludwig Foundation in the Museum of Modern Art

Sculpture as a by-product

Although in Max Klinger, Auguste Rodin, and Georg Minne the most renowned European sculptors were being presented to the public, it was not until after World War I that sculpture was able to establish itself as an autonomous art form. The majority of sculptural work during the Secession period was used mainly for decoration on architecture. Exceptions such as the bronze sculpture *Mark Antony* by Arthur Strasser, which has been displayed since 1901 in the Secession garden, convince more through their symbolic content than their sculptural quality.

In the years after 1910, Anton Hanak achieved great recognition; in his early days he created works of great monumentality, such as the sculptures for the building owned by the *Vorwärts* publishing firm. It is to Hanak's credit that from 1918, after many years of restraint, sculpture once again took up a self-confident

position in Austria. The decisive factor in his success was that he succeeded in translating the Expressionist language of form into the sculptural medium. Many works in the parks of Vienna are by his hand, such as the impressive *Ecce Homo* sculpture dating from 1916, which stands in front of the Historisches Museum der Stadt Wien.

Style, surface, ornament

The discovery of Oriental art, with its emphasis on surface and ornament, was of vital importance for the development of the Austrian Secession style. The sixth exhibition, held in 1900, was dedicated to Japanese art and with it, stylized forms of expression reached a definitive breakthrough. From this point onward, artists preferred the two-dimensionality of surface and line as a moving force of expression. This implied the negation of spatial forms, and decoration became a creative challenge. The estheticism which was thus triggered, and which increasingly gained momentum over the years, displaced the consciousness of social responsibility which the Secession had urged at its formation.

The esthetic object

In the realm of the crafts, however, which attracted increasing interest from 1900 onward, the Secessionists continued to be concerned with fulfilling the aims of mass culture. Here, their mentor was Charles Rennie Mackintosh, the founder of the Glasgow School of Art. The presentation of international craftwork at the Eighth Secessionist exhibition, and the appointment of Josef Hoffmann and Koloman Moser to the School of Arts and Crafts, allowed Austrian crafts to achieve a breakthrough. Support came from the *Museum für Kunst und Industrie* (Museum for Art and Industry) founded in 1864 (today the *Museum für angwandte Kunst*) (Museum of Applied Art). Its aim was to encourage industrial design and to educate the taste of purchasers. The leading manufacturers of furniture and glass were also influential; the progressive firms of Thonet, Kohn, and Lobmeyer allowed themselves to be convinced by the simplicity and elegance of craftsmen's designs. In 1903, the *Wiener Werkstätte* (Vienna Workshops) were founded by Hoffmann, Moser, and the industrialist Fritz Waerndorfer.

The Workshops soon began to receive major decorative commissions. One of the first significant projects was the building of the church of St. Leopold in 1903. The building was designed by Otto Wagner, in the grounds of the psychiatric clinic Am Steinhof. The monumental windows designed by Moser are particularly noteworthy. The decoration of the Westend sanatorium at Purkersdorf (1904) and of the

Painting and Sculpture, 1890–1918

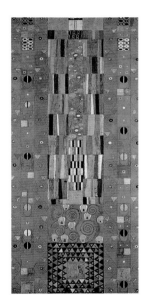

Gustav Klimt
Design for the Stoclet frieze,
ca. 1905/09
Tree of Life, right-hand section
with plant, 73 x 46 in
(194 x 118 cm).
Tempera, watercolor, gold paint,
silvered bronze, pastel, pencil,
opaque white on paper
Museum für angewandte Kunst

Palais Stoclet in Brussels (1905-11), for which Hoffmann was responsible together with Moser, Klimt, and Jungnickel, are among the outstanding achievements of the *Wiener Werkstätte*, which continued to exist until 1939. Klimt's famous frieze in the dining room of the Palais Stoclet is harmoniously incorporated into the total concept of the house and the rooms. Apart from a number of other Werkstätte items, the Museum of Applied Art contains nine designs for this frieze.

At the very beginning of their activity, the *Werkstätte* craft designs, in parallel with the Secessionist language of forms, was influenced by the floral, flowing lines of Art Nouveau, but soon ornamental yet functional forms came to be preferred. The agenda of attempting to appeal to a wider public, however, proved to be as illusory for the *Werkstätte* as it had been for the creations of the Secession. Outwardly the *Werkstätte* preached the subjection of form to function, but the use of costly materials was substituted for a reduction of formal elements. Only an elite section of the public could afford these items. It was this consideration which induced Moser to resign from the *Werkstätte* as early as 1906. Hoffmann, Moser, Otto Prutscher, and later Dagobert Peche, developed a highly individual language of forms, which was close to Cubism, and was known as the *Neue Sachlichkeit* (New Objectivity), and *Art Deco*. The designs and those of the Secession shared a preference for the square and rectangle as decorative elements.

The extremely successful metal workshop of Hagenauer, founded in 1898, rivaled the *Wiener Werkstätte*, and soon produced items in the Viennese Art Nouveau (Jugendstil) style . During the 1920s, the Hagenauer workshop undertook commissions for all the important architects, and especially for Clemens Holzmeister.

Space is art
he craft exhibition, where among other things Mackintosh's "Scottish Room" was displayed, was followed by a gradual "minimalization" of exhibition design. Its aim was a harmonious combination of architecture and the graphic arts In 1902 this development reached its high point in the "Beethoven exhibition," a "Gesamtkunstwerk" combining architecture, graphic arts and music. The project was based on Max Klinger's statue of Beethoven. The Beethoven Frieze created by Klimt for the exhibition, which is today displayed in the Secession building, is one of the best-known works of the Art Nouveau era.

After the exhibition had closed, increasingly violent conflicts blew up among the Secessionists. The Wiener Werkstätte's project to allow art to penetrate the realm of everyday objects induced discomfort among many members of the Secession, since they saw in it a degradation of art. In addition, stylistic splinter groups within the group resulted in the loss of common interests. When, in 1905, some members formed an association with commercial galleries, the time for a split had arrived for the

Gustav Klimt
Beethoven Frieze, 1902
Central narrow wall
Detail: Unchastity, Sensuality,
and Intemperance
Casein paint on plaster ground
Height: 87 in (220 cm)
Vienna Secession, permanent loan
by the Österreichische Galerie,
Belvedere

Secession. With the departure of the so-called "Klimt group" the Secession lost its most valuable creative potential. The remaining members admittedly continued in business in the traditional style up to 1914, but further successes were denied them.

A year after the split, Klimt and his followers founded the Austrian Artists' Union, which however was never able to take up a prominent position in Austrian art history. Tired of the everyday business of the organization, its members at first concentrated on their individual enterprises. Its first common project was the *Kunstschau* (Art Show), realized in 1908 and arranged in two stages: the first part, shown in 1908, presented exclusively Austrian art, while international trends were showcased in 1909.

Dissolution into downfall

As a result of the Secession's activities, the Viennese art-loving public had now become more sensitized to developments in the art world. The new works exhibited at the *Kunstschau* therefore attracted great interest from the beginning. The artists were encouraged even further by the fact that Klimt presented himself as the friend of a younger generation of unknowns.

The Kunstschau was held in a temporary structure designed by Hoffmann. It introduced to Austria the artistic era of Expressionism. In 1908, paintings by Oskar Kokoschka were shown for the first time on a grand scale, and in the following year, Egon Schiele presented his work to the public. Through the simultaneous presentation of works by former Secessionists and young Expressionists, the transition from the over-estheticized art of surfaces and lines to the radical language of images of Expressionism was easily accomplished. The Expressionists responded to the Secessionist cult of beauty with a frighteningly open individualism, with which Adolf Loos and Karl Kraus, as well as the young artists Albert Paris Gütersloh and Anton Kolig, identified themselves. At this time of extreme political and social tension, the younger artists rejected the role of harbinger of "healing" beautification.

In comparison with German Expressionism and the French *Fauves*, the Austrian version created an independent language of expression. Apart from the insistence on the manifestations of reality, a significant factor is represented by the relationship between innovation and tradition. The roots of Expressionism lie in the pessimistic variations on the Secession style, predominantly interpreted by Klimt, in which morbid, repellent content was conveyed. The figures in the Beethoven Frieze, far removed from beauty, marked by disease, death, and madness, already demonstrate early

Expressionist features. Here, as in the early work of Schiele, Minne's *Jünglingsfiguren* (Figures of Youths) exerted their influence.

It should not be forgotten, however, that Klimt's portrayals of horror served as a contrast to a glorified, purified life. The threats of day-to-day life, which the Secessionists sought to suppress, were accepted by the Expressionists as an unalterable reality. The prevailing sense of doom in relation to the monarchy, the threat of impending war, as well as social evils, were graphically portrayed. The Expressionists were not only protesting against the "beautiful" paintings of Art Nouveau and against social injustice; they did not shrink either from gazing into the darkest corners of the human psyche. The shortcomings of mankind were mercilessly exposed by means of painting. Freud had prepared the way, and the young, sensitive, and visionary artists saw it as their mission to delve into the most distressing emotions with all the wounds that these might cause to appear.

Oskar Kokoschka, who encountered the greatest opposition and who was designated the "chief savage" by a critic, overthrew all hitherto valid concepts of painting with his expressive force. Even before the *Kunstschau*, he had caused a stir in 1917 with the works of art he had created at the *Wiener Werkstätte*. For the illustrations to the story he wrote entitled *Die Träumenden Knaben* (The Dreaming Boys), he had used strongly expressive lines whose sharp, angular appearance created tension-laden rhythms. In these works, the line, whose origin is undoubtedly to be found in the tradition of Art Nouveau, already serves to express the inner content rather than a superficial beauty. In 1909, Kokoschka continued his career with psychological portraits, including

Oskar Kokoschka [1886-1980]

Oskar Kokoschka
Pietà - Poster for the Mörder
Hoffnung der Frauen
Color lithograph
Museum der Moderne Salzburg

Bertold Löffler
Poster for the Kunstschau,
Vienna 1908
Lithograph, 27 x 38 in
(68 x 96 cm)
Private collection

Painting and Sculpture, 1890–1918

those of Loos and Kraus. In a number of his works, he reflected the morbid condition of society, as for example in the still-life *Hammel und Hyazinthe* (Ram and Hyacinth), which encountered strong opposition from the public. Today, this work is one of the most valuable possessions of the Österreichische Galerie in the Upper Belvedere. While in his compositions and in the themes of his pictures Kokoschka made continual references to Baroque and classical traditions, his unusual choice of colors and dynamic brushstroke became a model for many of the artistic movements of the twentieth century. In this context, the "New Wild Painting" of the 1980s immediately springs to mind. Max Oppenheimer, who called himself "MOPP" from 1912 onward, was an artist who was stylistically very close to Kokoschka. Oppenheimer first exhibited at the Secession in 1906, but thereafter spent little time in Vienna, as he traveled a great deal. Oppenheimer became well-known mainly through his portraits of personalities in the worlds of art and literature.

In the creative work of Schiele, which at the outset was still very strongly influenced by the ornamental style of Klimt, Expressionism did not come to the surface until 1910. Soon Klimt's imagery began to appear too "purified" for him and thus incompatible with the content of his paintings. What followed was dominated by his preoccupation with his own state of mind, but also that of others. The themes of sexuality and death, both of which simultaneously aroused fascination and horror in him, run through his works like a red thread. His orientation toward the expressive color surfaces of Gauguin, the genre painting of Henri de Toulouse-Lautrec, and the dramatic figures of Munch, Minne, and Rodin, led Schiele with amazing rapidity to an

unmistakable style of his own. He developed a restless, broken line, emphasized by an intensely bright color scheme. Through his friendship with the art critic Arthur Roessler, Schiele soon became widely known. In 1909 the critic encouraged Schiele to found the *Neukunstgruppe* (New Art Group), introduced him to a number of galleries and collectors, and organized exhibitions of his work.

The young Richard Gerstl was the least committed, yet the most radical, of the Expressionists. Unlike Kokoschka and Schiele, Gerstl never reached Expressionism by taking the decorative Secession route. From the outset, his painting was free of standards and rules. With enormous force, he discovered the tactile qualities of painting and was the first to use them to express his own private emotions. His later work even borders on abstraction, from which the other representatives of Austrian Expressionism always kept their distance. Like Kokoschka, Gerstl applied the paint thickly, modeling it, as it were, on the canvas. He gave painting lessons to Arnold Schönberg. In 1909, after an unhappy love affair with Mathilde Schönberg, the composer's wife, Gerstl committed suicide.

Within a very short time, Expressionism had won a place on the Viennese art scene; but its practitioners found greater recognition beyond Austria's borders. Thus, Kokoschka left Vienna as early as 1917 in the hope of a professorship in Dresden, which he was able to take up in 1919.

After Gerstl's untimely death, the interest of the Viennese art world was primarily concentrated on Schiele, who experienced the last high point of his career in 1918 with an exhibition of his works at the Vienna Secession. He died shortly thereafter in the great epidemic of Spanish influenza which swept through Europe and killed more people than World War I. Schiele was not the only artist to leave Vienna prematurely and for ever in 1918, for Klimt, Wagner, and Moser also died in this fateful year. With their death, the heyday of artistic innovation in Vienna temporarily came to an end.

Austrian artists of the early twentieth century had not yet dared to take the great step into abstract art, which had already become established throughout the rest of Europe. They never demonstrated enough desire to associate themselves with the radical solutions of the international avant-garde. This is particularly true of the abstract formulations of Cubism and Futurism, which, leaving aside the hesitant gestures toward these trends made by the *Wiener Werkstätte*, were for a long time practically ignored in Austria. An unequivocal tendency toward abstraction did not gain ground in Austria until after 1945.

Egon Schiele
Poster for the 49th Exhibition of the Secession, 1918
Lithograph, 27 x 21 in (68 x 53 cm)
Historisches Museum der Stadt Wien.

Egon Schiele (1890-1918)
Photograph, Historisches Museum der Stadt Wien.

Gustav Klimt in the garden at his studio
Photograph, Print Collection, Albertina

Klimt's early work

In Vienna, the drift into modernism which was characteristic of international art at the turn of the century took place only hesitantly, gradually, and comparatively late in the day. Gustav Klimt, who was one of the initiators and co-founders of the Vienna Secession, at first developed his artistic language of forms in the tradition of historicism, before becoming the symbolic leader of a new artistic awakening.

Gustav Klimt was born in 1862; his extraordinary gift attracted attention while he was still in high school, and he was awarded a scholarship to study at the Kunstgewerbeschule (School of Arts and Crafts). One of his fellow-students was Franz Matsch, and another, a year later, his own brother, Ernst Klimt. Studying in the Department of Painting and Decorative Art, which Matsch and the Klimt brothers entered three years later, was a definitive experience for them. Their professor, Ferdinand Laufberger, was one of the most successful decorative painters of the newly-built Ringstrasse. He recognized the talent of his three students and soon allowed them to help with his public commissions; in 1879, they contributed to the so-called Makart procession, on the occasion of the silver wedding of the Emperor and Empress.

Laufberger's recommendation of the young painters to the theater architects Fellner and Helmer proved crucial. Between 1872 and 1915 this extremely successful architectural practice built well over forty new theaters in the provinces of the Austro-Hungarian Empire. The architects subsequently became the most important clients of Franz Matsch and the Klimt brothers.

A year after graduation from the Art School, in 1881, the young painters founded a studio community, known as the *Malercompagnie* (Company of Painters) which became very successful. This was due to the fact that their highly efficient studio offered the work of three painters but could nevertheless guarantee unity of style. Their concept of their role as purely decorative painters and their shared training allowed them to dispense, at first, with the development of an individual language of forms. Over a ten-year period, at first in the studio at 8, Sandwirthgasse, in the sixth district of Vienna, and from 1892 in premises in the Josefstädterstrasse, which later became Klimt's studio, the *Malercompagnie* played a significant part in the historical decorative painting of the time. There was an enormous amount of building activity, and a corresponding desire on the clients' part for artistic embellishment.

After lucrative commissions for theaters in Karlsbad (Karlovy Vary), Brünn (Brno), Fiume (Rijeka), and Bucharest, the studio community endeavored to obtain commissions in Vienna. The two great museums, the Burgtheater, and the University were all nearing completion. In 1886, at only 24 years of age, Klimt, together with his brother and

LEFT, ABOVE:
Gustav Klimt
Renaissance, 1890-91
Spandrel and inter-column painting
Oil on plaster ground, each spandrel painting 90 x 90 in (230 x 230 cm), each inter-column painting 90 x 31 in (230 x 80 cm)
Art-Historical Museum of Vienna

LEFT, BELOW:
Gustav Klimt
Auditorium of the old Burgtheater, 1888
Gouache on paper, 32 x 36 in (82 x 92 cm)
Historisches Museum der Stadt Wien

Gustav Klimt
Profile and back view of a gentleman with opera glasses, sketch of a right hand, 1888/89
Black chalk with white highlights 17 x 11 in (43 x 28 cm)
Print Collection, Albertina

Franz Matsch, received a commission from the Court Building Committee to produce ten ceiling paintings for the two main stairwells of the new Vienna Burgtheater. The theme, which was chosen by the current director, Adolf von Willbrand, was the development of the theater. In order to portray the style and costumes in the contemporary historical context, the Klimt brothers frequently used their friends, relations, or siblings as models. For example, Klimt immortalized his brother as

Gustav Klimt
The Hofburg Actor Josef
Lewinsky as Carlos, 1895
Oil on canvas, 25 x 17 in
(64 x 44 cm)
Österreichische Galerie, Belvedere

Romeo in the scene entitled *Shakespeare's Theater*. This painting also includes the only depiction of Klimt among his fellow painters. In 1887, Klimt was commissioned to document the interior of the old Burgtheater before it was demolished, and at the same time to portray 250 prominent theatergoers in this painting. This brought success and substantial prize money to the *Malercompagnie*. Finally, in 1890, there followed the decoration of the spandrels and inter-columnar areas of the Kunst-historisches Museum (the Museum of Art History). In the Museum, the work of the young *Malercompagnie* was placed in direct proximity to paintings by Makart and the ceiling painting by Mihály Munkácsy. The theme was the history of fine art. In addition to "Egyptian" and "Italian" art, Klimt also covered the classical period; individual figures, such as his Athena, hinted at his later artistic development. In 1891, the year in which this project was completed, the Klimt brothers and Franz Matsch joined the *Künstlerhaus* cooperative.

Two early panel paintings
The change of style in Klimt's work is generally dated to about 1900, but the severe, rectangular forms in the stairwell ceilings of the Museum already contains indications of a Symbolist language. Klimt's leanings toward Art Nouveau are particularly noticeable in the portrait of the Hofburg Actor Josef Lewinsky in the Role of Carlos in Goethe's *Clavigo*, as well as in the oil study *Love*, both created in 1895. In both paintings, a dark background is framed by a pale band and the effect of the diffused space is thus strengthened. In the lower half of *Love*, the lovers embrace, while above them float heads which represent three ages—childhood, youth, and old age. This motif, like that of death, was to preoccupy the artist. Here Klimt was inspired by Munich *Art Nouveau* (Jugendstil), and for the figure of the woman he used a sketch by Fernand Khnopff.

Gustav Klimt
Love, 1895
Oil on canvas, 24 x 17 in
(60 x 44 cm)
Historical Museum of the City of Vienna

Gustav Klimt
Schubert at the Piano, 1899
Sopraporta painting in the music
room, Palais Nikolaus Dumba,
Parkring
Oil on canvas, 59 x 79 in
(150 x 200 cm)
Destroyed by fire at Schloss
Immenberg in 1945

Gustav Klimt
Music I, 1895
Oil on canvas, 14 x 17 in (37 x 44.5 cm)
Munich, Bavarian State Art Collections,
Neu Pinakothek

Decorative art at the Palais Dumba

After the death of Ernst Klimt died in 1892, the
studio community struggled on for only another
two years. In 1893, it was commissioned by the
industrialist Nikolaus Dumba to design the music
room and dining room at his mansion on the Vienna Parkring. Klimt was responsible for the complete decoration of the music room, and used the
most costly materials for it. Nothing is left of this
valuable interior, because all the furnishings and
fittings were disposed of in 1937; the two sopraporta paintings were destroyed by fire in 1945.

When Klimt received this commission he was
at the height of his success as a decorative
painter. The first sketches for the design, however, were not produced until 1897, the year in
which the Secession was founded. The work
itself was completed in 1899 and thus already
exhibits a new, modern language of forms. In the
Schubert painting, for example, Klimt dispenses
with historical authenticity of detail, which had
been obligatory in the days of historicism. The
women wear contemporary dress, and the style
of the painting is influenced by Neo-Impression-
ism. Immediately after completion, the painting
Schubert at the Piano was exhibited at the Fourth
Secession exhibition, and honored by Hermann
Bahr as "the most beautiful picture ever painted

Gustav Klimt
Detail from Music II, 1898
Sopraporta painting in the music
room, Palais Nikolaus Dumba,
Parkring
Oil on canvas, 59 x 79 in
(150 x 200 cm)
Destroyed by fire at Schloss
Immenberg in 1945

by an Austrian." Not every critic was as enthusiastic. Karl Kraus, for instance, wrote in 1899 in the journal *Der Fackel*: "He [Dumba] had commissioned the paintings from Klimt when the latter was still working in the worthy manner of the Laufberger school. In the meantime, however, the painter had been bitten by the Khnopff bug, and, not to put too fine a point on it, has become a Pointillist. And Herr Dumba has become a Modernist." The painting Music II (see page 366, below) shows a tendency toward Symbolism. The dissolution of the space into an ornamental, two-dimensional background gives clues to Klimt's further development.

The Secession

Around 1900, a style developed in the urban centers of Europe that incorporated Impressionist, Symbolist, and decorative design elements. Art Nouveau (called *Jugendstil* in German-speaking countries) undoubtedly contained elements unique to each country, but in general it can be seen as an epoch-making phenomenon, crossing national boundaries. The foundation of artists' communities, known as "Secessions", in Munich, Berlin, and Vienna, was a simultaneous, parallel development.

Through the publication of journals such as *Ver Sacrum* in Vienna, and of exhibition catalogs, a new discourse was introduced. Furthermore, there was an attempt to introduce a general appreciation of modern art among the general public. Only a year after the foundation of the *Compagnie*, the exhibition building of the Vienna Secession, designed by Joseph Maria Olbrich, opened its doors. As a typical example of Art Nouveau, it became almost a symbol of a new awakening. Here, for the first time, was an opportunity to exhibit international art, too, in Vienna.

Gustav Klimt was generally regarded as the greatest talent in the ranks of the Vienna avant-garde of his day. He became the undisputed central figure of the early Secession and, in 1897, its first president. Together with Josef Hoffmann and Carl Moll as vice-president and secretary, he was responsible for the organization of the exhibitions over the years that followed, and thus for their sensational success.

The first *Kunstschau* was held in March 1898, in the rooms of the Horticultural Association on the Ring. Klimt designed the catalogue, as well as the poster that has become so well known through the scandal and censure it attracted. Using the classical theme of the *Battle of Theseus against the Minotaur*, it depicts the battle of the new art with the old. Only the second version of the poster could be printed. The exhibition, entitled "European Art of the Time", was a resounding success, and during its run Klimt was reelected as president. In addition, under his leadership, a flourishing art dealership developed, whose sales, both domestic and foreign, contributed a substantial amount to the exhibition budget. The Secession members shared the urge to free themselves from historicism and the eclecticism of their predecessors. Thus the painting *Nuda Veritas* (1899) is also to be seen as an expression of the new self-confidence of this young union of artists. Like the *Minotaur* poster, it is a strong statement about the politics of art. In *Nuda Veritas*, Klimt depicted a woman not only as the moving force of an allegorical statement, but also emphasized her femininity and eroticism.

In its search for new, individual paths, the younger generation now also had the opportunity to show what it could do. Its ambitious and extensive agenda was to bring world art to Vienna and familiarize the Viennese public and the artists themselves with the contemporary international art scene. This was not without influence on the stylistic development of art in Vienna.

Gustav Klimt
Nuda Veritas, 1899
Oil on canvas, 99 x 22 in
(252 x 56 cm)
Theater Collection, Österreichischen Nationalbibliotek.

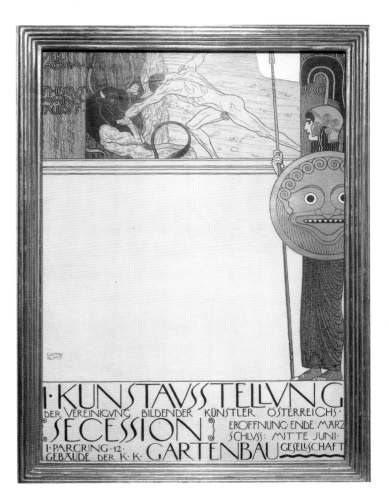

Gustav Klimt
Poster for the 1st Exhibition of the Secession (before censorship), 1898
Lithograph, 24 x 17 in
(62 x 43 cm)
Private collection

Pallas Athene and Judith

Klimt's early allegories not only contributed decisively to the development of his individual language of forms, but also conveyed the idea of a female type other than that found in his portraits of women. By portraying allegorical subjects no longer in terms of historical figures, but as naturalistic depictions of the female, he was distancing himself from the ideals of Historicism in both content and form.

This became increasingly clear in his monumental paintings and finally lead to paintings such as *Pallas Athene* (1898) and *Nuda Veritas*, a year later, as a seductive, red-haired temptress. The square canvas of *Pallas Athene*, in the metal frame designed by Georg Klimt, is occupied by the head and upper part of the body of Athene. She wears golden armor and holds in her hand the small figure of *Nuda Veritas*. Klimt places the figure full frontal severity at the very forefront of the picture; her right arm is cut off by the frame. As with the *Portrait of Sonia Knips*, created in the same year, the artist is working with the tension between the figure and the blank space. But Pallas Athene seems here to be part of an ornamental scheme. Naturalism is suppressed and there are strong references to the later, so-called "Golden Period."

This painting, whose theme is the victory of true art over established society, became the symbol of the Secession and found further use as the title page of *Ver Sacrum*, and thus as a poster. *Pallas Athene* was first shown to the public at the Second Exhibition of the Vienna Secession and aroused violent reactions. Viennese society perceived the grotesque, Medusa-like head, in particular, as a threat. Ludwig Hevesi, however, defended the picture in his review of the exhibition: "The large picture of the seated, rose-colored lady is actually much appreciated. But near her hangs the *bête noire* of the public at large, the notorious Pallas Athene. How beautiful she is! But even this lady in armor is not accorded approval. The public is familiar with Pallases who are easily recognized as actually being painted marble statues. But Klimt has designed his Pallas as the evident woman Secessionist of today."

The painting entitled *Judith I* was created in 1901. Klimt uses the same full frontal pose of Pallas Athene, but intensifies the contrast between the naturalistic portrayal and the ornamentation. Deviating from the historical view, Judith is shown not as a fighter, not at the moment of the act of murder, but as a sensual, lascivious woman. The attribute of Judith, the head of Holofernes, has been relegated to the lower right edge of the painting and drastically cut off by the frame. The subject of the *femme fatale* was a popular one at the turn of the century, and influenced the possibilities for artistic portrayal of eroticism and sensuality.

LEFT:
Detail from Judith I

Gustav Klimt
Judith I, 1901
Oil on canvas, 33 x 16 in
(84 x 42 cm)
Österreichische Galerie, Belvedere

Gustav Klimt
Pallas Athene, 1898
Oil on canvas, 30 x 30 in
(75 x 75 cm)
Historisches Museum der Stadt
Wien

The Faculty Paintings

When the new university was opened in 1883 on what is now the Karl Lueger Ring, the decoration of the Aula (great hall) had not yet been carried out, having been postponed on grounds of cost. Splendid ceiling paintings were envisaged, representing the four faculties of theology, philosophy, medicine, and jurisprudence. In 1894, the commission was finally offered to Franz Matsch and Gustav Klimt.

Klimt's work on *The Faculty Paintings* was produced during the time of his artistic turmoil. The designs which were exhibited set off a conflict

awarded the Grand Prix at the Paris World Exhibition during the same year.

In Vienna, however, the conflict escalated during the following year as a result of the exhibition of *Medicine* at the Vienna Secession. The depiction ran counter to the self-image of the faculty. Nothing in the painting refers to medicine as the art of healing; the life cycle is symbolized mainly by the use of female figures. The hieratic figure of Hygeia appears at the edge of a group of human figures, in the center of which Death, shown as a skeleton, confronts the free-standing, or rather floating, allegory of life.

LEFT:
Gustav Klimt
Medicine (final state), 1907
Oil on canvas, 169 x 118 in
(430 x 300 cm)
Destroyed by fire at Schloss
Immendorf in 1945

which was to continue for years. Klimt's portrayal of *Philosophy* no longer has anything in common with his earlier decorative painting. Thus, he completely dispenses with the rendering of historical associations as well as with a glorification of the faculty. His enigmatical allegory even discards any concept of spatial order, but rather illustrates a leitmotiv of the *fin de siècle*—human life, bound up in the cycle of nature. Through the impressive portrayal of the old man at the edge of the human group, Klimt intensifies the theme to the highest theatricality. The painting of *Philosophy* was

When the depiction of *Jurisprudence* was also rejected and *Philosophy* was not shown at the 1904 World Exhibition in St. Louis, Klimt withdrew the paintings. Thus, as a result of historical events, all three ended up in the Österreichische Galerie. In 1944, together with other works of art, they were stored at Schloss Immendorf, in Lower Austria to protect them from air raids. On May 8, 1945, the retreating SS forces set fire to the Schloss. The paintings, together with others by Gustav Klimt, were destroyed.

Gustav Klimt
Jurisprudence (final state), 1907
Oil on canvas, 169 x 118 in
(430 x 300 cm)
Destroyed by fire at Schloss
Immendorf in 1945

The Beethoven frieze

Together with the *Faculty Paintings*, the *Beethoven Frieze* represents a turning point in Klimt's work; it introduces the "golden period" which reached its zenith with the painting *The Kiss* in 1907-08. At the same time, it demonstrates in exemplary fashion the concept of the *Gesamtkunstwerk*, which was decisive for the artists of the Secession.

The frieze was part of the famous "Beethoven exhibition" of 1902. A ceremonial site in memory of the composer was created in the form of a temporary *Gesamtkunstwerk* around Max Klinger's statue of Beethoven. At the turn of the century, Beethoven was the object of a cult of adoration that had been fostered mainly by Richard Wagner and Friedrich Nietzsche.

Klimt did not restrict himself to single anecdotal scenes, but interpreted Beethoven's Ninth Symphony, with the ode by Friedrich Schiller, in a very free, personal manner. Its central theme is the redemption of "feeble humanity" through art

and love. The allegories of the longings and desires of mankind lead at last to the final image of redemption on the long wall, the embrace of man and woman, the kiss symbolizing the whole world, flanked by the choir of angels in paradise, chanting Schiller's ode. The woman is almost completely obliterated by the back view of the nude male figure. Both are bound up in the ornamentation which encompasses the whole image, and which reduces even the choir of angels to motionless rigidity. In between, on the shorter wall, the hostile powers are to be seen. The longings and desires of mankind are seen flying overhead, represented by floating figures, which are hardly distinguishable from the pale background of the frieze. They form the transition to the final scene. The portrayal of the figures diverges markedly from a naturalistic representation. The placing of blank space and figures, or groups of figures, in contrast to each other, had already been attempted in Klimt's paintings ca. 1898. Here, Klimt intensified the effect by dispensing

with spatial effects of depth. The figures are for the most part shown in motionless rigidity and are subjugated to a predominant decorative ornamentation. The artistic effect is suppressed and henceforward the line becomes the dominant characteristic of Klimt's language of forms. This two-dimensional, draughtsman-like style, together with the incorporation of the medium itself, in which Klimt leaves some areas of plaster blank and almost untouched, shows the artist's increasing tendency toward abstraction.

Of the frescoes that were painted for the exhibition, only the frieze has been preserved. It was left in place for the eighteenth exhibition of the Secession, dedicated to Klimt's work, which was already being planned at that time. After the Klimt show it was broken up into eight parts and sold. In the 1970s, it came into the possession of the Österreichische Galerie and was extensively restored. Today it is considered one of the major works of late nineteenth century European art.

Gustav Klimt
Beethoven Frieze, 1902
Second long wall, detail:
Genii, This kiss to the whole world,
Angels of paradise
Casein paints on plaster ground
Vienna Secession, permanent loan
from the Österreichische Galerie.

Gustav Klimt
Beethoven Frieze, 1902, detail:
Longing for Happiness
Casein paint on plaster ground
Vienna Secession, permanent loan
from the Österreichischen Galerie

Gustav Klimt
Danae, 1907-08
Oil on canvas, 30 x 32 in
(77 x 83 cm)
Vienna, Dichand Collection

Danae

A further major work in the exhibition was the painting of *Danae*, which was created at the same time as *The Kiss*. The theme of the painting is the mythological story of Danae, to whom Zeus made love in the form of a shower of gold. It is typical of Klimt that he dispenses with any form of narrative setting, concentrating instead on depicting the act of love and, as with *The Kiss*, stylizes it into a timeless moment.

The red-haired female had already become the symbol of womanhood for Klimt in his portrayal of *Nuda Veritas*. Here, the curving outlines of form, the flowing streams of ornamentation, and the unusual choice of area of the image contribute to the erotic effect of the scene. Through the stylization of the image, in which the naked body itself becomes part of the formal design, Klimt overcame the moral prejudices of the public. While Schiele was later to depict the union of man and woman in its reality, here Klimt tends toward the symbolic encoding of the masculine element.

For Klimt, Moser, and Hoffmann, who were by now well-established artists, the *Kunstschau* was a great success. There was criticism, however, from the younger artists who, thanks to Klimt, had also been able to exhibit, such as Oskar Kokoschka and, in 1909, Egon Schiele. The same year also saw the end of Klimt's "golden period." Under the influence of the art of the younger generation he rejected Art Nouveau in favor of a more expressive style.

Painting, 1890–1918

Gustav Klimt
Hope I, 1903
Oil on canvas, 74 x 26 in
(189 x 67 cm)
Ottawa, National Gallery of
Canada

Klimt's "golden period" and the Kunstschau of 1908

In 1907-08, with the famous painting *The Kiss* (page 374) Klimt's "golden period" reached its climax. The color gold had already played a significant part in paintings such as *Pallas Athene* (1898) and *Judith* (1901). Klimt now intensified this tendency and used gold, together with real gold leaf, in a much more pronounced manner. He thus achieved the effect of sumptuousness and lent his paintings an aura, a golden glow. This effect, combined with the theme of the painting, enforces a shift in the interpretation of the content. Further characteristics of his style are the division of the surface by means of ornament as well as the avoidance of deep perspective, an element of style that Klimt retained right up to the time of his last work.

The renunciation of any reference to historical or social reality had been a characteristic of Klimt's art since the *Faculty Paintings*. By picking out one moment in the destiny of humanity, Klimt isolates the scene, making it into a symbol of endless happiness, frozen in timelessness. The painting was first shown to the public at the Kunst-schau of 1908 and acquired direct from the exhibition for the Modern Gallery.

In the wake of the celebrations for the sixtieth anniversary of Emperor Franz Joseph's accession to the throne, Klimt's circle, with the help of subsidies, organized the largest exhibition in Vienna in the grounds of the Vienna Concert House on the Heumarkt which were not yet built over. In the meantime, the group had resigned from the Secession in 1905. As president of the organizing committee, Klimt gave the opening speech. Josef Hoffmann built 54 pavilions, which were connected to each other by gardens and cafés.

The center of attention was Room 22, designed by Koloman Moser, which was dedicated exclusively to the work of Gustav Klimt. The Viennese literary figure Peter Altenberg described the room as the "Church of Gustav Klimt" and showered the sixteen paintings by Klimt, which included some landscapes, with effusive praise.

A significant theme in Klimt's life continued to be his interpretation of the life cycle, which is heightened into a statement in pictures such as *Death and Life* or the two paintings *Hope I* and *Hope II*. Although Klimt rearranges the subjects and uses more progressive stylistic devices, the elements themselves had been familiar for some time, as a leitmotif in his work since the *Faculty Paintings* and the *Beethoven Frieze*.

Death and Life

In the painting *Death and Life*, completed in 1916, Klimt adopted the massed group of figures as a symbol of humanity from the *Faculty Paintings* and places them opposite Death. The empty space between them additionally heightens the tension of the arrangement. The golden ornamentation now becomes a collection of colorful elements of decor, from which individual figures emerge more or less powerfully.

A man and woman are lying on a deeply sloping flower-bed, absorbed in an intimate embrace. A golden aura surrounds them and at the same time distances them from the world around them. Within this closed configuration Klimt separates the bodies by means of a differentiated ornamentation of their garments. The rectangular white, gray, and black forms are allocated to the man, while the woman is given colorful, flowery, circular motifs. Naturalistic rendition is restricted to the depiction of the faces and arms, which stand out even more strongly in their expressiveness through the contrast with the ornamentation.

Comparing this work with contemporary pictures by Egon Schiele, one realizes that while Klimt handles similar themes, the intended content becomes subsidiary to the heightening of the formal effect. In the same way, in the painting *Hope I*, completed in 1903, Klimt relativized the nakedness of the red-haired woman by means of ornamentation and the allegorical female figures in the background. Nevertheless the subject was daring, to say the least, at that time, and Klimt refrained from public exhibition of the work, which was bought by Fritz Waerndorfer; for one thing, he probably did not wish to exacerbate the scandal which had blown up over the *Faculty Paintings*.

Gustav Klimt
Death and Life, completed 1916
Oil on canvas, 70 x 77 in
(178 x 198 cm).
Leopold Museum, Vienna
Private foundation

ILLUSTRATION PAGE 374:
Gustav Klimt
The Kiss, 1907-08, oil on canvas,
70 x 70 in (180 x 180 cm)
Österreichische Galerie, Belvedere

ILLUSTRATION PAGE 375:
Gustav Klimt
Portrait of Adele Bloch-Bauer I
1907, oil and gold on canvas
54 x 54 in (138 x 138 cm)
Österreichische Galerie, Belvedere

Painting, 1890–1918

Portraits of women

Since receiving the commission to paint the interior of the old Burgtheater, which included the portraits of important personalities in Viennese society, Klimt had had a reputation as a painter of beautiful Viennese women. This soon brought him a series of commissions for portraits. The depiction of the woman, in the most multifarious interpretations of the female or the allegorical, played a central part in Klimt's total œuvre. Yet between 1883 and his death in 1918, he actually painted only twenty-eight portraits, in addition to a few uncommissioned pictures of women, which are probably portraits of his models.

The stylistic development of Klimt's work can be documented on the basis of his portraits. One of his earliest portraits, created in 1898, was the *Portrait of Sonia Knips.* For this, he chose the square format which was to become so typical of his work. This portrait is also the only one in which Klimt attempted to incorporate the figure into an imaginary garden landscape. In 1902, he portrayed his lifetime companion, Emilie Flöge. For this painting, he used a tall rectangular format. Together with her sisters, Emilie Flöge ran a very successful fashion boutique on the Mariahilferstrasse. They bought model garments from Coco Chanel in Paris, and designed the famous "reformed gowns," liberated from the corset, which are to be seen in some of Klimt's portraits. This portrait shows a self-confident woman, who establishes a relationship with the observer by the full frontal pose of her face. Her family, and Emilie herself, were displeased with the portrait, and in 1908, Klimt sold it to the Historical Museum of the City of Vienna. He wrote to Emilie at the Attersee: "Today you are being sold off, or rather exchanged for cash — yesterday I had a complaint from Mother. Mother has indignantly placed an order for a new portrait, to be done at all possible speed."

The portrait of *Margaret Stonborough-Wittgenstein* was created in 1905 and is typical of Klimt's way of looking at the women he painted. With the exception of the case of Emilie, he did not deal with the personality. Using extreme perspective, he enlarged the women from the observer's point of view and distanced them at the same time. The resolute and unconventional Margaret Stonborough-Wittgenstein could not recognize herself in her own portrait, and rejected it.

The change in Klimt's style around 1909-10 can also be observed in the *Portrait of Adele Bloch-Bauer II* (page 375). Adele Bloch-Bauer was the wife of a leading industrialist Ferdinand Bloch. In the painting, the figure disappears almost completely behind an arrangement of two-dimensional ornamentation, while the face and hands are accentuated by their naturalistic depiction and unnatural pose. Klimt uses a wider range of color and a looser brushstroke than usual.

Gustav Klimt
Portrait of Margaret Stonborough-Wittgenstein, 1905
Oil on canvas, 70 x 35 in
(180 x 90 cm)
Munich, Bavarian State Art Collections, Neu Pinakothek

Gustav Klimt
Portrait of Emilie Flöge, 1902
Oil on canvas, 71 x 33 in
(181 x 84 cm)
Historical Museum of the City of Vienna

Gustav Klimt
Portrait of Adele Bloch-Bauer II,
1912
Oil on canvas, 75 x 47 in
(190 x 120 cm)
Österreichische Galerie, Belvedere

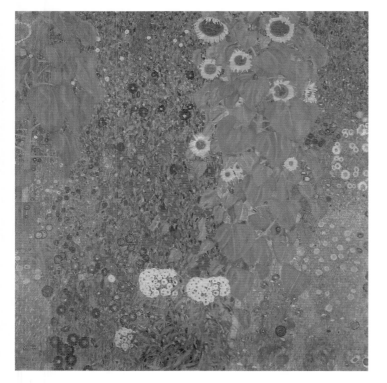

Landscapes

Klimt's landscapes form a separate group within his work. The fact that Klimt did not begin to paint landscapes until 1898 is explained by his training and activity as a decorative painter at the Vienna Ringstrasse. Another reason may be found in the fact that it was not until 1897 that Klimt spent the summer months outside Vienna. His earlier journeys had always been related to work commissions. From 1897, however, he visited the Attersee with the Flöge family almost every summer. Most of his landscapes were created there, or at least started there and completed at his Vienna studio. Klimt seems to have restricted his landscape painting to the summer months, since the paintings have exclusively summer or fall settings. Although the landscapes account for one fourth of his work, only three drawings of landscapes have been found in his sketchbooks.

This has a great deal to do with Klimt's working methods. He painted landscapes directly from nature onto his canvas, as he explains in a letter to Mizzi Zimmermann from his summer resort: "Early in the morning, usually about six, maybe a little earlier or a little later, I get up — if the weather is fine, I go to the forest — I am painting a little beech grove there (when there is sun), with a few conifers intermingled, this takes up to eight o'clock. Then there is breakfast, then bathing in the lake, taken with great caution." From 1900, he used the square format exclusively, thus making his landscapes into objects of meditation. Klimt largely dispensed with narrative content or figures. His nature is motionless, and reproduced at very close quarters.

Farmhouse with Birch Trees was created in 1900 and is characteristic of Klimt's early landscapes. The horizon is shown very high up on the canvas and the farmhouse is placed at the upper edge of the image and in the background, concealed by trees. The picture is dominated by the pale green meadow and the slender birch trunks, whose leafy crowns are cut off by the edge of the picture. The melancholy feel of the painting is similar to that conveyed by *Beech Wood I.*

Not until after the turn of the century do the pathos and distance gradually disappear. Klimt's flower paintings are transformed into painted mosaics, consisting of countless elements of color. There are many references in the literature to the parallel with tendencies to dissolution in Klimt's contemporary figure paintings of the "golden period," in which everything except the face and hands seems to dissolve into ornament. Klimt used gold in only one landscape painting. *The Golden Apple Tree* was created in 1903 and was one of the works which was lost when the Schloss Immendorf was set on fire by the retreating Germans in 1945. Klimt's later landscapes mainly depict Schloss Kammer on the Attersee.

OPPOSITE:
Gustav Klimt
Houses at Unterach on the Attersee
ca. 1916
Oil on canvas, 43 x 43 in
(110 x 110 cm)
Österreichische Galerie, Belvedere

Gustav Klimt
Farmhouse with Birch Trees, 1900
Oil on canvas, 31 x 31 in
(80 x 80 cm)
Österreichische Galerie, Belvedere

Gustav Klimt
Farmhouse Garden with Sunflowers
ca. 1905-6
Oil on canvas, 43 x 43 in
(110 x 110 cm)
Österreichische Galerie, Belvedere

Max Kurzweil
Woman in Yellow Dress
(Martha Kurzweil), 1899
Oil on canvas, 67 x 68 in
(170 x 172 cm)
Historisches Museum der Stadt
Wien

Max Kurzweil

Max Kurzweil was one of the founder members of the Vienna Secession and collaborated on its journal *Ver Sacrum*. Yet in his work, the Symbolism that characterizes many Secession artists appears only in the lithographs, while compared to Klimt, his landscapes seem more restrained, without the radical rejection of the traditional pictorial illusion.

The time Kurzweil spent in Paris and in Concarneau in Brittany was crucial in Kurzweil's development. The light and the formal language

of late Impressionism that he encountered there had a lasting impact on his work. Around 1900, he produced two large canvases, and these are his most important works. One of them is the *Lady in Yellow* (1899), which despite its large format avoids any sense of the monumental. The composition focuses on the curving flower-like structure of the pale yellow dress and is enclosed by the outspread arms of the woman, who is depicted facing the viewer. Kurzweil committed suicide in 1916 after a love affair with one of his students.

Richard Gerstl

Richard Gerstl
Laughing Self-Portrait, 1908
Oil on canvas, 15 x 12 in
(39 x 30.4 cm)
Österreichische Galerie, Belvedere

Richard Gerstl
The Schönberg Family, 1907
Oil on canvas, 35 x 43 in
(88.8 x 109.7 cm)
Museum moderner Kunst
Stiftung Ludwig

Most of Richard Gerstl's paintings were produced between 1904 and 1908. While Schiele and Kokoschka were quick to gain favorable attention, Richard Gerstl's art was hardly noticed by his contemporaries; he refused offers of exhibitions, and never showed is work during his lifetime. Those paintings that he did not destroy before his suicide in 1908 were only rediscovered in 1931, by the art dealer Otto Nierenstein. Gerstl was then celebrated as an "unknown Van Gogh," and in his deliberate rejection of the decorative style of turn-of-the-century painting he is now considered, along with Schiele and Kokoschka, as one of the most important exponents of early Modernism in Austrian painting.

Gerstl first studied under Professor Christian Griepenkerl at the Vienna Akademie der Bildenden Künste (the Academy of Fine Arts). Finding his relationship with his teacher unsatisfactory, he spent two summers in search of alternative approaches at the school of art that formerly existed at Nagybánya in Hungary, where he came into contact with Impressionism and Post-Impressionism. He painted his first important work, the *Portrait of the Sisters Karoline and Pauline Fey*, in the winter of 1905. The dematerialization of the room and the contrast between expressive faces and bodily rigidity of the subjects stand in the strongest contrast to the decorative curvilinearity of Art Nouveau.

Early paintings, such as the *Double Portrait of Mathilde and Gertrud Schönberg* (1906), are distinguished by Gerstl's confrontation with Pointillism.Whilst Gerstl maintained a great

reserve toward fellow-artists, he was willing to join the circle which had formed around the composer Arnold Schönberg, to whom he gave lessons in painting and whose family he painted in group and individual portraits.

Gerstl later went beyond the formal rigor of Pointillism to develop an ever more forcefully gestural brushwork that was increasingly unconcerned with either figurative depiction or the representation of spatial perspective. His inner turmoil found autonomous expression in the line, and in the landscapes and group portraits painted during the summer of 1907. Gerstl pushed his painting to the verge of the non-representational.

In 1908, his friendship with Schönberg ended as a result of his affair with Mathilde Schönberg. *The Laughing Self-Portrait*, one of his last paintings, can be seen both as a symbol of despair over the doomed love affair and as a protest against the established esthetic. Gerstl was a loner, both as an individual and an artist, and he had no successors.

Richard Gerstl
The Sisters Karoline and Pauline Frey, 1905
Oil on canvas, 69 x 59 in
(175 x 150 cm)
Österreichische Galerie, Belvedere

Oskar Kokoschka
Child with Parents' Hands, 1909
Oil on canvas, 28 x 20 in
(72 x 52 cm)
Österreichische Galerie, Belvedere

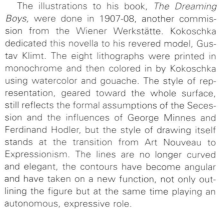

The illustrations to his book, *The Dreaming Boys,* were done in 1907-08, another commission from the Wiener Werkstätte. Kokoschka dedicated this novella to his revered model, Gustav Klimt. The eight lithographs were printed in monochrome and then colored in by Kokoschka using watercolor and gouache. The style of representation, geared toward the whole surface, still reflects the formal assumptions of the Secession and the influences of George Minnes and Ferdinand Hodler, but the style of drawing itself stands at the transition from Art Nouveau to Expressionism. The lines are no longer curved and elegant, the contours have become angular and have taken on a new function, not only outlining the figure but at the same time playing an autonomous, expressive role.

For the new generation, the focus would no longer be the *Gesamtkunstwerk* but man as an individual, in his psychological and existential existence. In 1908, Kokoschka had the opportunity to exhibit his work at the *Kunstschau* for the first time; it was generally met with rejection. Ludwig Hevesi called Kokoschka a "super-savage," and Kokoschka himself shaved his head and claimed to be an *artiste maudit*, an outsider on the Viennese art scene. His play, *Mörder, Hoffnung der Frauen* (Murder, Hope of Women), received its first performance at the 1909 *Kunstschau*. The poster he designed for it confirmed his reputation as a rebellious young artist.

Oskar Kokoschka's Viennese years

Austrian Expressionism has its origins in Vienna, in the so-called "Early Expressionism" of the first decade of the century. Today, it seems self-evident to classify the work of Gerstl, Schiele, and Kokoschka in this way, but the word ""Expressionism" itself entered the vocabulary of art criticism only around 1911. It was the appearance of the word in German-language critiques of international exhibitions that led to its being applied to Austrian artists. "Austrian Expressionism" was seen as an individual variety of a more general European movement, and now designates Austrian Modernism from Oskar Kokoschka through Herbert Boeckl. It therefore covers the most divergent trends in the history of art.

The 1908 and 1909 exhibitions of the Vienna *Kunstschau* marked a fundamental break, the first appearance of a new generation which took a deliberate stance against the flat and decorative art of turn-of-the-century Vienna. Significantly, this was also the last joint appearance by the Klimt group, whose patronage had made this public presentation of Modernism possible.

Kokoschka had been working with the *Wiener Werkstätte* since 1907, and his training at the Kunstgewerbeschule (School of Arts and Crafts) was marked by the stylisation of the Vienna Secession. His earliest works are prints and postcard designs, and he wrote his first one-act play *Sphinx und Strohmann* for the Cabaret Fledermaus established by the *Wiener Werkstätte* in 1907. The growing formal radicalism of his postcard designs then led on to Kokoschka's first important graphic work.

Oskar Kokoschka
Illustrations for The Dreaming Boys, 1907-08

Oskar Kokoschka
Poster design
Historisches Museum der Stadt Wien

Oskar Kokoschka
Still-life with Mutton and
Hyacinth, 1910
Oil on canvas, 34 x 45 in
(87 x 114 cm)
Österreichische Galerie, Belvedere

At the *Kunstschau*, Kokoschka first encountered the architect Adolf Loos, who became one of his most important mentors during his years in Vienna, also introducing him to the literary circle around Karl Kraus and helping him obtain many portrait commissions. It was as a result of Loos' persuasion that in 1909 Kokoschka left the School of Arts and Crafts and the *Wiener Werkstätte*, traveling with Loos to various spas in the Alps to paint portraits of the aristocracy.

Although Kokoschka was very little inclined toward society portraiture as a genre, within a few months he nonetheless became the most significant portrait-painter of his time. Between 1909 and 1911 he painted many portraits of prominent scientists and academics, including the leading figures of the Viennese intelligentsia. Kokoschka's subjects are not accessorized. He isolated them from their worldly environment, drawing everything from inside, frankly and honestly, and creating an atmosphere around them which crackled with tension, which he intensified by scratching and scraping at the painted surface.

In 1909, also through the mediation of Adolf Loos, he painted the *Child with Parents' Hands* (page 383 top) for the master-tailor Goldmann. The *Still-life with Mutton and Hyacinth*, painted a year later, is one of Kokoschka's most important works. Generally interpreted as a memento mori, a symbol of the transitory nature of life, it demonstrates Kokoschka's deliberate

Oskar Kokoschka
Portrait of Artists' Mother,
Romana Kokoschka, 1917
Oil on canvas, 44 x 30 in
(112 x 75 cm)
Österreichische Galerie, Belvedere

adoption of a traditional genre of painting which in its "emancipation of dissonance" (H. Giese) stands opposed to the predominant artistic style of the time, which subjected even death to decorative treatment. Here, Kokoschka breaks with the conventions of his day; the color increasingly begins to lose its relationship with the shape of the object, a new development in which a claim is made for the expressive power of painting per se.

In 1911, the Hagenbund Artists' Association staged a Kokoschka exhibition. The work was condemned by the conservative press, but Kokoschka became known abroad. Unlike Gerstl, however, he was anything but isolated, even in Vienna. He obtained numerous commissions through the intermediary of Viennese intellectuals and in 1910 he started to do work for the Berlin publication, *Der Sturm*. His *Portrait of the Duchess of Montesquiou* was purchased by Karl Ernst

Osthaus, and he was given a major show by the renowned art dealer Paul Cassirer.

In April 1912 Kokoschka met Alma Mahler, widow of the composer and step-daughter of the painter Carl Moll. His passionate relationship with Alma, seven years his senior, provided him with the theme for a series of paintings, one of the most important of these being the *Wind Bride* produced in 1914, which hangs in the Kunstmuseum in Basel. He began the painting after his travels in Italy with Alma Mahler, and his encounter with Venetian painting, and especially the work of Tintoretto, would have a profound influence on his work. Kokoschka worked over the painting several times; he originally called it *Tristan and Isolde*, and it was Georg Trakl who gave it the name by which it is now generally known. In its dynamic formal language the painting strikingly records Kokoschka's extremely fraught relationship with Alma. He

Oskar Kokoschka
The Wind-Bride, 1914
Oil on canvas, 71 x 87 in
(181 x 221 cm)
Kunstmuseum, Basel
Public collection

himself called it the "masterpiece of all my Expressionist efforts."

Kokoschka's relationship with Alma broke up when she had their child aborted at a Viennese clinic, and it may well have been his despair at this that drove him to volunteer to serve in the army in World War I. A year later, Alma Mahler married the respected German architect of the Bauhuas, Walter Gropius.

Kokoschka was seriously wounded in battle, and in 1916 he was discharged from the army. He then traveled to Berlin and signed a contract with the art dealer, Paul Cassirer, which provided him with a monthly income. In the meantime, his participation in international exhibitions abroad had made Kokoschka one of the most well-known Expressionist artists.

Kokoschka's literary work was also well-received, particularly by the Dadaists, and his plays were performed in Zurich, Dresden, and elsewhere. In 1919 he obtained a professorship at the Dresden academy, and left Vienna for good.

Max Oppenheimer

Kokoschka's Expressionism had a particularly strong effect on the younger artists, including Max Oppenheimer. Max was the son of the writer Ludwig Oppenheimer; he called himself MOPP, and signed his paintings in the same way. He studied at the Prague Academy until 1906 and it was from there that he sent two paintings to the Vienna *Kunstschau* which already bore the stamp of an unambiguously expressive style. Shortly afterward, he returned to Vienna, joining the circle around Egon Schiele and Albert Paris Gütersloh.

During his time in Vienna, Oppenheimer mostly painted portraits of well-known literary and musical figures, and in 1910 he paint-

ed Schiele's portrait. Schiele made sketches of him and the two become firm friends, even sharing a studio for a short time. Schiele's head and shoulders take up the whole of the canvas, and the expressive effect of the portrait is reinforced by the choppy outline and the forceful body language. The hatching scratched into the freshly applied paint is reminiscent of Kokoschka's work. In the early days Oppenheimer was indeed accused by contemporary critics of being an "imitation Kokoschka."

Oppenheimer is one of the very few Austrian artists to display the influence of Cubism and Futurism in his paintings, even if this is generally no more than a matter of formal quotation. He was especially interested in Futurism and its attempt to represent dynamic processes and movement in a painting. He explored these dynamics, however, in characteristically Viennese subject-matter, such as his frequent depictions of musicians playing.

In 1911, encouraged by the art dealer Paul Cassirer, Oppenheimer moved to Berlin. After brief periods spent in Switzerland, he returned to Vienna in 1924, where the Hagenbund gave him a one-man exhibition. In 1939, he emigrated to New York.

Max Oppenheimer
Mother and Son (Frau Malvine Reichel with Raimund), ca. 1910
Museum moderner Kunst
Stiftung Ludwig

Max Oppenheimer
Portrait of Egon Schiele, 1910
Oil on canvas
Historisches Museum der Stadt
Wien

The painting *Interieur* dates from 1907, and shows the apartment of his aunt and uncle, Marie and Leopold Czihaczek. The study is one of Schiele's few paintings of interiors and it demonstrates his interest in the effects of light and mirroring. His early work also demonstrates his later, intense preoccupation with the human form, in the treatment of which Schiele at first gave ample scope to the flat and decorative tendencies of the prevailing style.

For Schiele, as for Kokoschka, Gustav Klimt was the towering figure of the Viennese art scene. Schiele made contact with him as early as 1907, and Klimt became his mentor, introducing him to important art collectors. Much more strongly than Kokoschka's work, Schiele's early figurative paintings show a direct confrontation with Klimt's formal language, and *The Water-Ghosts* of 1907 is directly related to Klimt's painting *The Water-Snakes* completed the same year. Here however Klimt's ornamental richness is translated into a more sober and more angular formal language.

Schiele had four paintings in the 1909 *Kunstschau*. One was the *Portrait of the Painter Anton Peschka*. Peschka had studied with Schiele and later became his brother-in-law and a member of the *Neukunstgruppe*. He is shown in sideview, sitting in a patterned armchair. Schiele had borrowed this style of portrait from Klimt and had already used it several times. Alongside such demonstrable points of contact, other works show an individual, abstract formal language which, in its rendering of outline, distances itself unambiguously from the decorativeness of the Viennese style. Here, the new importance of the poster, which required the clear and emphatic representation of content, was an essential influence. Schiele himself designed very many posters and postcards during this period. They include *Two Men*

Egon Schiele
Two Men Standing on a Pedestal
(Klimt and Schiele), 1909
Black ink wash, 6.1 x 3.9 in
(15.5 x 9.9 cm)
Graphische Sammlung Albertina

Egon Schiele
Interior (view of Leopold and
Marie Czihaczek's apartment),
1907
Oil on card, 15.39 x 12.28 in
(39.1 x 31.2 cm)
Österreichische Galerie Belvedere

Egon Schiele: early works and the beginning of the Expressionist style

Like Kokoschka, Egon Schiele began his artistic career under the influence of the Viennese At Nouveau. He was one of the younger generation whose views had been influenced by Modernism, for the stylistic forms of the Secession had already gained acceptance, and these provided the basis for the development of Schiele's impressive formal language.

Schiele was born in 1890, at Tulln on the Danube. He trained as a painter at the Akademie der Bildenden Künste (Academy of Fine Art) under Christian Griepenkerl, a conservative artist rooted in the traditions of Historicism. Growing tensions between student and master lead to Schiele's departure in April 1909 and to his joining up with like-minded fellow-students to set up the *Neukunstgruppe* in that same year. Schiele's early work is characterized by Post-Impressionist tendencies, particularly evident in the small-scale landscapes on cardboard which he painted until 1908.

Egon Schiele
Portrait of the Painter Anton
Peschka, 1909
Oil, silver and gilt-bronze and
pencil on canvas, 43 x 39 in
(110.2 x 100 cm)
Private collection, courtesy of St.
Etienne Gallery, New York

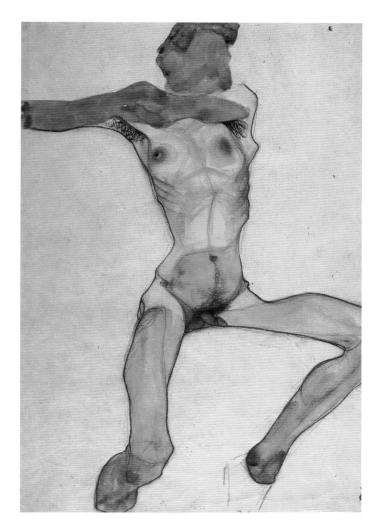

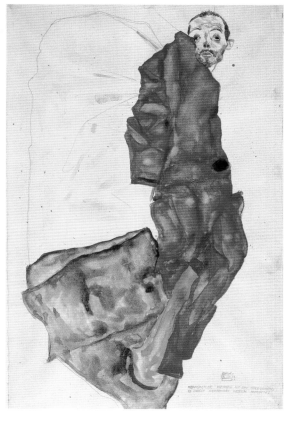

Egon Schiele
Seated Male Nude, 1910
Oil and gouache on canvas,
60 x 59 in (152.5 x 150 cm)
Leopold Museum, Vienna.
Private donation

Standing on a Pedestal (page 386, top right), one of a series of four designs, similar in style though not in execution, which was interpreted as a representation of Klimt and Schiele.

During the winter of 1909-10 the artists of the *Neukunstgruppe* had their first combined exhibition at the gallery of the art-dealer Pisko on the Schwartzenbergerplatz, and it was here that Schiele met the collector Carl Reininghaus, the publisher Eduard Kosmack, and the art critic Arthur Roessler. Roessler became a committed supporter of Schiele's art and did much to gain recognition for his work.

For Schiele the year 1910 marked his definitive breakthrough into Expressionism. The *Seated Male Nude* (1910) in the Leopold Collection is one of the more important works of this period. Schiele dispensed with any kind of props and allowed the human figure speak

solely through posture and position. The nude seems to float in a totally autonomous space from which it emerges, accentuated by the starkness of the contours; the effect of this bizarre outline is supported by the highly varied accentuation of the individual body parts through color.

Schiele "shatters" the ideal of beauty that was still central to Klimt's stylized art. The organic unity of the body is broken up by the extreme position of the hands, the projection of the hip-bones and ribs, and by the abrupt termination of the legs. Here, the body becomes a manifesto of an uncompromising self-expression. The original source of this language of gesture was Expressionist dance, which had quite significant effect on the fine arts, as can be seen in Schiele's enthusiasm for the work of the dancer Ruth Saint-Denis, for example.

Egon Schiele
Self-Portrait as Prisoner, 1912
Legend: It is a crime to impede
the artist, it kills the shoots of life!
Pencil, water-color, 12 x 19 in
(31.7 x 48.7 cm)
Print Collection, Albertina

Female Nudes

Schiele was one of the great draughtsmen of the twentieth century, able to give self-confident expression to his figurative intentions in a few precise lines. This can be seen particularly in his drawings of nudes, where the line not only outlines the complexity of bodily form but at the same time fixes it as a volume within the space of the white drawing paper.

The female nude was of central importance to both Klimt and Schiele. In Schiele's case, it even represented the greatest part of his work. Klimt, however, tamed the sexual element through different types of stylization and his drawings aim at a more sensual, erotic effect. Schiele, on the other hand, emphasised the frank, uncompromising representation of sexual reality. The gaunt bodies of his female subjects, with their hard lines are sometimes uneasily folded up on themselves, represented in postures intended to generate an expressive immediacy of great formal force. Items such as hose, thrown-back skirts, and shoes underpin the eroticism but also give the opportunity to introduce color and graphic excitement and interest

These sketches were always subject to accusations of obscenity, and in 1912 Schiele even had to defend himself in court. He was first accused of having seduced an underage girl, a charge which was proved to

Egon Schiele
Nude against Colored Cloth, 1911
Watercolor and pencil, heightened in white, 18 x 12 in (46 x 31 cm)
Private collection

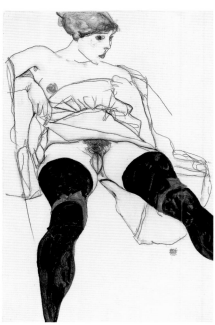

Egon Schiele
Woman with Black Stockings, 1913
Gouache, water-color and pencil, 19 x 13 in (48.3 x 31.8 cm)
Private collection, courtesy of St. Etienne Gallery, New York

be without foundation. Schiele was sentenced to three days' imprisonment, however, for "publication of immoral drawings," probably because the children who sometimes sat as models for him could at times have seen nude studies in his studio. He was convicted, despite the fact that when the prosecutor's office had objected to the publication of Klimt's erotic drawings in the journal *Ver Sacrum* — these were the studies on medicine — the case had been decided on appeal in favor of the artist, it being held that artistic freedom was not to be in any way restricted. At the end of Schiele's trial, an aquatint of a naked girl was ceremonially burned in the courtroom!

The Lovers

This painting is not dated but is generally ascribed to the year 1917, on the basis of its stylistic resemblance to *Reclining Woman*. It was exhibited in March 1918 as part of Schiele's big one-man show at the Vienna Secession, where it was purchased by a private collector. It was acquired by the Österreichische Galerie in 1950.

Schiele had worked on the theme of the embracing couple before, in the *Death and Maiden* (1915), but this painting has a totally different significance. If earlier man and woman were shown at the mercy of an ineluctable fate, the painting of 1918 shows the ecstatic embrace of two lovers whose bodies are clasped together in dynamic movement. The crumpled bed-sheet surrounds them like an aura, introducing a strong contrast between the figures and the painted background. The woman's loose, dark hair takes up the whole of the upper right corner of the painting and finds a formal echo in the complex folds of the sheet in the bottom left-hand corner.

The same theme is found in two watercolors now in the Albertina in Vienna. *The Lovers* (1914-15) have the features of Schiele and his lover, the model Wally Neuzil. As in *Death and Maiden*, the woman holds the man tightly. In the watercolor *Seated Couple* (left) of 1915 the collector Rudolf Leopold recognized Schiele's wife, Edith Harms. The man's body, hanging as if lifeless in the arms of the woman, is obviously influenced by the Pietà motif. Here, as in many of his paintings, Schiele depicts himself as silent, his empty gaze directed into the distance. This passive indifference of the man contrasts with those self-portraits in which Schiele confronts the viewer with provocatively expressive movement.

These studies by Schiele are probably responsible for the idea that the lovers in the oil painting are not an anonymous couple but a portrayal of Schiele in the arms of a female, identified either as his wife Edith or as a recollection of Wally.

Egon Schiele
Seated Couple
Pencil and gouache, 20 x 16 in
(52 x 41.1 cm)
Print Collection, Albertina

Egon Schiele
Embrace (The Lovers II), 1917
Oil on Canvas, 39 x 67 in
(100 x 170 cm)
Österreichische Galerie Belvedere

Models for the subject-matter can be found in the paints of Edvard Munch, and in the contemporary example of Klimt's *Mother with Children*, but with the drastic realism of his own picture Schiele wanted to broach a much more tragic theme. In the use of color, too, the composition is totally determined by the confrontation between life and death, Schiele contrasting the palid, ashen body of the mother with the luminous body of the child. In a letter written in 1912 published by Arthur Roessler, Schiele talked about the significance of colour in his paintings: "The picture must give off light, bodies have their own light, which they use up in living; when they burn up, the light is extinguished."

In 1915, Schiele broke up with his longtime companion Wally Neuzil and married Edith Harms. In the same year, he painted *Death and Maiden*, in which he showed himself together with Wally. His purpose here, however, was not portrayal but the representation of a more general theme. There are obvious affinities with similar subjects in the art of Rodin or Munch, but in Schiele's painting, death is no longer depicted as a skeleton and so emerges from beneath the cloak of anonymity. The woman embraces a man dressed in something like a penitent's habit, the two crouching on a white sheet against an ocher background. The symbolic force of the color underpins the impression of deep despair and ineluctable hopelessness.

Egon Schiele
Sketch for The Family, 1918

Egon Schiele
Death and Maiden, 1915
Oil on canvas, 59 x 71 in
(150 x 180 cm)
Österreichische Galerie Belvedere

Egon Schiele
Dead Mother (I), 1910
Oil on wood, 12.6 x 10.1 in
(32 x 25.7 cm)
Leopold Museum, Vienna
Private gift

Death and Life

One of the subjects that occurs again and again in Schiele's work is the polarity of life and death. Even if Schiele's interest in this theme is also a matter of purely artistic tradition, it can be partially explained in biographical terms. As a child, Schiele witnessed the death of his older sister, and when he was a young man his father also died, after many years of mental illness.

In 1910 Schiele's acquaintance with the gynecologist Erwin Graf brought him the opportunity to draw in a women's hospital. The drawings of ill and pregnant women that he did there led to the 1910 painting *Dead Mother I*, and from then on Schiele constantly returned to the theme of motherhood and more particularly to the contrast between life developing, suffering, and death. The extremely tight composition fills the whole canvas, the mother's head inclined and the bony hand positioned parallel to it enclosing a black circular form in which lies the child.

The Family

This painting was first exhibited at the Vienna Secession in 1918, under the title *Crouching Human Couple*. The title, chosen by Schiele himself, suggests that the artist was not essentially intending to produce a self-portrait with family, even if the man's features are clearly Schiele's own. The woman, indeed, bears no resemblance to Edith at all, reminding one rather of the women who sat for Schiele's painting *Pair of Seated Women* (1918). The addition of the small child at the mother's feet—there had earlier been a bunch of flowers at the same spot—has encouraged a sentimental interpretation, it being thought that Schiele had added the child on hearing of his wife's pregnancy. As in the case of most of Schiele's child portraits, the model was his nephew, Anton Peschka.

Formally speaking, the group constitutes a masterly compositional unity that makes use of motifs from earlier paintings. The sitting position of the man can be found in the painting *Blind Mother* (1914), and also in the *Seated Man,* the self-portrait of 1912, and the subject-matter can be traced back to Rodin's sculpture *Femme accroupie* (1882). The figures are lined up one behind the other, yet with no communication between them. There is, however, a greater cohesion between mother and child, which finds support too in the color. The man, the only person who is the only one looking out of the picture, seems strangely withdrawn and removed from his surroundings.

Egon Schiele
The Family (Crouching Human Couple), 1918
Oil on canvas, 59 x 63 in
(150 x 160 cm)
Österreichische Galerie Belvedere

Self-Portraits

"There is no self-portrait of me. I am not interested in my own person as a subject for a painting. I am convinced that I am not particularly
interesting as a person." Thus Klimt explained
the absence of this kind of painting from his
own œuvre. Though the succeeding generation
had no greater interest in the self-portrait as a
representational form, it was very much committed to reflexive self-analysis.

After 1909, the painted or drawn self-portrait
became one of the most important subjects in
Schiele's work. The formal influences which led
to his unmistakable habitual distortions are manifold. It will be enough here to refer to Georges
Minne and Ferdinand Hodler. In 1910 and 1911,
Schiele made a series of visionary self-portraits
in which he started each time with his own likeness but represented himself metaphorically as
a lyric poet, prophet or seer. In their rendering of
world-weariness and melancholy, these introduce new expressive content into his work.

Egon Schiele
Portrait of Dr. Victor Ritter von
Bauer, 1918
Oil on canvas, 55 x 43 in
(141 x 110 cm)
Österreichische Galerie Belvedere

Portraits

It was at the suggestion of the architect Otto Wagner that Schiele took up the portrait form for the first time in 1910, producing a series of large paintings of well-known Viennese personalities, amongst others the art critic Arthur Roessler and the publisher Eduard Kosmack. Both of these paintings are related to the seated male nudes of the first half of that year, and in his portraits Schiele makes use of the expressive poses of the self-portraits painted around 1910.

The emphasis of the composition is firstly based on formal considerations, which leads Schiele to a constructivist conception of the portrait. The publisher Eduard Kosmack is shown in full frontal in an extremely tightly self-contained pose, his hands pressed between his knees. Schiele reduces formal pictorial construction to the minimum, to give a greater expressive force to the sitter, which derives mostly from the captivating strength of the eyes which look out of the picture with their hypnotically fixed gaze. The facial expression and the position of the body give the impression of an introvert collapsing inward into himself. Schiele's tendency toward symbolism manifests itself here again in the wilted sunflower he grants his sitter as an attribute.

Otto Wagner himself agreed to sit for his portrait (ill. p. 275), but soon lost patience and suggested that as the head had already been finished someone else should sit in his place. A watercolor study for Wagner's portrait survives in the Albertina, but the painting was never completed. Disappointed, Schiele gave up the planned series and only returned seriously to portraiture in his later work.

It was more especially in the last two years of his life that Schiele gained recognition as a portraitist and was given important commissions. This started with Schiele's drawings of Russian prisoners and Austrian officers during his military service, which brought him wide public recognition. In the late portraits, Schiele replaces the pale background with the representation of an interior, and in almost all the paintings the sitter is perched on a square, wooden studio chair, which is rendered in detail in the Portrait of Dr. Victor Ritter von Bauer.

All in all, the later portraits are characterized by a free, painterly approach which does not restrict itself to the area enclosed by the outline but extends to the whole surface of the canvas. In 1918, Schiele exhibited at the Vienna Secession with great success, and the portrait of his wife Edith which he showed there was purchased directly from the exhibition for the Österreichische Galerie.

Egon Schiele
Portrait of Eduard Kosmack,
1910
Oil on canvas, 39 x 39 in
(100 x 100 cm)
Österreichische Galerie Belvedere

Egon Schiele
House Wall (Windows), 1914
Oil on canvas, 43 x 55 in
(110 x 140 cm)
Österreichische Galerie
Belvedere

Egon Schiele
Four Trees, 1917
Oil on canvas, 44 x 55 in
(111 x 140 cm)
Österreichische Galerie
Belvedere

Landscapes

The formal development of Schiele's landscapes
followed on from the Secessionists' depictions
of nature around 1900. His conception of the
limit of the pictorial space was influenced both
by the works of Ferdinand Knopff and his knowledge of Japanese prints. Klimt had created contemplative objects contained within themselves
by the constraint of the pictorial space, showing
nature in extreme close-up and moving the horizon up to the upper edge of the painting.
Schiele's landscapes, however, are closer to the
character of his figure paintings.

In a letter to Franz Hauer (1913) Schiele
explained his view of nature: "I find and I
know that working from nature is of no importance for me, as I can paint better pictures
from memory, as a vision of the landscape...
Deeply, with all one's heart and soul, one
imagines a fall tree in summer; I would like to
paint this melancholy."

His Krumau cityscapes are allegories of
human loneliness. The oil painting *House Wall*
(1914), which probably also makes use of
motifs from Krumau, differs from paintings like
Dead City or *The Little Town (II)* in content as
well as form. Schiele himself called the painting *Window*. The wall of the house takes up
almost the entire canvas, only a small part of
street can be seen. The decorative character of
the painting and the extreme close-up are reminiscent of Klimt's *Attersee Landscape*. *The
Four Trees* (1917) is one of the most beautiful
of Schiele's late landscapes. The rendering has
become more lyrical yet the symbolism of the
content has not been abandoned.

Wiener Werkstätte gallery in the
Museum für angewandte Kunst,
Vienna, redesigned by Heimo
Zobernig, 1986-93

Wiener Werkstätte Poster

The Wiener Werkstätte

The end of the nineteenth century saw a search for new forms of expression to counter the decline in esthetic standards associated with the introduction of mass production and the availability of cheap imitation materials. In this, the socio-political ideas of William Morris were an essential point of reference, especially his call for simplicity and functionality of design.

Alongside a return to the domestic virtues of the so-called Biedermeier period in metalwork and fine furniture that found new formal solutions to meet the demands of middle-class daily life, inspiration was drawn from Japanese plastic and graphic arts, fulfilling the need for both exotic luxury and formal novelty.

This revival of crafts entailed both bringing craft production under more specifically artistic direction and the re-establishment of the dignity of craftsmanship in relation to the fine arts. The development of modern crafts and Viennese interior design were the work of Joseph Hoffmann and Koloman Moser and their pupils at the Kunstgewerbeschule (the

Vienna School of Arts and Crafts). Hoffmann's early furniture was characterized by floral decoration, yet in its construction it already pointed toward modern functional design. The furniture Moser and Hoffmann showed at the Secession exhibition in 1900 marked a clear break with the past and the emergence of clear, clean, linear design which in Vienna had already been anticipated by Adolf Loos. Another significant stimulus to development came from the furniture and architecture of Charles Rennie Mackintosh, who also exhibited at the Secession. Furthermore, art publications of the English-speaking world enthusiastically received the *Wiener Werkstätte*, thus helping its members to exert an even greater influence.

At the turn of the century, both Hoffmann and Moser had established reputations as artists and they received numerous interior design commissions. In 1901, the industrialist Fritz Waerndorfer had them redecorate his villa, which was to be furnished by Mackintosh. It was probably as a result of this collaboration that in 1903, Hoffmann, Moser, and

Waerndorfer established the *Wiener Werkstätte*. The aim of this "producer co-operative" was to develop close collaboration with craftsmen so as to revive Austrian craftsmanship, to reform it in accordance with new artistic criteria and, not least, to adapt objects in daily use to the changing needs of a new age. Such fixtures, fittings, and furnishings were to gain esthetic richness from reductive simplification and would become bywords for sober elegance.

First to be set up were an office and workshops for metalwork, bookbinding, cabinetmaking, and lacquering. The plan provided for the sensible use of machines and promoted handwork in opposition to the mass production of low-quality goods. The early style of the *Wiener Werkstätte* is characterized by the use of basic geometrical forms in household objects, whose emphatic three-dimensionality is enlivened by glittering decoration or punched-out squares. The furniture is characterized by clarity of proportion, and was often created as part of an ensemble. Moser and Hoffmann's designs are stylistically very similar in this respect, so where their authorship is not documented it is difficult to arrive at an unequivocal attribution.

Around 1905, there was a relaxation of geometrical rigor in favor of a freer and more curvilinear style, which became more marked after Moser's departure, reaching its high point in the work of Dagobert Peche, who after 1915, together with Hoffmann, shaped the formal language of the *Wiener Werkstätte*.

Koloman Moser
Vase, 1903-04
Brass and citrine
Museum für Angewandte Kunst,
Vienna

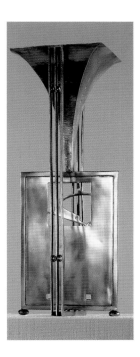

Koloman Moser
Bureau for Waerndorfer family,
1903-04
Varnished Macassar ebony, with marquetry of Madagascar ebony, boxwood, mahogany, and ivory.
Maker's nameplate, brass fittings.
Museum für angewandte Kunst,
Vienna

Josef Hoffmann
Two armchairs, ca. 1905-10
Upholstered in silk, feet covered in beaten silver
These two armchairs resemble those in the vestibule of the Palais Stoclet in Brussels

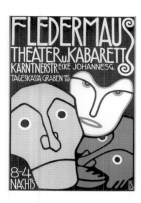

Bertold Löffler
Poster for Cabaret Fledermaus,
1907, lithograph
Historisches Museum der Stadt
Wien

Cabaret Fledermaus

In 1907, at Fritz Waerndorfer's suggestion, the *Wiener Werkstätte* opened a theatre-bar at 33, Kärntnerstrasse. In its furnishing and decoration, the Cabaret Fledermaus was the very embodiment of the demanding, exclusive standards of the *Wiener Werkstätte*. In the spirit of their conception of art and life, their cultural message was now to be extended to the performing arts, the Cabaret becoming a meeting point for the Viennese avant-garde.

The architectural design of the basement auditorium abolished the separation between actors and audience, placing every seat at an ideal distance from the stage. This space, which because of its great success soon proved to be too small, was decorated by Hoffmann in gray-and-white marble, whose luxurious effect was stylistically similar to that of the Palais Stoclet. The architecture, indeed, based on simple square and rectangular shapes, was on the whole closely related to that of the Brussels palace. The bar, however, was designed in a markedly less conventional style. The floor was laid with square black-and-white tiles, while the walls were clad up to head height in colorful ceramic tiles of varying sizes, which covered the surface in a crazy and dazzling pattern, abolishing the subordination of decoration to architecture.

These tiles were made by the *Wiener Keramik*, founded in 1906 by Michael Powolny and Bertold Löffler, a former pupil of Moser's. Their ceramics were subsequently sold by the *Wiener Werkstätte*, and Löffler and Powolny were brought in for all the *Wiener Werkstätte*'s major interior design projects. In addition to ceramics, Löffler produced prints, costumes, and jewelry, while Powolny's ceramic works, his putti in particular, became a trademark of the *Wiener Werkstätte*. A Powolny putto also stood at the entrance to the anteroom of the Cabaret.

Like the Palais Stoclet, the Cabaret enabled a theme to be carried through consistently in the design of every artefact from table ornaments to lamps to cutlery. Even the posters, tickets, programs, and menus were designed in a consistent style which became unmistakably identified with the Cabaret.

One of the artists whose work was performed there was Oskar Kokoschka. In 1913, the Cabaret Fledermaus was forced to close and was turned into a revue theatre, yet most of the items designed for it are today regarded throughout the world as the definitive expression of the *Wiener Werkstätte* style. An example is Joseph Hoffmann's "Fledermaus chair" with the characteristic spheres beneath the armrest and seat. Originally designed in black and white, it was later produced in other colors.

Michael Powolny
Putto "Fall," ca. 1907
Porcelain, white shards, colored
underglazes, on plinth by entrance
to ante-room at Cabaret
Fledermaus

Josef Hoffmann
Cabaret Fledermaus, 1907
Ante-room and bar

Josef Hoffmann
Café chair, the so-called
Fledermaus chair, ca. 1906,
Painted bentwood, seat cover in
red leather
Originally designed for Cabaret
Fledermaus

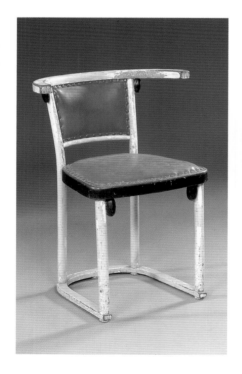

Arts and Crafts, 1890–1918

Josef Hoffmann
Tea service, 1903
Silver, coral, and ebony
Museum für angewandte Kunst,
Vienna

Koloman Moser
Decorated box, 1906
Silver, enamel, and
semiprecious stones
Museum für angewandte Kunst,
Vienna

FAR RIGHT:
Koloman Moser
Pendant, 1903,
Silver and opal
Museum für angewandte Kunst,
Vienna

Glass

The turn of the nineteenth and twentieth centuries saw the production of a great deal of household glass. Most of the traditional glassworks in the Austro-Hungarian Empire were located in Bohemia. Bakalowits Söhne were the suppliers of glassware to the *Wiener Werkstätte* until 1910, producing work to the designs of Kolo Moser and his students in particular. This glass is often combined with silver and distinguished by its sparse decoration.

The glassware most closely associated with the *Wiener Werkstätte*, however, is the bronzite glass produced by the Lobmeyer company. Ludwig Lobmeyer had already established a relationship with the architects and artists working on the Ringstrasse project in Vienna. His nephew, who took over the firm in 1917, was very fond of the Art Nouveau and Art Deco and was responsible for the production of glass for the *Wiener Werkstätte* after the great period of the Vienna Secession. Among their classics, produced

Josef Hoffmann
Vase, 1914
Opaline glass, vermilion glass exterior decoration etched on the white inner layer.
executed by Johann Loetz' Witwe, Klostermühle

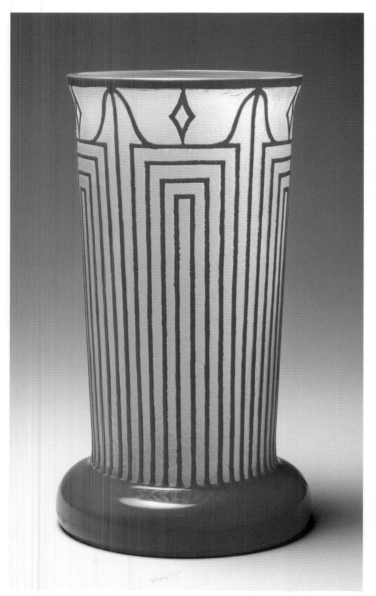

Josef Hoffmann
Vase, 1911-12
Opaline glass, black glass exterior decoration etched on the surface of the white inner layer.
executed by Johann Loetz' Witwe, Klostermühle

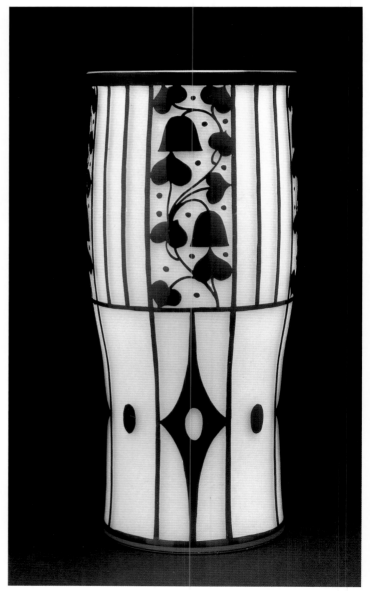

to this day, are Hoffmann's *Patrician* service and the range of glasses, tumblers, and carafes in matt glass with simple linear decoration in black bronzite designed by Hoffmann in 1912. The bronzite technique was developed around 1910. The glossy, metallic, pattern is made by coating the glass with bronzite, which is then etched away where a protective lacquer has not been applied. Bronzite glassware was also produced for the *Wiener Werkstätte* by the Loetz' Witwe company. Their glasses, unlike Lobmeyer's, are lipped glasses in a severe, linear style; designed by Josef Hoffmann and Jutta Sika among others. They are characterized by their glowing blues, reds, and yellows, while Michael Powolny remained loyal to his black-and-white striped decoration. The arrival of Dagobert Peche caused the production of a more decorative style in glassware.

Glass, ceramics, silver, and metal, jewelry, textiles, and fashion—the artists of the *Wiener Werkstätte* produced designs for every area of the arts and crafts. The Backhausen fabric company produced Koloman Moser's designs, and made the carpets for the Palais Stoclet as well as a wide range of fabric patterns which can still be purchased from the firm today. The *Wiener Werkstätte*'s first city shop was opened in 1907 at 15, Wiener Graben and in 1910 a very successful fashion department was added under the supervision of Eduard Wimmer-Wisgrill. Branches were opened elsewhere in Austria and abroad, but the *Wiener Werkstätte* never really succeeded in building up a large customer base.

After the departure of Waerndorfer, who emigrated to America in 1914, the *Wiener Werkstätte* was turned into a partnership of clients, patrons, and collaborators, and in this form, under the leadership of Otto Primavesis, it survived into the 1930s, the severe, unified style of the early period giving way to a stylistic pluralism. While the formal language of Dagobert Peche was dominant in the early years, the ceramicists of the *Wiener Werkstätte* in particular developed a highly individual, modern style in the 1920s which showed the influence of such movements as Cubism and Expressionism. The artists created individual pieces of the highest quality and short runs of everyday objects.

The *Wiener Werkstätte*'s 1932 exhibition was also a closing-down sale, the business having failed as a result of unprofessional management and the very difficult economic climate. During the World War II, its archive was placed in storage with the Museum für Angewandte Kunst, to which it was later donated. The archive includes design drawings, photographs, pattern books, textile patterns, and graphic art.

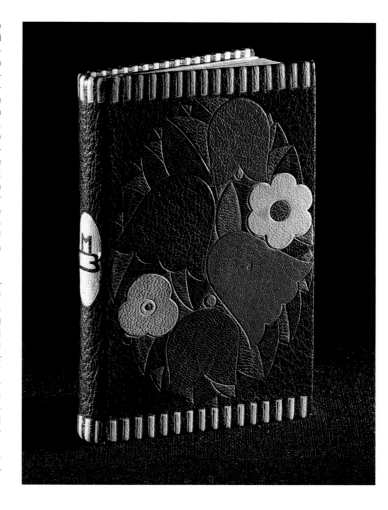

Josef Hoffmann
Bookbinding, ca. 1914,
Max Brod, Der Bräutigam
Multicolored morocco leather with flowers and linear decoration
Museum für angewandte Kunst, Vienna

Dagobert Peche
Vase and lidded bowl, ca. 1916
Enameled glass, executed by
Johann Loetz' Witwe, Klostermühle

Anton Hanak
Venus Vindobonensis, 1924–31, Laaser marble, h. 83 in (209 cm)
Österreichische Galerie, Belvedere

Anton Kolig
Family Portrait, 1928, oil on canvas 72 x 80 in (180 x 200 cm),
Österreichische Galerie, Belvedere

Awakenings: Eight Centuries of Austrian Painting and Sculpture

With the end of World War I, Vienna found itself in the grip of hunger and economic crisis. Artistic life deserted Vienna for the provinces of the new Austrian Republic, and it was in Styria, the Tyrol, and especially in Carinthia, that the artistic energy emerged that was mostly responsible for maintaining the continuity of Austrian art until 1945. Of the new artistic centers the *Nötscher Kreis* in Carinthia, whose tendencies were Expressionist, deserves particular mention. Its most important member was Herbert Boeckl, an artist much influenced by Schiele and Kokoschka, who first came to public attention with his exhibition in Klagenfurt in 1918, and to whom Austrian art would be indebted for much of the energy that made possible its new beginning after 1945.

For quite some time after 1918, the Viennese art world suffered from the loss of its outstanding artists — Klimt, Moser, Schiele, Wagner, and Kokoschka. They had dominated Vienna to such an extent that after their death or departure for abroad it was difficult to credit the viability of the Viennese art tradition. The *Hagenbund*, established in 1900, was still active alongside the now insignificant Secession, however, and a number of talented artists were still living in Vienna. Their struggles for independence, recognition, and artistic freedom were very much harder than those of their predecessors. From the very beginning, their efforts were always compared to the achievements of the Secessionists and the Expressionists. Later, after a short period of success, many were outlawed and driven away by the Hitler dictatorship.

The Hagenbund and Neue Sachlichkeit

The Hagenbund lived for almost a decade of its life in the shadow of the popular and successful Secession, and only in the years that followed the damaging resignation of the Klimt group from the Secession did its members succeed in developing a "more moderate", independent line, in which atmosphere at first played a major role.

After 1918, however, the formal language of the Hagenbund came to dominate artistic activity in Vienna, and in the 1920s it provided the most important focus for new artistic currents. Its members, among them Carry Hauser, Georg Merkel, Sergius Pauser, the sculptor Franz Barwig, Oskar Laske, Otto Rudolf Schatz, and Albin Egger-Lienz, disassociated themselves from both the Secession and Expressionism on essential questions of esthetics. They may have approved of the Expressionists' search for realism, but the expressive formal solutions they found conflicted with the Hagenbund's own artistic objectives. After the War, in particular, many works by Hagenbund artists show a lucid, sometimes

monumental, realism which brings them close to the *Neue Sachlichkeit* school. Many artists in Austria reacted to the deeply distressing events of the War and its aftermath, with depictions of a seemingly permanent and ordered world, usually without any hint of social critique. Their output was dominated by a magical realism and a transfigurative approach to nature, coupled with the introduction of popular iconographic motifs which would meld almost seamlessly with the figurative propagandistic art of the Third Reich. The muscular farmers of Egger-Lienz's paintings and the moralistic bourgeois tone of Pauser's works are exemplary in this respect. Today, in the Österreichische Galerie, the Historisches Museum der Stadt Wien, and in the Stiftung Ludwig at the Museum Moderner Kunst the works of the Hagenbund, whose significance in terms of the history of art was long misunderstood, hang alongside works of the Secessionists and the Expressionists, as the Austrian variant of the *Neue Sachlichkeit*.

Apart from groups like the Hagenbund, the *Künstlerhaus*, and the Secession, individual artists such as Anton Kolig and Albert Paris Gütersloh also played a role in the revival of the Viennese art scene in the inter-war period. Kolig, a member of the *Nötscher Kreis*, was given major commissions in the 1920s. These included Clemens Holzmeister's crematorium, for example. Gütersloh, a writer, director, actor, set-designer, and painter who would play an even more important role than Boeckl after 1945 as a go-between between tradition and Modernism, had already exhibited his early Expressionist works at the *Kunstschau* (Art Show) in 1909. Like Kolig, he had been promoted by Klimt. Their well-behaved Expressionism, however, had no chance against the excitement generated by Schiele, Kokoschka, and Gerstl. Together with a few other members of the *Hagenbund*, Gütersloh therefore left Vienna for a short time, returning only when realism purged of emotion had gained acceptance. Only Gütersloh continued to distance himself from this "sensible" objectivity with his atmospheric, ironically sentimental water-colors and gouaches.

At a time when abstract, constructive, and geometrical tendencies were asserting themselves almost everywhere in Europe, artists in Austria turned to either a detached realism or continued to pursue an expressive, painterly style, determined by subjective content. Abstraction, Constructivism, Cubism, and Kinetic Art received little attention in Austria at the time of their emergence. Hauser and Alfred Wickenburg, as representatives of Cubism in painting, were exceptions, but they were closer to Czech Cubism, which remained loyal to the object as the painting's maxim, rather than to the Cubist dissolution of form that developed in France.

Painting and Sculpture from 1919 to the Present Day

Franz Cizek's master class at the Kunstgewerbeschule was extraordinarily receptive to the formal language of Cubism and Kinetic Art, and the formal experiments undertaken by his students culminated in the early 1920s in Viennese Kineticism, comparable to the German Bauhaus. Erika Giovanna Klien, one of the most outstanding representatives of Kineticism, had been a pupil of Cizek's. Her emigration to New York in 1929 ended the modest beginnings of Viennese Kineticism; its geometrical analysis of form, however, would influence the everyday design of the Fifties.

On the annexation of Austria by Nazi Germany the majority of contemporary artists were designated as "degenerate," the Hagenbund dissolved and the Secession merged with the *Künstlerhaus*. This caused art in any real sense to disappear over the next few years, and it was replaced by an "esthetic" of Nazi dogma and propaganda.

Approaches to a New Era

When the dictatorship ended, the shock at events, the desire to catch up with what had been missed, and the force of repressed energies combined to usher in the beginning of a new artistic era. In 1945, Vienna immediately returned to the center of European cultural life, as notable artists took up teaching posts at the Kunsthochschule. In addition to Boeckl, who had returned from Carinthia in 1927, the most important figures were Gütersloh and the sculptor Fritz Wotruba. They encountered an artistic milieu that had been culturally starved by the National Socialist terror and which was looking for new tasks and new subject-matter. A new beginning beckoned, but first there had to be a reconnection with the tradition of Austrian art which could then be developed and progressed. Great efforts were also made to deal with Cubism and Surrealism, which had received little attention in Austria before World War II. From the fear of not being able to keep up with international Modernism and of thus surrendering to provincialism there emerged the terrific driving force and optimism of all those who were working with innovative forces for a renewal of Austrian culture.

Despite the harsh economic circumstances, Boeckl was able, as rector of the Akademie der Bildenden Künste and organizer of the famous *Abendakt* (evening life-classes), to relaunch art education and to convince many colleagues of the existence of new opportunities. Boeckl was a colorist, whose search for the spiritual dimension of painting often took him to the edge of abstraction, and he was understanding of the younger people who threw themselves enthusiastically into Abstractionism. In a teaching career that spanned more than thirty years, the gestural freedom of his painting and his sometimes symbolic handling of color deeply influenced the vision and representation

of several generations of students. As a professor at the Akademie, Gütersloh too had a great influence on artistic development, with, for example the *Wiener Schule des Phantastischen Realismus* (Viennese School of Fantastic Realism) and its main representatives. Arik Brauer, Wolfgang Hutter, Anton Lehmden and Ernst Fuchs were graduates of his classes. Even more important than his teaching was Gütersloh's role as president of the *Art Club* founded in 1946, the first forum for artistic debate after the War.

It was Boeckl who arranged in 1945 for Wotruba, one of the internationally acknowledged sculptors of the twentieth century, to take over one of the master-classes at the academy. Wotruba had at first continued in the Expressionist tradition of his own teacher Hanak, the trend-setting sculptor of the pre-war years, but he soon developed a distinctive formal vocabulary of his own based on strict geometry. Even in his early work, there is an analysis of the human form, borrowed from Cubism, which would later come to dominate his whole œuvre. He saw the body as a structure comparable to architecture, and the vigorous elimination of the superfluous led to strong, archaic figures.

Although Vienna has no museum specifically dedicated to the works of this great sculptor — an honor he richly deserves — examples of Wotruba's work can be seen in the sculpture garden of the Museum des 20. Jahhunderts (Museum of the Twentieth Century). Among the most interesting is the *Heiligsten Dreifaltigkeit* (Holy Trinity) church in Wien-Mauer, whose plans Wotruba began to work on 1965 but which was only completed in 1976, after his death.

Wotruba never imposed a style on his pupils, though the stele-like male torso which defined

Fritz Wotruba
Torso, 1928/29
Limestone, h. 56 in (140 cm)
Österreichische Galerie, Belvedere

Fritz Wotruba
Large Seated Female Figure,
1949. Limestone, h. 61 in (153 cm)
Österreichische Galerie, Belvedere

Albert Paris Gütersloh
Heavenly and Earthly Love, 1924
Gouache on paper, 8 x 25 in
(20 x 62 cm)
Klosterneuburg, Essl Collection

Roland Goeschl
Figure in Movement, 1965
Painted wood, h. 110 in
(274 cm)
Österreichische Galerie, Belvedere

his work was a fundamental element adopted by almost all the sculptors of his school. The works of Joannis Avramidis, Rudolf Hoflehner, Josef Pillhofer, Wander Bertoni, Andreas Urteil, and Roland Goeschl all show their teacher's influence. The same is true of the restless Alfred Hrdlicka, who already had completed studies in painting before he went to Wotruba's master class.

All his students nonetheless developed distinctive individual styles. Hrdlicka, seen from the start as an eccentric and an agitator, at first took his lead from Wotruba's work in the 1930s, although his own work, even the drawings and the prints, had always been distinguished by its exaggerations and expressive content. In 1983, Hrdlicka received a commission from the Austrian government for the Memorial Against War and Fascism at the Albertina. Wotruba and his pupils established an expressive and self-confident sculpture in Austria that had nothing to fear from international comparison. In 1975, Wotruba's master class was taken over by the painter, draftsman, and sculptor Bruno Gironcoli. Artists like Manfred Walkolbinger, Hans Kupelwieser, and Karl Prantl, and as well as those who operate in more indefinable areas, such as Franz West and Erwin Wurm, together bring energy and pluralism to contemporary Austrian sculpture. For all those mentioned, and for many others who cannot be included for lack of space, the fundamental emphasis is on sensuality and sensitivity to materials, often in the service of almost incommunicable conceptual or meditative themes.

Approaches to a New Era

Once World War II had ended, the Austrians were at pains to restore their reputation abroad as a land of culture, rich in traditions. Exhibitions in Zurich, London, Brussels, and Paris presented a historical panorama of the Austrian Baroque through Makart to Klimt and Schiele. This backward-looking approach was countered by the avant-gardist and internationalist endeavors of the thriving Viennese art scene, which by the beginning of the 1950s had already been able to connect self-confidently and surprisingly quickly to international developments in art.

Collaboration with artists of the occupying powers proved helpful in surmounting psychological and esthetic barriers. Such foreign artists wanted to establish a positive general impression of their own countries, and art played a role in this; alongside their traditional culture each offered contemporary work, thus providing encouragement to Austrian art.

In 1947, the first Exhibition of Modern Art was held in Vienna. It was under the patronage of the French, and included works by Picasso and Braque among others. The exhibits proved a shock for many people, positively for some as a

stimulus to explore the unknown, negatively for others by provoking a total rejection. A great deal was achieved in particular by the French Institute in Innsbruck, which is today acknowledged as one of the birthplaces of the Informal style of painting in Austria. Here the Tyrolean artist Oswald Oberhuber, a pupil of Wotruba's, was one of the first to come across the Informal school, and by 1949 he had begun to produce his own Informal painting and sculpture. The diversity of his work, the fruit of a ceaseless drive for change, his teaching at the Hochschule für Angewandte Kunst in Vienna (where he was rector for many years), and his activities as a curator and gallery owner, make Oberhuber one of the most glittering personalities on the art scene of Austria's Second Republic.

The Art Club

Any consideration of the various movements of those years has essentially to focus on two groups. One is the Art Club founded by Gütersloh and the Surrealist Edgar Jené, which brought together seventy or more individualists, among them many who would be responsible for the future development of Austrian art.

Their numbers included such artists as Maria Lassnig, herself a pupil of Gütersloh's, the draftsman Kurt Moldovan, Rudolf Hauser, and Wolfgang Hutter, who would become the principal representatives of *Phantastischen Realismus* (Fantastic Realism), and the sculptors Bertoni and Schmeller. Some were non-artists, like the art critic Alfred Schmeller, future director of the Vienna Museum of Modern Art.

The Club's inaugural exhibition in 1948 gave Austrians their first chance to see the contemporary art of their country. There were works by Gütersloh, Fuchs, Hutter, Hausner, Bertoni, and

Oswald Oberhuber
5 x Me, 1964
Mixed media on canvas, 60 x 50 in (150 x 125 cm)
Klosterneuburg, Essl Collection

Wotruba among many others. From 1950 through 1951, the Art Club had its headquarters in the rebuilt Secession building, moving to the *Loos Bar*, which had been nicknamed *Strohkoffer*, due to its covering of straw mats, and was for years almost synonymous with the world of the Viennese avant-garde. While the club's first exhibitions were dominated by figurative painting, mainly represented by the works of the *Phantasten* (Fantastic Realists), by the time the group moved to the *Strohkoffer*, Abstraction had taken over.

In 1951, the Art Club saw the arrival of the self-taught Friedensreich Hundertwasser, one of its most individual members, who had already developed his ideas about the humane environment, producing not only artistic and architectural but also ecological manifestos.

Hundertwasser first made a widespread impact in 1958, with his *Verschimmelungsmanifest gegen den Rationalismus in der Architektur* (Decay-Manifesto Against Rationalism in Architecture), in which he provocatively rejected functional architecture and pure form. In his view, buildings of the Modern Movement were the very embodiment of sterility. Hundertwasser's work during these years, at a time when he was concerned with the philosophy of an unending cycle, symbolized in the spiral, are among the most innovative of the time.

One of the high points of this period of work was the *Endlose Linie* (Endless Line) event at the Hochschule für Bildende Künste in Hamburg. For this, Hundertwasser drew an unending line through the spaces of the Hochschule. This provoked such a scandal that he resigned from his teaching post. His alternative architectural designs would only come to fruition in the 1980s and 1990s, with the building of the *Hundertwasser Haus*, the *Kunsthaus Wien*, and many other architectural projects.

The Fantastic Realists

Hundertwasser has no direct link with the *Wiener Schule des Phantastischen Realismus* (Viennese School of Fantastic Realism), despite claims to the contrary. However, almost all the members of this movement also belonged to the Art Club. In fact, they never saw themselves as a group, though all of them acknowledged the influence of Gütersloh.

The *Phantasten* saw their adoption of the classical painting and traditional painterly methods as an important demonstration of their acceptance of tradition. For many of them, Hieronymus Bosch - whose masterpiece, the *Weltgerichtstryptichon* (Triptych of the Last Judgement), can be seen at the Akademie der Bildenden Künste, was the touchstone of technical and "fantastical" skill.

For all of these artist the most important thing was perfect technique. This obsession caused

them to be dubbed *Technik Fetischisten* (Technique Fetishists). Their work tended toward figurative Surrealism — Max Ernst and Paul Klee were important role-models — which they developed along distinctly Austrian decorative and psychological lines.

Despite being committed to pictorial tradition and technical skill, the "Fantastics" were seen as being progressive in terms of their imagery. After some initial difficulties, the remarkable virtuosity of the most famous of them — Brauer, Fuchs, Hausner, Hutter and Lehmden — gained them unusually rapid recognition. Works by Hutter, Fuchs, and Lehmden had been exhibited at the Venice Biennale in the early 1950s. After the mid-1960s the *Phantastischen Realisten* became the post-war group of Austrian artists who were the best-known outside their own country.

The Forward March of Abstraction

Not only the Fantastic Realists but almost all Austrian artistic circles were indebted to Surrealism. Realistic currents represented, for example, by Hrdlicka, Fritz Martinz, and Georg Eisler, who had been taught by Kokoschka in London, were ignored. The encounter with *automatic* Surrealism led to the *Informal*, to *Abstract Expressionism* and to *Action Painting*, the dominant artistic movements of the early post-war years.

The establishment in Austria of these international currents was the responsibility of a group of young artists who had been unknown hitherto. They included Josef Mikl, Markus Prachensky, Wolfgang Hollegha, Arnulf Rainer, and the Carinthian painter Maria Lassnig. These ambitious artists were the "movers and shakers" of their time, first at the Art Club and then at the St. Stephan's Gallery, which opened in 1954 (and which, at the request of the Archdiocese of Vienna, has been known since 1963 as the *Gallerie Nächst St. Stephan* (the Gallery Next to St. Stephan's)).

In the 1950s, under the directorship of the progressive Monsignor Mauer, the gallery became a forum for predominantly abstract contemporary artists. Mauer was persuaded of the close relationship between culture and religion, and he believed that all artistic tendencies were compatible with Christianity, the abstract and contemplative ones in particular. The opening of the Galerie im Griechenbeisl in 1960 gave Mauer's gallery its first friendly competitor on the art market and in 1962, the opening of the Museum of the Twentieth Century provided them with an institutional counterpart.

At the time, Mikl was painting almost abstract *Maschinenfiguren* (machine figures) that took their formal language from Cubism and found their inspiration in burned-out automobiles, motorcycles, and tanks, as well as nudes formed out of geometrical volumes. Hollegha

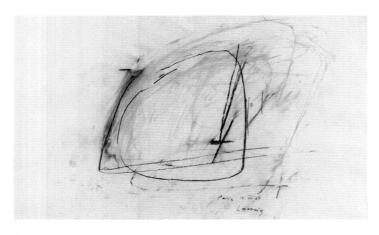

Maria Lassnig
Untitled, 1960

Arnulf Rainer
Purple overpainting, 1961
Oil and pastel on canvas, 80 x 33
in (201.5 x 81.5 cm)
Museum moderner Kunst
Stiftung Ludwig

turned toward the organic and vegetative, soon abandoning his comparable constructive beginnings, The monumentality of his large-scale paintings causes him to be seen as a successor of the Baroque painters.

Prachensky is the only real Tachist among them all, He has also painted as a public performance, as when in 1959 he appeared as part of the supporting program for one of George Mathieu's displays. Lassnig and Rainer traveled to Paris in 1950, intending to meet the Surrealists and André Breton. Once there, however, they felt more strongly attracted to Informal painting, whose extreme subjectivity and anti-authoritarian execution appeared to them to be a reaction to Nazi totalitarianism.

An introduction to Informal thinking followed in the shape of a happening in March 1951, at the first and last exhibition by the *Hundsgruppe* (Dog Group). This was organized by Rainer and Fuchs as a protest against what they saw as the dullness of the Viennese art scene. In the course of Fuchs's speech at the opening, Rainer suddenly jumped up and shouted, "Ich spuche auf euer Hemd". (I spit on your shirt). The public was outraged, and the artistic theme of the 1950s and 1960s, the destruction of every form and norm, was born. The exhibition itself consisted mostly of Rainer's compositionless decentralisations and concentrations of lines by Lassnig.

From then on, Rainer saw the negation of the traditional image as the only conceivable response to the Third Reich and to developments on the art scene, and he started his famous *Übermalungen* (overpainting) series. At the same time, Lassnig produced her first informal auto-receptive paintings which led later on to her distinctive and highly self-referential *Body Awareness Paintings*.

In November 1951, this group of artists organized an exhibition in Klagenfurt, which showed the progress made by Austrian art in the space of just a few months. Mikl and Hollegha were among the artists represented in Klagenfurt, and soon they would also come to influence many developments as spokesmen for the St. Stephan's Gallery.

Hans Staudacher adopted an independent path in Informal painting. Staudacher was a self-taught painter from Carinthia, who had spent some time in Paris, where he had become close to the *Lyrischen Informel* (Lyrical Informal) group. His poetic and semi-realistic collages, characterized by a rapid painting technique, still show traces of his literary activity.

Viennese Actionism

Aktionismus (Viennese Actionism), the Austrian variant of Happening Art and Fluxus, emerged at the beginning of the 1960s. It derived from the external manifestation of subjective states through Informal painting and the actions of Tachism. Actionism was introduced to Vienna in 1958 at the *Junge Generation*, a Socialist art gallery established as a counterpoint to the *schwarzen* (black) St. Stephan's Gallery. In 1960, the *Junge Generation* gallery exhibited Analytical Cubist works by Otto Mühl and Adolf Frohner, but in 1961 it was showing rough refuse-sculptures by the same artists.

Soon after, Mühl, Frohner, and Hermann Nitsch drew up the *Blutorgel* (Blood-organ), the first manifesto of Viennese Actionism, which argued for the equivalence of art and life as a logical continuation of the body-relatedness and the spatiality of painting. In 1962, as a protest against Vienna's Festwoche festival, Mühl, Frohner, and Nitsch organized a *Three-Day Action*, which turned into the first great Actionist scandal, amongst other reasons because Nitsch used the carcass of a lamb in his performance. The artists were accused of scandalous behavior and the police brought the performance to a premature close.

While the Fantastic Realists dominated the art market, the Austrian cultural scene of the 1960s was affected by the shocking, offensive performances of Günter Brus, Mühl, Nitsch, and Rudolf Schwarzkogler. If this decade saw political and social unrest in the United States and in most countries of Europe, in Austria feelings generally ran high about art.

In Viennese Actionism, art acquired a hitherto unknown political dimension for the first time. The Actionists challenged not only the traditional concepts of art but also the authority of the Austrian state and its Catholic character. The Actionists wanted to provoke, they wanted to shock and shake people up, but they were equally concerned with going beyond traditional limits and finding new modes of artistic expression.

Günter Brus
Viennese Stroll, 1965
3 photos from a series of 16
Klosterneuburg, Essl Collection

BELOW:
Hermann Nitsch
4th Action, 1963
Documentation, 8 color photographs, 24 x 20 in
(60 x 50 cm)

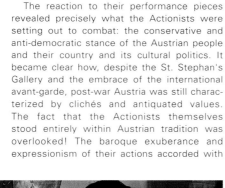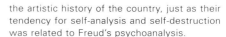

The reaction to their performance pieces revealed precisely what the Actionists were setting out to combat: the conservative and anti-democratic stance of the Austrian people and their country and its cultural politics. It became clear how, despite the St. Stephan's Gallery and the embrace of the international avant-garde, post-war Austria was still characterized by clichés and antiquated values. The fact that the Actionists themselves stood entirely within Austrian tradition was overlooked! The baroque exuberance and expressionism of their actions accorded with the artistic history of the country, just as their tendency for self-analysis and self-destruction was related to Freud's psychoanalysis.

In performances like *Blutorgel* and *Zock-Exercises* or the fateful *Art and Revolution* at the University of Vienna in June 1968, the artists wounded and painted their own bodies or carried out bodily functions in front of the public. After the famous *Uni-Ferkelei* event in 1968, which was planned as a discussion forum and then ended in excesses, Brus and Mühl were prosecuted for libel against the state, upon which Brus left Austria, and at about the same time Nitsch too left for Munich. Viennese Actionism, as a group phenomenon, had come to an end. Historically, it is now seen as the most important artistic movement since 1918. More intensively and more consistently than other tendencies of the 1960s, Viennese Actionism demonstrated the artistic use of the body as a form of creative expression.

A Different Reality

The end of the 1960s, the end of Actionism, and the artistic decline of the *Phantasten* left scope for new artistic developments in Vienna. In 1968, as a counter-reaction to abstraction and to the extreme positions of Actionism, the art historian Otto Breicha had organized an exhibition with six young artists on the theme: *Wirklichkeiten* (Realities). With their figurative, and at times socially critical paintings, Kurt *Kappa* Kocherscheidt, Franz Ringel, Peter Pongratz, Wolfgang Herzig, Robert Zeppel-Sperl, and Martha Jungwirth provided a strong contrast to Actionism.

In their exaggerated interpretations of consumer society Pongratz, Herzig, and Zeppel-Sperl took up the modes of representation of Pop Art and made use of kitsch and decorative

Peter Pongratz
Rock'n' Roll heart, 1992
Acrylic on canvas, 96 x 76 in
(240 x 190 cm)
Klosterneuburg, Essl Collection

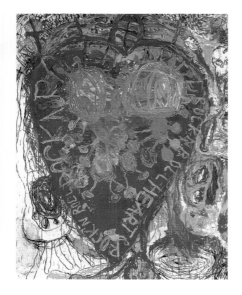

who identified with Actionism, Weibel and EXPORT took part in a few Actionist events in the 1960s, at the Vienna University in 1968, for example. As their work developed, performance, video and film became their privileged vehicles of expression.

VALIE EXPORT's unambiguously feminist standpoint and her fight for equality for women have won her a world-wide reputation. By the late 1960s, she had developed a performance art which took the relationship between the sexes as its theme. In 1968, she invited passers-by to reach into a box to grasp (and *comprehend*) her breasts for a few seconds; the artists called this *Tapp- und Tastkino* (Grope and Touch Cinema). In Vienna she led her male colleague Weibel across the Stephansplatz square on a leash. Weibel himself still expounds the Actionists' principle of anarchic provocation, questioning state structure, cultural policies, artistic subject-matter and social bonds. As an artist, curator, and teacher, Weibel's reputation has gone far beyond Austria.

motifs of the 1970s. Jungwirth's watercolors manifest her highly sensitive view of the world; always on the edge of abstraction, she continues to translate visual experience into subjective arrangements of form and color, thus endeavoring to define object and place, in order to fix her own moods and vision.

Ringel's work, first exhibited in 1968, was seen as being the most intense. He continues to be one of the most interesting individuals in Austria; his work reflects his outstanding talent as a draftsman and painter, yet is at the same time reflective and socially critical. Ringel's theme was, and is, radical social isolation. His works of the 1960s and 1970s show people enclosed in transparent skins who communicate with each other via hosepipes.

Since the 1980s, when painterly and expressive tendencies once again became dominant, Ringel has used opaque applications of color as well as the pastel and oil pastels he had used earlier. Kocherscheidt, who, like Pongratz, at first devoted himself to the trivial or exotic, turned in the 1980s to color-balanced, abstract forms which float freely in the picture plane.

The New Media

While the *Wirklichkeiten* (Realities) remained a merely regional phenomenon, media and video art once again brought Austria back in touch with the international art scene. VALIE EXPORT and Peter Weibel are two members of a generation of artists which includes Friederike Petzold, Richard Kriesche, Gottfried Bechthold, and Margot Pilz. They see the future in the new media. As very young artists

The Renaissance of Painting

After the 1970s, which were almost *Malerei-freien* (painting-free, being dominated by media art, photography, video, *Minimal* (Minimalism) and *Land Art*, many European countries experienced a renaissance of painting, which manifested itself in such movements as the *Neuen Wilden* in Germany, the *Nouveaux Fauves* in France, and the *Transavangardia* in Italy. In Austria, the so-called *Neuen Wilden* debated painting through the medium of paint, with a whole host of young artists who took up where painting had left off many years before with the Expressionism of Kokoschka and Gerstl.

This step was made easier for the younger artists by those artists of the older generation, such as Lassnig, Frohner, Hans Fronius, and Eisler, who had always clung to figurative painting and whose perseverance had meant that there was never a real break in the traditional art of painting in Austria.

As a professor at the Akademie in Vienna for many years, the Tyrolean Max Weiler, one of the very important figures in the history of twentieth century Austrian art, also encouraged his many students to concern themselves with painting. Weiler, who was born in 1910, had come from a classical tradition but had found his own abstract style in the 1940s. Always taking Nature as his example, Weiler still produces paintings which, without imitating Nature, empathize with its creative urge.

In the 1980s, Hubert Schmalix, Siegfried Anzinger, Hubert Scheibl, Erwin Bohatsch, and many others produced large-scale narrative

Max Weiler
Like a Father, 1980
Egg tempera on canvas
80 x 40 in (200 x 100 cm)
Klosterneuburg, Essl Collection

paintings of convincing spontaneity, which were eagerly lapped up by the art market and the wider public. Some rejected this recognition. Anzinger and Schmalix left Austria after considerable early success, while others, like Scheibl and Bohatsch, moved from a figurative and narrative pictorial language to an abstract and meditative position.

Johannes Zechne, although not a member of any particular school, also adopts a contemplative position. His work is distinguished by the use of text and of letters which mutate into mystical codes and ciphers. The text both exceeds and accentuates the painting and also gives structure to the composition. Here Zechner continues to explore the relationship between literature and fine art that has characterized the twentieth century.

The painter, graphic artist, designer, and musician, Christian Ludwig Attersee, is a pronounced individualist among Austrian artists, who exhibited works of great painterly intensity at *Dokumenta VI* in 1977. In the 1960s he created an Austrian version of Pop Art, one of the very few Austrian artists — apart from the Carinthian artist Kiki Kogelnik, who moved to America at the beginning of the 1960s — to reflect the emergence of American Pop Art. His paintings of the 1980s and 1990s sparkle with a wealth of color and sensual impressions, in which surreal subjects combine with expressive gesture.

In 1996, Attersee designed the façade of a large department store on the Mariahilferstrasse in Vienna, a mosaic several stories high, giving Vienna another artistically decorated public building, alongside Hundertwasser's architectural work.

Siegfried Anzinger
ML sitting, 1993
Distemper on canvas, 91 x 75 in
(227 x 188 cm)
Klosterneuburg, Essl Collection

Heinz Tesar
Model of new building for the
Essl Collection in Klosterneuburg

This extensive collection of Austrian twentieth-century art is at Klosterneuburg near Vienna. The collection contains more than 4,000 works which provide a comprehensive survey of Austrian painting, particularly post-1945, situating it in its international context.

Pluralism as a Principle

The early 1990s saw a reaction to the dominance of painting, one which could be attributed to the influence of Gerwald Rockenschaub, Ernst Caramelle, and Heimo Zobernig. The decade showed how Minimalist Art and Land Art had left their mark on the Austrian art scene and led to a reduction and minimalization of forms. Some conceptual works of great serenity are typical of this period.

Yet one cannot speak of a dominant tendency, since the Viennese art world of the late twentieth century is distinguished by a great pluralism of style and medium. The fast-moving pace of our times is reflected in contemporary art, in rapidly changing demands, fashions, and trends. After years of market uncertainty and reliance on famous names, many galleries and exhibition spaces are now daring to show new and experimental work. The Viennese art scene is extremely varied and exiting, and the range and programs of the city's galleries bear favorable comparison with the international art scene.

emphasis on realism of representation. At the Akademie, he quickly gathered round him those students interested in Surrealism, and he became the inspiration for the Vienna School of Fantastic Realists.

Herbert Boeckl, who is from Carinthia, was the great charismatic teacher of the Vienna Akademie, and his *Abendakt* (evening life-classes) were of almost legendary importance for the post-war generation. At first, Boeckl's painting followed on from Schiele and Kokoschka's Expressionism. One of his first large-scale paintings was the portrait of the art historian Bruno Grimschitz, which took up the esthetics of Schiele's constructive line. Later works from ca. 1918, however, are closer to Kokoschka's Expressionism. In contrast to Kokoschka's wide, rapid brushstrokes, Boeckl's painting uses small, broken up patches of opaque color which anticipate the move toward an abstract formal language.

It is only in the late 1930s and early 1940s that the dark, melancholic colors of Boeckl's early pictures begin to change, under the influence of travel and his encounter with the work of Cézanne. Paintings like Yellow Quarry near St. Margarethen (1938) and the series of Erzberg Paintings, begun in 1942, have a new luminosity. Boeckl's tendency to abstraction is documented by the series of Erzberg and Dominican paintings, in which formal elements of Cubism come to play an important role. The frescoes on the theme of the Apocalypse in the Engelskappelle at the Stift Seckau, a monumental work painted in 1951-52, also manifest Boeckl's affinity with abstraction.

Herbert Boeckl
Yellow Quarry near
St. Margarethen, 1938
Oil on canvas, 38 x 47 in
(94 x 117 cm)
Österreichische Galerie, Belvedere

Albert Paris Gütersloh
Portrait of Vera G., 1927
Oil on canvas, 29 x 24 in
(72 x 59 cm)
Museum moderner Kunst
Ludwig Collection

Herbert Boeckl and Albert Paris Gütersloh

Albert Paris Gütersloh and Herbert Boeckl both played a particularly significant role in the development of Austrian art after 1918. Their lives and work form a bridge from the beginnings of Austrian Modernism to developments in Vienna after 1945, which were considerably influenced by their teaching at the Akademie.

Gütersloh first trained as an actor and worked at the Deutsche Theater in Berlin under Max Reinhard. He also wrote, and he was friendly with Robert Musil and other writers. Back in Vienna, he joined the circle of *Neukünstler* around Egon Schiele, and in 1911 he published his essay, *Egon Schiele — Versuch einer Vorrede* (Egon Schiele — an Attempt at a Preface).

At first his painting was close to that of the Secessionists, but he soon adopted a Surrealist orientation. The mid-1920s saw Gütersloh move toward a more unified formal language, and, through the influence of the painting of the *Neue Sachlichkeit*, to a greater

Herbert Boeckl
Dominican, 1948
Oil on canvas, 53 x 40 in
(132 x 99 cm)
Museum moderner Kunst,
Stiftung Ludwig

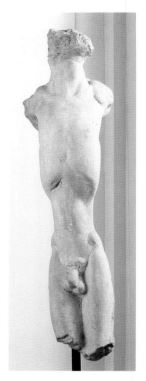

OPPOSITE PAGE:
Alfred Hrdlicka
Memorial against War and
Fascism, 1991,
Carrara marble
Vienna, Albertinaplatz

sense of three-dimensionality in the figure, which is cut directly from the block.

The disturbances of February 1938 forced Wotruba and his Jewish wife Marian into exile in Switzerland, where his studio in Zug quickly became a meeting-place for many other Austrian émigrés, such as Robert Musil and Fritz Hochwälder. In 1945, Herbert Boeckl brought Wotruba, by now an internationally acclaimed artist, back to the Vienna Akademie to teach the master class in sculpture. He arrived at the Westbahnhof train station with sacks of food, a homecoming that acquired legendary status, especially upon readng Wolfgang Kudrnofsky's account: "The starving Viennese standing in front of the Westbahnhof thought they were seeing some kind of French general. The man, however, was neither French nor a general, but Fritz Wotruba, a sculptor since his youth."

Under the impact of the bombed city, in 1946, the artist created the sculpture entitled *Weibliche Kathedrale* (Female Cathedral) (also called *Grosse Stehende* (Large Standing Figure)), in which Wotruba began to move away from the anatomical representation of the human form. The move toward the tectonic found its first climax in the sculpture *Grosse Sitzende* (Large Sitting Figure) of 1949, in which the artist reacted to the achievements of international Modernism and particularly to the solutions of Classical Cubism. From the 1950s onward, his blocks are composed of cubic and cylindrical elements, the play and interpenetration of these loosely assembled parts intensifying to develop into an abstract form, though man remains at the thematic center as the "secret of a firmly structured order of universal things."

Joannis Avramidis, Roland Goeschl, Rudolf Hoflehner, Wander Bertoni, Andreas Urteil, and Alfred Hrdlicka were among the students who attended Wotruba's class in the Böcklinstrasse studios near the Prater. Many of his pupils adopted Wotruba's prioritization of architectural structure and his tendency toward abstraction, leading them into even greater simplicity, and thus developing their own sculptural approach in close relation to Wotruba's own work. Others, like Alfred Hrdlicka, looked for a clear alternative to their teacher's formal solutions.

Hrdlicka had first studied painting under Gütersloh and then under Dobrowsky, attending Wotruba's sculpture classes after obtaining his diploma in painting. A fantastic draftsman, he also attended Herbert Boeckl's *Abendakt* (evening life-classes). Drawings and prints always remained an important element in his œuvre, but Hrdlicka is first and foremost a sculptor. His attachment to figuration stands in opposition to the abstraction to which the Austrian avant-garde of the Fifties felt itself more and more drawn.

Alfred Hrdlicka
Crucified Christ, 1959
Untersberg marble, h. 64 in
(160 cm)
Museum moderner Kunst
Stiftung Ludwig

Fritz Wotruba
Large Figure, 1966
Karst marble, h. 88 in (220 cm)
Museum moderner Kunst
Stiftung Ludwig

Sculpture and Non-figurative Art after 1945

At first, Austria played almost no international role in the development of modern sculpture. It was only after 1945 that a varied sculptural scene was established, strongly influenced by the personality of Fritz Wotruba.

Wotruba had enjoyed his first international success around 1930, with his torsos in limestone and marble. The purchase of the sculpture *Der junge Riese* (The Young Giant) by the City of Vienna allowed him to travel to Germany where the work of Lehmbruck and Maillol made a deep impression on him.

Wotruba's early works move on from a naturalistic understanding of the figure to a severe stylization. The surface of the stone is rough and unpolished at first; later he succeeded in stripping out detail and achieved a more marked

Hrdlicka rejected art which conveys no subject-matter, saying "I don't think things, I notice things." His themes are violence, power, and wrong-doing, and their place both in politics and in the relationship between men and women. More specifically he deals with the fate of outcasts from society, with mass-murderers, revolutionaries, the dishonored, his expressionism characteristically reflected in the fragmented treatment of the stone. Significant figures are worked out, while others are only hinted at in the roughly hewn material.

His sculpture of the *Gekreuzigten* (Crucified Christ) (ill. p. 412) was produced in 1959, part of a group of three with the figures of the two thieves. "In 1955, Wotruba provided me with a wonderful piece of pink marble. I carefully set about producing a Cubist work in the school's style", Hrdlicka remembered in 1993. "As soon as I had gotten this masterpiece of loyal student effort to my own studio, I beavered away at it to produce the Crucified Christ of 1959."

Yet Hrdlicka's expressive style has taken him further and further away from the classicism of the Wotruba school. His art is created in confrontation with themes of art history and the political realities of past and present, and his public works, such as the *Orpheus* in Salzburg, the portrait head of Karl Renner on the Ringstrasse in Vienna, and his Memorial Against War and Fascism on the Albertinaplatz (ill. p. 413), have always been sure to generate excitement.

Joannis Avramidis was born in Batum in 1922 and lived in Vienna after 1943. He, too, devoted himself to depiction of the human form, but unlike Hrdlicka he developed an abstract sculpture that aimed entirely at harmony and order, in which the formal concept was predominant. His figures have nothing at all of the theatrical gesture and expressive power so important to Hrdlicka. Starting from the laws of the sphere and the cone, Avramidis creates columnar groups of figures, segments constituting body parts being grouped around a vertical axis. These are *Absolute Figuren* (absolute figures) in compact, self-enclosed poses

Fritz Wotruba always stuck to stone as the starting point for sculptural work, and he was emulated by many of his students, while others, like Rudolf Hoflehner or Roland Goeschl, discovered new materials. Roland Goeschl is one of very few constructive artists on the Austrian art scene, which in general has shown no inclination toward a geometrical, constructive formal language.

Bruno Gironcoli
Large Column with inlaid artificial eyes, 1969
Cast aluminium, iron, polyester, glass, copper, cassette recorder, 126 x 120 x 59 in
(320 x 305 x 150 cm)
Generali Foundation Collection

Johannis Avramidis
Large Group of 3 Figures, 1961
Bronze, h. 25 cm
Museum moderner Kunst
Stiftung Ludwig

Walter Pichler
Portable Shrine, 1970
Wood, glass, metal,
Museum moderner Kunst,
Stiftung Ludwig

Karl Prantl
Parallels, meditationstone, 1960
Limestone, h. 19 in (48 cm)
Museum moderner Kunst,
Stiftung Ludwig

Roland Goeschl
Column, 1986
Lacquered iron, 92 x 4 x 4 in
(230 x 10 x 10 cm)
Generali Foundation Collection

After a period studying in London, where he saw the emergence of new art movements such as Pop and Op Art, color became an essential element in Goeschl's sculptures. He restricted himself to red, blue, and yellow. He came to a new understanding of sculpture in general, abandoning the concept of the isolated free-standing block in order to concern himself with the development of the figure in space.

In Vienna, the breaking up of sculptural unity and the application of color were tantamount to sacrilege. Goeschl recalls: "Wotruba used to talk about color mania when he visited my studio…" Goeschl has created many works for public spaces, such as the stele on the roof of the Technische Universität Wien on the Karlsplatz, or the facade of Humanic shoe company, which continues to make an impact on the street today.

These manifold new beginnings emerged in the 1960s and were later considerably encouraged by Bruno Gironcoli, who took over Wotruba's master class in sculpture in 1975 after the latter's death. Gironcoli had not been a pupil of Wotruba's, and, like Walter Pichler, he takes a conceptual approach. Since 1960, Gironcoli has been using iron and more novel materials such as aluminum, glass, and sheet metal. Like Walter Pichler's, his wire objects stand in the *Arte Povera* tradition.

Walter Pichler combines organic and techno elements in works which are often monumental in stature, to produce sculptures whose themes remain encoded. During an initial phase, Pichler assembled together mass-media equipment, using everyday objects to construct a menacing urban utopia. Around 1970, Pichler entered a second phase, in which he created cultic, ritual spaces around his sculptures, following a highly personal path, which finally led him to decide not to sell any more sculptures.

At St. Martin in the Burgenland he then constructed special buildings to hold his sculptures, with something of the feel of temples, total environments that go far beyond normal sculptural concerns. In 1991, with the *Tor zum Garten* (Door to the Garden) at the Museum für Angewandte Kunst, he created a sculpture that verges on an architectural concept. The *Tragbaren Schrein* (portable shrine) of 1970 is a tin case suspended inside a portable frame of wood and osier. Like a reliquary, the tin box contains a mirror, and the content of the shrine is therefore the mirror image of the viewer, compelling introspection in an atmosphere charged with religious overtones.

In Karl Prantl's stone blocks, the visible traces of sculptural intervention are reduced to a minimum. Like elements in surrounding nature, they stand monolithically and forcefully in the landscape. Their effect derives from the smoothness of the surface and from the different types of stone, which Prantl searches out from every corner of the globe. The objects bear contemplative temporal witness to an ancient natural history.

Ernst Fuchs
Psalm 69, 1949–60
Oil and tempera on wood,
30 x 21 in (75 x 53 cm)
Museum Moderner Kunst,
Stiftung Ludwig (on loan from
the Erste Österreichische
Sparkasse)

The Vienna School of Fantastic Realism

"The Fantastic Realists were the very first avant-garde," Alfred Hrdlicka once said of this group which emerged from the *Art-Club* after World War II. In the 1960s and 1970s *Phantastischen Realismus*, which saw itself as a counter-movement both to abstraction and to Viennese Actionism, was without a doubt the most successful Austrian art movement, both at home and abroad. Yet while Viennese Actionism would be granted an honored place in the history of Austrian art, art critics today ascribe no great significance to the Vienna School of Fantastic Realism.

The group emerged from the legendary split in the Art Club that also led to the establishment of the *Hundsgruppe* (Dog Group), whose most important members were the painters Arik Brauer, Anton Lemden, Ernst Fuchs, Wolfgang Hutter, and Rudolf Hausner. At first, they were called the Surrealists, and it was only in 1956 that the Viennese art critic Johann Muschik coined the term *Viennese School of Fantastic Realism*, which has since been generally adopted. During the Fifties, alongside its principal representatives, the group also included artists such as Arnulf Rainer and Maria Lassnig, who cannot really be counted as Fantastic Realists, though they had not then entirely broken with Surrealism.

The re-emergence of Surrealist tendencies after the Second World War was not a local phenomenon, but marked the whole of Europe and America. The most significant stimulus came from the circle around André Breton in France; in Austria, it was Gütersloh and the painter Edgar Jene who did most to establish Surrealism in Vienna. Despite their enthusiasm for mainstream Surrealism, however, the Viennese Fantastic Realists did not adhere to the Surrealist Manifesto's declaration of faith in automatism as the unmediated expression of unconscious artistic production. They turned rather to the realm of fairy tale, myth and fantasy, finding their formal exemplars in the Vienna Art-Historical Museum and in the art collection of the Akademie. Inspired by Brueghel and Bosch, they developed an old-masterly technique which increasingly distanced them from painters such as Rainer, Lassnig and Hundertwasser.

The public of the time, however, saw their art as neither traditional nor eclectic, feeling that the breaking of taboos, although encoded in metaphors of apparent absurdity, was no less shocking than the performances of the Viennese Actionists.

Ernst Fuchs was thought of as the *Wunderkind* of the group. Born in Vienna in 1930, he had begun his artistic education at the age of thirteen, later studying at the Academy under Gütersloh. His surreal cityscapes illustrate the brilliant draftsmanship that would characterize all of his work. His paintings draw their subject-matter from myths and legends and especially from the Old Testament, which Fuchs transformed into a personal world view. He draws his inspiration from the altar-pieces of the Quattrocento and from the old masters of the Netherlands: in paintings such as *Psalm* (1949-60) in which the disabled and the able-bodied stand side by side.

Anton Lehmden's painting is almost exclusively restricted to landscapes, which create a feeling of spaciousness in which the idyllic calm is always disturbed by unexpected events. He works with transparent glazes which allow underlying structure to

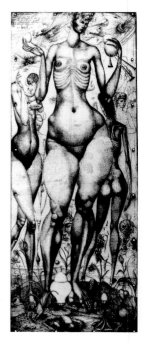

Ernst Fuchs
May, 1949
Etching, 30 x 21 in (75 x 52 cm)
Print Collection, Albertina

show through. The landscape is structured using strips of color which condense into turbulent whirlpools, clouds, and wind. Time is always present, as a slow force of change or as the sudden moment of eruption and violent collapse.

Arik Brauer's painting, on the other hand, is narrative, incorporating experiences from his extensive travels and interwoven with the mysticism of the Orient and the Bible. Dream and reality, consciousness and unconsciousness come together in his poetic and fantastical painting. Where Lehmden imagines gloomy apocalypses, Brauer conjures up earthly paradises. In 1954 Brauer went to Israel, where he worked as a singer and dancer, and later went on to Paris where he had his first successful one-man show. In the 1970s, Brauer painted backdrops for the opera houses in Zurich and Vienna, and 1995 saw the completion of the *Brauer-Haus* built to his design (ill. p. 350).

Anton Lehmden
Before the Storm, 1966-67
Oil on wood, 10 x 16 in
(25 x 39 cm)
Klosterneuburg, Essl Collection

LEFT:
Arik Brauer
Burning Woman as Flower, 1966
Oil on plywood, 25 x 28 in
(63 x 70 cm)
Klosterneuburg, Essl Collection

Rudolf Hausner
Forum of the Inwardly Turned
Optic, 1948
Tempera and gloss paint on
plywood, 25 x 48 in
(64.5 x 121 cm)
Historisches Museum der Stadt
Wien

Rudolf Hausner

"My painting is in fact a gnostic discipline. With it, everything can be analyzed and explored. Painting brings me insights and ideas. While painting I find the answers to my questions." This is how Rudolf Hausner once described his work. Hausner was a founding member of the Art Club and later a member of the Fantastic Realist group, but has always been seen as a unique phenomenon on the Surrealist scene in Vienna. In sixty years of work he created a relatively small œuvre of 160 pictures, which at times he would destroy with a razor blade immediately upon completion, only to submit them again to the creative process.

Hausner's paintings represent a series of uninterrupted self-examinations which started in 1948 with the two large pictures *Forum of Inward-Turned Optics* and *It's Me!* Both paintings are similarly encyclopedic yet at the same time profoundly personal. *The Forum of Inwardly-Turned Optics* is a first assessment of the artist's life and interrogation of his unconscious: "At that time, in 1947, I had arrived at a point where the compulsion to reappraise what lay behind me became overwhelming. I could no longer stand not knowing who I am and where I am."

Hausner's pictorial space is like a stage on which fantastic occurrences take place as in a play. Hauser subjects himself to an excessive self-analysis which, unlike that of the Expressionists' self-portraiture, operates using the styles and motifs of Surrealism.

In the late 1950s, Hausner found his alter ego in his representations of Adam. "All the Adam paintings were done with the help of a mirror and have to be seen as a mirror. Although all the Adam paintings have the facial characteristics of Rudolf Hausner, their use in self-experience is not limited to him alone, on the contrary all the Adam situations represented are really of a very general nature," he explained.

The artist uses Adam as a symbol of his own understanding of the world, provocatively transposing the figure from Genesis into the present day. "I looked into my face and I saw the world in it. Everything I know about me and the world I discovered while painting." Adam's head is almost always painted frontally and from below, the face sometimes deformed by distorted perspectives. Adam is the masculine component of the human existence, while the figure of the Anima is its female counterpart. Recurring memories of Hausner's own childhood appear like quotes from a faraway world. The mother's sewing needle, the row of houses in the Rögnergasse where Hausner spent his childhood, the Danube canal. Everything is painted with almost meticulous precision. References to the artist's own experiences are omnipresent. Anima has the features of his wife at the time of painting.

From 1974 until his death in 1995 Hausner often worked eight to ten hours a day in his studio in the Hinterbrühl near Vienna, and many of his pictures took years to paint. The complexity of content and technical skill in his painting confronts the viewer with ever-new, surprising insights. In retrospect , Hausner seems to bear but little relation to his erstwhile Fantastic Realist colleagues.

Abstract Painting after 1945

Max Weiler, seen today as the doyen of Austrian painting, holds a special place in Abstract painting after 1945.

Weiler was born in 1910, at Hall in the Tyrol, and began his studies in 1930 at the Akademie der Bildenden Künste in Vienna. Although he was already using color as a medium detached from the object in his early work, his definitive breakthrough to abstraction came in 1960 with the 29-part series, *Als Alle Dinge* (As All Things). The cycle is carried out in a free, gestural style which relies completely on the effect of color placed with bold brush strokes, establishing the foundations of the technique he used in paintings created between 1961 and 1967, which would later on be identified under the shared title *Wie ein Landschaft* (Like a Landscape). In these paintings Weiler made the essential breakthrough toward his aim at that time, the transposition of natural processes into painting. "This freedom of means — I saw that I had found what corresponded to my inner intention," he wrote in 1975.

Nature has always been the point of reference for his painting. Weiler wants to monitor the force and unfolding of its inner processes, which is why his color-world combines promptings from the real world with formal invention. For Weiler, landscape is a violet-pink stretching out against a blue-green ground, a red that lights up briefly, the dark silence of a mountain chain at twilight. He uses egg tempera, which permits a certain transparency however thickly the color is applied. Characteristic ambiguities arise in the instability of the transition between colors.

Weiler's tendency toward abstraction was shared by the younger artists Josef Mikl, Wolfgang Hollegha, and Markus Prachensky, another Tyrolean, who all belong to the group around the Nächst St. Stephan Gallery in Vienna. On closer examination, however, there appear significant differences both in the formal sense and in the handling of color. Hollegha at first worked from landscape as well, transposing similar themes into abstract painting. His colors however are always juxtaposed, monochrome fields which run into each other at their thinning margins. The color is often even poured onto the canvas and then smeared with a cloth. Hollegha likes to work in enormous formats. Unlike Weiler, whose color creates spaces that recede far into the canvas, Hollegha clearly places his luminous colors to the fore, using the background, which is always white, to delimit the space behind like a wall. In 1959. Hollegha visited to New York and met artists such as Helen Frankenthaler and Morris Louis. When he was awarded the Carnegie Medal he found international recognition.

Max Weiler
Like a Landscape, Proximity, 1962,
Egg tempera on canvas, 78 x 38 in
(195 x 96 cm)
Klosterneuburg, Essl Collection

Markus Prachensky
Red on White— Sebastianplatz,
1959,
Lacquer on canvas, 60 x 56 in
(150 x 140 cm,)
Museum moderner Kunst
Stiftung Ludwig
(Loan from the Austrian
National Bank)

In 1956, together with Markus Prachensky, Hollegha founded a collective in the Lichtenstein-strasse. Prachensky is certainly the most radical of the Nächst St. Stephan painters; his purified, total painting is forceful and extremely succinct. Prachensky completed studies in architecture and attended the master class in painting at the Akademie. His encounter with Wotruba led in the early days to a series of geometrical works, but after a stay in Paris, Prachensky developed his characteristic Tachist formal language. Vertical strips of color and thick horizontal strokes placed in the pictorial space so as to create tension are essential elements of his vocabulary, clearly differentiating his painting from Weiler's and from Hollegha's more lyrical conception. The colors, flowing into each other, generate not harmony but tension and dynamism, with red being dominant at first. Prachensky's color pourings led to painting "happenings." In *Peinture liquide* (1959, with Georges Mathieu) he poured buckets of paint onto an oversized canvas to the accompaniment of musical rhythms. Prachensky called this phase of work *Reise durch die Farbe Rot* (Journey through the Color Red). In the late 1960s, influenced by the deserts and salt lakes around Palm Springs, he created a series of two-color paintings.

Josef Mikl's early work was also influenced by Wotruba, making use of Cubism in a very individual manner. His paintings assemble man as a machine from geometrical volumes. The 1950s, saw a reinforcement of the gestural element which finally led to the dissolution of mechanical forms and to an Abstract Expressionism, which continue to be restricted to shades of blue and orange.

In 1994, Mikl was commissioned to create the painted decoration of the Redoutensaal in the Hofburg after it had been destroyed by fire.

Wolfgang Hollegha
Zottelhaube, 1979
Oil on canvas, 62 x 60 in
(155 x 150 cm)
Essl Collection,
Klosterneuburg/Vienna

Josef Mikl
Figure, 1952-53
Oil on hardboard, 34 x 52 in
(85 x 131 cm)
Museum moderner Kunst
Stiftung Ludwig, Vienna

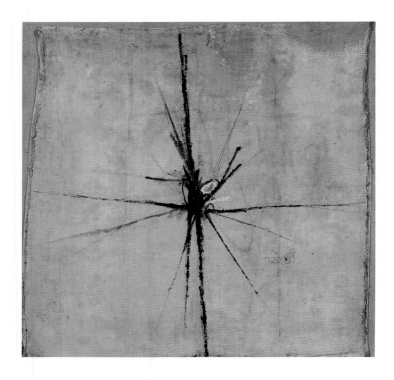

Arnulf Rainer

In the late 1940s, the self-taught artist Arnulf Rainer — who spent only three days as a student at the Viennese Akademie der Bildenden Künste where he would later become professor of painting — was working with Surrealist forms. However, in 1951, the *redselige Phantastik* (talkative fantastic) was overruled in favor of "blind painting" and the succeeding central designs which were strongly influenced by Informal painting.

In his search for the *Nullpunkt der Malerei* (zero degree of painting) described by Merleau-Ponty, Rainer went far beyond the language of the Informal. With his elementary gesture and broad mix of materials the artist was intent on achieving a homogeneous surface which, as it were, absorbed all earlier phases of painting. After 1953, he painted monochrome black paintings whose tension derives from corners and inner areas that disclose the bare white canvas — relics of the visible against which the black substance asserts itsel as a thick mass. Only apparently does the expressive, idiosyncratic painting inscribe a "beyond" behind the homogeneous surfaces, for it is the monochrome color, its slow build-up, and its coagulation that becomes the real content of the painting. The painting, freed of any figurative element, itself becomes the subject and so enters the hermetic realm in which interpretation is possible. *Malerei im Malerei zu verlassen* (Painting to leave painting), a phrase of Rainer's own from the early fifties, has become the standard formulation in the interpretation of his work.

After the monochrome background paintings, Rainer began to produce his first overpaintings, covering his own works and then those of other artists with layers of paint, thus creating a new type of dialog with art history. By partially covering up and erasing the old he also accentuated significant details of what remained.

In 1956, Rainer started overpainting large crosses. The cross — a traditional motif, though an unusual one in modern art — became a central element in his work, as did his preoccupation with his own face, photographed in a grimace and worked over with aggressive brushstrokes. This working over, and also the direct painting of his body, allowed the exploration of the inner substance of being through artistic communication with his own body.

Rainer's self-portraits, executed as what he called *Face Farces*, finally led to an intensive preoccupation with the theme of death as a form of artistic self-questioning, using portraits of mummies and photographs of the death masks of celebrities which were then worked over.

OPPOSITE PAGE:
Arnulf Rainer
Cross I, 1988/89,
Oil, wood on board, 74 x 50 in
(186 x 124 cm)
Klosterneuburg, Essl Collection

ABOVE LEFT:
Arnulf Rainer
Centralisation, 1951
Oil on canvas, 41 x 40 in
(102 x 100 cm)
Klosterneuburg, Essl Collection

BELOW LEFT:
Arnulf Rainer
Angels buzz around the Artist,
1992
Oil-paint applied to wood,
80 x 49 in (200 x 122 cm)
Klosterneuburg, Essl Collection

BELOW:
Arnulf Rainer
Death mask of HI. Joseph von
Calasanz, 1978
Photograph, pastel, 24 x 18 in
(59 x 45 cm)
Museum Moderner Kunst
Stiftung Ludwig

Painting from 1945 to the Present Day

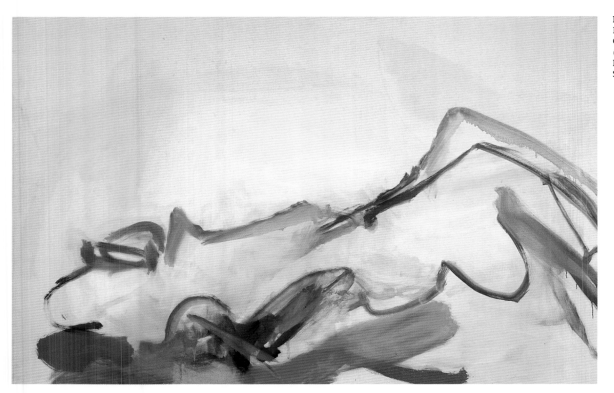

Maria Lassnig
Reclining Woman, 1961-62
Oil on canvas, 52 x 78 in
(130 x 195 cm)
Museum moderner Kunst,
Stiftung Ludwig

Maria Lassnig

Lassnig's works of the fifties are usually ascribed to Informal painting. If the works shown at the one-man show of 1952 at the *Art Club* still seem to be formally related to those of Arnulf Rainer, their esthetic aim and basic existential stance were really opposed to the Informal.

The *Statische Meditationsbilder* (Static Meditation Paintings) have associations to bodily forms. With pictures like *Etwas Masse im Raum* (Some Mass in Space, 1951) Lassnig soon found an individual form of expression in mass as a sensual bodily feeling, transposed into abstract pictorial language. In 1960, in Paris, where Lassnig spent more than ten years, the representation of her own bodily awareness and perception increasingly took center stage. "I was searching for a reality which would be more mine than the outside world, and so I came to the bodily shell that I inhabit. I had to become aware of it in order to be able to project and fix its imprint as a pattern of stresses in the picture plane."

The oil painting *Liegende* (Reclining Woman) belongs to the series of Parisian *Strichbilder* (Prostitution Paintings) of 1961. These emerged from authentic bodily feeling, as Lassnig strove to consciously experience the pressure on individual body parts as they are acted upon from outside, for example by the adoption of a particular posture, and to translate this tension into graphic language. Lassnig had found her subject: the self-portrait as a complex image of her relationship to the world (H. Weskott). As well as designating form, color gained an additional significance. According to Lassnig, in these paintings there are "pain-colors, torture-colors, thought-colors,

Maria Lassnig
Double Self-Portrait, 1974
Oil on canvas, 72 x 72 in
(180 x 180 cm)
Österreichische Galerie, Belvedere

crushing-colors, and bulging-colors." The body's limit was therefore not that visible from the outside, but was a line of force between inside and out.

In the 1970s, Lassnig painted her New York studio paintings which showed her dealing with the formal solutions of Pop Art, without absorbing their content. In these, Lassnig presented herself in ever new roles and characters. Compared to her previous abstract formal language, these pictures are realistic paintings, in which the white canvas is replaced by flat painted backgrounds. Against these, Lassnig created expressive paintings whose static figures, outside any everyday context, are used as illustrations of semantic associations. This is when Lassnig invented the expression "body awareness" for her work. In 1980, with VALIE EXPORT, she represented Austria at the Venice Biennale.

Hans Staudacher

Hans Staudacher is considered to be a loner on the Viennese art scene. He was neither a Nächst St. Stephan artist nor a member of the *Art Club*. What linked him to artists like Mikl or Hollegha was his abstraction and his admiration for the paintings of Georges Mathieu and Jackson Pollock. In this, however, he remained closest to the Informal Painting movement, extending its pictorial language through the inclusion of sculptural elements and legible symbols. Staudacher developed a "unique subjective pictorial style without parallel in Austria and still highly regarded in Parisian artists' circles to this day" (W. Skreiner).

Even in the immediate post-war years, the artist returned to Paris again and again. His paintings at that time still clearly refer to tangible objects and contain a generosity of design. The late Fifties found him with an intensified concern with form and a preoccupation with the *Lettrism* that was then current in Paris introduced a continuum of abstract signs.

Staudacher developed a visual alphabet freely inserted within dynamic, gestural painting. This was soon followed by the use of collage to integrate sentences, letters, or logos into the painting. His works are free-floating compositions in a completely open pictorial space. In spite of the impression of spontaneously placed brushstrokes, these are not accidental but rather subject to a long developmental process.

Since the 1980s, Staudacher's painting has been characterized by a minimal, almost delicate coloration. The lyrical element, however, always accompanies vigorous gesture, the delicate accord of a hand-written note alongside sweeping letters of the alphabet.

Hans Staudacher
Painted Feelings, 1988
Oil on canvas, 160 x 68 in (200 x 170 cm)
Klosterneuburg, Essl collection

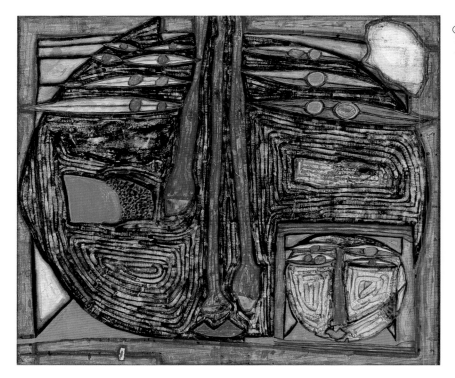

Friedensreich Hundertwasser
(477) The three-nose rivers, 1961
Mixed media on paper, mounted on
canvas, 18 x 21 in (46 x 53 cm)
Klosterneuburg, Essl Collection

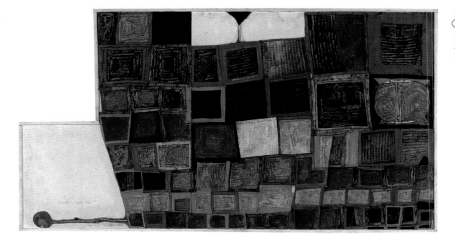

Friedensreich Hundertwasser
(176) Bus, 1953
Oil on plywood,
20 x 36 in (49 x 91 cm)
Klosterneuburg, Essl Collection

Friedensreich Hundertwasser
KunstHausWien, Vienna,
1989–1991, Interior

Friedensreich Hundertwasser

Since 1949, Friedrich Stowasser has used the name Hundertwasser (the word "sto" meaning a hundred in the Slavonic languages), under which he has become known far beyond Vienna.

At first Hundertwasser was thought to have something to do with the Vienna School of Fantastic Realists, but although he socialized with some of its members, in artistic terms this was not the case at all. His early work dealt with his impressions from numerous trips to Tunis, Morocco, and Italy; his formal language borrowed elements from the Secessionists and received a certain stimulus from the work of Paul Klee.

The urban environment was one of his main subjects even then. Pictures like Der Autobus (The Bus, 1953) are a good example. The theme becomes the starting point for an arrangement of blocks of color that form a modified geometric pattern. In this stylization, the bus loses any connection with its everyday context.

In 1953, Hundertwasser had great success with paintings like these in Paris, and his first Spiralbilder (Spiral Paintings), inspired by the spiral paintings of schizophrenic patients he had seen in a French documentary film, were created the same year. In Hundertwasser's work, the spiral became the symbol of everything organic and vegetative, at the same time expressing a demand for a new architectural principle that would eliminate the straight line.

Just as he stood for the abandonment of the geometric straight line, Hundertwasser fought fiercely in word and in art for architecture that is more oriented to people and nature, and for protecting the environment. Manifestos like Los von Loos (Away from Loos) of 1968, or Dein Fensterrecht — deine Baumpflicht (Your right to a window — your duty to trees), published in 1972, were offensives on behalf of an environment-friendly philosophy which he put into practice in the way he lived his own life in New Zealand.

Hundertwasser's paintings manifest an intense concern with color as material. To achieve the particular luminosity of his paintings, he never uses tubes of ready-mixed paint but returns to the techniques of the old masters: "This manufacturing process is of the utmost importance for the artist, for it is the starting-point," he says.

In 1981, Hunderwasser formulated his principles of architecture in harmony with nature in the text Farbe in der Architektur (Color in architecture). The artist was already working at the time on the Hundertwasser Haus project in the Löwenstrasse in Vienna. This "architectural physician" (as Hundertwasser called himself) also transformed the former Thonet furniture factory, which stands very near this house, in his own distinctive style; it opened as a museum in 1991.

Viennese Actionism

In some phases of their work, the Viennese Actionists shared with a number of painters close to them, such as Arnulf Rainer and Adolf Frohner, a certain idiosyncratic tendency toward abstraction. In the spirit of Rainer's dictum, "Painting to leave painting behind," the Actionists also sought the limits of painting precisely to revitalize or re-invent the greatest diversity of means of expression. From the start these included the artist's own body, an original contribution by the Viennese Actionists to international endeavors in this direction.

It is in the works of Hermann Nitsch, Günter Brus, Otto Mühl, and Rudolf Schwarzkogler in particular that one sees the emergence of an idea that is today synonymous with the *Wiener Actionismus*, though from the very outset, it was based on different conceptual considerations, which while enabling the move from painting to performance, gave rise to highly individual artistic statements. In 1962, Nitsch worked on a series of large paintings, the paint being applied by squeezing out a sponge at the top edge of the painting or by pouring it from a bucket onto a canvas flat on the floor, the composition emerging from the theatrical gesture.

That same year Nitsch, together with Mühl and Frohner, took the step into performance. The artists had themselves locked up for three days in Mühl's basement studio to paint together. Later, Nitsch used his own body as a surface, wearing a white shirt and having Mühl pour blood over him while he was tied to a cross. This "feast of psycho-physical

Naturalism," staged in 1963, is seen as the first piece of performance art, as it was performed before an audience. Further performance art sessions were planned, but even this first was prematurely halted by the intervention of the police. Mühl and Nitsch were then forced to come up with alternative models in which photography played a central role as the medium of documentation, but performance before an audience remained the most important feature during the whole Actionist phase.

During the 1960s, Mühl developed his "material actions", in which he made the human body a medium of expression alongside the other materials. He was the only one of the four Actionists to show an early interest in the possibilities of the cine-camera as a means of expression, and some of his performances were filmed by the Austrian filmmaker Kurt Kren. Unlike Nitsch, Mühl hardly ever appeared in these as a performer, but acted rather as the director of the action.

In 1966, the Viennese Actionists were invited to the "Destruction in Art" symposium in London, gaining attention for the first time as part of the international tendency represented by Fluxus and Happening Art. Inspired by this international break-through, they organized a series of events in which performance was now extended to include an element of socio-political critique. This reached its high point in the *Art and Revolution* event at Vienna University in 1968. Popular outrage led to prosecution and conviction. Mühl nevertheless remained in Vienna, and in order to continue the development of his material actions, he eventually founded a commune at Friedrichshof in the Burgenland as an alternative model for living.

Unlike Mühl and Nitsch, when Günter Brus and Rudolf Schwarzkogler executed their first performance pieces in 1965, it was without an audience, which is why photography was more important for them from the start, and for Schwarzkogler it would be so for the whole of his Actionist work.

Schwarzkogler constructed photomontages from black-and-white photographs documenting the event, tying these to the actual theatrical artwork to form a complete entity. His photo series were often created at "action sessions" organized specifically for the photographer. In 1969, the artist died as the result of a fall from the window of his apartment.

Unlike Schwarzkogler, whose work exhibited these parallel processes, Brus perceived the act of the performance as an end in itself, despite the calculated introduction of photography. His *Selbstverstümmelung* (Self-mutilation) performance of 1965 is a high point in Viennese

Actionism. Like Nitsch, Brus broadened the possibilities of the medium by using his own body, on which he placed drawing-pins, razor blades, and other sharp everyday objects. White paint was applied to these with a palette knife, transforming him into a white canvas. In the *Wiener Spaziergang* (Viennese stroll), also created in 1965, he broke up his monochromatically painted body (clothed, as in the illustration) with a black jagged line and walked through the city like this until he was arrested by the police. Brus' actions went beyond the limits of painting and broadened the general concept of a "work

of art" as hitherto understood to include its idea and concept. After his conviction in 1968, Brus fled to Berlin, concluding his Actionist phase with the Acid Test happening in Munich. This was followed by a return to the traditional medium of drawing in the picture-poetry which he continues to create. The *Selbstumkehrung* (self-reversal) of 1988 is an example of his colored pencil drawings, which combine surreal and decorative elements. In Brus' words, "Picture-poetry is the ideal form for me, because the unthinking drawing process is interrupted and counteracted by thoughtful writing."

Hermann Nitsch
Pour-Painting, 1990
Oil on canvas, 160 x 240 in
(200 x 300 cm)
Klosterneuburg, Essl Collection

Whilst for Brus and Mühl the end of the 1960s saw a transformation in the formal possibilities of Actionism, Nitsch implemented a logical extension of the principle of his early actions, characterized by their extensive symbolic content, to organize and create a "theater of orgies and mysteries". The events he has organized since 1973 at Schloss Prinzendorf in Lower Austria are concerned with bringing about a dynamic estheticisation of life with all its destructive and reconstructive force, taking the mythological Dionysus as their theme.

Symbols, such as the painter's smock, also took on a central importance after the blood-painting action: "My great admiration for Klimt and my conviction that the production of art is a priestly activity led me as early as 1960 to put on a simply-cut, almost monastic smock for my painting performances. Later, the wearing of this smock took on even deeper significance when the Theater of Orgies and Mysteries came to deal with relics." The smock, Nitsch continues, is hung on the painting as the most precious jewel and trophy, enriching its composition.

In 1998, he put on his biggest event ever in the context of the Theater of Orgies and Mysteries at Schloss Prinzendorf.

Günter Brus
Self-Reversal, 1988
Pastel on card, 40 x 28 in
(99.5 x 70.5 cm)
Klosterneuburg, Essl Collection

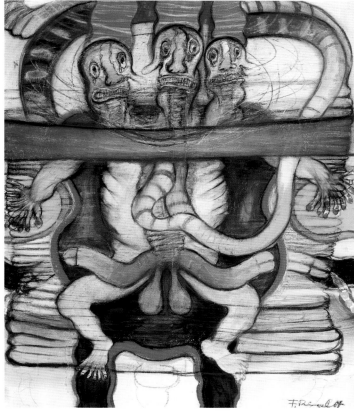

Franz Ringel
Manipulated Woman, 1979
Mixed media on paper, mounted
on board,
60 x 48 in (150 x 120 cm)
Österreichische Galerie, Belvedere

Franz Ringel

Of the artists of the *Wirklichkeiten* (Realities) group Franz Ringel is certainly the most radical. He attended Gütersloh's masterclass at the Akademie der Bildenden Künste, and his painting is characteristic of the work of the generation that emerged after the first wave of Tachism and Informal painting had passed. Ringel sticks to the artist's canvas and to painting, though he is no traditionalist. "I am a respectable painter," he wrote in 1969, only to note right away, "In my case the art work is certainly the product of a total loss of inhibition."

His painting is no search for an esthetic concept by the development a theme through a lengthy working process. His drastic realism transforms individually interpreted reality in a gestural and expressive act of painting, characterized by an intense, almost euphoric coloration. His paintings are oppressively forceful. His deliberately *Verhässlichten* (uglified) creatures, part-Punch and Judy puppets, part-worm, part-human being, are placed in front of the white canvas. They have abnormally elongated limbs, feeding tubes, and monstrous heads. Otto Breicha wrote of Ringel's paintings: "He tracks the metabolism and the paths through the body, the most inward is turned outward:

muzzle-flash at eye level." This last phrase comes the title of one of the paintings.

Since then Ringel has concerned himself with great themes, with death, or with the journeys of mythological heroes such as Orpheus or Homer's Odysseus, and he has worked a great deal on Elias Canetti's *Masse und Macht* (Masses and Power). His paintings have become more reflective. The explosive linear tangles of his earlier paintings start to consolidate, and the movement of the figures becomes stabilized on the surface. The tubular beings gain in strength; the massive bodies support small, distorted heads, sometimes with horrified, wide-open eyes. The head becomes the focus of expressive force, in which the ugliness of deformity always conflicts with the coloration of the painting. Ringel's own fears and anxieties become creatures on the canvas.

As Breicha said of him in the 1970s, Ringel does not paint to create something he wishes for, but to be rid of something. Bunches of fingers vibrate, three heads rise up, medusa-like, from the body. But these are not the aggressor, for they themselves bear the horror of the world on their distorted faces. A bar across the shared body forces them back into the seat, condemning them to remain where they are.

Franz Ringel
Triplets, 1967
Oil on canvas, 64 x 54 in
(160 x 134 cm)
Klosterneuburg, Essl Collection

The New Media

The "Intermedia" movement that ran in parallel with Viennese Actionism in the 1960s brought together a group of artists from different fields, such as the writers around Oswald Wiener, later to become known as the *Wiener Gruppe* (Viennese group), and the experimental film-makers Kurt Kren and Peter Kubelka. The young media artists VALIE EXPORT and Peter Weibel emerged a little later. They shared an approach based on media theory, and were part of the general reaction on the European art scene to early forms of media art in the USA.

One of the most important things they tried to do was to work in an interdisciplinary fashion, to liberate the various artistic orientations from their static postures, and bring them into dialog with each other, as VALIE EXPORT put it. If, at the start, they still shared some common ground with Viennese Actionism, the emphasis very quickly shifted from an expressive vocabulary that dealt in apparent self-mutilation toward a conceptual approach put into effect through the use of new technologies.

VALIE EXPORT was one of the pioneers of media art in the 1960s. She became interested very early on in photography, film, and color transparencies as autonomous means of expression. She was particularly interested in the space-and-time aspects of photography and in the possibilities of combining this medium with the semantics of language. That is why she called her work "photo-literature". A very clear example of this is her series of photographic works, which, like *Space-Jump* (1971), combine the lapse of time with linguistic expression. The balconied façade is not photographed frontally from a vantage point opposite, but vertically from above.

VALIE EXPORT
Space Jump, 1971, conceptual photograph

VALIE EXPORT
Wirbelsäulenflöte
Body-Configuration, 1982, photograph

Her *Körperkonfigurationen* (Body Configurations) series of 1972 is an important early example of work with photography, in which EXPORT combines geometric architectural features with bodily attitudes. EXPORT also called this work the "visible externalization of internal states," by which she meant a way of coming out of oneself, not seeing oneself as being a kind of external visual interlocutor to architecture, but rather as transcribing its structure in the body.

VALIE EXPORT always introduced a political dimension in her work, and her performances were responses to the cultural and political system in Austria at that time. In her actions, she used the body as an independent medium of expression, and coined the expression *feministisch Aktionismus* (feminist actionism). Some of her actions in the 1960s were performed jointly with Peter Weibel. Both artists at first met fierce public criticism, although they quickly established themselves at the international level.

Since then, EXPORT has had a great influence on the development of media art through her teaching (she is now a professor at the Hochschule für Medien in Cologne) and her writings on art theory. In the case of both artists, film was the medium of their earliest experimental work. In 1998, VALIE EXPORT received the Austrian prize for achievement in art photography. Peter Weibel became director of the Institut für Neue Medien in 1989 and has been curator of the Austrian Pavilion at the Venice Biennale since 1993.

Peter Weibel
Tortured Square, 1976
Iron, glass, rubber
Exhibition at Ludwig Museum, Budapest, 1996

VALIE EXPORT, Self-Portrait, 1970, Photograph, Stiftung Ludwig

Günter Damisch
Bright World-Field, 1988
Oil on canvas, 100 x 100 in
(250 x 250 cm)
Essl Collection,
Klosterneuburg/Vienna

Painting in the 1980s and 1990s

"In my first year as a student in Vienna in 1954 I secretly went to Boeckl's evening life classes. Although I was studying under Gütersloh, I felt at home in Boeckl's class. In all my four years as a student I tried never to miss this evening class. It replaced cinema, social life, and dinner." This is how Kiki Kogelnik described her time at the Akademie. Kogelnik, born in Carinthia, was part of a generation of Austrian artists who pursued abstractionism, and this is how she started too, first with large canvases on which she placed rings and circles with energetic brushstrokes. She was one of the group around Prachensky and Mikl, and was briefly engaged to Arnulf Rainer. During a stay in Paris she met the American artist Sam Francis and moved to New York at the beginning of the 1960s, subsequently commuting between Vienna, Carinthia and New York.

Reacting to the all-pervasive Abstract Expressionism of the USA, and influenced by the Pop Art that was emerging in New York, Kogelnik developed her own figurative language. The colors are gaudy, the figures impressed onto the surface — she would often "print" them from blocks. Her work from now on would be characterized by reduction and stylization, the mask, a head stripped down to the bare minimum, becoming a central motif that would preoccupy her throughout her life and become the trademark of her later work, appearing in paintings such as *Display* (1989), in her ceramics, and in the famous *Venetian Heads* of Murano glass. These heads can be interpreted as self-portraits, but in their expressive range they go far beyond this, becoming general symbols of human existence.

Sculpture and painting were always closely linked in Kogelnik's work, and her perfectionism led to her taking up traditional craft techniques once more. In the late 1980s, the heads became emblems of a laughing *danse macabre*. Kogelnik died in Vienna in 1997.

The 1980s saw a renaissance in painting. Claiming to be producing "simply good paintings," a young generation came to public attention whose work was characterized by the unhampered exploitation of painterly resources. Their large canvasses declared their faith in traditional painting, without, however, falling into an outdated academicism. Concepts of esthetic form and content were questioned and harmonious composition not even attempted.

The Austrian painters described as the *Neue Wilde* were promoted in particular by the Ariadne, Pakesch, and Krinzinger galleries in Vienna, and were presented to an international

Kiki Kogelnik
Display, 1989
Oil, acrylic on canvas, 45 x 41 in
(112 x 102 cm)
Essl Collection,
Klosterneuburg/Vienna

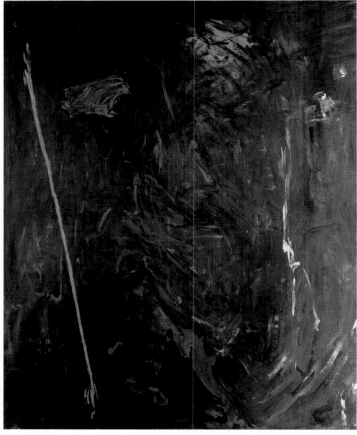

Siegfried Anzinger
Horses, 1982
Acrylic on viscose, 78 x 58 in
(195 x 145 cm)
Museum moderner Kunst
Stiftung Ludwig

public at various art fairs. Gunter Damisch, born in Upper Austria, studied with Arnulf Rainer at the Akademie in Vienna. Compared to the colorful paintings typical of his early work, the large-scale work of the late 1980s is dominated by a reductive simplicity of form and color. Narrative, figurative themes gave way to a few generally amoeba-like objects which float into the picture from outside. Titles like *Weltenbilder* (World Painting) or *Helles Weltenfeld* (Bright World Field) refer one immediately to a intellectual form of pictorial comprehension. The bright color fields have become denser through several overpaintings and radiate particles from the different layers of color. Like geological strata, the picture is made up of layers, which in the end do not all reach the surface. Compared to the rapidly laid-down brushstrokes of the early 1980s the effort at painterly intensification now becomes the most significant factor.

Siegfried Anzinger is considered to be the chief representative of this new painting in

Hubert Scheibl
Untitled, 1983
Acrylic on canvas, 199 x 80 in
(251 x 200 cm)
Klosterneuburg, Essl Collection

Gottfried Helnwein
Self-Portrait, 1983
Watercolor and acrylic on paper,
84 x 60 in (210 x 150 cm)
Klosterneuburg, Essl Collection

OPPOSITE PAGE:
Christian Ludwig Attersee
Weather-Trader, 1996
Two million hand-broken pieces of
Murano glass
63 sq. ft (210 m2)
78–80, Mariahilfer Strasse,
Vienna

Austria. Until the mid-1980s, his paintings were dominated by the expressive style of the gestural brushstroke, and the principal motifs are tragic, isolated individuals, treated with great pathos. The *Rotes Bild* (Red Painting, 1982), created with rapid, broad brushstrokes, is a good example. First drafts are often overpainted. The figure is placed against a strongly colored surface, the figurative element not yet being totally dissolved into the painted background. It is still intended as a discrete form, and motif and painting stand alongside each other as equals.

At a time when many painters were turning to abstraction or the new media, Anzinger chose a path between abstraction and figurativeness. From one series of paintings to the next, Anzinger developed his own painterly vocabulary in a context marked by what might be called *Herbststimmung* (Fall mood). After its early triumphs, figurative painting was once again being called into question and attacked. "You had to know exactly what you really wanted, if you wanted to continue along this subjective path," says Anzinger, who remains interested in the physical and emotional aspects of his painting, even if he has abandoned narrative excess. For him, figurative painting is, and has to be, more than just a pretty picture on the wall.

Anzinger's painterly interests become explosively manifest in the *Madonnenbildern* (Madonna paintings) and in the portraits he painted in the second half of the 1990s. Anzinger himself coined the term *versenkte Malerei* (sunken painting) for his work, in which the subject is merged with the painted background, a few details such as hints of color or the position of the sitter being sufficient to establish the spatial situation.

Like Anzinger's work, Hubert Scheibl's paintings of the early 1980s were also characterized by a broad, gestural application of color which covered the background with dense brushstrokes, in which the figurative starting point is perceptible only by association. The works he painted in the mid-1980s show a distinct tendency toward monochrome, and from then on his pictures, like those of his colleagues, Anzinger, Bohatsch, and Damisch, became calmer. Relief-like impasto was succeeded by large canvases in flat colors. The original painterly approach, the interaction of light and color, survives, but this is supplemented by a new intensity of content, which clearly owes much to meditative tendencies. Scheibl usually arranges his paintings as diptychs or in groups of three in which metallic surfaces contrast with painted or monochrome

canvases juxtaposed with more eventful and expressive painting.

Hubert Schmalix has been a professor at the Akademie der Bildenden Künste in Vienna since 1986, and since 1987 has divided his time between his studio in Vienna and his studio in Los Angeles. His painting declares his belief in figuration. Even if Schmalix has left behind his "wild beginnings," his paintings of the 1990s remain linked to his early work in their various areas of subject-matter.

Schmalix uses signal-like primary colors, often contrasted with a strict composition along architectural lines. In the 1990s, his painting was dominated by a confrontation with the representation of Christ, begun in 1987, which achieves its highest intensity in the *Alphaomega Paintings*.

Herbert Brandl studied in Vienna under Peter Weibl, at the Hochschule für Angewandte Kunst. Like Scheibl, he generally assembles his paintings into groups. His starting point is the landscape, but his heavy impasto is not intended so much to imitate nature as to represent the atmospheric, the workings of the forces of nature, and the mood created by wind and weather, yet without falling into a lyrical-poetic pictorial language. That type of landscape painting is now only thinkable as a painting that negates the landscape, because he has come to understand its essential features, requiring a reduction of the object to its essential, most generi, basic form.

In the late 1980s, Brandl produced paintings jointly with Gerwald Rockenschaub and Franz West. Today, West is one of the most important object artists at the international level. His first works in the 1970s were photo-collages, in which he mounted different clichéd images on a two-dimensional medium. West then developed a critique of Viennese Actionism, believing that the "events" maintained spectators in passivity. This led to the idea of the "usable" artwork. These were first made of plaster-like polyester and later of aluminum, and were shaped to the body.

With the idea of the usable object, West went beyond the limits of the classical concept of sculpture, turning against an interaction with art that was no more than "passive perception based on clichéd associations." Here, the sculptures act as catalysts for processes of movement that take the user as well as the artist into another reality. These first "adapted pieces" were forerunners of the artist's tables and furniture for sitting and lying upon. These invite use, yet remain objects in their materiality and bulk.

In the 1990s, West merged such furniture into large-scale installations, for example the seats covered in African fabrics at Documenta X in Kassel and the *Telephonskulpturen* (Telephone Sculptures) for the Carnegie Institute in Pittsburgh. West's art is always an invitation to use and is thus appropriately presented, that is to say, as furniture. It is only after the fact that the

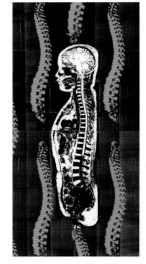

viewer perceives it as a work of art. As the artist says: "If they sit down on it, they are sitting in the middle of art."

In addition to West, there were others, like Gerwald Rockenschaub, Franz Graf, Brigitte Kowanz, Ernst Caramelle and Heimo Zobernig, who extended classical sculpture and painting through the inclusion of such elements as time, space, sound, light, and language. In using new media, such as video and computers, they continued the developments initiated in the 1960s by Peter Weibel and VALIE EXPORT.

In Brigitte Kowanz's light installations, the work of art is no longer present as formed material. The works are neither sculptures in the classical sense nor paintings on two-dimensional media. Light itself becomes the instrument of a technique of artistic creation which always includes a spatial element, through the configurations of shadow which are created. The light source itself is presented as the object, but at the same time creates a non-material spatial organization through the way the light is designed to fall.

Peter Kogler works in the area of combined media, adopting the computer as a medium after his graphic and sculptural works of the early 1980s. The digital images he creates in this manner are printed on various media, as large format computer graphics on paper, or as silk-screen prints on colored canvas. Using the computer's binary system Kogler develops both figurative motifs and abstract signs. These elements range from the already legendary *Ameise* (Ant) to techno labyrinths of

branching tubular forms or brain-like convolutions. These types of element are frequently combined, and they may be printed on fabric. In his designs for curtains and wallpaper, Kogler uses conventional spatial arrangements and plays with traditional models of interior decoration and design, only to strip them of their functionality and decorative character, turning them into autonomous works of art through the intervention of his digitally generated universe of themes and patterns.

Kogler has for a long time been prominent on the international art scene, his large-scale installations with wallpaper modules at Dokumenta X in Kassel generating a great deal of critical attention in 1997. Kogler may set up his modules either in already-existing spaces or in spaces specially constructed for the purpose, linking his work to the idea of the *Environment*.

Hubert Schmalix
Alphaomega V, 1993
Oil on canvas, 69 x 53 in
(172 x 132 cm)
Klosterneuburg, Essl Collection

Herbert Brandl
Untitled, 1992-93
Oil on canvas, 64 x 64 in
(160 x 160 cm)
Klosterneuburg, Essl Collection

Modern sculpture in public spaces

The idea of transferring the art object into public space was developed in Britain in the 1940s. Art in the urban space was, and always is, a compromise between the built environment and the modern idea of the autonomous artwork, and sculpture for Viennese public housing projects of the 1950s generally offered rather backward, "harmonious" solutions to this tension.

The sculpture by the British artist Henry Moore erected in front of the Karlskirche church was the first of a series of commissions awarded to contemporary artists of international stature. By piercing the self-enclosed figure, Moore deliberately created a relationship between sculptural mass and space through tectonic structuring and integration. Another modern accent is provided by the sculpture by Philip Johnson, erected in September, 1998. In the *Viennese Trio* (ill. page 440) the city has an expressive late work by the internationally renowned American architect, which stands on the border of art and architecture, again articulating the tensions of art in public space, which steps beyond its inherent artistic nature to enter the concrete social praxis of everyday life.

Sculpture is thus, simultaneously, an architectural detail on the Schottenring, a monument at the end of the Wiener Ringstrasse, as well as an expression of artistic interest by a large Viennese insurance company, which has a sculpture standing in front of its headquarters in the Ringturm Tower. It was the financial backing of the insurance company for the project that enabled *Viennese Trio* to be erected, in collaboration with the Museum für Angewandte Kunst. Formally, this work marks a surprising foray into sculpture by a nonagenarian architect, who made his mark on New York's cityscape with the Trump Tower and the AT & T building amongst others, reflecting Johnson's long-standing fascination with the monumental and with the link between architecture and the fine arts.

Public art in Vienna has been strongly influenced by the city's history, as witnessed by Hrdlicka's memorial on the Albertinaplatz or Rachel Whiteread's long-discussed monument to the Holocaust now planned for the Judenplatz, and such art gives rise to arguments that go well beyond debate on esthetic questions.

In late twentieth century city building projects, art has also been integrated with architecture, often giving younger artists their first chance to present their works in a broader context. Examples of this development are *Nike* by Thomas Hoke, born in 1958, and the extension of the U3 subway line, whose stations have been decorated by contemporary Austrian artists.

OPPOSITE PAGE ABOVE:
Hubert Schmalix
The Father Shows the Child
the Way , 1996
Sculpture in gray concrete and cast
blue concrete, h. 124 in
(310 cm),
plinth (40 cm)

BELOW:
Donald Judd
Stage Set, 1991
Steel, fabric, 3 x 25 x 40 ft
(10 x 7.5 x 12.5 m)
Wiener Stadtpark, 1996

RIGHT:
Thomas Hoke
Nike, 1995
Steel, sheet metal
Max. h. 280 in (700 cm)
Karlsplatz, in front of the
Kunsthalle, Vienna

ILLUSTRATION P. 440:
Philip Johnson
Viennese Trio, 1996
Max. h. 20 ft (6 m)
Polyester resin, plywood construc-
tion, fibreglass, Franz-Josefs-Kai/
Schottenring, Vienna

Appendix

Bibliography

EHRENFRIED KLUCKERT
Art and Architecture from the Antiquity to the Renaissance and Art and Architecture in the Seventeenth and Eighteenth Centuries. Baroque and Rococo.

Alewyn, R./Sälzle, K.: Das grosse Welt-theater. Die Epoche der höfischen Feste, Munich 1989
Anon, St. Stephen's in Vienna, Cathedral and Metropolitan Church, Schell, Regensburg, 1998
Aurenhammer, H.: Johann Bernhard Fischer von Erlach, London 1973
Baldass, P. von/Buchowiecki, W./Mrazek, W.: Romanische Kunst in Österreich, Vienna 1962
Brook, Stephen: Eye Witness Guide, Vienna, London 1998
Brucher, G.: Barockarchitektur in Österreich, Cologne 1983
Coudenhove, G.: Die Wiener Pestsäule, Vienna 1958
Czeike, F.: Geschichte der Stadt Wien, Vienna 1983
Donin, R. K.: Venedig und die Baukunst von Wien und Niederösterreich, Vienna 1983
Dworschak, F.:/Kühnel, H. (ed.): Die Gotik in Niederösterreich, Vienna 1963
Ernst, R./Garger, E.: Die früh- und hochgotische Plastik des Stephansdoms, Munich 1972
Feuchtmüller, R.: Der Wiener Stephansdom, Vienna 1978
Fillitz, H.: Die Schatzkammer in Wien, Vienna/Munich 1964
Georg Raphael Donner 1693–1741, Exhibition catalog: Österreichische Galerie Belvedere, Vienna 1993
Ginhart, K.: Die Fürstenstatuen von St. Stephan in Wien und die Bildwerke aus Grosslobming, Klagenfurt 1972
Grimschitz, B.: Johann Lukas von Hildebrandt, Vienna 1959
Hajós, B.: Die Schönbrunner Schlossgärten, Vienna/Köln/Weimar 1995
Hempel, E.: Baroque Art and Architecture in Central Europe, Bungay 1965
Kleiner, S.: Das Belvedere zu Wien, Dortmund 1980
Koepf, H.: Die gotischen Planrisse der Wiener Sammlungen, Vienna 1986
Kraus, W.:/Müller, P.: Wiener Palais, Munich 1991
Leitisch, A. T.: Vienna Gloriosa. Weltstadt des Barock, Vienna 1963
Loidl, F.: Geschichte des Erzbistums Wien, Munich 1983
Lorenz, H.: Johann Bernhard Fischer von Erlach, Zürich 1992
Ludwig, V. O.: Klosterneuburg, Vienna 1951
Oettinger, K.: Das Werden Wiens, Vienna 1951
Oppl, F.: Nachrichten aus dem mittelalterlichen Wien, Vienna 1995
Polleross, F. (ed.): Fischer von Erlach und die Wiener Barocktradition, Vienna 1995
Praschl-Bichler, G.: Wien. Architektur des Barock, Vienna 1990
Rapf, P. C.: Das Wiener Schottenstift zur Babenberger Zeit. In: 1000 Jahre Babenberger in Österreich, Stift Lilienfeld, Vienna 1976, 301–305
Raschauer, O.: Schönbrunn. Der Schlossbau Kaiser Josephs I., Vienna 1960
Sedlmayr, H.: Johann Bernhard Fischer von

Erlach, Munich 1956
Stephan, P.: "Ruinam praecedit superbia". Der Sieg der Virtus über die Hybris in den Bildprogrammen des Prinzen Eugen von Savoyen. In: Belvedere 1, 97, 62–87
Tietze, H.: Alt-Wien in Wort und Bild. Vom Ausgang des Mittelalters bis zum Ende des 18. Jahrhunderts, Vienna 1924
Timmermann, B.: Die Begräbnisstätten der Habsburger in Wien, Vienna 1996
Zöllner, E.: Wien zur Zeit der Babenberger. In: 1000 Jahre Babenberger in Österreich, Stift Lilienfeld, Vienna 1976, 296–300.

PETER PLASSMEYER
Architecture in the Nineteenth Century. From Classicism to the Ringstrasse Era

Benjamin, W.: Reflections: Essays, Aphorisms, Autobiographical Writings. New York: Harcourt Brace Jovanovich, 1978.
Bösel, R./Benedikt, C.: Der Michaelerplatz. Seine städtebauliche und architektonische Entwicklung, Vienna 1991
Bürgersinn und Aufbegehren. Biedermeier und Vormärz in Wien. 1815–1848, Exhibition catalog, Vienna 1987
Das Zeitalter Kaiser Franz Josephs, 1. Teil, 1848–1880, Von der Revolution zur Gründerzeit,Exhibition catalogue Schloss Grafenegg, Vienna 1984, 2 Bde.
Das Zeitalter Kaiser Franz Josephs, 2. Teil, 1880–1916, Glanz und Elend, Exhibition catalog Schloss Grafenegg, Vienna 1987, 2 Bde.
Boyer, John W.: Political Radicalism in Late Imperial Vienna. Chicago: University of Chicago Press, 1981.
Crankshaw, E.: The Fall of the House of Habsburg. New York: Penguin, 1983.
Hoffmann, H.-C.: Die Theaterbauten von Fellner und Helmer, Munich 1966
Im Schatten der Weilburg: Baden im Biedermeier, Exhibition catalog, Baden 1988
Janik, A./Toulmin, S.: Wittgenstein's Vienna. New York: Simon/Schuster, 1973.
Jenni, U.: Theophil Hansen. Entwürfe zur Akademie der Bildenden Künste in Wien, Vienna 1985
Johnston, William M.: The Austrian Mind: An Intellectual and Social History, 1848-1938. Berkeley, Los Angeles, and London: University of California Press, 1972.
Keller, H.: Die Kunst des 18. Jahrhunderts (Propyläen Kunstgeschichte),Frankfurt/Main,/Berlin 1990
Kräftner, J.: Joseph Kornhäusel. Ein vergessener Biedermeierarchitekt. In: Parnass 3, 1987, 48–67
Kraus, K.: The Last Days of Mankind by Karl Kraus. Edited buy Frederik Ungar. New York: Ungar, 1974.
Kraus, K.: In These Great Times. Edited by Harry Zohn. Manchester: Carcanet Press, 1976.
Kraus, K.: No Compromise: Selected Writings of Karl Kraus. Edited by Frederik Ungar. New York: Ungar, 1977.
Kraus, W./Müller, P.: Wiener Palais, Vienna 1991
Kriller, B./Kugler, G.: Das Kunsthistorische Museum. Die Architektur und Ausstattung. Idee und Wirklichkeit des Gesamtkunstwerkes, Vienna 1991
Luft, D. S.: Robert Musil and the Crisis of European Culture, 1880-1942. Berkeley, Los

Angeles, and London: University of California Press, 1980.
McGrath, W. J.: Dionysian Art and Populist Politics in Austria. New Haven and London: Yale University Press, 1974.
Musil, R.: The Man Without Qualities. Translated by Eithne Wilkins and Ernst Kaiser. New York: Perigee, 1980.
Nielsen, E.(ed.): Focus on Vienna 1900: Change and Continuity in Literature, Music, Art and Intellectual History. Houston German Studies, no. 4. Munich: W. Fink, 1982.
Olsen, D. J.: The City as a Work of Art–London, Paris, Vienna, Newhaven 1986
Austria during the period of emperor Franz Joseph II., Regent of Empress Maria Theresia, Sovereign and Ruler, exhibition catalog of the Melk Diocese, Vienna 1980
Pascal, R.: From Naturalism to Expression. Expressionism: German Literature and Society, 1880-1918. New York: Basic Books, 1973.
Plassmeyer, P.: Die Wiener Fernbahnhöfe des 19. Jahrhunderts. Architektur zwischen ökonomischem Zwang und bürgerlicher Selbstdarstellung, phil. Diss., Marburg a.d. Lahn 1990
Revolutionary Architecture. An aspect of European Architecture at about 1800, Exhibition catalog, Munich 1990
Roschitz, K.: Vom Glanz des Wiener Lebens. Die Wiener Weltausstellung 1973. In: Parnass 5, 1989, 52–58
Rozenblit, M. L. The Jews of Vienna, 1867-1914: Assimilation and Identity. Albany, N.Y.: State University of New York Press, 1983.
Schild, E.: Zwischen Glaspalast und Palais des Illusions. Form und Konstruktion im 19. Jahrhundert, Braunschweig/Wiesbaden 1983 (2nd edition)
Traum und Wirklichkeit. Wien 1870–1930, (Exhibition catalog) Vienna 1985
Schmidt, J,/Tietze, H.: Dehio-Handbuch. Die Kunstdenkmäler Österreichs: Wien, Vienna/Munich 1973 (6. edition)
Der Traum vom Glück. Die Kunst des Historismus in Europa, Exhibition catalog, Vienna 1997
Elisabeth von Oesterreich. Einsamkeit, Macht und Freiheit, Exhibition catalog, Vienna 1987
Freiheit, Gleichheit, Brüderlichkeit auch in Österreich. Auswirkungen der Französischen Revolution auf Wien und Tirol, Exhibition catalog, Vienna 1989
Schorske, C. E.: Fin-de-Siècle Vienna: Politics and Culture. New York: Basic Books, 1973.
Shedel, J.: Art and Society: The New Art Movement in Vienna, 1897-1914. Palo-Alto, Calif.: Society for the Promotion of Science, 1981.
Wagner-Rieger, R.: Wiens Architektur im 19. Jahrhundert, Vienna 1970
Wagner-Rieger, R.: Vom Klassizismus bis zur Sezession. In: Geschichte der bildenden Kunst in Wien, Band 7, Vienna 1973
Wagner-Rieger, R./Reissberger, M.: Wien 1850–1930. Photography by Roberto Schezen, Text by Peter Haiko, Vienna 1992.
Werfel, A. M.: And the Bridge Is Love. New York: Harcourt, Brace, 1958
Wiribal, N./Mikula, R.: Heinrich von Ferstel, Wiesbaden 1974
Zeitler, R.: Die Kunst des 19. Jahrhunderts (Propyläen Kunstgeschichte), Frankfurt/Main/Berlin 1990

Zweig, S.: The World of Yesterday: An Autobiography. New York: Viking, 1943; reprint, Lincoln, Nebraska, University of Nebraska Press, 1964

SABINE GRABNER
Paintings and sculptures of the Nineteenth Century 1790–1890

Aurenhammer, H.: Anton Dominik Fernkorn, Vienna 1959
Becker, E./Grabner, S. (ed.): Wien 1900. Der Blick nach innen, Van Gogh-Museum Amsterdam, Von der Heydt-Museum Wuppertal, Zwolle 1997
Billcliffe, R./Vergo, P.: Charles Rennie Mackintosh and the Austrian Art Revival. The Burlington Magazine (London), 119 (November 1977), pp. 779-44.
Birke, V.: Josef Danhauser (1805–1845). Gemälde und Zeichnungen, Vienna 1993
Bisanz, H./Krapf, M.: Johann Evangelist Scheffer von Leonhardshoff, Österreichische Galerie Belvedere und Historisches Museum der Stadt Wien, Vienna 1977
Bürgersinn und Aufbegehren. Biedermeier und Vormärz in Wien 1815–1848, Historisches Museum der Stadt Wien, Vienna 1988
Bilder des Lebens. Johann Baptist Reiter und der Realismus des 19. Jahrhunderts, Museum Francisco Carolinum, Linz 1990
Braunegger, T./Hörmann-Weingartner, M.: Theodor von Hörmann, Vienna 1979
Buchowiecki, W.: Geschichte der Malerei in Wien. In: Geschichte der bildenden Kunst in Wien, Vienna 1955
Burg, H.: Der Bildhauer Franz Anton Zauner und seine Zeit. Ein Beitrag zum Klassizismus in Österreich, Vienna 1915
Chipp, H. B.: Viennese Expressionism, 1910-1924 (exhibition catalogue). Berkeley: University Art Gallery, University of California, 1963
Comini, A.: From Façade to Psyche: The Persistence and Transformation of Portraiture in Fin-de-Siècle Vienna. In Tobor Horvath, ed. Evolution générale et développements regionaux en histoire de l'art. Acts of the Twenty-second International Congress of Art Historians, 1969, Budapest. 1972.
Comini, A.: Vampires, Virgins and Voyeurs in Imperial Vienna. In Thomas B. Hess and Linda Nochlin, eds. Women as Sex Objects. Art News Annual 38. New York: Macmillan, 1972
Comini, A.: The Fantastic Art of Vienna. New York: Knopf, 1978
Dreger, M.: Josef Führich, Vienna, 1912
Exhibition catalog:
Romantic and Realism styles in Austria. Paintings and sketches from the Schäfer Schweinfurt collection, Schloss Laxenburg 1968
Feuchtmüller, R.: Leopold Kupelwieser und die Kunst der österreichischen Spätromantik, Vienna 1970
Feuchtmüller, R.: Friedrich Gauermann, Vienna 1962
Feuchtmüller, R.: Ferdinand Georg Waldmüller, Vienna 1987
Fillitz, H. (ed.): Der Traum vom Glück. Die Kunst des Historismus in Europa, Künstlerhaus und Akademie der bildenden

Künste in Wien, Vienna 1996
Frodl, G.: Der Aussenseiter Anton Romako 1832–1889. Ein Maler der Ringstrassenzeit, Österreichische Galerie Belvedere, Vienna 1992
Wiener Biedermeier. Malerei zwischen Wiener Kongress und Revolution, Kunstforum Wien, Munich 1993
Hans Makart. Monographie und Werkverzeichnis. Mit einem Beitrag von Renata Mikula, Salzburg 1974
Frodl, D.: Wiener Malerei der Biedermeierzeit, Rosenheim 1987
Frodel-Schneemann, M.: Johann PeterKrafft 1780–1856, Vienna/Munich 1984
Fuchs, H.: Emil Jakob Schindler. Zeugnisse eines ungewöhnlichen Künstlerlebens, Vienna 1970
Giese, H.: Franz von Matsch. Leben und Werk 1861–1942, unprinted, Vienna 1976
Grabner, S.: Ferdinand Georg Waldmüller, Museum Carolino Augusteum Salzburg und Tiroler Landesmuseum Ferdinandeum, Salzburg 1993
Grimschitz, B.: Österreichische Maler vom Biedermeier zur Moderne, Vienna 1963
Grimschitz, B.: Ferdinand Georg Waldmüller, Salzburg 1957
Gurlitt, C.: Die deutsche Kunst des Neunzehnten Jahrhunderts. Ihre Ziele und Thaten, Berlin 1899
Hevesi, L.: Österreichische Kunst im 19. Jahrhundert, Leipzig 1903
Hoffmann, H.-C./Krause, W./Kapner, G.: Ringstrassendenkmäler, Wiesbaden 1973
Holsten, S.: Moritz von Schwind. Meister der Spätromantik, Staatliche Kunsthalle Karlsruhe und Museum der bildenden KünsteLeipzig, Ostfildern-Ruit 1997
Kallir, J.: Austria's Expressionism (exhibition catalogue). New York: Galerie St. Etienne; Rizzoli, 1981
Kapner, G: Ringstraßendenkmäler, Wiesbaden 1973
Kitlitschka, W.: Das Wiener Opernhaus, Wiesbaden 1972
Die Malerei der Wiener Ringstrasse, Wiesbaden 1981
Koschatzky, W.: Peter Fendi, Salzburg 1995
Krasa-Florian, S.: Johann Nepomuk Schaller, Vienna 1977
Koschatzky, W.: Rudolf von Alt. 1812–1905, Salzburg 1975
Krause, W.: Die Plastik der Wiener Ringstrasse von der Spärromantik bis zur Wende um 1900, Wiesbaden 1980
Kuhn, B.: Der Landschaftsmaler Michael Wutky (1739–1822). Leben und Werk, unprinted, Innsbruck 1980
Lutterotti, O.R.v.: Joseph Anton Koch (1768–1839). Leben und Werk, Vienna/Munich 1985
Mayr-Oehring, E. (ed.): Orient. Österreichische Malerei zwischen 1848 und 1914, Residenzgalerie Salzburg, Salzburg 1997
Moll, C.: Emil Jakob Schindler 1842–1892. Eine Bildnisstudie, Vienna 1930
Novotny, F.: Der Maler Anton Romako 1832–1889, Vienna/Munich 1954
Novotny, F.: Painting and Sculpture in Europe 1780 to 1880, Harmondsworth, 1960
Otten, F.: Ludwig Michael Schwanthaler 1802–1848, Munich 1970
Poch-Kalous, M.: Wiener Plastik im 19. Jahrhundert. In: Geschichte der bildenden

Künste in Wien, Vienna 1996
Pötschner, P.: Wien und die Wiener Landschaft. Spätbarocke und biedermeierliche Landschaftskunst in Wien, Salzburg 1978
Probszt, G.: Friedrich von Amerling. Der Altmeister der Wiener Porträtmalerei, Zürich/Leipzig/Vienna 1927
Rittinger, B.: Die Kreuzwegfresken Josef von Führichs in der Pfarrkirche St. Johann Nepomuk Wien II, Praterstrasse, unprinted, Vienna 1976
Schröder, K. A.: Waldmüller, Kunstforum Wien , Munich 1990
Strobl, A.: Das k.k. Waffenmuseum im Arsenal. Der Bau und seine künstlerische Ausschmückung, Graz/Cologne 1961
Zemen, H.: Leopold Karl Müller 1834–1892. Briefe und Dokumente, Vienna 1996
Zeitler, R.: Die Kunst des 19. Jahrhunderts, Berlin 1966
Zimmermann, H.: Das Alt-Wiener Sittenbild, Vienna 1923
Zimmermann, W.: Anselm Feuerbach, Karlsruhe 1961

BARBARA BORNGÄSSER
Architecture from the Late Nineteenth Century to the present day.

General works and further readings:
Achleitner, F.: Österreichische Architektur im 20. Jahrhundert, 4 Bde., Salzburg, Vienna 1980–85
Achleitner, F.: Wiener Architektur. Zwischen typologischem Fatalismus und semantischem Schlamassel, Vienna/Köln/Weimar 1996
Architektur im 20. Jahrhundert. Österreich, Exhibition catalog DAM Frankfurt 1995/96, Munich/New York 1995
Architektur Wien. 500 Bauten, Stadtplanung Wien (ed.), Vienna/New York 1997
Ankwicz von Kleehoven, Hans. Austria and 20th Century Architecture. Austria International (Vienna), 1950
Bode, P. M./Peichl, G.: Architektur aus Österreich seit 1960, Vienna 1980
Borsi, F./Godoli, E.: Wiener Bauten der Jahrhundertwende. Die Architektur der Habsburgischen Metropole zwischen Historismus und Moderne, Stuttgart 1985
Feuerstein, G.: Visionäre Architektur Wien 1958/88, Berlin 1988
Vienna Present and Past: Architecture, City Prospect, Environment. Vienna: Jugend/Volk Verlagsgesellschaft, 1974.
Frank, J. (ed.): Die internationale Werkbundsiedlung Wien 1932, Vienna 1932
Haiko, P.: Wien 1850–1930. Architektur, Vienna 1992
Hautmann, H./Hautmann, R.: Die Gemeindebauten des Roten Wien, 1919–34, Vienna 1980
Kapfinger, O./Kneissl, F. E.: Dichte Packung. Architektur aus Wien, Salzburg/Vienna 1989
Kapfinger, O./Krischanitz, A.: Die Wiener Secession. Das Haus: Entstehung, Geschichte, Erneuerung, Vienna/Cologne/Graz 1986
Neuer Wiener Wohnbau, Exhibition catalog, Bundesministerium für Auswärtige Angelegenheiten (ed.), Vienna 1991
Österreichische Architektur 1945–75, Öster-

reichischen Gesellschaft für Architektur (ed.), Vienna 1976
Peichl, G./Steiner, D. (ed.): Neuer Wiener Wohnbau, Vienna 1986
Pozzetto, M.: Die Schule Otto Wagners. 1894–1912, Vienna/Munich 1980
Swoboda, H. (ed.): Wien. Identität und Stadtgestalt, Vienna/Cologne 1990
Tafuri, M.: Vienna Rossa. La politica residenziale nella Vienna socialista, 1919–1933, Mailand 1980
Varnedoe, K.: Wien 1900. Kunst. Architektur. Design, Cologne 1987
Waissenberger, R.:(ed.): Wien 1890–1920, Vienna/Heidelberg 1984
Weihsmann, H.: Das Rote Wien. Sozialdemokratische Architektur und Kommunalpolitik 1919–1934, Vienna 1985
Widder, E.: Zeichen des Heils. Kirchenkunst der Gegenwart in Österreich, Linz 1963
Wien. Architektur. Der Stand der Dinge. Stadtplanung (ed.), Vienna 1995

Individual artists and themes:
Adolf Loos, Exhibition catalog der Graphischen Sammlung der Albertina Wien, Vienna 1989
Blohmensacht, F.: Hans Hollein, Stuttgart 1989
Clemens Holzmeister, Exhibition catalog, Vienna 1982
Clemens Holzmeister. Architekt in der Zeitenwende. Selbstbiographie, Werkverzeichnis, 3 Bde., Salzburg/Stuttgart/Zürich 1976
COOP Himmelblau: Architektur muss brennen, Graz 1980
Czech, H./Mistelbauer, W.: Das Looshaus, Vienna 1976
Fonatti, F.: Gustav Peichl. Opere e progetti 1952–1987, Mailand 1987
Fritz Wotruba. Kirche zur Heiligsten Dreifaltigkeit, St. Gallen 1976
Geretsegger, H./Peintner, M.: Otto Wagner 1841–1918, Salzburg/Vienna 1983
Graf, O.A.: Die vergessene Wagnerschule, Vienna 1969
Graf, O.A.: Otto Wagner. Das Werk des Architekten, 2 Bde., Vienna/Cologne/Graz 1985
Günther Domenig. Werkbuch, Museum für Angewandte Kunst Wien (ed.), Vienna 1989
Gustav Peichl. Bauten und Projekte, Bundeskunsthalle Bonn (Hrsg), Stuttgart 1992
Hans Hollein. Exhibition catalog, Historischen Museum der Stadt Wien (ed.), Vienna 1995
Hans Hollein/ Walter Pichler. Architektur, Exhibition catalog, Vienna 1963
Hübl, H.: Wilhelm Holzbauer. Porträt eines Architekten, Vienna 1977
Hundertwasser, F. (ed.): Das Hundertwasser-Haus, Vienna 1985
Kamm, P. (ed.): Roland Rainer. Bauten, Schriften, Projekte, Tübingen 1965
Karl Schwanzer. Architektur aus Leidenschaft, Vienna/Munich 1974 (2nd. ed.)
Kolb, G: Otto Wagner und die Wiener Stadtbahn, Munich 1989
Krecic, P.: Plecnik. The Complete Work, London 1993
Krimmel, B.: Joseph M. Olbrich, 1867–1908, Darmstadt 1983
Loos, A.: Ornament und Verbrechen, Vienna 1908

Moneo, J. R. u.a.: Boris Podrecca. Architecture, Exhibition catalog, Madrid 1992
Münz, L.: Adolf Loos. Mit Verzeichnis der Werke und Schriften, Vienna 1989
Oechslin, W.: Stilhülse und Kern. Otto Wagner, Adolf Loos und der evolutionäre Weg zur modernen Architektur, Zürich/Berlin 1994
Olbrich, J. M.: Architektur (complete reprint of the three original volumes of 1914) Tübingen 1988
Peichl, G.: Architektur und Technik. Die Bauten des Österreichischen Rundfunks, Vienna 1979
Pettena, G.: Hans Hollein, Mailand 1987
Podrecca, B. (ed.): Max Fabiani. Bauten und Projekte in Wien, Exhibition catalog, Vienna 1982
Pozzetto, M.: Max Fabiani. Ein Architekt der Monarchie, Vienna 1983
Roland Rainer, Arbeiten aus 65 Jahren, Salzburg, Vienna 1990
Rukschcio B./Schachel, R.: Adolf Loos. Leben und Werk, Salzburg/Vienna 1982
Seiger, H. (ed.) et al: Im Reich der Kunst. Die Wiener Akademie der bildenden Künste und die faschistische Kunstpolitik, Vienna 1990
Sekler, E. F.: Josef Hoffmann. Das architektonische Werk, Salzburg 1987 (2nd. ed.)
Spalt, J.: Josef Frank 1885–1967, Vienna 1981
Steiner, D. (ed.): Gustav Peichl. A Viennese Architect, Berlin/Tübingen 1993
Wagner, O.: Die Grossstadt, Vienna 1911
Wagner, O.: Moderne Architektur, Vienna 1895 (4th ed.)
Wilhelm Holzbauer, Bauten und Projekte 1953–90, Hochschule für angewandte Kunst (ed.) Vienna 1990
Pehnt, W./Strohl, H: Rudolf Schwarz 1897–1961. Architekt einer anderen Moderne, Stuttgart 1997

Architectural reviews containing articles about contemporary architecture in Vienna.
Architektur aktuell
Architektur und Bauforum
Baumeister
Bauwelt
Perspektiven
UM BAU
Wettbewerbe

GABRIELE BÖSCH/SILVIE STEINER
Paintings and sculptures of the late Nineteenth Century to the end of the Twentieth Century.

Badura-Triska, E. (ed.): Franz West, Exhibition catalog Museum moderner Kunst Stiftung Ludwig Wien, Vienna 1996
Breicha, O. (ed.): Gustav Klimt. Die goldene Pforte. Werk-Wesen-Wirkung. Bilder und Schriften zu Leben und Werk, Salzburg, 1985
Breicha, O. (ed.): Herbert Boeckl. Das Spätwerk. Bilder nach 1945, Graz 1988
Breicha, O. (ed.): Wirklichkeiten. Aspekte einer Gruppierung. Exhibition catalog Museum des 20. Jahrhunderts, Vienna 1988
Das Jahrzehnt der Malerei, Österreich 1980–1990. Sammlung Essl, Exhibition catalog Kunstforum Wien, Vienna 1991
Drechsler, W.: Ansichten. 40 Künstler aus Österreich im Gespräch, Salzburg/Vienna 1992
Einfach gute Malerei, Exhibition catalog moderner Kunst, Vienna 1982
Fahr-Becker, G.: Wiener Werkstätte 1903–1932, Cologne, 1994
Fleck, R./Smolik, N. (ed.): Kunst in Österreich. Künstler, Galerien, Museen, Kunstmarkt, Kulturpolitik, Adressen, Cologne, 1995
Fliedl, G.: Gustav Klimt (1862–1918). Die Welt in weiblicher Gestalt, Cologne, 1994
Fuchs, R.: Apologie und Diffamierung des "Österreichischen Expressionismus". Begriffs- und Rezeptionsgeschichte der österreichischen Malerei 1908 bis 1938, Vienna/Cologne 1991
Gorsen, P.: Jugendstil und Symbolismus in Wien um 1900. In: Wien um 1900. Kunst und Kultur, Vienna 1985
Habarta, G.: Frühe Verhältnisse, Kunst in Wien nach '45, Vienna 1996
Heller, R.: Recent Scholarship on Vienna's Golden Age: Gustav Klimt and Egon Schiele. Art Bulletin (New York), 59 (March 1977), pp. 111-18
Hevesi, L.: Acht Jahre Secession (März 1897–Juni 1905). Kritik, Polemik, Chronik, 1906. Nachdruck Otto Breicha (ed.), Klagenfurt 1984
Hoerschelmann, A./Weiermair, P. (ed.): Von Schiele bis Wotruba. Arbeiten auf Papier 1908–1938, Vienna/Frankfurt/Zürich, 1995
Konfrontationen. Neuerwerbungen 1990–1993. Museum moderner Kunst, Stiftung Ludwig Wien, Vienna 1993
Kunst aus Österreich 1896–1996, Kunst- und Ausstellungshalle der Bundesrepublik Deutschland, Bonn, 1996
Max Oppenheimer, Exhibition catalog Jüdisches Museum der Stadt Wien, Vienna, 1994/95
Museum moderner Kunst (ed.): The Austrian Vision, Positions of Contemporary Art, Exhibition catalog für das Denver Art Museum und das Museo Nacional de Bellas Artes Buenos Aires, Vienna 1997
Hofmann, W.: Modern Painting in Austria. Vienna: Kunstverlag Wolfrum, 1965
Jetztzeit. Exhibition catalog Kunsthalle Vienna, 1994
Holme, C.: The Art Revival in Austria The Studio (London), special issue, 1906
Howarth, T.: Charles Rennie Mackintosh and the Modern Movement. London: Routledge Kegan Paul, 1952
Neuwirth, W.: Wiener Werkstätte. Avantgarde. Art Déco. Industrial Design, Vienna 1984
Noever, P. (ed.): Die Überwindung der Utilität. Dagobert Peche und die Wiener Werkstätte, Exhibition catalog MAK–Österreichisches Museum für angewandte Kunst, Vienna 1998
Oskar Kokoschka. Symposium der
Hochschule für angewandte Kunst Wien, Salzburg/Vienna 1986
Schimmel, P./Noever, P. (ed.): Out of actions. Zwischen Performance und Objekt 1949–1979, MAK-Österreichisches Museum für angewandte Kunst Wien, Vienna 1998
Schmied, W. (ed.): Malerei in Österreich 1945–1995. Die Sammlung Essl, Munich/New York 1996
Schröder, K. A.: Richard Gerstl (1883–1908), Exhibition catalog Kunstforum Wien, Vienna 1993
Siegfried Anzinger Exhibition catalog Museum moderner Kunst, Stiftung Ludwig Wien, Vienna, 1998
Skreiner, W.: Österreichs Transavantgarde. In: Achille Bonito Oliva: Transavantgarde International, Mailand 1982
Smola, F./Rossi, A.: Österreichischer Expressionismus. Malerei und Graphik 1905–1925, Exhibition catalog of the Österreichischen Galerie Belvedere, Vienna 1994
Sotriffer, K. (ed.): Der Kunst ihre Freiheit. Wege der österreichischen Moderne von 1880 bis zur Gegenwart, Vienna 1984
Szeemann, H./Schröder, K. A. (ed.): Egon Schiele und seine Zeit. Österreichische Malerei und Zeichnung von 1900 bis 1930 aus der Sammlung Leopold, Munich 1988. Traum und Wirklichkeit. Vienna 1870–1930, Exhibition catalog, Historisches Museum der Stadt Wien, Vienna 1985
Weber, S. C. (ed.): Rudolf Hausner 1914–1995; Museum Würth, Künzelsau 1996
Weibel, P./Steinle, C.: Identität Differenz. Eine Topografie der Moderne, Vienna 1992
Werkner, P. (ed.): Kunst in Österreich 1945–1995, Vienna 1996
Werkner, P.: Richard Gerstl. In: Physis und Psyche. Der österreichische Frühexpressionismus, Vienna/Munich 1986
Wiener Secession (ed.): Secession. Das Jahrhundert der künstlerischen Freiheit, Munich 1998

Index of Names of Individuals

Place and Subject Index